2

Breaking Boundaries

A New Generation of Poets in the GDR

KAREN LEEDER

CLARENDON PRESS · OXFORD
1996

Oxford University Press, Walton Street, Oxford OX2 6DP
Oxford New York
Athens Auckland Bangkok Bombay
Calcutta Cape Town Dar es Salaam Delhi
Florence Hong Kong Istanbul Karachi
Kuala Lumpur Madras Madrid Melbourne
Mexico City Nairobi Paris Singapore
Taipei Tokyo Toronto
and associated companies in
Berlin Ibadan

Oxford is a trade mark of Oxford University Press

Published in the United States
by Oxford University Press Inc., New York

British Library Cataloguing in Publication Data
Data available

Library of Congress Cataloging in Publication Data
Leeder, Karen J.
Breaking boundaries: a new generation of poets in the GDR,
1979–1989/Karen Leeder.
(Oxford modern languages and literature monographs)
Includes bibliographical references.
1. German poetry—20th century—History and criticism. 2. German
poetry—Germany (East)—History and criticism. I. Title.
II. Series PT3719.L44 1996
831'.914099431—dc20 95–32025
ISBN 0–19–815910–2

1 3 5 7 9 10 8 6 4 2

Typeset by Cambrian Typesetters, Frimley, Surrey
Printed in Great Britain
on acid-free paper by
Biddles Ltd,
Guildford and King's Lynn

'Unglücklich das Land, das keine Helden hat!' [. . .]
'Nein. Unglücklich das Land, das Helden nötig hat.'
(Bertolt Brecht, *Leben des Galilei*)

Acknowledgements

THIS book is based on a D.Phil. thesis submitted to the Faculty of Medieval and Modern Languages at the University of Oxford in the summer of 1993. I would like to thank the staffs of the various libraries and academic institutions I visited during the course of my research for their friendly co-operation: the Deutsches Literaturarchiv in Marbach am Neckar, the Staatsbibliothek in Frankfurt, the Akademie der Wissenschaften and the Humboldt Universität in Berlin, and the Taylor Institution in Oxford. For support during the writing of the thesis I am grateful to my family; also to the President and Fellows of Magdalen College, Oxford; The Master and Fellows of Emmanuel College, Cambridge; the F.v.S. Stiftung in Hamburg; the British Council; and the DAAD. Thanks are also due to colleagues and friends for their encouragement and suggestions: my supervisor Ray Ockenden, Jim Reed, Tom Kuhn, Ian Wallace, Martin Kane, Arthur Williams, Philip Brady, the 'Young Fellows' of Emmanuel College, and, for unfailing support and inspiration, David Constantine. Special thanks must go to the many poets and academics from the former GDR, who were generous with their time and comments before and after the fall of the Wall.

I owe a large and lasting debt of gratitude to my former tutor Malcolm Pasley, to whom this book is dedicated.

Permissions

I AM grateful for permission to quote the following material:

'Auf halbem Weg' from *Mit der Sanduhr am Gurtel*, 1983, and 'dem treuem medium' from *stoff der piloten*, 1989, © Thomas Böhme; 'Déjà Vu' and 'Sisyphos' from *Wasserstände und Tauchtiefen*, 1985, © Hans Brinkmann; 'Das Sonnet' from *Zweite Inventur*, 1987, © Kurt Drawert; 'rumor' from *mehr über rauten und türme*, 1991, © Andreas Koziol; 'Lied für meine Freunde' from *Poesiealbum*, 1979, © Steffen Mensching; 'Zangengeburt', 'Ich schlief', and 'Man(n) ist Man(n)' from *Zangengeburt*, 1984, © Lutz Rathenow.

Sascha Anderson, 'RECHNUNGEN' from *Jewish Jetset*, 1991; Bert Papenfuß, 'schriftbruch', 'wortflug', and 'rasender schmertz weiterlachen' from *SoJa*, 1990; Rainer Schedlinski, 'ich lief durch namenlose treppenhäuser', from *die männer der frauen*, 1991, © Duckhaus Galrev, Berlin.

Volker Braun, 'DAS EIGENTUM' from *Die Zickzackbrücke: Ein Abrißkalender*, 1992; Kerstin Hensel, 'Im Stau' and 'Gänze des Lebens' from *Angestaut*, 1993; Steffen Mensching, 'Erinnerung an eine Milchglasscheibe', 'Auf einem Bein, nackt, nachts', 'Angenommene Farbenlehre Erich Mühsams', 'So weiß war der Morgen', 'Unter den Linden', 'Traumhafter Ausflug mit Rosa L.', and 'Hölderlin', from *Erinnerung an eine Milchglasscheibe*, 1984, and 'Ist dir aufgefallen', from *Tuchfühlung*, 1986; Hans-Eckardt Wenzel, 'Wir suchten das Verbindungsstück', 'Ich braue das bittere Bier', and 'Dreidimensionales Bild einer Dorkirche bei S.', from *Lied vom wilden Mohn*, 1984, © Mitteldeutscher Verlag GmbH Halle (Saale).

Gerd Adloff, 'Selbstmord' from *Vogelbühne: Gedichte im Dialog*, 1985, © Verlag der Nation, Bayreuth.

Heinz Czechowski, 'Goethe und Hölderlin', from *Nachtspur*, 1993, © Ammann Verlag & Co., Zurich.

Michael Wüstefeld, 'Für Uwe Kolbe' from *Berührung ist nur eine Randerscheinung*, ed. Sascha Anderson and Elke Erb, 1985, © Verlag Kiepenheuer & Witsch, Cologne.

Uwe Kolbe, 'Hineingeboren' and 'Wir leben mit Rissen' from *Hineingeboren: Gedichte 1975–1979*, 1982, 'Ich war dabei' and 'Ein Gedicht, worum es mir geht' from *Bornholm II*, 1987, 'Gruß an Karl Mickel', 'Tübinger Spaziergang', 'Spiegelbild', and 'Berlin' from *Vaterlandkanal*, 1990; Barbara Köhler, 'Papierboot', 'Selbstportrait', 'Endstelle', 'Meer in Sicht', 'Rondeau Allemagne', and 'Anrede Zwo: Diotima an Bellamin' from *Deutsches Roulette*, 1991; Durs Grünbein, 'Fast ein Gesang', 'No. 8', and 'An diesem Morgen' from *Grauzone morgens*, 1988, 'O Heimat, zynischer Euphon', 'Zerebralis', and 'Die leeren Zeichen 1' from *Schädelbasislektion*, 1991; Rainer Schedlinski, 'die unvordenkliche lichtung der worte', 'dann leuchten die stätten', '(zungenfilm)', 'nun ist das bleiben ein standhafter weg', *die rationen des ja und des nein*, 1991, © Suhrkamp Verlag GmbH, Frankfurt/Main.

Bert Papenfuß-Gorek, 'innehalt', and 'strohtod im stiefel' from LED SAUDAUS, 1991; Róža Domašcyna', 'Budissin', from *Zaungucker*, 1992, © Gerhard Wolf Janus press GmbH, Berlin.

Bert Papenfuß, 'ich', and 'sußer odin' from Bert Papenfuß *tiské*, 1990, © Steidl Verlag Göttingen.

For permission to reprint the photograph 'Zwei Kinder am Stacheldraht', the Vereinigung zur Förderung der Wiedervereinigung Deutschlands, © Arbeitsgemeinschaft 13. August e.v., Haus am Checkpoint Charlie.

Earlier versions of some of the material included here have appeared in *Neue Ansichten: The Reception of Romanticism in the Literature of the GDR*, *German Literature at a Time of Change 1989–1990*, and *The Individual, Identity and Innovation: Signals from Contemporary Literature and the New Germany*.

It has not been possible to trace some authors and obtain all the necessary permissions. Any omissions will be rectified in future editions.

Contents

Orthography and Abbreviations

MANY of the primary sources quoted in this study are written in forms which deviate from standard orthography and grammar. I have adhered strictly to the forms, orthography and lay-out of the manuscript or published versions of these texts.

The following abbreviations have been used:

ABznG	*Amsterdamer Beiträge zur neueren Germanistik*
DB	*Deutsche Bücher*
FAZ	*Frankfurter Allgemeine Zeitung*
NdL	*Neue deutsche Literatur*
SitZ	*Sprache im technischen Zeitalter*
SuF	*Sinn und Form*
Temperamente	*Temperamente. Blätter für junge Leute*
WB	*Weimarer Beiträge*
ZfG	*Zeitschrift für Germanistik*, Neue Folge

Introduction

> Die Geschichte der DDR-Literatur muß neu geschrieben
> werden. Bisherigen Interpretationen fehlte der exakte Stasi-
> Kontext.[1]

WHEN I started work on this project, I thought of it as the chance
to present and analyse some of the most exciting contemporary
European poetry I had read. It is now as much about writing
literary history. The end of the German Democratic Republic, the
acrimony of the 'Was bleibt' affair and the revelations of
the *Staatssicherheit* ('Stasi') files have displayed those ideological
certainties upon which literary history has, up until now, relied. In
the East that history was the product of fragile negotiations
between 'Geist' and 'Macht'.[2] In the West it was sited somewhere
between the Cold War suspicion of the 'Dichter im Dienst'[3] and
ideological applause for the apparently dissident.

In Volker Braun's 1990 text 'Nachruf' there is the line: 'Und
unverständlich wird mein ganzer Text'.[4] This is not, however,
simply the misery of a single writer, unable to comprehend the
'text' of his own identity, his work, and his history: it has become
perhaps the fundamental paradigm of the 1990s. His moving
testament to loss concludes:

> Was ich niemals besaß wird mir entrissen.
> Was ich nicht lebte, werd ich ewig missen.
> Die Hoffnung lag im Weg wie eine Falle.
> Mein Eigentum, jetzt habt ihrs auf der Kralle.
> Wann sag ich wieder *mein* und meine alle.

In the 1991 poetry anthology *Grenzfallgedichte*, in which it is
included, one senses a multitude of texts, biographies, histories, and
'truths' unravelling themselves and escaping, almost as one reads.
For example, Heiner Müller's 'FERNSEHEN' contains a section
entitled 'SELBSTKRITIK':[5]

> Meine Herausgeber wühlen in alten Texten
> Manchmal wenn ich sie lese überläuft es mich kalt Das
> Habe ich geschrieben IM BESITZ DER WAHRHEIT
> Sechzig Jahre vor meinem mutmaßlichen Tod

Auf dem Bildschirm sehe ich meine Landsleute
Mit Händen und Füßen abstimmen gegen die Wahrheit
Die vor vierzig Jahren mein Besitz war
Welches Grab schützt mich vor meiner Jugend

Heinz Czechowski's 'Notiz' (p. 103) also looks anew at former truths:

Ich
Lese in alten
Büchern, die
Noch gestern die alte
Wahrheit ver-
Kündeten.

Once again the lyric subject is rendered an impotent spectator, unable to compose new meaning, a new text.

Einen Brief
An H. geschrieben. Be-
Deutungslos

But the centre, the 'Kern | Im Kern', is the 'text' of the self:

Texte
In zeitlicher Folge
Habe ich nicht
Zu verteidigen. Vielleicht aber
Werde ich vorkommen,
Nachdem ich mich selber
Vergaß.

Particularly striking in these texts, as in many others written in the years since 1989, is the opposition of possession and loss. This clearly has a concrete meaning, in remembering the failed ethos of communal ownership in the GDR, but also in documenting the acquisitive reality of the new German *Wende*. The references to Brecht in Müller's text ('im Besitz der Wahrheit') and to Hölderlin in Braun ('Mein Eigentum'), however, also point beyond, to the existential dispossession of the poet.[6] These are simply examples, the gesture is almost universal: the opaque or invalidated 'text' of a lifetime.[7]

Such gestures have been understood, on a global level, as a symptom of our age. The fashionable and sometimes seductive irresponsibility of the 'postmodern' encourages scepticism about those 'meta-narratives' rooted in Enlightenment thought. Instead we are presented with a reading of history (and of the subject) which recognizes only the cross-fire of discontinuous, unplaced, and heterogeneous discourses, a challenge to the very idea of a stable 'text'. However, if—to borrow an image from Kleist—there is no going back into the garden after the 'Fall', we are demonstrably on our way forwards, and clearly in the market for new 'texts'. In Germany, at least, they are already being written. As Günter Kunert points out, 'Die Legende ist im Entstehen';[8] a new text and a new history is already being formulated, somewhere between left-wing nostalgia for the lost utopias of socialism and the New Right's brutal dismantling of its realities.

The attempts to write a new history are matched by attempts to write a new literary history. Wolfgang Emmerich, whose *Kleine Literaturgeschichte der DDR* has long been the standard Western version of GDR literary history, has called for revision in radically new terms.[9] He explicitly dismisses those ideological schemes which have governed our understanding of GDR literary history up until now, and which have created a climate in which GDR literature was regarded primarily as a manifestation of 'gesellschaftlich-politische Verhältnisse'. He calls instead for 'eine Literaturgeschichte der DDR, die die Kategorie des Ästhetischen zum Fluchtpunkt macht'. In the same way he calls into question pivotal dates which have so far determined literary discussion (1961, 1968, 1971, 1976, etc.) and 'hilflose Metaphern' which have been used to bolster historical trajectories: 'Literaturen des *Abschieds*, der *Ankunft* und des *Anwesendseins*'.[10] Dismissing as inadequate the single teleological development that such co-ordinates imply, Emmerich calls instead for a form of reappraisal which would tolerate pluralism and could incorporate concurrent paradigms, competing strategies, and dominant and subordinate cultures, 'lauter neue Historien'. It is perhaps worth citing his terms here, because they look set to determine a new understanding of GDR literature.[11]

1. Literatur entfaltet sich weder linear und stetig, noch auf irgendein Telos hin. Es gibt nicht *eine* literarische Entwicklung, sondern ein System widerspruchsvoller, interferierender Bewegungen. Verschiedene ästhetische Strategien und Praxen existieren nebeneinander, konkurrieren miteinander. Ihre Entstehung und ihr Verhältnis zueinander korrespondieren mit der

4

Herausbildung unterschiedlicher dominanter und nichtdominanter Kulturen im Schoß der DDR-Gesellschaft.
2. Daraus folgt, daß es falsch wäre, eine literarhistorische (Teil-) Epoche nur von *einem* Paradigma bzw. von dessen Prädominanz her beschreiben zu wollen. Gewiß gibt es privilegierte und unterprivilegierte künstlerische Programme und Praxen; aber eben diese Struktur bewegter Widersprüche muß beschrieben und analysiert werden, ohne ein Paradigma absolut zu setzen. Das gilt auch für die DDR-Literatur.

Despite Emmerich's (albeit qualified) endorsement of the essential props of the postmodern—'Pluralität, Vielheit, Un-eindeutigkeit', and 'ein Denken und Forschen [. . .] ohne Zentrum'—one, in the context, surprisingly conservative organizing principle does survive his critical *Kahlschlag*, namely 'generations'.[12] Such a gesture would seem to run counter to the emphasis on 'Einzelheit und Einmaligkeit' which he and many other critics now place at the centre of their new methodological schemes.[13] Reference to 'generations' of writers has become as much a part of the critical discourse about GDR literature as have the metaphors of progress and the dates referred to above. It is, however, an equally suspect category; one which has never been comprehensively explained or examined. Here I focus on just one of the so-called literary generations of the GDR: those born in the 1950s and 1960s, those who were, to borrow Uwe Kolbe's phrase, 'Hineingeboren'.[14]

My examination, which spans the time between the official recognition of these writers in 1979 to their putative literary death in 1989, hinges on the semantic and metaphorical field of 'Grenzen', dubbed in literary terms 'das Motto der Achtziger'.[15] The discussion is marked by the tension between being born into these boundaries (*Hineingeboren*) and that of 'breaking out of them' (*Entgrenzung*). On one level Kolbe's pithy label for the experience of young writers 'born into' an established and closed socialist state speaks for itself. On another level it can be seen as the emblem of a pan-German experience. Reinhard Mohr, in a widely cited if idiosyncratic sociological essay about the same generation in the Federal Republic—what he calls 'die 78er'—describes them as 'born into' a historical vacuum which exists between the disillusioned revolutionaries of '68 and 'die postmodernen Neonkids' of '88.[16] Taken as a yet broader cultural paradigm, however, it also signals the paradoxical experience of a generation emerging from the crumbling monoliths of ideology to face the liberating but debilitating 'hyper-realities' of the postmodern. 'Entgrenzung', the breaking of boundaries and taboos, the vagabond expedition into the Unknown, is the most significant literal and metaphorical gesture of the 1980s.[17] Politically, it could be argued, it finds its ultimate manifestation in the breaching of the Berlin Wall. On a textual level it translates into the desire to radicalize accepted understandings of the subject, of history, of tradition, of poetic form, indeed of the poetic enterprise itself. One cannot understand these two motifs—'Hineingeboren' and 'Entgrenzung'—in isolation, nor in simple opposition. For where on one level the 'security' (the ambivalence is already there) of regulated schemes and patrolled boundaries provides an anchor for identity and meaning—even, perhaps especially, in opposition to those boundaries, on another level that security can become crushing and silencing imprisonment. Equally, what begins as a bid to rupture such boundaries can issue into the terrible anxiety of the void: formlessness, displacement, and atomization. It is the unresolved friction between all these levels of meaning which makes the poetry of this decade so extraordinary. The writers expose their texts (and often themselves) so fundamentally to these tensions that, where they do not withstand the dislocation (there is no hint of resolution), they are torn apart: new ground in the GDR. Indeed in some cases this was so brutal a violation of accepted forms and formulas, that the writers concerned were entirely excluded from the official culture, imprisoned, marginalized, threatened, and forced into the underground scene of the now notorious Prenzlauer Berg.

However, in a sense the story is only half written by the time the GDR, these writers, and the innovations they introduced were consigned to an early grave: 'Die BRDigung des DDR-Untergrunds'.[18] Christine Cosentino cannot have anticipated the full truth of her words when, in 1988, she cited the emergence of this young generation as 'ein brisantes Kapitel in der DDR-Literaturgeschichte'.[19] After 1989, the writing of this generation, which had become known as the 'alternative' literature of the GDR, 'die andere Sprache', was catapulted into the centre of the literary scene as *the* language, *the* literature of the new Germany.[20] It was celebrated for its postmodern aloofness, for refusing to accept the antagonistic deadlock of collaboration and dissidence, and for founding an autonomous realm beyond official discourses. In 1991, for example, in an influential survey which placed the implosion of the GDR and the fall of the intellectual under the sign of 'Melancholia', Wolfgang Emmerich pointed to the literature of the young writers as one of the few things which 'would remain'.[21] They, he claimed, had managed to extricate themselves from those allegiances to the utopian principle, to the State, and to a seductive 'hope', which had so long bound the older writers in the GDR.

But in the wake of the *Stasi* controversy a much more intricate relationship between the writer and the mechanisms of power in the GDR has been, in part at least, revealed. Most importantly, the much-touted 'autonomy' of the 'underground' writer has been exposed in many cases as simply a more precarious, and in some cases a more cynical, contract with power. The fall from grace was swift. Those young writers who had been so recently and so vociferously fêted by an emerging 'neudeutsche Literaturkritik' became almost at once the scapegoat for their now disappointed ambitions. At the same time they were exposed to the pointed hostility of those older writers and critics who had anyway despised their supposedly postmodern aesthetic.[22] In short they became the final *feuilleton* test-case for the integrity of GDR literature as a whole. The realization that even Prenzlauer Berg had been compromised, claimed Frank Schirrmacher, 'zerstört den letzten Glauben an eine genuine, intakte DDR-Kunst'.[23]

These writers are therefore not simply important as the last generation of the GDR, nor even as the initiators of radical new possibilities for poetry under censorship. They stand at the very heart of three of the most pressing literary discussions in contemporary Germany: the scandals concerning the relationship between literature and the *Staatssicherheit*, the postmodern debate, and the 'Sturz vom Sockel' of the intellectual.[24] The debate about the role of the *Staatssicherheit* in the underground has provoked a pitched battle between those who understand the moral and those who understand the aesthetic as the primary basis for literary judgement. The experimental texts produced by young writers have, for some, embodied the essential shift from a modern to a postmodern aesthetic. Finally, the anti-Enlightenment nihilism espoused by many of them has been seen as a key factor in the 1990s 'Intellektuellendämmerung'.[25] I would argue that these are all facets of the question which has dominated German literary history since 1945: the relationship between political engagement and literary autonomy.

At the moment various distinct voices are attempting to give form and meaning to the political and literary histories of the 1980s, and beyond them to the existence of the GDR itself. But they represent approaches and understandings which meet head on, with very little room for negotiation. This battleground is important, for critics are not simply writing literary histories of the 1980s, they are rewriting the historical 'text' of the two German states. This is intended as a contribution to that discussion.

In writing about the lyric poetry of the 1980s in the GDR, one becomes immediately aware of the treacherous terms of classification which have become the norm. In this discussion I am chiefly concerned with two. The first is the use of the term 'generation'. Amongst critics it has enjoyed a remarkable currency as a means of organizing GDR history, the more remarkable for the extent to which the writers themselves have also fallen in with it. The first extensive—although by no means logically consistent—use of the word 'generation' as a critical term in the GDR was to identify the controversial 'Volker-Braun-Generation' in the early 1960s. The term has found an extended life in discussions about Braun's successors. However, the reason for its use, its ideological implications and the validity of the methodology underpinning it, have never been subject to comprehensive scrutiny. As a result, it has long obscured the diversity of political and poetic aspirations among young writers.

The second term is related. It is the notion of the 'Prenzlauer-Berg-Connection' (Endler).[26] In the early 1970s Prenzlauer Berg might still have been thought of as simply a run-down workers' quarter in East Berlin. During the 1980s it became home to a shifting unregistered population of (mostly) young people and the centre for an artistic underground, which expressed itself in punk, illegal performance, multimedia experiments, but above all in a network of unofficial magazines and literature. In 1981 Ingrid and Klaus-Dieter Hähnel signalled the importance of Prenzlauer Berg in one of the first critical essays to discuss the emergence of the young poets: 'Prenzlauer Berg ist—und das hier ohne jede Ironie gesagt—längst nicht mehr nur eine Wohngegend, sondern eine Haltung.'[27] Although they were careful to play down the most blunt formulations of that attitude—elsewhere described simply as 'Null Bock auf alles Offizielle'—the Hähnels themselves probably under-estimated the extent to which Prenzlauer Berg would become a political icon of the 1980s—and beyond.[28] The notoriety of the place became a magnet for the disaffected. Writers, artists, and film-makers, ostracized from the official GDR culture industry, congregated there and earned the area a bohemian chic in both East and West, which still looms large in many appraisals of its literary worth. The fascination engendered by the possibility of an emphatically (post-)modern 'Bohemia in East Berlin' is borne out by the many books devoted to it as a social or, more recently, as a tourist phenomenon.[29] The idea of 'Prenzlauer Berg' is seductive, but one does not have to be as sceptically disposed towards the writers associated with it as Wolf Biermann, for example, in order to recognize that its cachet has been in part engendered by the attention of Western media and Western academics.[30] Yet quite apart from the reality of the place, 'Prenzlauer Berg' has become a metaphor: one in the long line of metaphors (although this time unofficial), upon which the literary history of the GDR has been based. In the most recent critical discussions this has become even more acute. The term has developed into a cipher for a marginalized, autonomous existence outside the discourses of state and of opposition. Thus at the 1992 Bad Godesberg conference organized by the 'Internationaler Arbeitskreis Literatur und Politik in Deutschland', 'Prenzlauer Berg' became a virtual space, to be found somewhere apart from or between the positions inscribed in the conference title: 'Dableiben? Weggehen? Weiterschreiben'.[31] Ultimately, the term has been adopted as a form of critical shorthand for an aesthetic understanding: one which might be broadly identified with experimental 'language-centred'[32] texts and an engagement with French post-structuralist thought.

If the emblematic value of the term has given it a currency in which the distinction between the biographical, political, and poetological has been progressively condensed and confounded, it is almost redundant to say at this point that the reality of Prenzlauer Berg was (is) much more complex. The literary scene there has evolved over more than fifteen years, involving a large number of authors whose dates of birth span at least two so-called generations. It has a sometimes turbulent and in any case shifting history of competing political and poetic positions which confound any attempt to define it in stable or singular terms. In April 1991 Peter Böthig, a critic and writer closely associated with the underground scene, commented:

> eine literatur des prenzlauer bergs hat es in wirklichkeit nie gegeben. aber es gab und gibt den prenzlauer berg als einen ort der literatur. er ist zunehmend ein ort in der mitte europas [...], in dem die sozialen, kulturellen und semiotischen widersprüche und prozesse in besonderer form aufeinanderprallen.[33]

From the vantage point of 1994, the demystification and contextualization he invokes is even more pressing. The revelations of the archives of the *Staatssicherheit* have only served once again to obscure the complexity of the literary scene which had developed there. While some critics have simply gone on as before, others have condemned wholesale what they see as the corrupt aesthetic project of the place, and others have been forced into unsatisfactory and often absurd compromises.[34] 'Prenzlauer Berg' must be situated within the literary topography of the new Germany, as a place with a history (histories) and not as a critical myth. At the moment it is simply a fashionable label, which betrays the many poetic initiatives and the many damaged lives it obscures.

I have introduced these two problems straight away, because they are closely related. The notion of 'Prenzlauer Berg' has in part replaced, and in part become entangled with, the idea of a literary generation in the GDR. This slippage has had two major effects. On the one hand, it has eclipsed the many writers of more or less the same age who have expressly dissociated themselves from the radical linguistic experiment or the calculated provocation of the 'Szene' Prenzlauer Berg. This is especially true of the more overtly political poetry, to name one example, and of poetry by women as a whole. On the other hand, it has obscured the links between the young writers and those older writers, particularly Adolf Endler, Wolfgang Hilbig, and Elke Erb, but also Volker Braun or Heiner Müller, whose aesthetic practice shows marked similarities to that of the younger writers. In any case, both terms falsely suggest a stable and quantifiable whole, and both terms discourage any kind of diachronic study of the poetry, or a proper placing of it within the context of an ongoing literary development in the GDR as a whole. Ultimately both concepts—that of the 'Prenzlauer-Berg-Connection' and the 'new generation'—have been used to detach the work of the young writers from German literary history, as if they are an entirely unique phenomenon. A better understanding of the innovations and the weaknesses of their work can be gained by seeing it in relation to other literary 'avant-gardes'. I have tried to suggest some of the important influences and to signal at least some of the useful connections: with German expressionism, certain Romantic writers, Russian futurism, French symbolism—especially Rimbaud, and the postmodern 'Language Poetry' from the United States. One would not be far wrong in seeing the extraordinary efflorescence of language-centred poetry in the GDR of the 1980s as an important development of the whole controversial phenomenon of twentieth-century 'avant-gardism'.[35]

Where the notions of 'Prenzlauer Berg' and of a 'generation' of poets certainly need clarification, there is also the problem of the matrix of critical jargon which has evolved to describe their literature. 'Szene', 'Avantgarde', 'Ost-moderne', 'Postmoderne', 'Post-Avantgarde', 'Untergrund', 'zweite Kultur', 'dritte Literatur', 'subversive Literatur', 'autonome Literatur' have all been regularly used, along with the adjectives 'alternativ', 'inoffiziell', 'subkulturell', 'nicht angepaßt', 'oppositionell', and 'dissident'. One of the aims of this book is to negotiate a path between the unstated ideological intent of these terms.

The terminology is complex. That complexity is compounded by three further factors. The first is the question of dates. Operating within date boundaries is particulary restricting in GDR literary criticism. This is partly due to the often inordinate delay between the completion of a text and its eventual publication. The volume *Zensur in der DDR* has begun to give an insight into the long and painful gestation of many GDR texts.[36] Some texts which may date back to the early 1970s but never found their way past the censors, have recently been published in a number of anthologies and collections. Sometimes no dates are provided and older texts are published alongside much more recent work. Even where dates are provided for the texts, they are sometimes contradictory or inaccurate and editions sometimes fail to indicate where material has been significantly reworked between the original publication and the later anthologized version. The dates within which I have chosen to locate this study (1979–1989), do not, then, mark hard and fast demarcation lines. They signal instead the centre of interest, and, once again, can be understood as a contribution to the discussion surrounding the development of GDR literature. I have attempted to set this decade in literary context by casting back three years to 1976 and casting forward three years into the 1990s. It has been widely argued that the enforced expatriation of Wolf Biermann in 1976 marked a fundamental caesura in GDR cultural history. It also had a profound effect on the literary beginnings of the writers under consideration. From the vantage point of the present one can follow the development of the young writers in the new Germany and reappraise their work in the light of the literary controversies and revelations of 1990 and 1991.

The second pragmatic decision concerned the scope of the texts to be studied. Some limitation has been necessary. I have concentrated on a body of some fifty writers born between 1950 and 1966. The Bibliography lists the dates of birth of those writers, and the titles of their collections of poetry, individual publications, manuscripts, and the anthologies of their work which have formed the basis of my research. I have focused especially on texts written and published in the GDR by authors living in the GDR. This has two important consequences.

First, although I have often discussed individual texts published privately in the many unofficial magazines, 'Künstlerbücher', and 'Lyrik-Grafik-Mappen' of the GDR, I have not been able to examine this phenomenon in the detail it deserves. At this stage it is impossible to have an overview of the anarchic and constantly shifting alternative publishing scene, which flourished from the beginning of the 1980s, and which has provided one of the most invigorating impulses in the literary scene of the new Germany. The spectacular *D1980D1989R Künstlerbücher und Originalgrafische Zeitschriften im Eigenverlag* (1991) lists more than thirty magazines, some of which had twenty or more editions, and over 150 'Künstlerbücher'.[37] Even this is only a beginning, as many texts, films, photographs, recordings, and multimedia works have yet to be recovered from private collections and, in some cases, the archives of the *Staatssicherheit*. There will doubtless be a great deal of academic work done on this phenomenon in the future. Secondly, my decision to focus the study on texts produced by GDR authors in the GDR means that, as a general rule, writers ceased to be central to my project if they moved to the Federal Republic. An exception to this is Sascha Anderson. Both his central status as controversial 'guru' of the underground scene, which continued even after he had left the GDR in 1986, and his place at the centre of the *Stasi* revelations mean that he merits special consideration.

A final question to be addressed is that of genre. Jan Faktor pinpoints the dilemma most clearly in his first collection when he claims, 'Gedichte schreibe ich eben nicht'. He calls his texts instead 'positive texte'. Gabriele Kachold's 1989 collection *zügel los* carries the subtitle 'prosatexte', Johannes Jansen labels the work in different collections as 'spottklagen', or 'Materialversionen', and Bert Papenfuß[-Gorek] created the notion of 'Ark', later 'Arkdichtung', as a genre definition for his early work and as an anarchic gesture in the face of literary convention.[38] Many of the texts are explicit attempts to write a way out of those forms approved by political and poetological prescriptions. In a characteristically wry interview of 1992 Durs Grünbein claimed that for a long time he called his texts 'Versuche' and explained: 'Das Euphemismus Gedicht bleibt lange tabu'. Whether as 'Versuche', essays, or even assaults on literary convention, or rather, as one reviewer claimed of Kachold, 'Entfesselungsversuche', it is clear that the texts are, and are meant to be, a provocation to formal literary definition. I have chosen to write about what I have called poetry, but it is clear that the boundaries here as elsewhere when one is dealing with the literature of this decade are not fixed. This aspect of the work, of course, brings it close to the historical 'avant-garde'.[39]

As I have indicated, one of my main aims is to question the generalizations which have been used in discussing the young writers up until now, and to set these against the reality of individual texts. There appeared to be several possible ways of tackling this. They are worth mentioning here, in order to illuminate my own approach.

The model which at first most readily presented itself was Gerrit-Jan Berendse's pioneering *Die 'Sächsische Dichterschule'*. It might be imagined that Berendse's line of analysis for the work of his 'Sächsische Dichterschule' until 1979 could simply be translated into the terms of the 'Prenzlauer Berg Schule' for the following decade up to 1989.[40] However, there are many factors which make such an approach inappropriate. The particular writers of the 'middle generation' who in fact form the focus of Berendse's study offered themselves for study as a coherent body, partly because of their geographical provenance, but also, primarily, because of their established and unique intertextuality—'Aufeinanderbezugnehmen' (Endler).[41] Quite simply, they saw themselves for a long time, in some cases even after they had left the GDR, as a group.[42] Berendse signals the demise of such an understanding among GDR writers in his conclusion, and indeed the younger writers are generally much more wary of such groupings. Although temporary and intense collaborations do occur and also leave their mark on the work (particularly between writers and musicians or writers and painters), there is no sustained collective feeling in quite the same way. Anneli Hartmann (following Harald Hartung) went so far to call the younger writers a generation of ' "Einzelgängern" oder "Vereinzelten" '.[43] In this light alone Berendse's model is inappropriate for a study of the later poets. Furthermore, although Berendse's study is unique in its attention and sensitivity to textual detail, there are other factors inherent in his methodology which seem to me problematic. His painstaking tracing of 'soziologische', 'szenische', and 'literarische Dialogizität' between the chosen writers, in opposition to what he (following Peter V. Zima) calls the 'machtgeschützte Monosemie' of the GDR, encourages too clear a sense of fixed patterns. Correspondences threaten to obscure differences.[44]

The second obvious possibility would have been to pursue certain aspects of the texts of the 1980s, written by writers of all ages, and to set out a detailed comparison. This is the approach employed by the innovative Leipzig academic Peter Geist in his dissertation analysing poetry of the late 1970s and early 1980s (1987). While he acknowledges that generations are a question to be addressed, he chooses instead a perspective privileging 'generationsübergreifende Erfahrungen', and thus sacrifices the possibility of distinguishing specific generational differences of approach or form, if they could be shown to exist.[45]

Neither of these approaches seems satisfactory alone. I have chosen instead to insist on and to draw out difference. This is not a new thought. The editors of the provocatively titled anthology of GDR prose-writing *Schöne Aussichten*, which features many of the same authors referred to here, conclude their introduction (dated November 1989) as follows:

schöne aussichten—es gibt keine zirkel mehr. keine ismen. keine sächsische dichterschule. keine prenzlauer-berg-connection. es geht nur noch von text zu text. von autor zu autor. von autorin zu autorin. was sich am ende verbinden läßt, ist eine neue literatur aus der ddr. andere zeiten sind angebrochen.[46]

Although this approach suggests a useful antidote to the distortions of large-scale schemes, carried to such an extreme, it nevertheless makes the writing of literary history impossible. A compromise is necessary. In this spirit, while I endeavour to explore the attitudes invoked by the term *hineingeboren* and sketch the emergence of a collective identity in Part I, the individual chapters of Part II follow a variety of literary *Entgrenzungen*, while at the same time testing the ground for continuities, comparisons, and broader groupings. If there has not been the scope to study the development of individual writers in the detail they deserve, I have nevertheless tried to balance a broad range of reference with a more concentrated focus on a handful of those poets whom I have found most interesting and stimulating on repeated reading, in particular: Sascha Anderson, Thomas Böhme, Stefan Döring, Durs Grünbein, Kerstin Hensel, Barbara Köhler, Uwe Kolbe, Steffen Mensching, Bert Papenfuß-Gorek, Rainer Schedlinski, Kathrin Schmidt, and Hans-Eckardt Wenzel. Similarly, while I have offered readings of recurrent topoi, widespread concern with certain aspects of literary tradition, or marked use of particular forms, I have been concerned not to obscure the diverse political and poetological aspirations of the writers concerned. Although, from the beginning, I point forward to the revelations of the *Stasi* files, the main discussion of their importance for understanding the work of the young generation is contained in Part III. There is a tendency, signalled most memorably by Hans Mayer in his *Der Turm von Babel*, to judge the literature and history of the GDR solely in the light of its demise: 'Ende schlecht, alles schlecht'.[47] The same problem now exists with Prenzlauer Berg. The temptation to interpret it 'vom Ende her' has led critics either to treat it nostalgically, as a failed utopian project, or to dismiss it out of hand as corrupt and worthless. It is important—especially now—to allow the literature to stand, or fall, on its own merits.

In part my approach has been inspired by Emmerich's call for the integrity of contradictory impulses and concurrent paradigms to be respected and represented in the formulation of new histories.[48] But it is also a reaction against the political irresponsibility that can be the ultimate product of Emmerich's tack. For while the theoretical constructions of Enlightenment thinking are, in 'DDR-Germanistik' at least, long overdue for adequate deconstruction, the arrival in the 'postmodern condition', as it has been dubbed, has equally serious political consequences. What starts as impartiality, a refusal to engage, however principled that may be, almost inevitably becomes capitulation to the status quo.[49] Recently this has been demonstrated by the curious alliance between a freshly theoretical brand of *feuilleton* journalism, those stalwart defenders of High Modernism, and the respectable face of the new political Right as they set about dismantling the literature of the GDR. Notwithstanding, it seems to me that it must be possible to challenge the structures of meaning which have dominated German literary history up until now, without sacrificing the notion of structure altogether. One can create alternatives: structures more modest, more temporary and unsure of their ground. In other words, it must be possible to challenge our traditional understandings of the subject, truth, progress, meaning, and of history without completely abandoning these as useful categories. This is one way forward: the integrity of difference set alongside, and against, the possibility of broader structures, histories, and 'texts'.

There has been no comprehensive academic analysis of the work of the young 'generation' of GDR poets as a whole, and the work which was published, and the research which could be done within the GDR, was often very partisan in its line of enquiry. For the most part research into the poetry of the 1980s focused on the teenage poetry associated with the officially organized 'Singebewegung' and 'Poetenbewegung' of the 'Freie Deutsche Jugend' (FDJ). As late as 1985 in a thesis examining young writers' poetry Katrin Hagemann refuses to consider texts which might function in the hands of the class enemy, 'als Belege für seine These von der Krise der Wertorientierung des Sozialismus sowie von der Sozialismus-müdigkeit der jungen Generation'. Such texts, she asserts, 'sind als solche kenntlich zu machen und prinzipiell zurückzuweisen', preferably in the form of responsible suppression.[50]

In contrast the critical anthologies and catalogues which were published after the fall of the GDR have concentrated on bringing to light the work of many of those suppressed writers who, until 1989 at least, were scarcely known outside the GDR or even, in some cases, Berlin. They have also brought to wider attention the many 'Maler-' and 'Künstlerbücher', the literary magazines, and the picture and poetry folders, each one unique, which very quickly became collector's pieces, and have often since vanished into private holdings.[51] These anthologies also contain accounts by a number of the writers involved in the history of the literary constellations and disputes which surrounded the unofficial publishing scene. Such accounts are now the only contemporary evidence of at least ten years of suppressed literary activity. Some of them also offer the first perspectives for critical analysis in the future. Many of the most insightful of these are by the writers themselves and by critics intimately associated with the underground scene such as Klaus Michael and Peter Böthig. This brings with it advantages and problems of its own. In the mid-1980s Jan Faktor identified a pervasive stagnation in the literary scene around Prenzlauer Berg, which he dubbed 'die neue Kritiklosigkeit'. It is noticeable that, with the exception of Faktor, there was, before 1991 at least, very little sustained attempt to identify the weaknesses of the texts under discussion or of the scene as a whole, or indeed to discuss either of these in a larger context.[52] There will doubtless be a large amount of academic work devoted to the various literatures of 'Prenzlauer Berg' in the future. This will offer a useful alternative to the sometimes over-incestuous nature of commentary up until now, but, more important, it will provide a necessary redress for the literature which was so long excluded from the literary history of the GDR.[53]

However, for the purposes of this project I am most indebted to the indispensable if quixotic 1991 anthology of GDR poetry from the 1970s and 1980s, edited by Peter Geist, *Ein Molotow-Cocktail auf fremder Bettkante*.[54] The creative structure of the anthology and Geist's 'Epilogue' seem to me the most cogent and illuminating presentation of this decade of poetry to date. Articles on particular writers and aspects of the poetry which have contributed to my understanding will be discussed individually in the course of the study.

PART I

Hineingeboren: Writers in Context

I

Hineingeboren: A New 'Generation' of Poets in the GDR

IN 1979 the existence of a new 'generation' of writers in the GDR was given the official blessing of Siegfried Rönisch, the influential editor-in-chief of *Weimarer Beiträge*. In his article 'Notizen über eine neue Autorengeneration', he welcomed their coming to prominence as one of 'die gewichtigsten und weittragensten [*sic*] kulturellen Ereignisse des zurückliegenden Jahrzehnts'.[1] These were writers who had been 'born into' the established socialist state, to borrow Uwe Kolbe's much quoted term 'hineingeboren'.[2] Since 1989 and the collapse of the GDR, it is this generation which has been at the centre of literary debates in Germany. In the run-up to German unification many older and established GDR writers came under sustained attack from literary commentators and critics. They were accused of being 'Staatsdichter', who were now implicated in the brutalities of a corrupt regime. The young writers whom the regime had tried to silence and write out of the literary history books, 'eine *beinahe* weggeschwiegene Generation' (Leonhard Lorek),[3] could be rescued from the obscurity of the underground where they had survived, to become the morally unimpeachable representatives of a new German literature. With the revelation, in 1991, that some of the leading figures of this literary scene had been implicated in the operations of the GDR *Staatssicherheitsdienst* and could thus no longer be celebrated as heroes of cultural autonomy, it was once more as a 'generation' that they were discredited.

Ever since the early reviews in 1979, the critical reception in East and West of young writers has been based upon the broad understanding of them as a generation. On the whole, this has been an understanding that the writers themselves were happy to go along with. Towards the end of the 1980s, however, several writers showed themselves very wary of the generalizations that such categories imply. In 1988, during a round-table discussion of writers born between 1953 and 1961, the concept came under fierce attack.[4] While the moderators of the discussion sketched out the contours of literary generations in the GDR, a number of writers spoke out explicitly against the notion of the themselves as 'Vertreter einer Generation', 'Generationserfahrung', and even the very concept of a generation itself. For example, Kerstin Hensel: 'Ich habe schon Schwierigkeiten mit dem Wort "Generation", kann mir keine Antwort darauf geben, was meine Generation ist. Sie ist so in sich gespalten. Die, die wir hier sitzen, sind nicht meine Generation [. . .] Ich glaube, daß ich vollkommen andere Erfahrungen habe im Leben als die Mehrzahl meiner Altersgruppe.'[5] In the same year Jan Faktor also agitatedly dismissed 'das G-Wort', as he called it.

Es regt mich immer wieder auf, wenn jemand ernsthaft das Wort Generation benutzt oder dieses schon so ausgelutschte, ziemlich bombastische Wort sogar zum zentralen Begriff irgendwelcher Verallgemeinerungen macht. Ich warte schon Jahre darauf, bis dieses für mich tabuisierte Wort endlich allgemein verpönt wird. [. . .] Ich komme im weiteren also ohne das G-Wort aus.[6]

A number of writers have subsequently complained that the notion of a collective identity has always been a fiction. Bert Papenfuß-Gorek understands it as 'eine synthetische Solidarität': a temporary consensus forged under the pressure of State intervention, Detlef Opitz, on the other hand, sees it rather more sceptically as 'eine Kreation der bundesdeutschen Journaille'. In a recent poetic retrospective on the end of the GDR Barbara Köhler reflects on the ambivalence in the need for solidarity and individuation.

Immernoch sage ich WIR: Du und Du und Du und Ich, als ob Generation schon zuviel gemeint wäre für ein paar Jahrgänge um 1959, Freundinnen und Freunde, die das Wort Schicksal vermeiden; wir wollen nicht übertreiben. Ein Wir das die Defensive des Ichs beschreibt, unser Wir gegen das allgemeine Einvernehmen, die Einbahnstraße VOM ICH ZUM WIR gegen die Anfechtbarkeit die Unanfechtbarkeit ein kleiner Plural der Vergewisserung.[7]

In addition, it has been pointed out that, if anything, the cycle of generations is speeding up, and the youngest among the writers, those born in the 1960s, already appear to have recognizably different concerns from those even slightly older, and might be said to belong to a different generation again.[8] Johannes Jansen

(b. 1966), for example, does not consider himself 'ein in die DDR Hineingeborener', and describes himself in a poem—ironically perhaps—as 'fast nur noch ein ich'.[9] In tracing below the emergence and reception of these new writers in the GDR, I would like, at the same time, to explore how the rhetoric of generations has up until now conditioned—and perhaps distorted—our view of the writing concerned, and how far it can usefully be used as a category of literary history.

Literary Generations in the GDR

On the one hand, classification by generation is a standard methodological tool in the study of the sociology of literature.[10] On the other hand, a rhetoric of generations has long been used more or less metaphorically in order to signal evolution and revolution in literary practice. This finds its way into German literature as, for example, the topos of the expressionist 'Vatermord', the judgemental father–son motif of the 1950s, or the radical reckoning with the fathers of 1968. It is interesting to note how concretely the writing of the 1980s extends and expands this motif into the context of the contemporary GDR. Kurt Drawert's *Spiegelland* of 1992 charts the reflective fictionalized biography of a rebellious generation at odds with their 'hochbeamteten Vätern'. An epilogue describing the way the text has run away with itself concludes: 'Denn der Gegenstand des Denkens ist die Welt der Väter gewesen, von ihr sollte berichtet werden, und wie verloren sie machte und wie verloren sie war—als herrschende Ordnung, als Sprache, als beschädigtes Leben.'[11] But beyond the biographical specifics, perhaps Uwe Kolbe is right when he concludes: 'Der Vatermord ist eine von jeder Generation zu erliegende Aufgabe.'[12]

In the GDR, on the other hand, the word 'generation' was for a long time absent from literary discussion. Where a historicization of GDR literature was attempted, the terms of periodization were for many years governed by the 'Großmetaphern' of railway, river, building, and machine. These metaphors, stemming from the philosophical and economic studies of Marx and Engels, were intended to embody the evolution towards a Communist society in plastic forms. They served to validate the idea of progress—construction, a journey—but always along a preconditioned track, and with a fixed goal in mind: 'Die Geschichte verläuft in diesen

Bildern eindimensional'.[13] Wolfgang Emmerich also highlights the prevalence of terms like 'Aufbau', 'Suche', 'Übergang', and 'Reife' in accounts of GDR literary history, which are of course less mechanical, but no less teleological in their implication.[14] The notion of distinguishable generations in GDR literature, however, was thought to jeopardize both the image of the successful and homogeneous socialist collective, but also the fluent or organic progress towards a Communist future. As Hans Richter concludes: 'Die ausdrückliche Bestätigung von Generationsunterschieden kollidierte mit dem lange erwünschten Bild eines grundsätzlich harmonischen und kontinuierlich verlaufenden gesellschaftlichen Lebens.'[15] Distinct 'generations' could be seen to imply heterogeneous perspectives, and difference of perspective was all too easily interpreted as the kind of antagonistic conflict normally reserved for relations with the West.

This attitude changed as a result of the cultural liberalization at the beginning of the 1970s. The validity of a personal experience of reality (as against politically approved versions of it) was increasingly recognized in literary discussion. And it was in the same spirit that the distinct experience of different generations was recognized, and became a standard category of literary criticism in the GDR. The Leipzig academics Christel and Walfried Hartinger pioneered this approach to lyric poetry. In an essay of 1976 detailing the relationship between 'Zeitgenossenschaft und lyrische Subjektivität', they explicitly understood 'eine solche Generationssicht' as 'ein aufschlußreiches, unentbehrliches methodisches Prinzip'.[16] An example of the shift in attitudes can be seen in the reactions to what has now almost universally become known as 'die Generation von Volker Braun'.[17] Kurt Hager had been quick to condemn what he called the 'künstlerische[s] Aufbauschen des Generationsproblems' in the work of the young writers who came to prominence during the 'Lyrikwelle' of the early 1960s.[18] By 1970 the influential writer and critic Günther Deicke paid tribute to Volker Braun and his companions, precisely for having brought a distinct experience and distinct expectations to GDR literature. He placed this explicitly within the context of a new historical generation. Deicke's tribute demonstrates, however, that the recognition of different generations in the GDR also served a useful political and cultural purpose. Reference to the divergent experience of generations could be used to demonstrate the positive trajectory of the socialist state. Braun and his compatriots were seen to be overcoming the remaining non-antagonistic contradictions which still persisted in really existing socialism. 'Volker Braun und seine Altersgenossen wuchsen bereits in dieser Welt auf—wo wir uns vornehmlich mit der Vergangenheit auseinandersetzten, fanden sie in dieser ihrer Gegenwart bereits Reibungsflächen, endeckten wo wir Fortschritt sahen, schon Unvollkommenheiten.'[19] Even if Communism had not yet been realized, it was thus at least seen to be recognizably under way. For Western critics too the terminology of generations had a cultural political function. It had been introduced as a means of periodization in GDR literary history in the early 1970s.[20] During the 1980s and since the Wall in particular, it has increasingly served as an oblique method of marking stages in the disintegration of the socialist project.

In East and West, then, critics have set 'literary generations' against each other largely in order to mark out pieces of cultural history.[21] Uwe Wittstock, for example, delineates the evolution from 'die großen Alten' to 'die mittlere Generation' and finally to 'die zornigen Jungen'. Most recently, Rüdiger Thomas takes up the same three generations with more ideological tags: 'die Gründer- und Aufbaugeneration, die Generation der Desillusionierten und die Generation der Autonomen'.[22] It is rhetoric less politically charged than that of the early GDR cultural historians, but no less suspect in literary terms. For, in focusing on ideological and aesthetic rupture, critics have inevitably obscured three things: the continuities between writers of different generations, the simultaneous development of writers of different generations, and the very different approaches and aims of writers from within the same generation.

A New Generation of Poets in the GDR

In an intense and fragmentary poem, published in the West in 1982, Sascha Anderson juxtaposes a jumble of disturbing dream images with a more sober formula to describe himself and his fellow writers: 'der | buchstabe x das absolute zeichen meiner | generation'.[23] It is the bald and yet elusive quality of Anderson's formula, which I would like to understand as programmatic. In mathematics, 'x' is after all the unknown quantity still to be sought and defined.

Siegfried Rönisch's resounding tribute to 'eine neue Autorengeneration', in the *Weimarer Beiträge* of September 1979, was marked by the simultaneous publication of five round-table discussions, with representatives of the generation in question from different fields. In defining the characteristics which distinguished the writers concerned, Rönisch concentrated on biographical coordinates. 'Nach 1944/45 geboren, wuchs diese Generation ausschließlich in unserem Lande auf. Ihre Kindheit verlebte sie im ersten Jahrzehnt des sozialistischen Aufbaus, und mit den Begriffen Klassenkampf, Faschismus und Krieg usw. verband sie keine direkten Eindrücke und Erfahrungen mehr' (p. 7). Within the next two years a very large body of criticism from the GDR built up, which clearly identified the contours of a new generation of writers in very similar terms.[24] This was the 'vierte Generation' of the GDR, as distinct from the generations of Becher, Deicke, and Braun, respectively. Very quickly critics drew a further distinction between a 'Zwischengeneration', born in the late 1940s, and those born in the 1950s.[25] The writers highlighted in the subsequent discussions shared one overriding experience in common; they were, to borrow a phrase from Biermann, 'unvermischte DDR-Produkte'.[26] These were writers whose dominant experience was having been 'born into' the established socialist state, writers for whom the Second World War, the anti-fascist democratic struggle of the founding years, the Cold War, the building of the Berlin Wall, even the events of 1968, were all textbook history. It is worth perhaps stressing their relative ignorance of 1968, for the disillusionment that set in amongst writers in the GDR after the Warsaw Pact countries invaded Czechoslovakia marked the lives of writers even only slightly older than the ones who are the focus of attention here. Both Thomas Brasch and Andreas Reimann, for example, were imprisoned, and Bettina Wegner was expelled from University, on account of their protests.[27] In a laconic note of 1991 Uwe Kolbe sums up the situation of the youngest authors. 'Jene, meine Generation läßt sich übrigens durch drei Daten eingrenzen: wenig oder kaum Bewußtsein der Zeit vor dem 13. August 1961; zu jung, 1968 eine Meinung zu haben; gereift in der letzten Tauwetterperiode der DDR, also zwischen Honeckers Machtantritt und, etwa, der Biermann-Ausbürgerung 1976.'[28]

The year 1976, which saw the forcible expatriation of Wolf Biermann, marked a critical watershed in the cultural and political history of the GDR. It was, as Günter Kunert put it: 'Ein Datum wie eine Geschichtswende: Vor Biermann und nach Biermann'.[29] For this was the date on which the official rhetoric of an equal and intimate relationship between 'Geist' und 'Macht' in the GDR was demonstrated to be an illusion. The repressive measures taken against those who had openly supported Biermann, and the subsequent exclusions from the Writers' Union in 1979, led to increasing disillusionment amongst GDR intellectuals and a conspicuous exodus of many of the leading writers of the day, mostly under pressure from the authorities. Even for those who stayed, it represented a calamitous rift with the State.[30] Christa Wolf, for example, talks of suffering 'eine Krise, die existentiell war', and feeling at a stroke entirely extraneous to the political and cultural process: 'dieses ins Extrem getriebene Zum-Außenseiter-gemacht-Werden'.[31] It was at this point for many writers that the illusion of the much-touted 'Übergangsgesellschaft' gave way to the anticipation of an 'Untergangsgesellschaft'.[32] It is no chance that images of a 'Waste Land' of sorts—physical, spiritual, and linguistic—began to appear in GDR literature in particular profusion at this time. Günter Kunert's 1977 collection *Unterwegs nach Utopia*, for example, distils ecological pessimism, glimpses of the end of history, a disturbing 'Sprachskepsis', and profound loss of political illusion into a bleak dystopian topography.[33] In his 1985 Frankfurt lectures, looking back to this time, and to these poems in particular, Kunert signals a fundamental caesura: 'der endgültige Abschied von der Utopie, vom Prinzip Hoffnung'.[34]

The profound loss of illusion which many older writers suffered in these times was something quite different from the experience of the younger writers. Many of them simply had no illusions to be shattered. They had had no part in the absolute belief of those who had fought through the war years, nor the belief of the newly converted after the war. They were never infected by enthusiasm for the *Aufbau*, nor the crisis of seeing it fail. They were 'born into' that state of radical marginalization and alienation which the older writers had just begun reluctantly to acknowledge. Sascha Anderson's comment of 1986, 'Meine Jugendzeit fiel nicht in die Aufbauphase der DDR. Ich mußte mich nicht identifizieren mit diesem Staatsgebilde', finds an echo in an essay by Rüdiger

Rosenthal: 'Eine Identifizierung mit der "sozialistischen Aufbauphase" konnte bei ihnen kaum oder gar nicht entstehen', and,
quite simply, in a poem by Johannes Jansen: 'ich war nie ein land
und ich war nie ein wir'.[35] As Heiner Müller, reviewing Thomas
Brasch's 1977 collection *KARGO. 32. Versuch, auf einem
untergehenden Schiff aus der eigenen Haut zu kommen*, put it: 'Die
Generation der heute Dreißigjährigen in der DDR hat den
Sozialismus nicht als Hoffnung auf das *Andere* erfahren, sondern
als deformierte Realität'.[36] Many of them were never disabused,
they started without 'hope', and expressed this quite openly: 'Diese
Enttäuschung ist für mich kein Erlebnis mehr, sondern eine
Voraussetzung'.[37] In the crackdown after the Biermann *Ausbürgerung*, however, such radical scepticism could scarcely be
tolerated, and a series of measures were initiated to keep the
remaining writers in check. In 1979 literature published privately,
without permission of the authorities, was criminalized. At almost
the same time efforts were made to draft a 'Gesetz zum Schutz der
Berufsbezeichnung Schriftsteller', and it is now clear that this is the
point at which a concerted campaign to contain and direct the
literature of the nascent Berlin scene was put into operation by the
cultural authorities.[38] Gabriele Kachold was given a prison
sentence for her protests against the Biermann *Ausbürgerung* and
Sascha Anderson was, he claims, imprisoned and beaten for
printing and circulating Biermann's songs. Karl-Wilhelm Schmidt
points out the alarming over-representation of young authors (born
after 1949) in the figures for those who left the GDR during the late
1970s and 1980s.[39] Yet despite, or rather precisely because of, the
extremities of that time, the decade after Biermann saw not only the
excoriation of the intellectual élite in the GDR, but also another
quite different reaction. Paradoxically enough, many of the young
writers also had their first (often abortive) opportunity to publish at
this time. It was ideologically important for the authorities to find
another generation waiting in the wings.[40] Bernd Wagner, a writer
who left the GDR in the mid-1980s, claimed, however, that the
response of those young artists remaining in the GDR was neither
conformity nor retreat into a poetic refuge, but rather, 'eine neue
Radikalität'—a fundamental break with the structures of power.[41]

Dieser längst überfällige Verlust von Illusionen, der Entzug eines
gemeinsamen Konsenses zwischen Macht und Kultur brachte aber auch die

Entlassung aus der 'Eidgenossenschaft sozialistischer Schriftsteller'. [. . .] die Entbindung vom fast priesterlichen Amt als stets waches soziales Gewissen, von den Folgen der dialektischen Zwangskrankheit, dem ständigen Abwägen objektiver Faktoren, die dieses oder jenes rechtfertigen oder nicht rechtfertigen, dem noch in der Abwendung auschließlichen Fixiertseins auf dem Marxismus als Leitschnur eigenen Handelns. (p. 110)

Nowhere was this more in evidence than among the young writers. Many (though not all) of them also looked to settle their literature outside the restrictive dialectic of State and official (or critical) writer. They initiated the search for a new, autonomous language: 'die Formulierung einer eigenen Sprache, die die Korrespondenz mit der Sprache der Macht abgebrochen hat'.[42] This gesture of rupture was also translated into the physical circumstances of their lives. Whereas writers even only slightly older had generally completed their studies or done their military service before following the prescribed route into industry or an apprenticeship, many of the younger writers had opted very early for a precarious but more independent existence '*am Rande* der DDR Gesellschaft angesiedelt'.[43] Writing was no longer simply a profession, but a way of escaping the regulated public sphere and creating a different way of life. In pursuit of 'dieses andere Leben' many writers chose not to go on to further education: the prerequisites for study and the authoritarian structures involved alienated many young writers. Of those who did start studying several were subsequently *exmatrikuliert*, including Lutz Rathenow and Gabriele Kachold.[44] Others were originally involved in the FDJ poetry seminars in Schwerin (Anderson and Döring even held 'Förderpreise') or were proposed for membership of the Writers' Union, but either distanced themselves from the organizations or found themselves on black-lists on account of their political stance.[45] Many had a series of manual jobs, others were simply *asozial*, and squatted illegally and, they hoped, anonymously, in the old housing stock of one of the major cities. In most cases they saw themselves to some extent as marginal to the established social norms.[46] The Hähnels spell out the effect it had on young writers: 'Man fühlt sich unnütz in dieser Gesellschaft, resigniert, zieht sich zurück'. From the distance of West Berlin Sascha Anderson put the case more forcefully by speaking of a generation of 'Aussteiger', of 'Nicht-Einsteiger', and Bert Papenfuß-Gorek's characteristically uncompromising text 'forwiegend aber' claimed quite bluntly: 'aber

aberarkdichter schreiben seit jahren | nur fon & ueber was sie
ankotzt | & ueber eine gesellschaft | die sie forwiegend auskotzt'.[47]

'Positionsbestimmungen' and Critical Responses

The arrival of the new generation of writers onto the literary scene
signalled a fundamental, and controversial, paradigm shift in the
literature of the GDR. A number of critics have discussed the
changes which emerged in the understanding of young writers and
artists at this time; here I want simply to summarize some of the
most important tendencies.[48] If the writers had felt marginalized by
their society, the critics were almost unanimous in recognizing a
fundamental retreat from that social reality on the part of the
writers. Ursula Heukenkamp's description of a shift from 'Lebens-
erfahrungen' to 'Kunst als Refugium' might stand as a single
example here.[49] Broadly speaking, critics identified this retreat in a
number of distinct areas of the writers' work: in their presentation
of the subject, and of their social reality, their understanding of
history, of politics, and of the function of literature, and their
attitude towards language.

It was in the 1979 round-table interviews that this shift in
attitudes crystallized (and provoked a determined response from
the cultural departments of the *Staatssicherheit*).[50] Far from feeling
themselves to be the subject of history, the ministers of social
progress, as they had learnt at school, the young writers felt that
they were manipulated daily by forces beyond their control.[51] It
was particularly a sullen and much-quoted riposte by Uwe Kolbe
which gave vent to this political and existential displacement and
shocked critics in the GDR:[52]

Meine Generation hat die Hände im Schoß, was engagiertes (!) Handeln
betrifft [. . .] Ich kann noch weiter gehen und sagen, daß diese Generation
völlig verunsichert ist, weder richtiges Heimischsein hier noch das
Vorhandensein von Alternativen anderswo empfindet.

As a response to the existential unhousedness and insecurity Kolbe
describes, writers emphasized the importance of the private
realm—apart from, and even at odds with, the public one.[53] A
distinctive emphasis on the representation of the subjective was
highlighted more or less aggressively by a number of critics who

noted in the poetry: 'der Drang des Einzelnen nach Selbstverwirk-lichung' (Hartinger), 'stärkere Ich-Bezogenheit' (Dau), and 'die Erörterung des eigenen Standpunkts' (Hähnels).[54] Beyond the immediate subject, writers appeared reluctant to venture into a broader social sphere in their work. They contented themselves with a sober focus on the concrete reality of immediate surroundings. 'Man wendet sich nicht an eine abstrakte Gesell-schaft oder einen abstrakten Sozialismus', claimed Bernd Wagner.[55] Again this was taken up by the critics, who commented positively on 'die Konkretheit des einzelnen Lebens' (Dau) as it appeared in the poetry, and the 'Geradlinigkeit und Unbestech-lichkeit' of poetic observation (Rönisch).[56] Social problems appeared only to interest the poets to the extent that they impinged directly on their own lives. However, the intention to focus on a microcosm of reality, with which the poet was intimately familiar, brought with it for many critics a loss of necessary historical perspective. A number of commentators blamed the ideological shortcomings of the writers on their inability to draw from the past, or project from the present.[57]

In contrast to writers of previous generations, these young writers appeared to dissociate themselves politically from the extravagance of what they called the 'DDR-Messianismus' of the *Aufbau* years: 'Kein früher Braun heute', exclaimed Uwe Kolbe.[58] Stephan Ernst, for example, broke with orthodox traditions of socialist literature along notoriously radical lines.

Die Literatur ist eine Art Opposition. [. . .] Sie ist Gegenwehr zuerst zu den Erwachsenen, zur Schule, später auch ideologisch [. . .] Ein bestimmtes Bewußtsein von einem Ungenügen braucht Literatur als Gegenwehr gegen ihre Umwelt, auch gegen politische Konzeptionen und meinetwegen auch gegen die marxistische Philosophie, sagen wir: gegen kollektive Vereinnahmung.[59]

Other writers also rejected a traditional Marxist understanding of the role of literature, and focused instead on its importance as an individual enterprise, as 'Verantwortung vor sich selbst', as 'Stütze des Individuums, nicht der Gesellschaft'.[60] In interpreting such comments as these many of the GDR critics were concerned to tone down the most outspoken of the views. Dau, Rönisch, and the Hartingers, for example, are all at pains to integrate these tendencies as part of an ongoing search for political and social

positions. Dau concludes her article by insisting on the conscious
role these writers see for themselves in constructing a socialist
future: 'Überall sind auch sehr verschiedene "Vorschläge" im
Angebot, Signale für die Gesellschaft, die nicht von einer unbeteiligt
oder gar zynisch beobachtenden "lost generation", die ihre Ideale
verloren hat, abgegeben werden, sondern von selbst "Betroffenen"
und Mitgestaltern ihrer eigenen Zukunft.'[61] In the reference to
'Vorschläge', Dau is undoubtedly thinking of the Brechtian use of
the term, and situating these writers in a line of non-antagonistic
socialist criticism. Similarly, both Hartinger and Dau also turn to
the Brechtian phrase 'eingreifendes Denken' to anchor the work of
the young writers in a socialist tradition.[62]

However, especially where the writers dealt with the function of
poetry, other critics were often forced to radical conclusions. The
Hähnels, for example, conceded: 'Das Gedicht wird verstanden als
persönliche Lebenshilfe, als Versuch, sich durch die poetische
Artikulation im alltäglichen Leben besser zurechtzufinden. [. . .]
Der Akzent liegt hier auf *persönlich*, denn um mehr geht es bei den
meisten der jungen Autoren wirklich nicht.' The primary impulse of
the young writers' poetry they defined, not as solidarity or
construction, as Dau or Hartinger had done, but rather as 'Not',
'die "Risse" und "Nöte" des Ichs'. 'Die wirklichen Kunstanlässe',
they continue, '[sind] in den Nöten, im Defizit gelebten Lebens zu
sehen'. Finally, it is clearly an admission that essential bench-marks
of socialist literary policy are being erased when they conclude of
the young writers: 'Ein Funktionsverständnis, das der Literatur eine
Aufgabe und Möglichkeit im Hinblick auf die fortschreitende
Veränderung der Gesellschaft einräumt, steht für sie vorerst nicht
zur Diskussion.'[63] The conclusions offered by the Hähnels were
fiercely contested by Rudolf and Mathilde Dau in an article of the
following year. Their main criticism is that the Hähnels do not take
into account the songs and poems of the (officially sponsored)
'Poetenbewegung', 'Singebewegung', or annual 'Poetenseminar' in
Schwerin.[64] However, the signal for discussion of the shift in
literary direction had clearly been given.

The apparently programmatic shift to inwardness in the young
writers' work was also identified in the fabric of the texts. Ursula
Heukenkamp noted the absence of words like 'Jahrhundert',
'Epoche', 'Zukunft', or 'Geschichte' in the young writers' work—
concepts which had formed the very basis of earlier generations'

poetic understanding.[65] Instead she saw the cultivation of a deliberately hermetic language, a private dialogue between like-minded poets and an apparent disregard for the reader. Suspicious of the abandonment of traditional poetic forms and of the preoccupation with word play, unorthodox orthography, and graphical presentation in their work, Heukenkamp came close to accusing the writers of a bourgeois 'l'art pour l'art' aesthetic: 'das Gedicht erhält seinen Mittelpunkt in sich selbst'.[66] The Hähnels were far more conciliatory in their treatment of two early texts by Bert Papenfuß, cautiously citing a productive interaction with the traditions of concrete poetry in the West. However, even they warn against the 'dangers of his method', namely: 'die Veruntreuung von Wirklichkeit', and 'eine sehr vermittelte Kundgabe von Subjektivität'.[67]

Where some critics had attempted either to play down, defend, or even contain and reintegrate this shift in aesthetic understanding, a degree of more outspoken opposition to the perceived inwardness, insubstantiality, incomprehensibility, and pessimism of the writing was not surprising. A letter published in the journal *Temperamente* accused the young writers of a lack of courage, of coquetry and superficiality, the then cultural secretary of the FDJ attacked their alienation from ordinary people, and even Heinz Plavius, in an otherwise sympathetic piece, voiced acerbic asides for 'künstlich-eskapistische Existenzen wie Bohemians und Playboys'.[68]

A more serious problem for the cultural establishment was the move from Socialist Realism as a model. Where the veteran writer Jurij Brězan noted this with sadness and consternation, Inge von Wangenheim railed against the young writers' 'abandonment of the fundamental positions of Socialist Realism'. In particular, she highlights the breakdown in the continuity of generations. The relay of responsibility, what she calls 'die Weitergabe der Fackel', essential to the very survival of the socialist project, she sees as endangered.[69] 'Entweder verfehlten die Nachkommenden den Treffpunkt, oder die Fackel wurde angenommen, bevor die Kraft, sie zu halten, genügend entwickelt. So fiel sie in den Sand.' At the cultural conference of 22 October 1982 Egon Krenz, in his capacity as first secretary of the FDJ, countered the dangers even more robustly: 'Der Stafettenstab, den sie von den älteren Genossen übernahmen, wird dabei nicht mit pseudo-avantgardistischer Pose beiseite geworfen, sondern fest wie eine Fahne in der Hand gehalten.'[70] The outspokenness of such important figures testifies to the acute alarm which the work of the young writers had caused in some sections of the cultural establishment. What had begun as an enthusiastic welcome for a new generation of socialist literature had become a struggle to defend the basis of Socialist Realism itself. The anti-political bias perceived in the work of many of the young writers, the rupture with traditional socialist aims and orthodox aesthetic models, were provocations that demanded a response. That response was certainly not as high-profile as the Biermann affair—the authorities wanted to avoid a similar scandal—but it was none the less effective. For certain writers (Kolbe, Mensching) this meant opportunities to publish and perform as long as they were prepared to compromise.[71] For others it meant almost a decade of censorship and the virtual eradication of their names from official literary criticism.[72]

The 'Prenzlauer-Berg-Connection'

It was the writer Adolf Endler who coined the term the 'Prenzlauer-Berg-Connection',[73] and it is he who has been perhaps most bitter about what he sees as a mixture of ignorance and cowardice on the part of those academics and critics in the GDR who colluded in attempting to silence so many young writers.[74] In fact, many of those writers and their texts went 'underground' and became part of an alternative culture which flourished for almost a decade in the large cities: Dresden, Leipzig, and, especially, Berlin–Prenzlauer Berg. One of the most important aspects of this culture was undoubtedly the network of magazines which grew up over the years (*Anschlag*, *Ariadnefabrik*, *Bizarre Städte*, *liane*, *Entwerter-Oder*, *schaden*, *Und*, etc.). They were produced in editions of between thirty and two hundred, some handwritten, others, later, on computer, and were passed from hand to hand. Both Wolfgang Emmerich and Klaus Michael cite *1979*, the year that the generation was first officially recognized in the GDR, as the 'eigentliche Geburtsstunde der originalgrafischen Zeitschriften'. Nevertheless, it has taken over a decade for this 'alternative' literature of the young generation to become accessible to widespread critical discussion.[75] Although it has often—mistakenly—been treated as a fixed or homogeneous body of work, there have already been a number of more differentiated attempts to catalogue the work that appeared in such publications and to recuperate the 'other' history of GDR literature in the 1980s.[76] I do not want to rehearse those accounts here. Instead I would like to present some of the problems in approaching this vast body of work: in particular, the notion of it as a (single) literature, and its relationship with the work that appeared 'above ground' during the same period.

The poem 'Gruß an Karl Mickel' by Uwe Kolbe was written in 1979:[77]

> Zugeb ich, daß ich ganz privat
> so reflektiere nah am Hochverrat,
> und meine Gerade nenn ich Grat:
> Am einen Fuß die Schelle klirrt,
> der andre nimmt ein Bad
> in Eselsmilch.

The first three lines, the 'confession' of the lyric subject, are clearly to be understood against the political situation at the time: 1979 was the year of the expulsions from the Writers' Union and increased restrictions placed on publishing. The lyric subject's obstinate integrity, his 'Grat' (recalling Bloch's 'aufrechten Gang'), turns at the colon to become also a 'Gratwanderung' of sorts. The private truth is to be safeguarded against the intervention of the State with traditional poetic tools: what Brecht might have called 'List'. With the 'Narrenfreiheit' of a court jester and a semblance of innocence, the poet hopes to make it through the net of censorship.[78] The irony of this text is that it did not enact its own poetic quite well enough. Held back by the 'Verlagslektor' at work on Kolbe's 'Bornholm' manuscript, it could only exist in limbo in an illegal pamphlet entitled 'Kabarett', until it was finally published in the West in 1990.[79] The fate of this poem crystallizes the dilemma facing writers pitted against hostile censorship at the beginning of the 1980s. The protection afforded by a kind of 'Sklavensprache' was precarious.[80] For those poets—and texts—excluded from the official sphere and unwilling or unable to achieve that 'balancing act' there could only be an alternative existence in the underground.

It would be wrong to overemphasize the significance of the term 'alternative'. One of the failings of work done so far on the young writers is the exclusivity of the categories which have been used. Whereas, of course, some writers suffered an *ad hominem* 'Verbot', and, until the late 1980s at least, had very little chance of publishing in any official organ, one should not understand the boundary between official and unofficial publication in the GDR as watertight. Just as some of the younger writers who wrote for or edited the unofficial literary magazines also had an official publishing profile (Kolbe himself is a good example here), so a number of more established (and older) authors also contributed to the unofficial scene. For some writers at least, there could be a two-way traffic of sorts. Nevertheless, it is important to underline the significance of the term 'existence'. As is clear from the comments above, the unofficial publishing network which developed in Berlin and the other cities was not simply a response to censorship, but part of a much larger project: an alternative way of life. That existence was to be found in a community situated beyond the stagnant social reality of the older generations: 'hingehalten von frustration & orgonomie, politikant | unsere väter: verweser, wir: die verwesten . . .' (Papenfuß-Gorek).[81] What began as informal 'collaborations' between artists and writers and musicians turned into an expanding alternative culture which included experimental rock, theatre and cabaret, films, photography, and painting.[82] Artists found their audience in a network of unofficial and impromptu readings, meetings, and performances in private flats, cafés, or church halls.[83] Peter Böthig has described the anarchic beginnings of the underground scene as 'einen kollektiven prozeß des mündig werdens'.[84] It is a useful starting-point for the complex dynamic of existence and aesthetic which was generated beyond the controlled public sphere. While many of the texts printed by official publishing houses thematized their own 'Entmündigung' (to take one example, Christiane Grosz's 'Blatt vor dem Mund'), the focus for those young writers excluded from publishing possibilities was on discovering a new language, unconditioned by the dominant discourse.[85] Many commentators have emphasized the link between the assertion of an alternative way of life and an alternative language formed through dialogue: 'eine Form des Zusammenlebens', 'Versuch eine "Kommunikationsidee" zu leben'.[86] Aesthetics and existence are understood as a creative interplay: as Papenfuß-Gorek puts it, 'das ist mein Leben mit dem ich experimentiere'.[87] The intense commitment of self and life in such an understanding of literary creation can have costs of its own.

Peter Geist has recently highlighted the cases of a number of writers whose frustrated 'Lebensexperiment Kunst' turned back on them and eventually destroyed them: particularly "Matthias" BAADER Holst and flanzendörfer.[88] More mundanely, the sense of communicating only within a closed network of largely like-minded people can breed complacency and stagnation.

On the other hand, the mixture of practical existence and conscious aesthetic manifests itself positively in two very interesting formal aspects of the work. The need, at the beginning, to reproduce texts laboriously by hand meant that poetry, especially, became a favoured form. This later became justified as a programmatic turn towards experimental poetic texts and a rejection of 'der zentrale Roman' (Schedlinski).[89] Similarly, what began as the exploitation of a loophole in the publishing laws, which meant that elements of text within a painting or drawing did not require the same licence as a written text, led to an extensive collaboration between painters and poets and a deliberate aesthetic programme.[90] The same is true of the format of the magazines and 'Lyrik-Grafik-Mappen'. The holdings of *schaden* in Marbach, for example, consist of individually painted card covers tied with ribbon, and a loose-leaf collection of handwritten or typed texts, collages, scraps stuck in, photos, drawings, poems on silver foil or graph-paper, screen prints, watercolours, sometimes with cassettes or badges tucked inside: in short an artistic 'production' in itself. In the late 1980s this form of production, what Klaus Michael has called 'das Unikat-Syndrom', became one of the major sources of revenue for the underground scene, as the folders and magazines were smuggled out by diplomats and sold to private collectors in the West.[91]

As indicated above, what Birgit Dahlke, for example, calls the 'gegenkulturelle Anfangsphase' of the underground scene was not originally conceived as an 'opposition' to the official culture, but rather as the opportunity to create an 'Ergänzungskultur', 'eine dritte Literatur', 'eine andere Öffentlichkeit'.[92] The terminology is difficult; the most important aspect, however, is the sense of moving into an autonomous and unregulated sphere: 'Weg mit der Ersatz- und Sklavensprache' (Kolbe).[93] In a letter introducing the magazine *ariadnefabrik* to the Akademie der Wissenschaften of 1988 (when the underground culture was already semi-acknowledged by the State), Rainer Schedlinski insists that the unofficial literary scene had never understood itself as 'eine alternative zum offiziellen [. . .] eine art *gegenliteratur*'. To define it simply as 'der abfall, der mangel oder der auswuchs der anderen' would be to implicate it in a dialectic which it had consciously sought to escape.[94] That is not to say, however, that the unofficial publishing scene was not regarded in its totality as a provocation, even perhaps a threat, by the cultural authorities and the cultural division of the *Staatssicherheit*. Whatever might be produced out of it, the very existence of such an alternative network meant that writers were operating not only outside, but against, the law.

The political status of the writers in question and their literature is complex. I deal with it in greater detail later. It is worth noting, however, that there were very different factions and splinterings within the underground which gravitated somewhere between the two 'Szene-Fürsten', the explicitly political Lutz Rathenow and the postmodern guru Sascha Anderson.[95] It would be wrong to divide the underground simply into a political and an unpolitical literature. Most of the writers wrote for or edited a large number of the magazines; the spectrum of publications allowed for very different understandings, and these often generated political and aesthetic debates between them.[96] On the other hand, the increasing influence of the writers around Sascha Anderson meant that a dominant aesthetic was formed, and that those who did not fit in with it were sometimes marginalized. In 1988, for example, Jan Faktor spoke disparagingly of 'die Allmacht des Penckismus' and darkly about 'Kontroversen mit Sascha'.[97] The 'misogyny' of the inner Prenzlauer circle deserves special note and has led to several recriminations by leading women writers against 'das gesetz der szene'.[98] The term 'Zersammlung', the title given to the first 'unofficial literary congress' held in Prenzlauer Berg in 1984, perhaps sums up best the shifting and various allegiances, political and poetic, of the unofficial literature of the GDR.[99]

If the many different factions of the underground culture are important, so too is the evolution of its publishing network. Klaus Michael identifies four phases of development: an early phase (1979–82) in which the first experiments were made, the development phase (1982–4), the main phase (1984–7) when many of the most famous magazines were published, and the late phase from 1988, when some of those alliances were formed which would go into the founding of new magazines and publishing houses after the fall of the Wall. Michael distinguishes a quite different character for each of the phases and the magazines born out of them, generally due to the changing political climate. There is a fascinating literary history to be written about the evolution from the first unique 'Künstlermappen' and magazines, which accepted the work of anyone who cared to provide fifteen copies, to the editorial experiments (and wranglings) of the mid-1980s, and finally, the sophisticated word-processed literary aesthetic journals of the final years. Significant co-ordinates in that development are perhaps *Und, Mikado, schaden, liane*, and *ariadnefabrik*, although the picture is complicated by the many special-interest magazines ranging from church-sponsored publications to the (relative) mass circulation of the green political magazine *Umwaldblätter*.[100] The year 1984/5 marks a caesura of sorts. Many of the leading writers and artists had moved to the West or had applied for visas, and the euphoria of the collective identity became dissipated in 'das fehlende "Danach" ' (Faktor).[101] In other essays Faktor paints a particularly depressing picture of the disillusionment, internal squabbling, and provincialism of the scene after 1985. He stresses the 'beziehungslose Atmosphäre', the desultory 'Herumpinseln und Herumsurrealisieren', and the lack of creative 'Selbstkontrolle', which, he claimed, had led to creative stagnation: 'Alle sind wunderbar cool, nehmen sich gegenseitig nicht allzu ernst, meiden in eigenem Umkreis offene Auseinandersetzungen (Kleinkriege nicht gerechnet) und testen, wie sich Verzweiflung am besten betäuben läßt.'[102] In a later essay, he links the increasing lack of energy and the aesthetic complacency with the fact that the self-understanding of the underground had been so thoroughly undermined by the *Staatssicherheit*.[103] The shift in emphasis was also caused by a gradual recognition and partial reintegration of some of the authors into the official publishing culture. By 1988 *ariadnefabrik* was presented to the Akademie, and the late magazine *Bizzare Städte* (1987–1989) also understood itself as a semi-official publication, seeking dialogue with the official publishing industry and often including work by older writers. By 1988–9 a number of the young writers had been taken up into Gerhard Wolf's 'Außer der Reihe' series with Aufbau.

The anthology *Berührung ist nur eine Randerscheinung*, which appeared in the West in 1985, edited by Sascha Anderson and Elke Erb, marked a turning-point in the literary scene of Prenzlauer

Berg. This project had its origins in 1980, when Franz Fühmann, long a champion of controversial texts by younger writers, worked with Anderson and Kolbe to present a selection of material to the Akademie der Wissenschaften. This failed but some of the material went forward to the later anthology.[104] The extraordinary six-page 'Strategiepapier' of the Büro für Urheberrechte, which came to light after 1989, demonstrates the anxiety and hostility with which the young writers and their texts were viewed by the GDR authorities, and also the extraordinary detail of the authorities' literary analysis:

Das Manuskript enthält Texte, in denen die Positionen des 'Außenseiters' bzw. 'Aussteigers' aus unserer sozialistischen Gesellschaft zur Schau gestellt werden. Es wird ein Lebensgefühl artikuliert, in dem resignative und nihilistische Züge vorherrschen, Elegisches und Bitteres, Gefühle des Eingesperrtseins kommen zum Ausdruck, Selbstmord und Tod sind bevorzugte Motive.

Das Manuskript kommt aus diesem wie auch aus Gründen der Autorenzusammensetzung für eine Veröffentlichung in einem Verlag der DDR nicht in Frage.[105]

Despite attempts on the part of the GDR authorities to prevent publication in the West by pressurizing the publishing house Kiepenheuer & Witsch and the editor Elke Erb, this anthology did serve to bring the young writers to the attention of the West German media. Up until then commentators had been reluctant to recognize a new generation in the GDR. In 1983, for example, Harald Hartung concluded that there was no 'new generation' in evidence, a conclusion he reiterated almost word for word two years later in his *Die Deutsche Lyrik seit 1965*: 'Die Generation Volker Brauns ist bislang nicht abgelöst worden. Die jüngeren Talente, die diesen Namen wirklich verdienen, sind gering an der Zahl, und nicht alle können in der DDR publizieren; es sind Einzelgänger oder Vereinzelte.' In the same year Wolfgang Emmerich also considered the literary scene too unstable and fragmentary to identify a distinct new generation.[106] The publication of *Berührung ist nur eine Randerscheinung*, however, marked the beginning of a keen critical interest in the underground scene on the part of Western critics, and a realization that—however controversially—the generation of Volker Braun had been supplanted.[107]

The initial judgement in the *feuilletons* was cautious and

sometimes hostile. In particular critics were concerned about what they saw as an immaturity and superficiality, a lack of historical awareness: 'private Anspielungen [. . .] Plattheiten' (Franke), but also a wilful hermeticism which appeared to be appropriated directly from Dada and concrete poetry: 'gesuchten Tiefsinn [. . .] geistige Avantgardismen' (von Matt). Roland Mischke put it most bluntly; for him the poetry was exhausted in the violence of its fundamental gesture of negation: 'Die geopolitische Gefangenschaft macht bitter böse [. . .] die sich entladende Aggression verdrängt die Poesie.' These strands of scepticism have persisted up to the present, and are a useful check on the often uncritical reception which has greeted subsequent publications in the West. However, the principle of a 'Generationswechsel' (von Matt), the notion of retreat from the outside world, and the idea of a new postmodern avant-garde at the heart of Socialist Realist citadel, have fired the imagination of Western academic criticism from the mid-1980s onwards.[108]

Those same traits of resignation, flight, and the cultivation of a safe haven in the closed sphere of art, which had been noted by GDR critics in the officially published work of the young writers, were now identified in an intensified form by Western observers in the unofficial work. Cosentino, for example, discerned a growing 'Desorientation und Ziellosigkeit', Berendse 'Verweigerung', Cohen-Pfister 'the individual's retreat from society into the private realm', and Hartmann the fixation on 'Textkonstitution' at the expense of 'Sinn'.[109] Over the last two years this same perception of the writers and their work has persisted, but has been turned aggressively against them. Their 'inner emigration' has been understood as the very precondition of their complicity with the *Stasi*. In his Mörike Prize speech of 1991, for example, Wolf Biermann, one of their chief accusers, contrasted the unpolitical inwardness of Mörike ('echt und wahrhaftig') with that of Prenzlauer Berg:

Nun erfahren wir, daß die bunte Kulturszene am Prenzlauer Berg ein blühender Schrebergarten der Stasi war. [. . .] Die Stasigärtner mendelten dort einen manierierten Stil für demoralisierte Genies und eingeschüchterte junge Leute, die vor sich hinblödelnd dadaistisch entschliefen, als der große Streit mit der Obrigkeit drohte, endlich ernst zu werden.[110]

Conclusion

The reception of this 'generation' has been marked by political considerations in both its positive and its negative versions. Since the middle of the 1980s, and certainly since the collapse of the GDR, it is those writers who were for so long officially silenced in the GDR who have now almost entirely eclipsed the other representatives of the generation, those previously acknowledged and discussed by the official GDR culture industry. The writers associated with Prenzlauer Berg have become the exclusive representatives of the 'generation'. Where critics have attempted to make distinctions, these have generally been schematic and hinge crucially on the frequent and shifting antagonisms between the experimental and largely unpublished writers of the underground, and those more established and explicitly political writers like Mensching and Wenzel. Thus in 1988 Jan Faktor, for all his criticisms of the 'provincialism' of the underground scene, noted that it was free of the 'penetranten Didaktik' of older generations, and far from the 'neuen Penetranz der jüngeren Didaktiker, die in den Spuren der älteren (fleißig publizierend) nachstolperten—wie Mensching, Wenzel usw.'.[111] Adolf Endler, in a characteristically provocative outburst, also dismisses Mensching and Wenzel as 'jugendliche Musterhelden' of 'eine schon einäugige [. . .] jetzt aber endgültig debil—"parteilich"?—gewordene Literatur-Propaganda'. His scorn is amplified in the often quoted text by Papenfuß-Gorek which satirizes various of the young poets:[112]

> steffen mensching ist im untergrund
> ein arschloch & wenzel der entsprechende
> stöpsel, im untergrund
> wird überdacht & nachempfunden
> wie im überbauch auch. . .

Approximately the same divisions—although less scurrilously expressed—were taken up in the 1980s by notable critics in the West. Emmerich takes Kolbe and Bert Papenfuß-Gorek as paradigmatic for two strands—'gegenläufige Tendenzen'—in the work of the young generation, contrasting on the one hand 'eine neue Erlebnislyrik der Unmittelbarkeit mit stark expressiver Tendenz', and on the other 'das artistische, oft manieristische Hantieren mit dem Sprachmaterial, das Sprachexperiment'. Anneli

Hartmann uses the same polarization but this time under the labels 'Lyrik der Unmittelbarkeit' and 'Entpersönlichung'.[113] While serving as a basis for discussion of the young writers' work, however, these divisions obscure the variety of forms and approaches which many of the poets use. Significantly, in discussions since the end of the GDR, Emmerich and others have once again reinforced and perpetuated these divisions under a new aspect. For Emmerich in 1991, for example, it was those writers of 'einer *alternativen literarischen Kultur* der [. . .] nach 1950 Geborenen' who would be guaranteed a place in the canon of the new Germany. For those young writers who had dedicated themselves to 'vertrauten Formen des gesellschaftlichen Engagements' and subscribed to utopian notions of progress enshrined in GDR cultural policy—however critically that had been done—he had little to say.[114] This attitude has been borne out in the reception of writers since Emmerich's article.

The second difficulty in defining and analysing the contours of the young 'generation' is the tendency in many critics to characterize it by default, that is by contrasting it with the arrival of an earlier generation in the 1960s: that of Volker Braun. The sense of distance between the young writers and Braun (in particular) as a representative of the pathos of the *Aufbau* was made very clear in the anthology *Berührung ist nur eine Randerscheinung*, notably by Fritz Hendrik Melle: 'Volker Braun?—da kann ich nur sagen, der Junge quält sich. Dazu habe ich keine Beziehung mehr.'[115] A sense of mutual incomprehension was brought to the fore in the dispute over Braun's essay 'Rimbaud. Ein Psalm der Aktualität'. Similar discrepancies became evident between younger poets and those outspoken dissident writers who had left the GDR; this rift manifested itself in the opposition between Sascha Anderson and Wolf Biermann.[116] However, the clear differences in emphasis should not obscure the many links between the generations. A number of writers take up an active dialogue with some of the older writers: Mickel, Endler, Czechowski, Müller, and Braun, in particular.[117] By the same token, many of the more established writers were important protectors for their younger colleagues.[118] The approach whereby critics set out to define a new generation of poetry by comparing the emergence of the young writers with that of the generation of older writers some two decades before can, in some cases, be a useful starting-point. However, it runs the risk of simply demonstrating the difference between the poetry written in the 1960s and that written in the 1980s.[119]

Here I would like to argue for a new understanding of the literature of the young generation in the GDR, one which works against the dominant critical paradigm on three levels. First, the division between a (simplistically homogeneous) understanding of 'Prenzlauer Berg' on the one hand, and the other more established 'political' or 'conventional' poetry on the other, must be dissolved, in order to see a continuous gradation of different perspectives, aims, and forms, all of which are important for understanding the generation as a whole, and the variety of GDR literature as a whole. Secondly, the often cited contrast with the positions of older writers (especially positions taken in the 1960s) must be balanced by comparison with the developing perspectives of those writers, in order that the continuities (and simultaneities) might also be established (I hope simply to point to some of those here). Finally, the dominant critical understanding of the literature of the young writers as a programmatic retreat within fixed boundaries cannot stand alone: it must be understood dialectically with the impetus of 'Entgrenzung'.

2

'ich fühle mich in grenzen wohl':[1]
The Metaphors of Boundary and the
Boundaries of Metaphor

IN his idiosyncratic autobiographical text of 1992, *Krieg ohne Schlacht*, Heiner Müller comments on the young generation of writers, and those of Prenzlauer Berg in particular.[2]

> Die DDR hat für diese Generation nicht existiert, aber etwas anderes kannten sie auch nicht. Das ist so wie bei diesen holländischen Tomaten, die ohne Boden wachsen, nur mit Luftwurzeln. [. . .] Ihre Existenz in der DDR war eine Scheinexistenz. [. . .] Mein Problem mit den Texten der Jüngeren in der DDR war, daß sie keinen Gegenstand hatten. Die Wirklichkeit der DDR konnte es nicht sein, weil sie die nicht auf etwas anderes beziehen konnten. Die Voraussetzung für Kunst ist Einverständnis, und die Jungen hatten nichts, womit sie einverstanden sein konnten.

One aspect of Müller's assertion closely recalls Uwe Kolbe's words during the controversial round-table discussion of 1979, when he also signalled his generation's existential homelessness: 'Ich kann noch weiter gehen und sagen, daß diese Generation völlig verunsichert ist, weder richtiges Heimischsein hier noch das Vorhandensein von Alternativen anderswo empfindet.'[3] However, Müller goes further than Kolbe and indicates that the lack of acquiescence in the terms of reality, 'Einverständnis, in Haß oder Liebe, mit dem Gegenstand' (p. 289), is missing not only in the lives, but in the texts of the young generation. The 'Mangel an Gegenwartsstoffen', which Kolbe ironically signals in one of his own texts,[4] is one of the most frequent complaints brought against the young writers, and not only those publishing in the underground. Ursula Heukenkamp notes 'Mangel an Konkretheit' in the published work of the young generation, Rönisch similarly condemns 'Wirklichkeitsverlust', and Michael Franz is discouraged by what he sees as 'erschreckend stofflose Poesie'.[5] Writing in 1989, however, Uwe Kolbe insists that it is exactly 'unsere Biographien [. . .] unsere Nicht-Biographien, unsere Poetik gegen das eben noch und immer wieder verordnete Nichts', which it is the duty of his generation to bring to language.[6] Indeed, far from lacking a subject, much of the poetry of the young generation is engaged in the struggle to bring their ambivalent biographies (and non-biographies) to their work, and to forge a language adequate to express them. What the critics miss perhaps, and what is often lacking in the work, is the broad socio-historical reflection of earlier generations: 'größere Gegenstände'.[7] These writers concentrate first and foremost on the examination of their own lived experience.

Programmatic in this sense is Kurt Drawert's 'Zweite Inventur' of 1986.[8]

> Ein Tisch.
> Ein Stuhl.
> Ein Karton für altes Papier, Abfälle,
> leere Zigarettenschachteln, Briefe,
> die keiner Antwort bedürfen.

Dedicated to Günter Eich, and resonant of Eich's poem in its low-key vocabulary and deliberate repetition ('Das ist mein Zimmer', 'Das ist mein Vorteil'), Drawert's text constitutes a stocktaking of really-lived socialism.[9] But in another sense it is also a reversal of Eich's text, in that it insists, not on that which has been salvaged, but rather on that which is in the process of being lost or eroded more finally ('endgültiger'). The insinuation of that comparative offers a clearly critical reading of GDR reality, but also of the language of which it is constituted, for this is also a 'Sprach-inventur'.[10] As Drawert puts it in another poem: 'Zu sagen die wenigen Dinge, | auf die morgens mein Blick fällt | mit einer Handvoll Vokabeln'.[11] Echoes of Eich's poem are also clearly to be heard in a number of poems, including Uwe Kolbe's 'inspiration', or a late poem by Kathrin Schmidt, 'Blickwechsel'; but even where Eich is not invoked directly, the sense that poetry is being used to record, to conserve, even to fix the banal but vulnerable details of lived reality pervades a great deal of the work:

> ein leeres zimmer
> das fenster zum hof
> ein stuhl und ein zettel
> drei straßen entfernt
> meine schritte
> früh gegen halb zwei

ein kommen und gehen
zwischen den wändern der häuser
zwischen gebäuden aus milchglas und sand

This extract from the poem 'Alibi' by Johannes Jansen makes it clear that, in fixing reality and language, writers are at the same time seeking to fix the contours of the self.[12] On the other hand, however, as with Braun's sprawling cycle 'Der Stoff zum Leben', many writers open up the 'material' of their own lives.[13] Their poetry moves beyond a documentation of surface reality to explore the dimensions of their experience.

At the centre of that experience is the fact of being 'hineingeboren'. It is this unique and most basic premise of their lives which links all the writers of the generation. It is expressed in very different ways. To take three examples: Uwe Kolbe, in his 'Auf ein paar alte Bekannte' (1979), ironically calls his comrades to revolution: 'Wir sind um Mitte Zwanzig, sind viele und denken | scharf'—but it is a revolution which must first be sanctioned by the FDJ, the 'ZK der SED', and the 'Gruppe Sowjetischer Streitkräfte in Deutschland'. Kerstin Hensel exploits a fairy-tale scenario. In her compelling 'Fieberkurve', a generation—'unsere Geburt liegt | In den Fuffzigersechzigern prinzenhaft heil'—is forced to conform to their 'story' and their bloody fate: 'RUCKEDIGUH! . . . BLUT IST IM SCHUH'. Durs Grünbein, on the other hand, plays out the generation's frustrated longings: '3 Jahrzehnte mit einer Hoffnung im Off . . .' within the shifting scenarios and displaced narratives of a postmodern metropolis.[14] However, even with such very different individual signatures, there are common co-ordinates to that experience. At its most fundamental, of course, this is the experience of the Wall. In a text entitled 'Kontext' by Uwe Kolbe, the lyric subject in the West is listening to recordings of poems from his former colleagues in Berlin: 'Kommt sie nicht vor, denkt er, während das Wasser abkühlt, kommt die Mauer nicht irgendwo vor bei einem Autor, der in dieser Stadt schreibt so lügt er.'[15]

In one sense Kolbe is right: the awareness of 'Grenzen'—those boundaries into which the young writers were born—is an extraordinary constant in the work; it is impossible to do justice to the treatment of the theme here. For many writers the 'Grenze' has migrated to become even part of themselves: 'ich bau mir meine mauer selber durch den leib' (Anderson), 'ICH BIN EIN KOPF IN ZWEI HÄLFTEN GETEILT | ICH BIN DIE SCHEIDEWAND IN MEINEM

HERZEN' (Annett Gröschner).[16] The most interesting texts, however, use this simply as the starting-point for an exploration of their experience. There are many ways to approach the very varied treatment of this theme. Here I want simply to take up the explicit motif 'hineingeboren', and then demonstrate how it is explored in three main ways: historically, spatially, and linguistically. It is difficult to construct a linear survey, because the categories tend to collapse into one another, creating a very dense network of allusion and echo. However, it is clear that, in concrete and in metaphorical form, the experience of being 'born into it', is one of the central topoi of the young writers' texts.

It was a text by Uwe Kolbe (b. 1957), the title of which became the signal for the experience of an entire generation. The poem 'Hineingeboren' is probably the single most-cited (although paradoxically little-analysed) text by any of the young authors.[17]

> Hohes weites grünes Land,
> zaundurchsetzte Ebene.
> Roter
> Sonnenbaum am Horizont.
> Der Wind ist mein
> und mein die Vögel.
>
> Kleines grünes Land enges,
> Stacheldrahtlandschaft.
> Schwarzer
> Baum neben mir.
> Harter Wind.
> Fremde Vögel.

The interest of the poem lies in the unresolved contradiction between the two strophes. This can be seen to represent the schizophrenia of a lyric subject, and on a larger scale, but with remarkably modest language, that of a country. In almost every respect the second strophe undoes the first. The sense of space and hope, along with a confident assertion of identity and freedom (birds, wind), make way for a sense of alienation and contingency ('hart', 'neben', 'fremd') and threat (the abrupt 'enges'). The oddly Expressionist tone associated with the fusing of sun and tree becomes darkness.[18] However, one can also read the text, not as a static contradiction, but as a progression of sorts—a shift of perspective, a loss of illusion. The strident and rather strained 'mein' of the first strophe is an act of willed blindness. It belies the limitations and distortions which already exist: 'zaundurchsetzte Ebene', 'Horizont', the sun, not fused with, but trapped in the tree. In the second strophe, the light has changed; things are simply revealed as they are, and the glib rhythms and confident syntax of the first strophe respond by becoming contorted and choked. This poem enacts the switch of perspective between horizons of belonging and horizons of menace, between safety and imprisonment, as Durs Grünbein puts it elsewhere: 'Gesehen ganz wie | von neuem (geschockt)'.[19] A 'sudden seeing' of sorts is, of course, a common literary device, but is used very frequently by the poets to signal a loss of illusion.

The same kind of schizophrenic double-take is self-consciously taken up in a poem by Michael Wüstefeld, 'für Uwe Kolbe'.[20]

> Hineingeboren wie hineingeborgt
> Eingenommen wie gefangengenommen
>
> Festgehalten nicht fester Halt
> Aushalten nicht Anhalt
>
> Ankommen wie wegkommen
> Ankunft wie Wegkunft
>
> Hierbleiben nicht dableiben
> Ausreisen nicht ausreißen
>
> Lachen wie Masken
> Maskieren wie Weinen
>
> Verrecken nicht um Ecken
> Umrunden nicht im Kreis
>
> Loseisen wie festrosten
> Geborensein wie totleben

This gives bitter expression, both to the inner 'division' of an individual and to the double-take of reality. But here there is no movement between illusion and loss, for there are no illusions to be lost. The rupture is not discovered; it is already buried deep in the flat and finished statements, simply waiting to be exposed. Gerhard Wolf claims that these 'Kennworte' between two members of the same generation spring from a common experience which excludes, and is unintelligible to, older writers.[21] It would be wrong to exaggerate this point. The text simply demands a rereading of very familiar terms 'Ankunft', 'Ausreisen', etc., and points to a political understanding, but also several complexes of imagery, which are commonly found in the work of the young writers: circles, masks, imprisonment, and escape. Wüstefeld's text does, however, demonstrate a linguistic short-circuit of sorts. Syntax, language, and movement are all caught up and forcibly checked.[22]

Like Wüstefeld, a number of writers exploit the conflict between the idea of birth and the weight of resistance against it.

Zangengeburt

Gegen mein Stemmen
ins Leben gezerrt Blutige Ankunft
drei Wochen zu spät (wie immer
ich komme zu spät) Gekappt dann
die Schnur Drei vier Schläge
auf das Gesäß—und ich schrie
Schrie Und schrei

This poem gave its title to Lutz Rathenow's first collection (published in the West) in 1982.[23] The brutality and sense of resolute, if bleak, endurance which mark this text dominate the collection as a whole. The idea of the forceps birth also conditions the three-part structure of the collection. Rathenow explains: 'Zuerst die—leicht gestörte—Heiterkeit des Wachsens. Dann die Überreife, das Überfällig-Sein jenes Wesens, das seine Geborgenheit zu verlassen nicht imstande ist. Obwohl es an dieser zu ersticken von dieser vergiftet zu werden droht. Endlich fast zu spät der Kampf um das Geborenwerden.'[24] The notion of the double-edged 'Geborgenheit', along with the 'Überreife', 'Überfällig-Sein', and the repeated 'arriving too late' are symptomatic. A similar mood finds its way into the tortured cycle of texts and images, 'Garuna ich bin', by Frank Lanzendörfer, which constitutes 'eine poetische Biographie, die sich vom Mutterleib bis zur Gegenwart erstreckt'.[25] If Rathenow's lyric subject actively struggles against suffocation and towards birth, a struggle which in the poem is continued with the slip into an open-ended present tense ('Und schrei'), the birth screams in Lanzendörfer's text are those of despair, pain and alienation.

gekrümmt im mutterleib, bin vollendet, will raus
durchkommen. laß mich raus. du hast angst & ich, ich
will raus [. . .]
aber
es ist kalt hier
wo bringt ihr mich hin
o furchtbare welt
sie bringen mich weg. ich will nicht weg. schreie, schreie
schreie (p. 2)

One of Durs Grünbein's most impressive poems, 'O Heimat,
zynischer Euphon', is dedicated to Thomas Kling, a young poet
from West Berlin.[26] Here the young generation are described quite
bluntly as the object of a cynical historical joke: 'der kranken Väter
Brut sind wir, der Mauern | Sturzgeburt':

Geröntgt, geimpft, dem deutschen Doppel-Klon,
Gebrochnen Auges, das nach Weitblick giert,
böse verfallen sind wir, pränatal dressiert.
›Deutschland?‹ . . . O Heimat, zynischer Euphon.

The poem is an unsettling mixture of 'brave new world' nihilism
and concrete political concern. It focuses particularly on the cynical
rituals which 'condition' the baby's undeveloped brain. A juxtaposition of mechanical aggression (particularly the verbs) and
vulnerability is used to brutal effect: 'mit Nervennelken tätowiert',
'Stachelgaumen, | In violetten Babyschädeln installiert', 'pränatal
dressiert'.

At its most extreme, the motif of birth is not used simply to
indicate the fact of having been born into it, being born too late, or
being born into a pre-programmed reality, but rather, it becomes a
kind of death: 'tödlich vereinnahmt & | tot geboren'
(Lanzendörfer).[27] In Papenfuß-Gorek's linguistic play, for example,
this ends up as 'hineinrichtung': a paradoxical fusion of birth,
execution, and the structures of state.[28] In the dark landscapes of
childhood generated in Ulrich Zieger's *neunzehnhundertfünfundsechzig* attempts to formulate an identity are constantly erased or
aborted: 'wir. sind. leider. gedanken. geblieben.'.[29] In Hensel's
haunting and densely alliterative sonnet 'Engelspuppen' an
unnamed 'wir' is sewn into a cocoon by the threads of 'Geduld'.
The poem ends: 'Wir leben aus und gehen langsam ein | und sterben
voll entfaltet, wie zum Schein'.[30] The critic Ursula Heukenkamp

and her daughter Marianne offer a fascinating insight into the power of this metaphor in a review of Hensel's collection, which explicitly addresses the problem of 'generations'. Heuekenkamp reads the 'Larvenzustand' as a representation of 'Sozialisierung' and finds it 'alienating' and 'shocking'. Her daughter, on the other hand, who is approximately the same age as Hensel, recognizes it immediately as the fundamental 'Lebensgefühl' of her own generation. In her comments on the metaphor of the 'Larvenzustand', she pinpoints some of the key issues surrounding the situation of the young writers:

Das Lebensgefühl unserer Generation entwächst stärker dem Gefühl einer Handlungsohnmacht ('Eingepuppt-Sein' ist eine überaus treffende Metapher), dem Eindruck, 'auf uns kommt es ohnehin nicht an', 'es ist alles längst entschieden' [. . .] Insofern bezeichnet die Metapher vom Larven-zustand, dessen einzige Metamorphose der Tod ist, schon einen 'Normal-zustand'.[31]

Insect larvae (in Hensel's text with resonances of the fall of angels and perhaps the backstreet 'Engelmacherin') make very powerful symbols, because of their fragility, their enclosed metamorphosis, and, in the case of Hensel (or Sascha Anderson, whose butterflies in 'das ist sicher ein traum' die under glass), because of their arrested flight.[32]

Born into it—Historically

Like Lutz Rathenow in the poem quoted above, a number of writers take up the thwarted experience of a generation, born into ongoing historical structures, but 'born too late'. Compare Gabriele Kachold's three-page prose poem 'an die 40jährigen':

wir sind die zu spät gekommenen, ein klein wenig zu spät für eure ordnung, um eintritt zu finden dazu, zutritt in den raum der geregelten abläufe. ihr hattet noch zeit, euch einzurichten, in das land, in das leben, in die zeit. ihr seid die generation, die eine andere generation in die welt setzte.[33]

Far from casting themselves in the role of Brecht's 'Nachgeborenen', as Braun and his contemporaries had done, and thus accepting their place as part of a continuing process of evolution and progress, the young writers place themselves much further down an attenuated and sorry line: 'Wir, die Nachundnachgeborenen'. This text, by

Ralph Grüneberger, takes the form of the poetic biography of a generation which starts with Brechtian idealism and progress, but gradually loses energy and tails off into senselessness.[34] This poem in particular triggered a dismissive review of Grüneberger's collection as a whole from Kerstin Hensel, which itself initiated a debate in the journal *Temperamente* about the concept of generations. 'Dieses WIR ist bedenklich. [. . .] Dieses WIR meint eine ganze Generation: die, die genommen haben, die sich verengt haben im Leben, die einen neuen Schritt nicht gehen wollen. Aber es stimmt so nicht, die Wahrheiten sind halbe.'[35]

What is pervaded with a sense of self-pity in Grüneberger, '[wir] . . . Gedenken unsrer | Mit Nachsicht', becomes in Kachold a more aggressive (and poetically convincing) frankness:

wir sind die generation zwischen einer generation, wir stehn zwischen zeiten, regeln, empfindungen. wir sind die zwittergeneration, wir sind ein zwittergeschlecht [. . .] wir sind die fruchtlos, sinnlos nachgeborenen.[36]

The young see themselves as caught in structures which were set up before they were born, and a future which owns little perspective for change. They are a generation born into a finished, resolved society, where there are no struggles to be fought or experiences left to be had.

Kurt Drawert expresses his frustration in 'Gedicht in Juni, Juli, August'. Once more this is a poetic (auto)biography of the lyric subject from birth and charts the search for a place in a 'Geschichte, die eine Geschichte ohne mich | war'.[37]

> Was war sie wert, meine
> Anwesenheit in einer Welt die dekliniert war,
>
> geordnet, in Definitionen, Tabellen,
> Schlagzeilen gebracht?
> Fertigbedingungen und Fertiggerichte.
> Die Geschichte war fertig. Die Gegenwart
> war fertig, die Zukunft, die Revolution,
> die Antworten waren fertig.

Unusually, and in poetic terms rather weakly, this piece ends by celebrating the eventual escape from 'Staub' and 'mathematischen Regeln' (p. 15). However, the weight of the text falls on the frustration which has preceded the unlikely release. Any notion of contributing as part of a team at work on ongoing, transitional structures, has been replaced by a sense of marginalization and despair. Where, in the 1960s, history had been 'unfinished' for Braun and his contemporaries, now it is not only completed, but also collapsed and without perspective: 'die Geschichte war fertig. Die Gegenwart || war fertig'. The future too is collapsed into a kind of 'still-life'. In Kerstin Hensel's striking 'Stilleben mit Zukunft', for example, the future is simply 'die alte | Kiste' washed up on the shore and gnawed by the sea like a bone. In a text, 'stilleben stellen', by C. M. P. Schleime, the perspectives of 'noch' (in a temporal sense) are subverted to become a grammatically ambiguous comparative associated with death and conformity: 'noch gleicher als grabsteine'.[38] The young generation is simply not part of an ongoing historical process. 'Die großen Dinge werden ohne dich getan' is the programmatic title of a text by Bernd Wagner; 'Wir sind nicht zu brauchen' are the provocative first words of an open letter from Uwe Kolbe to Lothar Walsdorf.[39]

Certainly the conviction of 'belatedness' is not a phenomenon confined to the GDR or even the twentieth century alone. Harold Bloom has argued that it is symptomatic of a recurring sense of envy and dismay in the face of what has gone before and has used it, famously, to define a general poetic theory of influence.[40] The sensibility of the young writers can perhaps be interpreted as simply one manifestation of this universal anxiety. But there are, nevertheless, biographical co-ordinates which would seem to fix the experience of this generation as an acute and particular historical belatedness. At this point it is interesting to compare a few sentences from an essay by the West German Reinhard Mohr, which describes the same generation (those born in the 1950s) as the 'Zaungäste' of the Federal Republic.

Wohin sie auch kamen—stets trafen sie als zweite ein. Sie waren die ewig verspätete Generation. [. . .] Intensiv empfanden sie die 'Nutzlosigkeit erwachsen zu werden', fühlten sich, stolz und bang zugleich, als unverbesserliche Weltverbesserer, als hoffnungslose Außenseiter, Solitäre einer vergangenen Epoche. [. . .] Die 78er, die heute auf die vierzig zugehen, kamen zu spät zur Revolte der sechziger Jahre und standen dann, in den Achtzigern, vor den verschlossenen Türen der reformierten Gesellschaft, die sie gar nicht zu brauchen schien.[41]

Although Mohr is considering only the Federal Republic, and refers to no literary texts, the correspondence is striking. It would suggest that this is the mood of a generation in Germany, even in Europe as a whole. There are differences, of course. If Mohr detects traces of utopianism amongst those in the West, 'unverbesserliche Weltverbesserer', many more young GDR writers responded to the experience of repudiation by the establishment by abandoning such aspirations altogether. In this case, a direct comparison with Volker Braun is instructive. In Braun's powerful text 'Allgemeine Erwartung', the worker, worn down at the machines all day, gives voice to his private aspirations in the quiet of his home. The conclusion of the text, however, signals his confidence in the power of collective aspirations and collective progress: 'Das meiste | Ist noch zu erwarten'.[42] By the late 1970s and early 1980s such confidence is scarce. Bernd Rump's 1979 song takes direct issue with Braun's text and turns Braun's programmatic 'Das kann nicht alles sein' on its head, focusing not on future progress, but on disbelief at present lack: 'Kann das schon alles sein?'[43] It is a question (or rather a rhetorical question, for no answer is genuinely sought) which underscores much of the poetry of the 1980s. What had been active participation, anticipation, the sheer enthusiasm of *Aufbau* ('*er*warten'), becomes, in the texts of the 1980s, a passive and alienated waiting ('warten').

The idea that contemporary life is not part of an unstoppable historical teleology but instead a kind of historical parenthesis is very common; the images used to describe it: 'ein großer Wartesaal' (Müller), 'ein gebremstes Leben' (Braun), 'auf dem Abstellgleis der Zeit' (Mensching) are remarkably consistent across the generations.[44] These images explicitly take issue with the mechanical and transport metaphors of historical progress, so beloved of GDR cultural historians.[45] More important, as Dieter Schlenstedt points out, they indicate a fundamental 'Zeitdifferenz': on the one hand stand the aspirations of socialist progress, a kind of utopian historical foreshortening, on the other, the experience of the individual trapped in the stagnation of the present. The dislocation of personal and historical time signals a radical disillusionment for some of the older writers, but it is the starting-point for the young generation.[46] In his seven-part essay 'Chiron oder die Zweigestaltigkeit', Hans-Eckardt Wenzel takes up the idea of the 'aufgeteilte Zeit' as a fundamental topos of the age. He projects it into a paradigmatic 'Warte-Situation': that of Hölderlin's 'Chiron', the immortal centaur waiting for his liberation (and his death) at the hands of Herakles.[47] If Wenzel's analysis is here primarily poetological (although also philosophical), he gives the theme a much more political edge in a text of 1987.[48] In 'Wartung eines Landes', five strophes give voice to the compelling and seemingly endless incantation of those waiting:

> Die Beschuldigten warten auf Recht
> Das Volk an der Straße wartet auf *ihn*
> Die Familie wartet auf den Zug
> Das Land wartet auf die Zukunft.

Striking is the conscious mixture of banality (individual time) and pathos (historical time). However, the many activities, the many aspirations are erased in the oppressive gesture of waiting. Waiting not only nullifies activity but also time. Or rather, not all time is erased: waiting erases the past and diminishes the present but aggrandizes the future, in which one supposes what is waited for will appear. Here, however, the perspective into the future is closed down with an abrupt couplet: 'Die Wahrheit erwartet die Aufwartung | Aber das Land wartet ab'. The text ends on a note of passivity (the ironic shift from 'Wartung', 'Erwartung', and 'Aufwartung' to 'abwarten') and hopeless waiting with, for the first time, no object in sight.[49]

Of course, senseless waiting, 'waiting for . . . waiting', has been understood, since Beckett at least, as a symptom of the essential condition of modern humankind.[50] Notwithstanding, it carries a special disenchantment when it comes from the GDR, home to the would-be 'Sieger der Geschichte'.[51] The ambiguities are captured by Stefan Döring in a series of linguistic texts, from his *Heutmorgestern* (1989).[52] As the title suggests, time has imploded to become a permanent unified singular condition. Compare the play on 'zeitfirmen' haggling over the 'gegenwert der gegenwart' (p. 12):

> all deine zugkunft und verlangenheit nach jetzt:
> erst heute das morgen schon heute das gestern
> heutmorgestern
> liebe mitverbürger eifriger geschicklichkeit
> begreift begeifert dies wunder zeit
> dass in der mitte zusammenfliesst
> in unser aller mitte liebe mitwürger der gegenwart

The very dense text is in part a treatment of transience: human mortality. However, it also sets the yearning ('Verlangen') to find a way out of the standstill of the centre, against those more human agencies who work to close it down: 'mitwürger der gegenwart'.

Born into it—Spatially

In the texts above I have demonstrated how common is the complaint of having being 'born into' a historical limbo, a pre-programmed reality without perspective for the future. But this is not the only expression of the generation's having been 'born into it'. The same sense of frustration at being born into closed structures is translated into a very striking physical topography. At its most obvious this is an awareness of 'Grenzen'—encroaching political and geographical horizons, walls, barriers, frontiers, perimeters, barbed wire, stone—but also a yearning for the open spaces beyond.[53] That this awareness manifests itself in very different ways is clear. Talking about the metaphor of 'Grenzen' in the work published in *schaden* in the early 1980s Egmont Hesse comments: 'früher hatte man die 108178 quadratkilometer "knast" genannt, heute sagt man öfters "heilanstalt" oder "enge": die situation ist aber die gleiche, über die man nachdenkt.'[54] Here I would like to focus on just one aspect of this massive theme: the ways in which the experience of being 'hineingeboren' is translated into the presentation of the city.[55]

To write about the 'city' is to place oneself within an important artistic tradition which goes back at least to the first decades of the twentieth century.[56] Many of the young writers work self-consciously with elements of this heritage: the Expressionist metropolis; Brecht's 'asphalt city'; Kunert's elegiac visions of a lost civilization; or Rolf Dieter Brinkmann's traumatized and inhuman cityscapes.[57] They are not, then, simply describing the very real cities of their experience: Dresden, Leipzig, and especially Berlin. Instead they are also mapping out an 'Unreal City' (Eliot) of sorts: as the landscape of their souls.[58]

That is not to say that the very particular characters of the writers, their cities, and the traditions within which they place them are lost. Michael Wüstefeld, in his collection *Stadtplan*, for example, presents a detailed and often nostalgic topography of the streets, towers, and fountains of Dresden in poems written between 1983 and 1987: 'Warum zögern mein enges Land zu beschreiben | Weshalb drängen mein von Grenzen geprägtes Wissen zu leugnen'.[59] Thomas Böhme's second collection captures the 'beklemmende ruhe' of Leipzig. The broken-down and over-crowded townscape is presented in choking heat, with blistered asphalt, and an air heavy with the toxic fumes of Bitterfeld which settle over the low ground there: 'Die stadt ist krank und ihr klebriger schweiß verstopft | jede pore'.[60] Both Böhme and Wüstefeld pay homage to the poets of the 'Beat Generation', and it is no chance that the open road becomes for them a primary symbol of escape from the claustrophobia of regimented life. In Böhme's 'Schwüle', for example, at the very centre of a picture of the teeming Leipzig suburbs, is the line 'Alle fernstraßen tragen die spuren von fluchten'.[61] In the collection *Hineingeboren*, Uwe Kolbe builds up a very low-key cityscape of the roofs, antennae, and derelict courtyards of East Berlin, while in his *Bornholm II*, with more than a passing debt to the Expressionist city of Meidner or Heym, he presents a city overshadowed by demons and portents of apocalypse. Kurt Pinthus's 1922 collection of Expressionist texts, *Menschheitsdämmerung*, was published in the GDR with Reclam in 1972, and in part occasioned the (second) 'Expressionismus-Debatte'. Kolbe recalls the impact this work had on him ('Die ersten Gedichte meines Lebens, die mich wirklich interessiert haben'), and points to his spontaneous feeling of affinity: 'Den Gott der Stadt—ich kannte ihn schon'.[62] But beyond the literary self-consciousness, perhaps more than any of the other young writers, Kolbe also exploits the symbolic resonances of Berlin, especially the district of Bornholm, as the quintessential 'deutsch-deutscher Ort': a physical manifestation of the split German consciousness.[63] Durs Grünbein, probably the most obsessive and bleak observer of the urban reality of the GDR, styles himself as a 'flâneur' of sorts, and presents a series of 'Glimpses and Glances' at a discontinuous urban wasteland.

> [du] . . . weichst
> Mülltonnen und Stapeln von
>   Bierkasten aus und vor all
> diesen Abrißhäusern und
>   öden Garagenhöfen
> Plakatschwarten an Litfaß-
>   säulen und
>   Schrebergärten
> peinlich umzäunt bist du
>   die meiste Zeit

nichts als
ein drahtiger kleiner Statist . . .

Another text focuses on the brooding claustrophobia of Dresden:

ich habe es satt so ganz
gramgesättigt zu leben von einem
undurchdringlichen Augenblick an den
nächsten gespannt in einer Stadt alternd
in notgedrungenem Schweigen in dieser
Talversunkenheit schwerer Kuppeln und
schmaler durchbrochener Türme—Dresden
grausam zurückgebombt um ein
weiteres kaltes Jahrhundert der Müdigkeit
und betriebsamen Enge die Straßen
voll Echos verhohlener Echos.[64]

Clearly, then, the cities are very different and very real. However, more interesting than the topographical detail, or even the literary dimensions of their presentation, is the extent to which the writers raid the 'City' as a symbolic landscape (and here the final Grünbein text is a good example) to find spatial correlatives for their experience.

Two critics have already hinted at this. As early as 1981, in a review article discussing Uwe Kolbe's collection *Hineingeboren*, Ursula Heukenkamp identifies the tension between interiors and exteriors as a kind of 'Grundfigur' in his poetry.[65] In the same year, analysing the work of a handful of the young poets, Ingrid and Klaus-Dieter Hähnel (famously) go a little further: 'Prenzlauer Berg ist—und das alles ist hier ohne jede Ironie gesagt—längst nicht mehr nur eine Wohngegend, sondern eine "Haltung": Die Risse in den Wänden der Hinterhofhäuser erscheinen nicht selten als die Korrelate für die "Risse" und "Nöte" des Ichs.'[66] I would like to take up a number of individual elements of the city topography and look at them in more detail, starting with the Hähnels' courtyards.[67]

In an essay of 1987 Dennis Tate came to a very different conclusion from that of the Hähnels and claimed that precisely the 'Innenhof' 'has become a new symbol of insulation from the conformist pressures of city life', both in women's literature and in the work of the youngest generation of writers.[68] On the surface this might seem to be true. In Kunert's 'Fahrt mit der S-Bahn', for example, glimpses from the train into the industrial courtyards had intimated the 'unbekannte Abgründe dieser Stadt'. Helga Schubert's prose piece 'Innenhöfe' is already quite different in tone.[69] 'Ein Innenhof, in dem man ankommt, in dem es ruhig ist und nicht verlassen. Die Tür nach draußen ist hinter uns und nicht vor uns. Sie ist geschlossen, aber nicht verschlossen. Hier könnten wir vielleicht leben, geborgen und ruhig und freundlich, ohne Schuldgefühl spotten, ohne Bitterkeit lieben, ohne böse Vorahnung glücklich sein, sogar genießen.' As an example of this new feeling Tate quotes part of a text by Uwe Kolbe, one of a number of texts by the young authors which deal with the many courtyards of Prenzlauer Berg.[70] It starts:

> Wir leben mit Rissen in den Wänden,
> ist es dir aufgefallen?
> wir leben auf sich entfärbenden Dielen,
> unter beweglicher Decke.
>
> Das Fensterkreuz ist längst
> von Fäulnis durchgefressen, es zieht
> im Sommer schon die kalte Nachtluft
> hindrungslos herein.
>
> Wir wohnen illegal, mach das
> dir täglich neu bewußt, daß sonst
> wir beide auf der Straße säßen
>
> Wir hausen in Prenzlauer Berg,
> vier Treppen hoch unter dem Dach. . . .

Tate points out that the poem is a 'romantic cliché' (p. 160). Indeed it does appear to owe something to a Spitzweg painting, or the image of the 'Dachstubenidyll' which has also dogged much of the literary criticism about Prenzlauer Berg. However, there are very different undercurrents in the poem, which are brought out especially in the abrupt turn of the final strophe:

> und lache noch im Hagelrauschen,
> wenn der Himmel finstrer wird,
> lache noch im Tränenfluß
> und lache in der Kälte zwischen uns.
> Im Staub der Körperdünstung lach ich,
> genießend unter Kraftaufwand
> die uns gebotne Sicherheit.

This is not one of Kolbe's best poems; yet neither is it the idyll which Tate tries to make of it. The 'Risse in den Wänden' are central expressions of the flawed security of a generation, but also of the fractures in the subject, the lovers' relationship, and in the fabric of socialism itself. Their significance is underlined by the rot, darkness, cold draughts, and woodlice which invade this shell of an existence. The whole text turns on the ambivalence of security and fragility: an ambivalence which is reflected in the uneasy structure of the last strophe: the abrupt first line 'und lache . . .', the pathos engendered by the rhythm which gathers momentum and then breaks down, and the telling reversal of word order which leaves a desperate and forced 'lach ich' at the end of the last line but two. This 'security' is anything but safe.[71]

A number of texts take up the Berlin courtyard and use it to explore the notion of blocked perspectives, and the potential for final escape, as in Pietraß's 'Berliner Hof'.[72]

> Fest gefügt vier Mauern.
> Noch immer
> Sinken Tage und Nächte
> in diese Stickkammer

The walls become a claustrophobic prison: 'Stickkammer'. However, the piece finally opens up to offer a sudden perspective:

> . . . Die Blicke
> Prallen an graue Wände
> und kehren
> Gespiegelt zurück. Im eckigen
> Kreis
> Irren die Augen und gleiten
> endlich nach oben
> Zum blauen Handtuch
> des Himmels.

The gaze evades the walls, the reflections turned in on themselves, and the enclosing circle. It searches up towards a scrap of sky, which is equated with escape and an almost utopian aspiration. From a world of stone, concrete, and decay—and certainly not idyll—Kolbe's 'Hoflied' concludes with another such an opening of utopian perspective:[73]

> Von Zeit
> Zu reicherer Zeit
> Holt der Himmelsfleck
> Sich eins meiner Augen

Hans-Eckardt Wenzel's 'Schmuggerower Elegie IV' is introduced
with the conviction, borrowed from Walt Whitman: 'ich glaube alle
Heldentaten wurden unter freiem Himmel erdacht.' In this same
spirit, his 1984 song about transience and loss, 'Feinslieb', ends
with the simple expression of a poignant longing: 'Ich will noch so
viel Himmel sehn'.[74]

Of course no one more than Christa Wolf has shown that the sky
is not immune to the interventions of politics: 'Den Himmel? dieses
ganze Gewölbe von Hoffnung und Sehnsucht, von Liebe und
Trauer? "Doch", sagte sie leise. "Der Himmel teilt sich
zuallererst." '[75] And yet, in much of the poetry, the sky becomes a
powerful intimation of hope, stretched above the urban landscape.
In some poems, it is true, those glimpses of sky do not promise
freedom or infinity, but rather reflect the contingency, or even
menace, of life on the ground. In Barbara Köhler's 'Ortung', for
example (with a passing reference to Büchner's *Lenz*), the world is
turned upside down, with asphalt above and the sky beneath:
'einen Himmel verworfener Hoffnung'.[76] Nevertheless, the poetry
of the young writers is remarkable for the preoccupation with
birds, angels, pilots, planes, and ultimately Icarus, sent up as
embodiments of escape, longing, hope or desperation, above the
blighted urban landscape. Kolbe, talking about the birds in his
work, comments that they are at once part of his real experience of
Berlin, but also inevitably a symbol of love, sexuality, freedom, and
movement.[77] As he himself points out, birds have an established
iconography, and are to be found in the poetic traditions of many
countries. However, in many of the texts of the young authors, they
become representations of the bid for a very specific form of
freedom. This is made explicit in Kolbe's 'ein vogel sein, fliegen so
wie er', or in 'Komm wir sind Vögel', for example, where the birds
'erwarten nicht länger | *Genehmigte* Jahreszeit' (my emphasis).[78]

The political resonances are also made clear in the many Icarus
poems by writers during the 1980s. 'Über die ganze Szene fliegt
Ikarus', claimed Dorothea von Törne in her introduction to the
1983 anthology *Vogelbühne*.[79] Icarus is a fascinating figure in the
mythological landscape of the GDR, for he is a divided figure: he
carries his soaring ambition, 'einen Anlauf für das Unmögliche', but
also his fall within him.[80] If in the early poetry of the GDR he was
taken to represent the utopian aspiration of flight (Arendt) or the
victorious ascent of *Aufbau* (Becher), the poetry of the younger

generation demonstrates a marked shift in emphasis.[81] There is no space to pursue this topos here. However, in general one can say that it is either the attempt of Icarus to escape the tyranny of slavery and the labyrinth, which is emphasized in much of the young writers' work, or his inheritance: age, disillusionment, and impotence, which mean that he will never fly.[82]

> So steht er da und hofft,
> daß sein Arm ein Flügel werde.
> Doch er altert nur
> und hinkt schon ein wenig.

Ultimately, he becomes a representation of the frustrated aspirations of a generation.[83]

Selbstmord

> Da fiel er uns vor die Füße:
> Ikarus, sah ich sofort
> rot, das Wachs, zerlaufen.
>
> Hat sich die Flügel verbrannt.
> Konnt sich nicht halten.
> Wollte zuviel wohl.
>
> Kam zu nah an die Sonne
> oder vom Boden nicht los.

A similar ambivalence surrounds rivers in the city. Rivers have a central place in any poetic tradition, as embodiments of eternal flux (Heraclitus's 'panta rei'), as the dividing line between the living and the dead, even as a representation of the poetic enterprise itself. Added to this, however, is the geographical reality of the modern German state. The River Spree, which winds its way through the divided city of Berlin, finds its way into an ironic Wenzel song as an expression of the divided German identity. The rondo form of Kolbe's 'Versorgungs-Rondo' underlines his bitter reflection on the standing Berlin water: 'Eschengraben, grünes Kaumgewässer, heißt das Rinnsal, doch sich selber fremd.'[84] However, it is the Elbe in particular which features in a large number of texts.

In an article entitled 'Zu neuen Ufern: Lyrik der "Sächsischen Dichterschule" im Spiegel der Elbe', Gerrit-Jan Berendse gives a very illuminating account of the place of the Elbe in the poetry of the 'middle generation'.[85] If in the work of the older writers the Elbe is still flowing from some kind of mythical, poetic, utopian source, in the work of the younger writers it is a city river, poisoned by pollution and disillusionment.[86] Durs Grünbein offers a vision of riparian decay in his 'Belebter Bach', for example, or 'An die Elbe'. Another text welcomes 'die Freude der Überschwemmung' (with a marvellous line break), as a turbulent liberation from the monotony of Dresden: 'die || Regenfluten brachten das Einerlei | des verdammten Elbalbkessels zum | Brodeln.'[87] However, it is Barbara Köhler who has written perhaps the most remarkable series of texts on the Elbe, texts which also embody the aspirations and frustrations of a generation: 'Den Flüssen hier glaubt man nicht, daß sie ins Meer | wollen'.[88] In two cycles of texts, 'ELB ALB' and 'Papierboot', and in a variety of forms—from rondo to prose poetry—Köhler explores the Elbe as potential escape from the city, but also as border, 'Grenzfluss' (p. 59). The river becomes a mirror of longing, but also a symbol of poisoned aspirations: 'Die giftige Schlammschicht am Grund der Flüsse, sagt jemand. | Die nicht ausgeführten Entwürfe', sagt jemand' (p. 52). In another text, later in the collection, Köhler appears to dismiss those metaphorical escape routes from their limited lives, which she and so many of her generation have followed: 'Der Himmel der Strom sind kein Ausweg mehr Ver- | seuchte Metaphern die unsre Sehnsüchte zurechtweisen' (p. 60). And yet, despite this, she sends out onto the water her 'Papierboot' (p. 54).

> Der ins Wasser gefallene Mond ist ein Boot. Eine leichte Barke, aber Grund genug für die Versicherung, daß auch Sachsen am Meer liegt. Grund genug—habe ich Grund gesagt, können wir auf einem Papierboot bestehen. Papier, das aus halbtoten Wäldern uns zuwächst, dem wir manchmal unser Sterben anvertraun: Nächtebücher, versiegelte Sätze, Briefe, nicht abgeschickt. Bilder ohne Rahmen, Entwürfe ohne Maß, die geheime Zerstörung der Proportionen. Papier voller Irrfahrten und Aben- teuer, wenn das Land uns verlassen hat und die Hoffnung uns fahren läßt; Papier auf dem wir zu uns kommen, Papier auf dem wir untergehen, unsere Barke unser ge- brechlicher Grund. Sachsen am Meer—Ahoi!

The promise of 'Sachsen am Meer' is a utopian promise which one should read with Ingeborg Bachmann's 'Böhmen liegt am Meer' in mind.[89] The 'paper-boats', like the birds discussed above, are expansive gestures of humanity's highest aspirations; aspirations which break down barriers and explode boundaries: 'Entwürfe ohne Maß, die geheime Zerstörung | der Proportionen'. Their extraordinary fragility is also that of the poetic enterprise itself.[90]

If the metaphors of sky and sea are to some extent 'poisoned' for the young writers, there is another locus within the confines of the city which is used as an image of enclosure, but also of escape. A very common motif in Berlin literature since the 1960s is the journey between Bahnhof Zoo and Friedrichstraße, encapsulating the very proximity of, and gulf between, the two halves of the city.[91] As Kunert puts it in his 'Gleisdreieck':

> Keiner ahnt
> bei der Fahrt mit der S-Bahn
> das metaphysische Ausmaß
> der Reise.[92]

Precisely because they were 'born into' a city in which that journey was not possible, the 'S-Bahn' and with it the 'U-Bahn' take on a very different aspect in the young writers' work.[93] Durs Grünbein's two sprawling texts 'Unten am Schlammgrund' and 'In Tunneln der U-Bahn' focus on the underground as labyrinthine soul of the city.[94] It is the understated brutality of his representation which first brings the reader up sharp. This is the place where a man is found dead, strangled with a wire, with music still spilling out of his ears, 'aus einem *walkman* irgendwo im Innern', or where the corpse of a baby scarcely a week old is found in a left-luggage locker: 'schon festverschnürt bereit zur Reise || In einen anderen Automaten-Limbo'.[95] The underground also becomes an image for the subconscious, and for the underworld, or rather (typically for Grünbein), 'Kulissen für einen Unterweltsfilm' (p. 32). The lyric subject is trapped within all of these: at once a wanderer in the circles of Hell and a fugitive in the labyrinth.[96]

> Ortlos, zeitlos,
> als seist du
> verdammt durch Geschichte
> Zu eilen . . . (p. 35)

But it is also a Hell of very German making: a divided Hell. A 1987 text by Elisabeth Wesuls is far less harrowing than that of

Grünbein, but also portrays the link between Berlin's underground and the self-understanding of the lyric subject. With a hand to the ground, the lyric subject feels it shiver with the vibrations of the S-Bahn as it travels beneath her feet between unknown stations in the West. She becomes aware of the fragility of the earth: 'unterhöhlt ist sie, sie tickt | wie eine Gasuhr'. Very soon one realizes that it is also the city, the earth, history, and the self which have been hollowed and undermined. The final lines are confusing, but seem at first to emphasize this vulnerability: 'und ich hab Wurzeln geschlagen, | mit den Händen, ich zittere leise | ich steh Kopf'. However, when one looks back at the title of the text, the poem suddenly turns to offer the promise of a passionate and liberating energy: 'Und im Kopf wuchern Wiesen'.[97]

In another, more powerful text, 'S-Bahn Frühling', Wesuls takes up the image of the filthy, discontinuous, ruptured city and produces a striking metaphor for collective yearning generated within its heart.[98]

In das Rissige dieser Stadt
gräbt sich ein
mit Gewohnheit und täglich neu
die schwarzrote Schnellbahn, reißt
einen Graben hinter sich her
Schlund an den wüsten Stellen der Stadt.

Da fällt nichts mehr auf,
Doch jahranfangs, als gäbe es
ein unter der Erdhaut gekochtes
Verlangen, unstillbare Sehnsucht
bricht es bricht in diesen
Gräben auf: Grün. Und kurz darauf
überall Flieder, nutzlos
und blau.

Den keiner hier greifen kann:
Die Schlünde sind rissig, verdreckt
der Flieder
blüht an den unzugänglichen
Stelln. So fährt man vorbei
ihn zu sehn, jauchzend
brausend und schneller als sonst
mit einer zehrend unstillbaren Sehnsucht
als gäbe es ein unterderhaut
empörtes Verlangen, wild, blau und verdreckt.

There are two complexes of vocabulary associated with the city in this text. The first depicts the monotony and resignation of those living within it: 'mit Gewohnheit und täglich neu', 'Da fällt nichts mehr auf'. The other is of decay and disruption: 'das Rissige', 'Schlund', 'Graben', 'wüst', 'verdreckt'. The 'Flieder' arrives in this bleak landscape of the soul as an extraordinary eruption of hope, expressed in violent, erotic terms: 'Verlangen', 'unstillbar', 'wild', 'zehrend', 'gekocht', 'unterderhaut', 'jauchzend | brausend und schneller als sonst'. Underscored by the repetition (l. 11) and the over-excited rhythms, this seems almost an appetite; certainly a kind of 'Frühlingserwachen'. Yet there is more to it. For the 'Verlangen' is also a 'Sehnsucht', and is linked with a blue flower, 'den keiner hier greifen kann', glimpsed only 'in unzugänglichen Stelln'. Is this an urban version of Novalis? In the last lines the longing merges with the flower: both are 'wild, blau und verdreckt'. The poem appears to be an intimation of utopia, escape, of redemption even, for the blasted places of the city and the blasted people within it.

'Born into it'—Linguistically

I do not want to pre-empt here the arguments of Chapter 5. Nevertheless, the examination of the motif of having been 'born into it' would not be complete without a brief discussion of having been 'born into' fixed structures of language. This theme is central to the anthology *Berührung ist nur eine Randerscheinung*, where Uwe Kolbe explicitly speaks of the need to find one's way out of what he calls the 'Metasprache': 'die Sprache der Sprachreglung, die Kollektivlüge der herrschenden Sprache' (p. 41). It is not simply a question of formulating a negative version with which to oppose it. Kolbe concludes: 'Ich zitiere ihre Versatzstücke, um zu sehen, wie sie in der veränderten Grammatik meines Denkens reagieren' (p. 41). The poets must dismantle the monolithic formulas of public rhetoric and test the single parts against experience. In her introduction to the anthology, Elke Erb takes up a similar position. She contends that the work of the young writers moves beyond 'folgenlose Kritik' and 'konfrontative Positionen' and that this is: 'die Konsequenz des *Austritts* aus dem autoritären System, der *Entlassung* aus der Vormundschaft eines übergeordneten Sinns' (p. 15; my emphasis).[99] The 'System' and 'Sinn' are clearly meant in political and philosophical terms, but are also linguistic, in the sense of Wittgenstein's celebrated phrase: 'Die Grenzen meiner Sprache bedeuten die Grenzen meiner Welt'.[100] Yet the only means of breaching the patrolled boundaries of language are through language itself. For many of the writers those 'Wege aus der Ordnung' are to be apprehended within the very mechanisms of that language.[101] It is striking how often the poetry documents enclosure, escape, or the tension between them, and how often this is inscribed into the very structure of the texts.

A kind of mirroring or repetition of language is used by a number of writers to signal the boundaries of their world. In Bert Papenfuß-Gorek's 'RAUS aus der Stadt', for example, the gesture of defiant energy in the first lines, 'RAUS aus der Stadt | über die grenze', is gradually corralled by the repetitions of the piece until it is modulated ('jenseits der stadt', . . . 'hier in der stadt', . . . 'rein in die stadt') to become a gesture of submission: 'kein abgang | durchBruch | leck mich'.

A similar effect is achieved in a text by Sascha Anderson.[102]

> geh über die grenze
> auf der anderen seite
> steht ein mann und sagt:
> geh über die grenze
> auf der anderen seite
> steht ein mann und sagt:
> geh über die grenze
> auf der anderen seite
> steht ein mann und sagt:

Here the impetus of the parataxis and repetition appears to push over the 'grenze'. However, the idea of an infinity of reflections, constantly turning back on themselves around the colon is in fact used to underline the imprisonment. In interview Anderson replaces the idea of two mirrors with that of 'zwei trichter, die ineinander verschoben sind. der mann in dem gedicht ist man natürlich auch selber, oder das ist dein grab, in das du gehst, oder das ist dein gott, mit dem du austauscht, das ist auch ein sehr mythologischer text'.[103] An interesting light is shed on this text in Uwe Kolbe's open letter to Anderson after Anderson's involvement with the *Staatssicherheit* was revealed in 1991.[104]

The search for ways 'aus der sprache | engpaß'[105] forms the basis of the theoretical and poetic work of Rainer Schedlinski. In a text from *die rationen des ja und des nein* he explores the theme of enclosure.[106]

```
                    . . .verdeckt
    schwarzen                siehst du
                 schnee                      den
                    auf den
                       seiten
    sind gitter                      die zeilen
                 des menschen
                    sprache
    gefängnis                      ein offnes
                 dort
                    gibt es
                       kein
                          draussen
```

With a passing reference to Derrida's 'il n'y a pas de hors-texte', Schedlinski details the prison-house of language. Yet the text itself, straggling in diagonals across the page, disrupts the fixed paths of linear reading. It allows for ungoverned connections to be made in different directions across the page. The spaces between the words—to borrow the title of the piece, 'diese unvordenkliche | lichtung der worte'—open up to offer a realm of movement within. The text becomes 'ein offnes . . . gefängnis'.

An even more concrete treatment of the theme appears in Frank Weiße's 'überdenken vergangener grundsätze auf die spitze getrieben' (see figure, overleaf).[107] This teasing pictogram is an example of the concrete poetry which flourished in the GDR in the 1980s. It is an ironic play on the formulaic language which the young generation have been born into, but also a scathing comment on the traditional *Aufbau* metaphor of the socialist project as 'Bauplatz unter unseren Händen'. On a first 'reading' one notices three things. The active 'überdenken' of the title becomes decisions already made ('über-dacht'), and ultimately a roof or enclosing lid (probably also a reference to the 'Überbau'). The foundations ('fundament' etc. . . . .), at once the 'grundsätze' of socialism, are undermined (the last line reads a repeated 'untergraben', or 'unter—graben') by the play on two idioms. The phrase 'baut auf beton' plays on the injunctions of *Aufbau*, but inevitably calls into mind an altogether more temporary result: 'auf Sand gebaut'.[108] Its corollary, 'beißt auf granit', sums up the frustration of those (to switch into the English idiom) who find themselves 'banging their heads against a brick wall'. The long, truncated build-up of the proverbial 'wo ein Wille ist . . .' (appropriately translated: 'wo EINE VILLA IST . . .') which forms, as it were, the fabric of the structure, appears to find an optimistic outlet in the continuation '. . . ist auch ein weg', which ruptures the contours of the form, and issues into a path.[109] On closer inspection, that opening is the result of a build-up of disturbances in the lower levels of the house itself. These take the form of questions, which rupture the blandly repeated 'proverb', and finally issue in an answer: 'wo EINE VILLA ZUGEMAUERT IST FEHLT DIE LUFT ZUM ATMEN'. The ambivalence is emphasized just above the point where the path breaks away, with the replacement of the word 'WEG' with 'WEH'. It is difficult in the end to assess the strength of that subversive force,

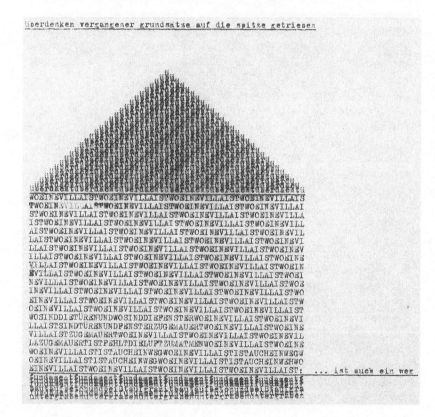

and the relationship between the blinded windows, the security of the structure, and the painful escape routes from it. However, the repeated patterns of lettering and close-set type, which at first cheat the eye into seeing only uniformity, but then reveal the subversion of language, are used to great effect. Such strategies demand very active forms of reading. One is made aware of the plasticity and ambiguity of structures (political and linguistic), and one is repeatedly forced to test one's ways of negotiating them.

If the texts discussed above demonstrate the difficulties of subverting language to escape traditional forms and meanings, a series of texts written between 1979 and 1984 by Stefan Döring, entitled 'komm geh', constantly test for means of escape: 'umwege hinzubiegen | sichtwenden zu durchschauen | feststehendes auf-zuheben'.[110] In his 'hochmut vor dem wall', for example, Döring ironically fixes the dilemma of a generation in language, but also playfully sets about 'undermining' boundaries, by undermining the signs which represent them.

> die grenzen begrenzen nichts wesentliches
> die fremden befremden nicht eigentlich
> die übergänge unterlaufen unumgängliches (p. 100)

One of Döring's most interesting texts is just such an attempt to find 'fortwege':

wortfege[111]

> weinsinnig im daseinsfrack
> feilt an windungen seiner selbst
> wahrlässig er allzu windig
>
> im gewühl fühlt er herum
> und windet sich nochmal heraus
> fund, kaum geborgen, bloss wort
>
> wasser, lauernd, von wall zu wall
> die spiegel mit fellen überzogen
> wetter, uns umschlagend, dunst
>
> die gewährten fegt es hinüber
> die bleibenden gefahren erneut
> der sich herausfand währt dahin

Gerhard Wolf has exposed an alternative reading of the poem (or, as he calls it, 'ein zweites Gedicht'), which is based on the interchangeability of the letters 'f' and 'w' (hence: 'feinsinnig im daseinswrack. . . | etc.).[112] Alexander von Bormann suggests that the subtext can be understood as the 'authentic' version, and equated with the author's own position. He bases this presumably on the emotive content. The poet's life is thus seen as a wreckage ('daseinswrack'); he is seeking means of escape ('fortwege'), which are clearly linked with leaving the GDR; but finds himself existentially unhoused: 'wund, kaum geborgen, bloss fort' (l. 6). Such an interpretation implies that the printed text is simply a 'Sklavensprache' of sorts. I would argue that the tension created between the levels of meaning should not be dismissed so lightly. There are, in fact, four possible poems here (the titles of which would be 'wortfege', 'fortwege', 'wortwege', and 'fortfege'), which are all grammatically, syntactically, and lexically coherent in themselves, but which are made the more powerful for being constantly mirrored one within the other. The very opposition of 'wrack' and 'frack', for example, highlights the discrepancy between official appearances and the inner state of the individual. This opposition is sustained in the references to what is hidden from view and what is revealed within the poem as a whole. Indeed, the text is a self-conscious exercise in balancing these. Adolf Endler compares the text to one of Escher's paintings in the multiple readings and awkward perspectives of the piece.[113] It is an extraordinary poem; one which manages to pinpoint the dilemma of an entire existence with economy and precision. To conclude, it is worth quoting Wolf:

Hier ist die Befindlichkeit einer Generation, die Döring durch die Wahl seiner Wörter, mit denen er umgeht, verwandelt, ziemlich treu wiedergibt, wenn er sie im Daseinsfrack als Daseinswrack erkennt, wenn findig und windig, Gefühl im Gewühl zu verschwinden droht, fund und wund Synonyme sind, für Windungen und Findungen in diesem Dasein, das zwischen Wall und Fall seine Wege zu suchen hat, f(w)ahrlässig oder f(w)indig. (p. 161)

The confusion and vulnerability which the text presents is not only existential in its broadest sense; it also has a concrete political dimension, and of course a linguistic one. However, Döring is not simply playfully shedding a layer of language. The 'fortwege' which are discovered and enacted in the ambivalences of the text itself are, as the text concedes, fragile, sometimes desperate, and perhaps ultimately inadequate: 'bloss wort'.

PART II

Entgrenzung: Breaking Boundaries

Introduction

THE critical reception of the young writers in the early to mid-1980s, in particular, was one dominated by the idea of a retreat from the broad scope of reality. Confronted with the limitations placed on their existence in real and metaphorical terms, the young writers appeared to turn inwards and take refuge in enclaves away from the structures and discourses of state. I have already indicated the dominant lines of critical response (see above, Chapter 1). Broadly speaking, critics identify a retreat in a number of areas of the work: the presentation of the subject, and of that subject's social reality, the understanding of history and tradition, of politics, of the function of literature and, finally, of language and form. Those same lines of argument persist in more recent criticism too. Particularly noteworthy is the emphasis placed on the writers' apparent rejection of social or political engagement. Anneli Hartmann speaks of a 'Rückzug von gesellschaftlichem Engagement und aktivem politischem Handeln', and Gerrit-Jan Berendse identifies a fundamental 'Verweigerung', which results, he claims, in the writers turning in on themselves as self-consciously marginalized 'outcasts'.[1] Common to all these understandings is a sense of literature as personal consolation, the fixing of identity within a closely defined realm: 'Literatur als Zuflucht in der Haft' (Wittstock).[2]

Set against this understanding is one which identifies precisely the opposite general impetus in the work. In 1988 in Cologne an exhibition and a series of readings and performances were organized which brought together many of the increasing number of writers who found themselves transplanted to the West. Among them were some of the most significant of the writers of the young generation. Its title was 'Entgrenzungen'. In the catalogue, Sascha Anderson, one of the central organizers commented: 'die veranstaltungen repräsentieren keine bestimmte art, sondern die möglichkeit verschiedenster arten miteinander. die fähigkeit einer generation, zu entgrenzen.'[3] Of course the notion of a poetic *Entgrenzung* of sorts is not something which can be ascribed exclusively to this generation of young writers, nor even to lyric poetry. Erich Arendt's 1981 collection *entgrenzen* is an important reference point for many of the young writers, and in his recent dissertation, for example, Peter Böthig fruitfully sets texts by Sarah Kirsch, Heiner Müller, and Arendt himself alongside the innovations from Prenzlauer Berg.[4] However, it is in the young writers' work in particular that a complex metaphorical field of containment and the breaking of boundaries has built up during the 1980s.

One of the most interesting and controversial reckonings with the young writers came in the form of Volker Braun's essay 'Rimbaud. Ein Psalm der Aktualität'.[5] In this essay Braun plays the notions of literature as 'Zuflucht' and 'Entgrenzung' off against one another. He explicitly rejects the idea of literature as any kind of sanctuary: 'Diese Poesie ist ja keine Zuflucht, sie ist ein Arbeitsraum, Laboratorium, wo nicht das Gold absoluter Wahrheit gesucht wird, sondern das akute Material der authentischen Erfahrung' (p. 997). In order to understand the nature of Braun's disagreement with what he perceives as the thrust of the young writers, it is necessary to outline the project of his essay as a whole. On one level it represents an exploration of Braun's affinity with the poet Rimbaud, whom he claims as a long-standing 'Gewährsmann meiner Erfahrungen' (p. 978). On another level the piece champions the legacy of the 'avant-garde'. This is understood as an impetus rather than a historical phenomenon; Braun's use of the concept embraces surrealism, modernism, and the work of the Beat Generation, for example. His aim is to reclaim its potential for the literary canon of the GDR. In doing that, however, he also sets out a response to the work of Heiner Müller and Elke Erb. In the case of Erb, he is also responding specifically to a paper read by her in 1981 about Anderson and the other young poets of Prenzlauer Berg. Braun's essay also passes an initial judgement on these writers, the 'vermeintlichen Neutöner' (p. 990) of the literary scene. Most important, as the subtitle, 'Ein Psalm der Aktualität'—from the second of Rimbaud's 'lettres du Voyant'—suggests, it is an essay which investigates the very premise of poetry and its function in the GDR.[6]

The affinity which Braun perceives between himself and this literary model is based largely on a political reading of Rimbaud, which highlights Rimbaud's revolutionary interest and translates his radical gesture of departure into a revolutionary act.[7] At the centre of Braun's reading is the opposition of stagnation— 'Geschichte auf dem Abstellgleis. Status quo' (p. 982)—and revolutionary movement—'Entgrenzung aller Sinne' (p. 984). This is metamorphosed into a concrete and political topography, in which 'Provinz' represents the ossified regimentation of the GDR, and 'Revolution' the vagabond expedition 'ins innerste Afrika' (p. 995). Rimbaud's incursions into that Unknown, his 'illuminations', are also translated by Braun into more concrete political visions.

Rimbaud's elusive goal, 'le lieu et la formule', becomes in Braun's essay 'die Formel für ein menschliches Leben, den Ort der Poesie', and is linked explicitly to a revolutionary socialist future (p. 983).[8] In doing this Braun claims Rimbaud firmly for the tradition of political poet-seer.[9]

Rimbaud's quest for a future 'langage universel', with which to articulate his vision, is taken up by Braun, significantly and polemically, in the central idea of a 'Gegensprache'.[10] It is here that he expressly rejects the 'poésie pure' (p. 996) which he sees as the domain endorsed by Elke Erb's poetological statements, and which he identifies with the young writers. He scorns the hygienic naïvety of poetry which refuses to engage (p. 986 and p. 990). Instead, he takes up Rimbaud's 'impure' poetry, which has been distilled from extremities of experience; and, by a sleight of hand, Braun then slips into the 'impurity' of revolutionary poetry. The poetry of the young writers, he claims, does not engage on behalf of change: 'Literarische Befreiungseffekte, nicht die Befreiung der Literatur; das Ordnungsmodell und der Harmoniezwang werden bei dieser Erb-Sache umgangen, aber nicht zerbrochen' (p. 996). When he claims, 'Die Gegensprache, sie wird auch Fürsprache sein' (p. 985), it is clear that the language he is seeking is not in any way an abdication, a retreat, or a simple opposition; rather, it is the enactment of a utopian alternative in the here and now: 'die Wirklichkeit öffnen' (p. 990).[11]

The key term in Braun's essay is *Entgrenzung*. It runs through almost all his arguments in different forms: 'ausbrechen aus den Zwängen. Aus den Panzern' (p. 992), 'Durchblick' (p. 989), 'die Wirklichkeit öffnen' (p. 990). Braun translates Rimbaud's 'dérèglement de tous les sens' into a revolutionary bid for new ground: 'die *Freiheit* beginnt jenseits' (p. 989).[12] The breaking of boundaries is, according to Braun, to be within the self, within history, within political understandings, and, importantly, also within language. Here, and in Braun's poetry of the same period, there is the fundamental injunction: 'Du mußt die Grenze überschreiten'.[13] Against this movement he sets the gesture of the young writers' poetry.

Unsere jungen Dichter, Kinder der administrativen Beamten, suchen auch das Loch in der Mauer. Sie verbrauchen ihre Fantasie an Tunnels und Fesselballons, ihre 'monologe gehen fremd'. Fluchten wieder, aber auf Hasenpfoten. 'Ein Stück, nur aus einem Schrei gebaut, das wäre ehrlich.' Das ist tierischer Laut. Gesang, ihr unfreundlich Asyl, nur ein privates Eigentum. Dabei wissen wir doch, daß uns die Freiheit nicht auf den Versen folgt. Wir müssen, gräßliche Vernunft, Provokateure bleiben. (p. 983)

The reference to a poem by Sascha Anderson ('ihre monologe gehen fremd') identifies Braun's target as the writers associated with Prenzlauer Berg.[14] He accuses the young poets of abdicating their responsibility to their society, and (recalling Hölderlin) to the tradition of revolutionary poetry—'Gesang, ihr unfreundlich Asyl, nur ein privates Eigentum' (p. 983).[15] In poetic terms he rejects writing which has degenerated into self-fulfilling monologue, or 'geistlosen Handbetrieb der Avantgarde' (p. 990).

Anderson's response to Braun's comments fixes on the difference between the two generations of writers. For Anderson, Braun's comments arise out of an inability to understand what the younger poets are trying to achieve, and a frustration at the failure of those ideals in which he himself had invested. It is noticeable, however, that Anderson does not take up any of Braun's individual points and argue them out. The lack of productive dialogue between the two writers is indicative of a fundamental and mutual incomprehension: what Gerhard Wolf has called 'die kluft zwischen den beiden sprachen'.[16] Braun's essay on Rimbaud is a compelling piece of writing. However, this does not necessarily mean that his analysis of the young writers is accurate or just. I would argue that, if one looks at the generation as a whole, it is precisely the energy for breaking boundaries which is the fundamental gesture of their work.

3

'Leib eigen & fremd': Breaking the Bounds of the Subject

ich
ist ein weites feld
mit breitem rand[1]

THE GDR literature of the 1980s saw an unprecedented crisis in the legitimation of the textual subject, 'der Irrweg des Aberglaubens mit Namen "Subjekt" ', as Emmerich, discussing Kunert, has called it.[2] Yet, when set against the discussions in other European countries or in North America, for example, the continued currency of terms like 'authenticity', 'self-realization', 'the search for identity', and 'subjectivity' in GDR writing is very striking.[3] More striking still is the assurance with which critics—particularly from the West—have treated these terms as aesthetic criteria and even, quite baldly, as indexes of literary value. This is partly a result of the unique role which the notion of the subject and its textual equivalent came to play in the GDR.

Faced with the total politicization of the public sphere and the degradation of the subject in favour of the collective, the private in the GDR—almost by default—became the site from which a different reading of reality could be formulated.[4] Many of the older writers in particular invested that private sphere, and the textual subject which became its insignia, with all the utopian promise which had been eliminated from the 'mega-machines' of state. Christa Wolf's 'subjektive Authentizität'[5] came to represent not merely resistance to dominant Socialist Realism, nor even a simple act of redress for the embattled individual, but also the goal of a utopian aspiration.

In lyric poetry the preoccupation with the subject can be traced in particular to the emergence of those writers associated with the 'Lyrik-Welle' of the 1960s, who have now become known as the 'Sächsische Dichterschule'.[6] 'Hier wird Neuhimmel gegraben und Neuhimmel angeschnitten,' declared Volker Braun in his 1965 collection *Provokation für mich*.[7] The publication of this collection and those other collections and anthologies which appeared at the beginning of the 1960s signalled a controversial shift in political, cultural, and aesthetic understandings in the GDR.[8] The new impetus in their poetry was primarily understood, especially in the early years, as the struggle to resurrect the rights of the individual voice—that 'gescholtenes, geschmähtes denunziertes Ich'.[9] Indeed, the notion of a 'Rehabilitierung des Ich' (Wünsche) conditioned the critical reception of these writers throughout the 1970s to such an extent that by the end of the decade the notion of a 'Lyrik der Unmittelbarkeit' had become the standard formula for discussing the poetry of the GDR.[10]

The interest of critics in the West can be explained, in part at least, by the comparable emergence of an emphatically subjective poetry in the West at the same time. Nicolas Born's poem 'Fahndungsblatt', which begins 'Gesucht wird ICH', can stand here as a single example of the impetus which was to become known in the West as 'Neue Subjektivität', and which was to dominate the literary scene throughout the 1970s.[11] Indeed, the marked emphasis on the subjective was one of the most important aspects of the much-discussed 'convergence' of the two German literatures in the 1970s and early 1980s.[12] In the face of an increasingly politicized and mechanized public sphere, for example, a number of critics identify a 'Rückzug vor der Realität' as the dominant literary gesture, and Heinrich Mohr, explicitly addressing the 'Prozeß der Angleichung' of the two German literatures, fixes on the preoccupation with 'das bedrängte Individuum' and 'das beschädigte Leben' as central to the literature of East and West.[13] However similar the approaches to the subject might appear on the surface, the poetry has been interpreted very differently in East and West. If the emphasis on the subjective in the West was understood primarily as the cultivation of a poetic refuge and was soon (disparagingly) described as 'neue Innerlichkeit',[14] the subjective impulse in the GDR was interpreted as part of a conscious political programme.[15] Wolfgang Emmerich, for example, emphasizes that the Braun generation forged a remarkable 'third way' between the political instrumentalization of the 1950s, on the one hand, and a removal from the social sphere on the other: 'nämlich eine Synthese aus Gesellschaftlichkeit und Subjektivität, aus Politik und Poesie, aus Einverständnis und Provokation'.[16] As a key to the understanding of this generation, and indeed the poetry of the 1960s and

1970s, he cites Georg Maurer's term 'arbeitende Subjektivität'.[17]
It is precisely this 'Amalgam aus Gesellschaftlichkeit und Ichbezogenheit' (Emmerich, p. 387) which critics found lacking in the subjective awareness of the youngest generation of poets in the GDR. Instead, although one or two critics explicitly took up the idea of 'arbeitende Subjektivität' and understood the work of the young writers as a more radical extension of that same impetus which had marked the work of their predecessors, many more identified an embattled subject seeking 'Rettung im Bereich des Privaten'.[18] Heinz Plavius was particularly concerned at the 'undialectical conception of the relationship between individual and society' in their work, an understanding which he condemned as 'anachronistisch', an affront to the very basis of socialist society (p. 144). He pointed out that for many of them literature had become 'Stütze des Individuums nicht der Gesellschaft', and had taken on an essentially defensive role as 'Anwalt und Verteidiger der bedrängten Individualität' (p. 143). Precisely these concerns have been echoed by a number of critics from East and West over the last decade. Here Anneli Hartmann's important 1985 article, 'Der Generationswechsel—ein ästhetischer Wechsel?', might serve as a single example.[19] She identifies 'Individualität in die Defensive gerutscht' (p. 109), 'Rückzug aus der Öffentlichkeit', and 'zunehmende Privatheit' (p. 132) as characteristics of the subjective understanding in the work of the young writers.

Most interesting in a sense is the method which many of the critics, including Hartmann, employ in order to set about exploring this subjective awareness. Very frequently the position of the young writers is delineated in contrast to that of the Volker Braun generation. The Hähnels, for example, comment in 1981 that the 'lyrische Innerlichkeit' of some of the young writers is 'verletzt-defensiv' rather than 'provokativ und eingreifend', and contrast this with the confidence which was an integral part of the poetry of Braun and his contemporaries. Ursula Heukenkamp, discussing Uwe Kolbe's work in the same year, misses a 'großen Weltentwurf' in his poetry and concludes: 'Auch würde man vergeblich nach dem Ich suchen, das sich mit seinen Ansprüchen und Entwürfen der Gesellschaft als Maß und moralische Instanz vorstellt und zugleich entgegensetzt.' 'Das Ich', she claims, 'in den Erstlingen der sechziger Jahre war ein anderes.'[20] Similarly Hartmann contrasts the subjective awareness of the older writers, which she claims has been won out of a confrontation with the public sphere, with that of the younger writers which she understands as 'nahezu autonom und absolut gesetzt' (p. 120).[21]

There are a number of problems inherent in using the work of older authors as a foil in order to judge the subjective awareness among later writers. I should like here simply to point out three of the most significant.

First, despite the emphasis on the subjective in their work, the 'I' of the older writers was never simply a retreat into subjectivity. Their protest was also against the representative function which had been foisted onto the lyric subject. Instead they set about negotiating a position within a more complex collective identity. The 'wir' of that collective has two distinct aspects. In the early years in particular, it is striking to what extent the poets articulated themselves as part of a generation.[22] This becomes clear in Adolf Endler's reference to a 'poetische Plejade der um 1935 Geborenen', or Sarah Kirsch's praise for the 'junge Dichter vom begabten Jahrgang 35'.[23] However various the individual idioms of the different writers concerned, from the melancholy halftones of Kirsch to the abrasive energy of Biermann, theirs was a 'Beschwörung ähnlicher Erfahrung'.[24] The rhetoric of generations also found its way into the work itself. A reference to 'Generationsproblematiker: der Braun z. B.', which appears in Braun's own 'Zueignungen: zu Vorläufiges', might be more ironic than anything else, yet the poetry of many of the writers is marked by the opposition of 'ihr' and the 'wir' of a youth made impatient by the regulations imposed by their old comrades.[25] As a kind of tribunal for truth, a 'Kontrollposten Jugend', that 'wir' sets out to review the decrees of 'steife Routine'.[26] The opposition of 'ihr' and 'wir' becomes a lever with which to force open an essentially closed reality. It is no surprise, for example, that one of the most controversial poems of the time was Rainer Kirsch's sonnet 'Meinen Freunden, den alten Genossen', which operates with just such a series of explicit and implied oppositions.[27] However, that 'wir' was not simply the badge of a 'generation'; it also looked forward to a community invested with the utopian aspirations of the present. 'Dem betont herausgekehrten Ich wurde ein selbstbewußtes Wir an die Seite gestellt, das eben nicht mehr auf die Harmonie zwischen Individuum und Gesellschaft abzielte, sondern

ein utopisches Wir einer noch zu verwirklichenden Menschengem-
einschaft meinte.'²⁸

There is a second problem. From the late 1960s into the 1970s
the *Aufbau* faith in the upsurge of new technologies gave way to a
wider-reaching scepticism. This provoked a review of the historical
progress of socialism to date and a concession that history, to
borrow the title of a story by Volker Braun, was 'unvollendet'.²⁹
The understanding of the Enlightenment project was also now
extended to include its pathological underside. Where collective
experience governed by rationalism and progress had once been
paramount, attention now began to shift to the individual, the
eccentric, and the partial. One manifestation of this, which I take
up in more detail later, is the widespread identification with the
figures of Romanticism—especially Günderrode, Hölderlin, and
Kleist. Notions of identity, particularly the collective and utopian
understanding of 'arbeitende Subjektivität' were in crisis. To speak
with Emmerich: '1977 [. .] sieht sich die "arbeitende Subjektivität",
die den Übergang vom *solitaire* zum *solidare* auf ihre Fahnen
geschrieben hatte, wieder auf die kontemplative, die räsonierende
Haltung des vereinzelten Einzelnen zurückgeworfen.'³⁰ By the
1980s this had gone even further, and Czechowski's programmatic
'Was mich betrifft' | So bin ich ich' of 1981, for example, represents
the agonized determination of an increasingly embattled lyric
subject.³¹ Throughout the 1980s Czechowski, along with Elke Erb,
Kito Lorenc, and even Braun, was forced to concede the erosion of
a stable and integral subject. The process is documented in the open
forms of their later work.³²

The third problem with the backward-looking comparison is that
it fails adequately to address the most radical developments in the
young writers' work. Recent criticism has placed their work firmly
under the sign of the postmodern. Many of the younger generation,
it is claimed, have never invested in the notion of a subjective
awareness, but have instead set about dismantling what they see as
the 'illusion' of an autonomous subject and the 'fiction' of a direct
lyric voice. With reference to Lacan's 'decentred subject', Michael
Thulin (i.e. the GDR poet and critic Klaus Michael) explores the
radical interrogation of the lyric subject in the work of Rainer
Schedlinski and concludes:

das vielbeschworene 'lyrische ich' erweist sich so mit seinen hermen-
eutischen umhüllungen als das, was es ist: der narzißtische spiegel einer

vorgeblich-vergeblichen identität. die fiktion eines in sich und mit sich identischen 'lyrischen subjekts' und der rückzug auf jene unbestimmbare 'subjektive authentizität' kann wohl nur noch als sündenfall des poetischen bezeichnet werden.[33]

This kind of position is too extreme to be addressed in those critical studies which concentrate on highlighting the continuities and differences between the subjective awareness of the earlier poets and their successors.

As I indicated in Chapter 1, a certain consensus has emerged, which provides a useful starting-point for discussion. Both Emmerich and Hartmann signal two dominant tendencies amongst the young writers. On the one hand stands 'Lyrik der Unmittelbarkeit', to borrow Hartmann's term, which can be understood as a continuation of the impetus of Braun and his colleagues, and which Hartmann dismisses very quickly as fairly conservative. Set against this is 'Lyrik der Entpersönlichung', which both critics understand as an essentially 'linguistic' poetry, in which the very notion of 'lyrische Subjektivität geschichtlich obsolet geworden ist'.[34] Although offering a first approach to the poetry of the generation, such a division does not stand up to investigation for very long. Some of those texts which Hartmann places in the first category as 'Verständigungstexte über die eigene Existenz' (p. 120) in fact explore the way the subject is constituted in language, and some of the most extreme of the experimental texts are clearly testing out formulations of meaning, personal and political. This is the problem with all schemes attempting to create meaningful patterns over such a large and various body of material. Nevertheless, in the following discussion of examples, some of the continuities and distinctions might suggest a new approach to the notion of subjectivity in the young writers' work, one which would attempt to do justice to the complexities of the question itself.

Working Subjectivity

There are of course a number of texts in which the lyric subject enacts a simple withdrawal from the world into a sentimentalized poetic refuge, in the manner of Eva Strittmatter, for example—notably pieces by Sonja Schüler, or even a few of the early poems from Kolbe's *Hineingeboren*.[35] However, a far larger number do not seek simply to eliminate the contradictions ranged against them, but rather to explore them. Kurt Drawert's 'Im Klartext' appears to set out (with an ironic reference to Czechowski's 'ich, beispielsweise') a programmatic 'Reise ins eigene | innere Land':[36]

> Mich beispielsweise, lieber Czechowski,
>
> interessiert tatsächlich nur noch
> das Privateigentum an Empfindung,
> der Zustand des Herzens, wenn die schwarze Stunde
> am Horizont steht . . .

Yet, on looking more closely at the text and the collection as a whole, it is clear that the poetry documents the gradual constitution of the lyric subject rather than a closed statement of it.

> Sobald ich mich bewege,
> überzeugend zwischen den Dingen,
> die ich kenne, bin ich überzeugt,
> mich zu bewegen.[37]

The sense of a lyric subject at work on, and changed by, a subjective acquisition of reality might be understood, with reference to Georg Maurer, as 'arbeitende Subjektivität' (see above). In some senses, this gesture can be seen as a continuation of the legacy of Braun and his contemporaries, but it is noticeable that, in many cases, the lyric subject is far more militant in insisting on the validity of its own experience. To speak with Uwe Kolbe, it is 'das radikale ich'.[38]

Common to a number of texts is what Siegfried Rönisch identified as 'Geradlinigkeit und Unbestechlichkeit' in their observation of reality.[39] As Kolbe comments in his 'Gespräch ohne Ende':

> Die Fahnen faulen die Zeichen
> sind abgenutzt die Losung
> bleibt gleich Tag für Tag
> soll ich das Ende dessen singen?[40]

In their poetry writers look to represent those ambiguous truths which are so neatly manipulated into the ideological black and white of the newspapers.

> (schwarz als reaktion auf weiss
> weiss als reaktion auf schwarz)
> vielleicht sollte man die wahrheiten

die durch die literatur verbreitet
werden grau auf grauem grund
drucken.'[41]

As Christine Cosentino confirms in an early article on the
Prenzlauer Berg poetry: 'Kunstwahrheit fängt die Welt des
Individuums mit ihren Rissen und Nöten ein und registriert die
Reaktionen des Individuums auf die verschrumpften Ideale des
unverbrämten DDR-Alltags.'[42] The 'Risse', as I indicated in
Chapter 2, are important. The 'cracks' are not simply that single
most fundamental German rupture, the 'Riß' which found its way
into the poetry of Reiner Kunze or Wolf Biermann, for example.
The poetry of the 1980s offers a reality complete with all the
contradictions, discrepancies, and fissures in the walls and houses,
and in the fabric of the socialist ideal. In discussion various of the
young writers claim the concrete and existential precondition of
their work as 'Zerrissenheit'. 'Ich schreibe lieber aus Rissen heraus',
declares Kolbe in 1979, and Gerd Adloff confirms 'Zerrissenheit' as
the core of his work. Mensching goes slightly further in signalling it
as the duty of the literature itself to reflect the 'Komplexität und
Zerrissenheit' of 'really existing socialism', and Sascha Anderson
goes so far as to claim, 'ich schaffe Risse'.[43] Faced with the
contradictory nature of lived reality, writers concentrate on a
subjective acquisition of that reality, and reject the retouched
picture which is fed to them through official channels. A key term
in this respect is 'wirkliches Erleben'.[44]

However, the various reactions to that experience of reality, and
the lyric subjects which are constituted in response to it, are very
different. It is important to identify the exact nature of this
subjective approach and the lyric subject which articulates it: to
distinguish between an essentially defensive poetic ego retiring into
the subjective, a rigidly oppositional lyric self, whose assault on
reality ends in stasis and silence, and the active espousal of the
subjective as a means of corresponding with a broader reality. It is
the third of these which one might call 'working subjectivity'.

A consideration of Lutz Rathenow's collection *Zangengeburt*
may serve to clarify these distinctions.[45] This collection is filled
with nightmare visions of the disintegration of the subject. For
example, the poem 'Ich schlief' (p. 47) is structured around
disjointed images of walls, soldiers and abysses, and ends:

Er vor der Mauer   Sie legten an
Die Hände hob er   Ich beugte mich vor
Dann fiel ich
Und der Fallschirm klinkte
                          klinkte nicht aus
Ich erwachte zerschmettert

In a discussion of Rathenow, James Knowleton speaks of writers who 'turn their backs on the social whole and take refuge in art, assuming what Konrad Franke calls "die Position des Beobachtenden, des Zuschauers; Wer genug gesehen hat, flieht in die Kunst" '.[46] To imply that a flight from reality is a pervasive tendency in Rathenow's work is to ignore the almost reckless resolve of his poetry. A short text stands as a kind of motto for the collection as a whole, and is called, quite simply, 'leben' (7).

Die rettende Insel suchen
um sie zu versenken.
So daß für die Flucht
nur eine Möglichkeit bleibt:
auszuharren

There is no mistaking this for a gesture of resignation. In an interview of 1983, Rathenow was convinced that such an intractable assertion of his individual awareness was vital in the GDR: 'My work is needed here. The Socialist form of society is not going to evaporate—one has to supply the impulses, lead the dialogue.'[47] The question is, however, whether such stridency does not ultimately lead to stasis, to a form of opposition, in which the identity of the subject is defined entirely in its gesture of negation.

The notion of the writer as one half of an antagonistic opposition was taken up by Günter Kunert, writing in 1988 about the dilemma of young authors coming from East to West. He warns against the danger of being forced into a static role as 'Gegenbild des Funktionärs', and allowing one's poetic self-understanding to be conditioned by restraints which regulate one's existence: 'Ihr ganzes Selbstverständnis möglicherweise auch ihre Intention resultieren aus nichts anderem als dem inneren Widerstand gegen das sie und alle unterdrückende System.'[48] Significant in this respect is Rathenow's poem 'Man(n) ist Man(n)' (p. 77). The title already suggests a kind of stasis, although presumably also (in its reference to Brecht's play) the mechanistic deconstruction of identity.

> Ein Mann, der an einer Mauer steht, seine Notdurft
> verrichten will, und verstört einen Polizisten betrachtet,
> der vor der Mauer steht, seine Notdurft verrichten will,
> und verstört einen Mann betrachtet, der an der Mauer
> steht.

Here the language is checked and thrown back on itself in the act of observation. The political force is emphasized in the shift from an indefinite to a definite article, 'die Mauer'. The result is that a momentary opposition is created, but also circularity, or rather stasis. The same fundamental gesture is a common feature of the collection as a whole and is perhaps best summarized in the end of a poem (ironically?) entitled 'Aussichten' (p. 76): 'Gefesselt an deine Zukunft | lebst du. Hier'.[49]

The lyric subject in Hanz-Eckardt Wenzel's 1984 collection *Lied vom wilden Mohn* is similarly resolute in confronting a damaged reality, but uses it as a basis for engaging with that reality.[50] In his 'Lebenslied (1977)', for example, 'Schmerzen', 'Herzweh', 'Ärger', 'Kummer', and 'Kater' are successively 'eingeplant' (foreseen, but not avoided) and each strophe ends with the obstinate resolution in upper-case: 'ABER VERZICHTEN WILL ICH DARAUF NICHT'. The lyric subject attempts to endure the contradictions and pains by exposing himself to them, and living them. In acquiescing in the totality of experience—the sorrows as well as the dreams—the lyric subject wins a sense of movement, the motivation to construct practicable ways of living, and ultimately a further dimension to his identity. In the final strophe, for example, the lyric subject is able to project beyond the narrow vistas of his own experience: 'ich greife verlockend weit aus meiner Zeit | Ich träume mir das Anderssein'. The mixture of passionate engagement and fierce melancholy, which informs this text, is one of the most compelling aspects of Wenzel's writing, and marks the presentation of the lyric subject in this and his subsequent collection.[51] A similar kind of mood is created in his 'Ich braue das bittere Bier'.[52]

> Ich braue das bittere Bier,
> Den Wehrmut, ich breche den Stab,
> Ich treib hinter meiner Tür
> Die sorglosen Kinder ab.
>
> Ich male mir Narben zum Fest.
> Vergeßt doch, wie schön ich noch bin.

Bis man von den Reden läßt
Und reicht mir Almosen hin.
Ich singe den Übermut her,
Und redet man laut von Gefahr:
Ich lache und stopf das Gewehr,
Ich tanze und häng am Haar.
Ich spucke die Galle, das Gift,
Ich streue den Sand in das Brot.
ICH LASS MEINE HOFFNUNG NICHT,
Ich raufe und leb mich tot.

In an illuminating essay, Steffen Mensching, who writes and performs with Wenzel in the *Liedertheater* group 'Karls Enkel', makes the link between this text, dedicated to Erich Mühsam, and the Mühsam cabaret programme which the theatre group performed.[53] Although he recognizes that Wenzel's text is fired by the 'Euphorie der Identifikation' with Mühsam, Mensching interprets it ultimately as a 'Bekenntnis des poetischen Ich zu seiner Situation' (p. 335). Mühsam himself expressed his revolutionary yearning in a text of 1909:

Ich möchte wieder vom Glücke gesunden,
Die Seele sehnt sich nach harten Streichen.
Die Seele sehnt sich nach frischen Wunden,
nach Kämpfen und Bängnissen ohnegleichen.[54]

In Wenzel's poem, the militant gestures, 'Ich breche den Stab', 'Ich male mir Narben zum Fest', 'ich singe den Übermut her', etc. are done at once in a spirit of melancholy (for the stasis which is his reality), but also of determination and self-determination (the play on 'Wermut', 'Wehmut', 'Wehrmut', and 'Übermut' is important here). The resolve to accept the full bitterness—of the beer, the gall, the poison—is not simply passive, however. It is an active desire. The lyric subject brews the bitter beer himself, and scatters the sand on his own bread. In the final image, one should not understand the lyric subject as being a puppet of historical forces, but rather, even in the midst of a painful awareness of the age ('ich häng am Haar'), he generates the freedom to laugh, battle, dance, and live—with an urgent hope which takes up Mühsam's own anarchic yearning: 'Von meiner Hoffnung lasse ich nicht'.[55] Mensching's own homage to Mühsam, 'Angenommene Farbenlehre Erich Mühsams',[56] insists on a very similar, again anarchic, determination:

Nennt mich Arschloch, Vollidiot. Schlagt mich auf und schlagt
   mich nieder.
Schlagt mich windelweich und tot. Nein ich streiche nicht das
   Schwarz.
Und ich streiche nicht das Rot.

The notion of contradiction, expressed here, is at the centre of
Mensching's poetic understanding. The world which finds its way
into his texts is the concrete and discontinuous reality of the city:
'Die in sich chaotische und sich widersprechende Wirklichkeit der
Großstadt, in der das tragische Moment des Verkehrsunfalls neben
dem Zeitungsblatt von vor sechs Tagen und dem Hund eines
Börsenmaklers erscheint.'[57] Yet both Mensching and Wenzel deny
a perception of reality as merely 'Splitter von Welt friedlich und
beziehungslos nebeneinander'. Instead they point to the creative
potential inherent in such disjointedness: 'Die Dinge kommen
willkürlich zusammen, und Ihr Nicht-Zusammenpassen läßt eine
viel tiefere Einsicht in soziale Bewegungen und Vorgänge, ein viel
genaueres Hinterfragen zu, als ihr logisch konstruierter Vorgang.'[58]
It should be noted that this potential is not generated by resolving
the contradictions, but rather exploiting the unexpected contigu-
ities. The short poem which introduces Mensching's first collection,
Erinnerung an eine Milchglasscheibe, demonstrates with what
degree of suspicion any form of opportune harmony is viewed.

So weiß war der Morgen so
Offensichtlich aus gutem Stoff, so blaß
Und unnütz, daß ich dich fragte, was
Haben sie dahinter versteckt (p. 5)

Instead the creative unrest generated between contradictions is
translated into an outward-looking energy. It is with a 'weltoffene
Haut' (Mensching), a 'Verlangen | Nach einem großen Platz'
(Wenzel), or a militant 'Sehnsucht' (Hensel), that these writers
encounter and act on their reality.[59] This is achieved in a constant
productive dialogue, one which works on all levels: within the self,
with a 'Du', with utopian aspirations for the future, and with
history. Here three examples might illustrate the approach.
   In the short poem 'Unter den Linden', Mensching fixes a concrete
moment and the core of the lyric subject in a laconic word picture:

An meiner Schläfe
Klebte ein feuchtes Lindenblatt.

> Ich bin, wie du,
> Mit einem Schlag, altgraue Stadt,
> Zu treffen[60]

The apparent simplicity of the text reveals, on closer examination, a precise rhythmic construction, a controlled synchronic and diachronic development and multi-layered references. It encompasses at once the Siegfried legend, the precarious political reality of Berlin, and ultimately (via the association of 'mit einem Schlag' and 'Erstschlag') the nuclear menace overshadowing all such cities. All this is done without ever losing sight of the lyric subject's own concrete vulnerability.

In a number of poems the dialogic interaction with a 'Du' unleashes a powerful utopian aspiration. An example is given in the final poem of Mensching's first collection, 'Auf einem Bein, nachts, nackt' (p. 88).

> Auf einem Bein, nachts, nackt
> In der Küche stehend, schöpfte ich wieder
> Seltsamen Mut, als du mir Ungelenkem,
> Tropfnassem, das Handtuch, wortlos, gabst,
> An das ich nicht ranlangen konnte

In concrete terms this is a very unremarkable gesture between lovers. It is, to use Dieter Schlenstedt's formulation, 'eine kleine Geste',[61] but one which illuminates the whole collection in retrospect. The resonance of the extraordinary 'seltsamen Mut' which the gesture engenders is an intimation of the possibilities which might be won for the future. As always with Mensching, this intimation is underplayed; the colloquial, blunt language stifles any uncomfortable sentimentality. The text is simple and without metaphor since the poem itself is a metaphor, and it stands as an emphatic contradiction to the brutalities and discrepancies which have come before. It is a gesture of hope towards a world to come, one 'wo der Mensch dem Menschen ein Helfer ist'.[62]

A very similar gesture is presented in more explicitly political terms in the poem 'Ist dir aufgefallen . . .' of 1986.[63] A nervous smile exchanged between the poetic subject and an American soldier in a children's bookshop transcends barriers of hostile prejudice and, in a gesture quite different from Rathenow's 'Man(n) ist Man(n)', reveals:

. . .daß dieser Augenblick
eine Sekunde oder zwei,
sehr seltsam war, so verzweifelt, utopisch, blödsinnig
hoffnungsvoll zeitlos kurz entwaffnend

The single breath of the poem culminates in a string of adjectives suspended unpunctuated at the end. The familiar formula, 'sehr seltsam', generated in the exchange, unleashes extraordinary possibilities. The final adjective: 'entwaffnend' acts as a triumphant bridge between the personal and political levels of the poem.

The Divided Self

If, in these texts, the subject manages to mediate between the competing impulses of reality, history, and intimations of the ideal, there are many texts in which irresolvable contradiction becomes inscribed within the lyric self. For Wenzel this is part of a programme for living: 'Ich leb bedroht, als ging die Welt entzwei | Ich leb! und das behalt ich bei'.[64] Indeed, he goes so far as to create the term 'Dualektik' in order to designate a state in which the independent integrity of opposites is safeguarded against the pressure of premature synthesis. Instead, he condemns the all-too comfortable misapprehensions of the socialist dialectic. 'Oft stellen wir Widersprüche vor, als ob es nur darum ginge, den schlechteren Teil von beiden herauszufinden und abzuschaffen. Das ist bequem und undialektisch. Die Suche nach dem versöhnenden Dritten ist falsche Harmoniesucht.'[65] For Wenzel, this determination to maintain the contradiction leads him to Romantic models such as Heine: 'im Herzen des Poeten, durch das bekanntlich ein Riß gehen soll', but particularly to Hölderlin.[66] I discuss the reception of Hölderlin amongst the young writers in more detail in Chapter 4. Here it is simply worth mentioning the significance of Wenzel's reception of Hölderlin's centaur poem, 'Chiron'. In an interview of 1984, discussing the significance of the writer for his thinking, Wenzel highlighted the contradiction inherent in Hölderlin's commitment to his concrete, lived reality on the one hand, and his revolutionary aspirations on the other.

Er hat bis ins Extrem ausgehalten, bis zur Krankheit, diese Schizophrenie, diesen Dualismus, der keine Dialektik werden will, wie in seinem Gedicht 'Chiron', halb-Mensch, halb-Tier. Ich lebe—unter grundlegend veränderten gesellschaftlichen Umständen, die andere Ausgänge ermöglichen aber nicht automatisch bereithalten—ebenfalls in solcher Spannung.[67] Wenzel's seven-part essay 'Chiron oder die Zweigestaltigkeit' can be seen as a response to Hölderlin's poem, but also as a vindication of his own existence. In Chiron Wenzel introduces a new mythological figure to the canon of GDR literature. This Chiron calls on the restless energy associated with the centaurs in Hölderlin's Pindar fragment 'Das Belebende', and asserts his 'zerrissene Doppelexistenz' as a positive expression of subjective integrity.[68] In a note on the dust-jacket to Wenzel's collection, Mensching mocks the attitude which would understand Chiron's fate as exclusively negative. Instead he clearly underscores the restless energy created by such an inner dichotomy: 'Armer Chiron, daß du die Extreme in dich hereinholen willst. Du weißt, wohin das führen kann, daß du es nach wie vor nicht *bequem* haben willst.' Mensching's identification of the 'unbequeme Dichter' indicates his own stance as much as it does that of Wenzel. This becomes clear in his own 'Anweisung an mein Mischpult': 'Hohe Höhen, Tiefe Tiefen. Dazwischen | Kenn ich wenig'.[69]

Wenzel is by no means alone in identifying the divided or schizophrenic self as a form of existence. The lyric subject in a large number of poems speaks out of a precarious existential position: 'ein Leben auf der Kippe' (Struzyk), caught 'auf halbem Weg' (Böhme) or trapped 'in unserer höllischen mitte', 'unserer scheinheilen mitte' (Schmidt).[70] Wenzel, however, is almost the only author who embraces that dilemma as something productive. More often it threatens to tear the lyric subject apart. Böhme's 'Auf halbem Weg', for example, begins with an almost casual aside: 'Er war jung und glaubte das auch noch' 'ne weile durch- | zuhalten'. One starts to read the text as an ironic lament for the half of life: disappearing youth and approaching middle age.

> ... seine rock'n'roll
> stars wurden nach & nach vierzig, lennon gekillt, andre
> bekamen in ihren neoantiken villen herzattacken ertranken
> erstickten

If the preoccupation with death appears to unsettle the studied nonchalance of this piece, the final section of the poem reveals a more sinister confrontation with another part of the self altogether.

Er kannte den anderen nicht aber er erkannte ihn auf
der vorderseite des spiegels
Er fürchtete sich als ob der andre ihn einholen könne
Er war unterwegs mit der sanduhr am gürtel
Er schaute sich um auf halbem weg & es war dunkel
Er schaute vorwärts auf halbem weg & sah nebel
Er schlug sein spiegelbild nieder blutete & kroch
weiter auf allen vieren

The sense of a schizophrenic existence has perhaps a particular
resonance in a state like the GDR. ͵Czesław Miłosz, in his
fascinating study of 'the captive mind', describes the schizophrenic
simulation of an outward self as the fundamental strategy for
survival in a dictatorship.[71] It is also notable in Antonia
Grunenberg's survey of the attitudes of young people in the GDR
that the identification of a 'Doppelbewußtsein', 'Acht-Stunden-
Ideologie', 'Persönlichkeitsspaltung', or even 'DDR-spezifische
Schizophrenie' is very common.[72] However, in Böhme's text the
most interesting facet of the divided self (also explicitly identified as
a writing self) is the way the other part of the subject has taken on
an independent existence: 'der andere'.

Where Wenzel identifies with Romantic models and their
existential 'Zerrissenheit', it is the 'Modernist' impetus of Rimbaud,
and particularly his celebrated 'Je est un autre', which ghosts
through far more of the texts.[73] The French poet had fascinated
Braun as a political comrade and as a model in the breaking of
boundaries.[74] The young poet Thomas Günther understood him as
as 'Freischärler', a rebel, who set his life on the line for art: 'Du
balancierst auf der Schneide des Messers bis zur Spitze—oder bis
zum Absturz. Der Boden, auf den du fällst, ist gefroren.' Sascha
Anderson dedicated a series of sketches and snatches of poetry in
French and German to Rimbaud, in a synaesthetic alchemy of
colour and sense impressions.[75] From these examples, it is clear
that the young writers' reception of Rimbaud is much closer to his
reception by the Dadaists than to that of Volker Braun, in that they,
like Hugo Ball for example, are attracted by 'Die Wüste, das
Nichts, die Selbstzerstörung seiner Persönlichkeit'.[76]

For, if the I is another, the notion of Romantic dualism is
replaced by a more fundamental displacement. Rimbaud's is not
just another version of the concept of the double, a familiar enough
Romantic topos; it is rather the creation of a verbal realm where the

identity of the I has dissolved into the world of objects, which nevertheless bear the imprint of its presence.[77] If, for Rimbaud, this offered a (generally) positive liberation from the contours of the self, for the young writers the result is far more ambivalent. This is typified in a text by Cornelia Jentsch entitled 'legespiegel', which begins programmatically: 'in den spiegel blicken: eine art, in die fremde zu gehen'.[78] Gabriele Stötzer-Kachold's second collection explores both the emacipatory potential and the notion of the displced self as is indicated by the title: *grenzen los fremd gehen*. However, whereas this exploration might appear to promise multiple possibilities for the lyric self, more often, especially for the women writers, it is rather the alienation of the self which is emphasized. This problem is already inscribed in the second meaning of 'fremd gehen' in Stötzer's title. She, and the other women writers, are forced to confront specifically sexual forms of identity, which have also been imposed from outside.[79]

An extraordinary number of poems in Barbara Köhler's *Deutsches Roulette*, including a series specifically entitled 'Elektra. Spiegelungen', take up images of the lyric subject, in masks, mirrors, photographs, or reflected in water.[80] In the exploration of this hall of mirrors,[81] the power of the reflective surface to double up meanings and release truant possibilities of the self becomes clear. The subject confronts itself in reflections of the mirror, but also from literature and myth: an ageing dipsomaniac Ophelia (p. 29), or a theatrical Electra who knows that, despite her bloody act of self-assertion, she will be edged out of history and silenced by her brother Orestes and his 'new gods', and so takes off her mask ('Vorspiel auf dem Theater', pp. 24–5). Both of these texts clearly owe something to a reading of Heiner Müller, and his explorations of identity and history in *Hamletmaschine*, in particular, but they can also be read with the Lacanian theories of individuation in the mirror-phase in mind: 'ich sitze im spiegel bin ich ein reflex | es ist nichts hinterm bild es ist | ein spiegel' (p. 26).

These possibilities of the self are, however, very vulnerable; if they are generated within complex matrixes of language, reflections, and desire, they are often accompanied by a longing for protective invisibility, loss of language, and androgyny. In some places the 'Spiegelbild' even becomes an undermining or tyrannizing force within the self, 'die Spiegelfrau verrät dich | an den Tod hinter deinem Rücken' (p. 15); and any attempt to destroy it, the destruction of the self: 'hast du die scherben | deines blicks gesehen' (p. 26). The collection offers little chance of escape. In a text which begins 'Das Ende ist | dem Anfang am nächsten' (p. 13), the lyric subject is trapped at the very centre of the text in the reflection of a mirror. The line where it appears, 'sitzt ich und schreibt', forms the central axis of the poem, about which nine lines are repeated exactly, but in reverse, just like a mirror reflection. The displacement of the self, which extends even into the grammar ('sitzt ich'), is explored again in 'Selbstportrait' (p. 17).

> ICH STELLE MICH VOR vollendete tatsachen (die mauer im
> rücken halbdunkel im kopf die hand zwischen den
> schenkeln nach welt schreien): undurchsichtig was ich
> gelegentlich durchschaue als tarnung einer gewissen ab-
> neigung TRANSPARENT zu sein um nicht zu verschwinden
> tauche ich unter agent provocateur in der dritten person
> ICH IST DAS SPIEGELBILD MEINES SPIEGELBILDS: ER SIE ES
> die unvollendete gegenwart als zeitform jeglicher revolte
> gegen das gesagtsein nach den gesetzen deutscher gram-
> matik gefoltert vom schweigen rede ich um mein leben
> bringe mich wort für wort um kopf und kragen müßten
> mal wieder gewaschen werden—DAS SIEHT MIR ÄHN-
> LICH

Here it is interesting to see how the lyric subject finds a militant alternative to the restrictions of the present ('mauer', 'das gesagtsein nach den gesetzen deutscher gram- | matik', 'schweigen'), in the possibilities of the reflected self. That 'agent provocateur' is a strategy for survival ('tarnung', 'rede ich um mein leben'), but also a challenge to those restrictions of language which threaten to inscribe and fix the subject. The subject slips instead into the underground of the displaced third person, and a continuous (and presumably infinite) present tense of reflections ('die unvollendete gegenwart als zeitform jeglicher revolte'). This is a guerrilla assault on the fixities of language which threaten to enclose the subject.

Köhler is not the only one to recognize such possibilities, even if in her texts they are often held in check. Sascha Anderson's use of the motif of the schizophrenic self is very striking. In an interview he explains how he uses the divided self as a means of engaging with experience:

man hat es gelernt, mit der schizophrenie produktiv umzugehen. Ich bin nicht schizophren, sondern ich bin der, der schizophrenie als mittel zur verfügung hat d. h., ich brauche nicht die zwei welten, in denen ich existiere und mich ausdrücke, und ich kann eine sterben lassen, welchen sinn das hat interessiert dabei erstmal weniger als die möglichkeit. ich verfüge über die mittel der schizophrenie, ohne selbst betroffen zu sein.[82]

A large number of his poems appear to play with these possibilities.[83] Recent revelations about Anderson's activities as an 'Inoffizielle Mitarbeiter' have led critics to concentrate on his use of the motif, as if it were exceptional amongst the young writers (cf. below, Chapter 7). Quite apart from the fact that many writers from Eastern Bloc countries have commented on the challenge which life in a dictatorship presents to any form of integral identity, such an awareness of 'Zerrissenheit', whether as productive possibility (or, more often, as lack) has been almost a constant in the literary imagination from Romanticism onwards.[84] The creation of a textual 'ich', at odds with the writing subject and even divided in itself, is recommended by a number of the young writers as a vehicle for dealing with experience. In an interview published in 1988 Uwe Kolbe takes up Rimbaud to insist, once again, on the fundamental *difference* of the textual 'ich', as a positive writing strategy: 'Das Ich ist ein Vehikel, überhaupt mit dem Sprechen beginnen zu können: es spricht eben [. . .] in jedem Text ist es ein anderes; jeder Text erfordert sein eigenes Ich, stellt es sich her (der Verfasser stellt es her, dann ist es textimmanent und selbständig).'[85]

The Pathological Subject

Where Kolbe or Köhler allow that textual 'ich' every opportunity, writers like Sascha Anderson, Ulrich Zieger, Raja Lubinetski, Frank Lanzendörfer, Mario Persch, or "Matthias" BAADER Holst seem more concerned with presenting the pathology of the lyric subject. In the posthumous collection *unmöglich es leben* (1992), Lanzendörfer presents the lyric subject as fundamentally fragmented and dispossessed: 'leib eigen & fremd'.[86] This phrase is taken as the title for a cycle of texts in which refractions of the subject, 'ausverstanden zerheilt', appear to be hounded by the language:

> trostlos eingewohnt &
> land vermessen ausgewandert
> von irgend nach wo aufn weg

verfahren bei leibe [. . .]
im fremden eigen
im eignen
fremd wie dort (p. 71)

Here, as in other texts, amidst a hypnotic stream of images and
macabre distillations of nursery rhymes and brutal slang, the
subject is under threat: 'das gehetzte tier'.[87] Indeed much of the
claustrophobia of the texts is produced by the way the language is
driven by the syntax itself, with encroaching repetition, and
grotesque reflections and distortions of everyday phrases.
Lanzendörfer seeks escape in the dissolution of the self:

spiegel spiegelt verkehrt meine fiktion
erfindet kreuzwege wegekreuze am
tatort (p. 58)

However, at the same time he is searching for 'eine schreibhaltung
die mich einschließt' (p. 180), a language in which to record (to
contain?), this dissolution.

A similar sense of pathological interest is demonstrated in Mario
Persch's 'Identitykit' or 'Autopsie', but perhaps finds its most
radical linguistic expression in the texts of "Matthias" BAADER
Holst. His 'Phosphor flieht' begins:

es gibt nichts was mich tötet: allein der text
als er SELBST ein ANDERER GENANNT
oder
. der versuc
h s—ICH zu nähern[88]

Here the extreme ruptures of the text come to represent the
ruptures of the self, a self often explicitly housed in the 'leichen-
schauhaus'.[89]

This attempt to approach the self in explicitly bodily terms leads
also, however, to texts of a very different tone, notably from a
number of women writers. Certainly the violence is still there. Raja
Lubinetski's 'eine haut', for example, begins 'eine haut ist mir
davongerissen', and ends with 'den tod meines leibes gar'.[90] And
whereas this is text marked by an elegaic tone, others translate the
aggression into a wounded and ruptured syntax. However, against
the threats ranged against the lyric subject, some writers focus on
the body as the site from which to assert a new sense of self.

Gabriele Kachold's *zügel los* of 1989 was fêted by a number of critics in the GDR (and in the West) as an innovative example of a 'feminine aesthetic'.[91] The collection is openly autobiographical, and is centred on the traumatic fight for identity during Kachold's time in prison as a result of her protests against the Biermann *Ausbürgerung*. Her incarceration, and the threat to her identity, awaken in her the desire to be a writer. Writing is understood as a kind of birth and offers a possibility to escape the physical confinement, to consolidate her identity, but also an explicitly feminist way to free the self from a less visible bondage: the prison of gender roles and patriarchal linguistic structures.[92] The dominant sphere of images is that of the female body: self-mutilation, sex, masturbation, pregnancy, birth, and, especially, blood. Ricarda Schmidt remarks tartly that 'blood flows twenty-three times on the first seventeen pages alone and continues to flow steadily in her later texts'.[93] The immediacy of the female body becomes the locus where a new identity and, significantly, a new language can be formulated. The writing is, as the title suggests, apparently unchecked: an energetic 'freischreiben freischwimmen freiwindeln freiwippen wüppen | wappen rängeln ringeln klingeln' (p. 105), often driven by sound association or rhythm rather than sense. This stream of consciousness is often also unbroken by aesthetic distance, as in the text 'reflexion 3, aus einem fortlaufendem text', where Kachold expresses her suspicion of simile and metaphor as a kind of linguistic adultery, an aesthetic disenfranchisement of the female voice:

damit fing es an: das ist wie . . . nichts ist wie es ist, es ist immer wie . . . erlebnisse sind nicht wie sie selbst, sie sind wie . . . eine frau ist nicht diese einmalige frau, sie ist immer wie . . . wie eine schon einmal erlebte, wie eine imaginierte, gewünschte, gesuchte . . . sie ist eine andere frau (p. 50).

This text ends with the rejection of an alien 'bild' and the assertion 'ich werde meine worte, dann meine sprache finden, wenn ich ganz im leben bin' (p. 51). The language of the texts is exactly that. A attempt to give voice to immediate experience, centred exclusively on the lyric subject, 'kein bild außer ich' (p. 28). It is not so much an exploration of identity as a statement of it in art: 'Kunst ist ein Rhythmus, in dem frau leben kann.'[94] Kachold's texts demand to be read against the background of Hélène Cixous's theories of 'écriture féminine'. In particular Kachold takes up Cixous's idea of 'writing the body': an exploration of physical 'jouissance' as the emancipation of the feminine. Nevertheless, both in their crude appropriation of feminist jargon, and their insistence on 'orgasmus', 'geilheit', and 'brunst' (pp. 41–2), Kachold's texts appear scarcely to go beyond the early feminist experiments of the 1970s, and rarely to be convincing as literature.

Probably none of the writers of the young generation pursues the lyric subject and its precarious strategies for survival with greater consequence than Sascha Anderson. From the early collections *Jeder Satellit hat einen Killersatelliten* and *totenreklame*, to the poem (play?) 'die erotik/der geier' in *waldmaschine*, which begins with the line (stage direction?) 'jeder, der spricht, stirbt', to the many interviews he has given, Anderson's preoccupations always seem to centre on the 'death of the subject'.[95] The 'formula of that death' he explores in a striking text 'wer ich bin':

> wer ich bin werden wir
> sehen auf der fotomontage mein herz
> kreuzt der graue schatten
> unserer achtundvierzig gestrigen stunden
> das gelb meiner ohnmacht
> ich kann mich erinnern eines tages
>
> ich selbst wollte die formel meines sterbens
> finden
> und nannte meine erinnerungen
> gelb
> ich erwarte nichts
> weisst du die dinge vergessen uns
> schneller als wir denken
> und ich weiß nicht wer es war[96]

Apart from the expressive use of colour, one of the most immediately noticeable aspects of this text is the apparent marginality of the lyric subject, despite the number of times 'ich' itself is actually mentioned. The key lies in the last lines, with the erosion of the subjective awareness in the 'things' around it, which then assume the active voice. In a telling passage from *totenreklame* (p. 53), Anderson elaborates: 'dann werden die dinge zeichen, und sie als das zu sehen, was sie sind, ist unmöglich. die erreichten denkmale werden spiegel, der weitere weg, schritte im labyrinth. die scherben spalten deine erscheinung und werfen deine abbilder in den sammelnden raum.' In the place of the mirror, the fragments of reflecting surface. In the place of the distance between self and reflection, the gap between signifier and signified. Despite the impact of the emotive vocabulary of 'wer ich bin', it is clear that Anderson's text is less concerned with the subject itself than the possibilities of its textual mediation.[97]

In an interesting essay on Anderson, Michael Thulin (i.e. Klaus Michael) interprets the predominance of death in Anderson's work as the result of the unique coincidence of three moments. Thulin pinpoints the historical moment: 'eine postphase allgemeinen schlachtens', a philosophical one: 'die umfassende krise des subjekts [. . .] und seine bedeutung als sozial handelndes wesen', but significantly also a linguistic one: 'der tod des subjekts und seine unmittelbaren folgen für die poetische struktur der texte, für ihre sprache und metaphorik'.[98] Looking back at 'wer ich bin', one might now emphasize the way the metaphorical intensity is in fact undermined. With the entry into the 'labyrinth' of representations and images, the fixing of meaning has become precarious and the harnessing of ideas into metaphorical structures perhaps most precarious of all. Thulin suggests that one reads the metaphors of death in the work of Anderson, as 'gravestones' to the subject and to the belief in a transparency of language (p. 7).

The Disintegrated Self

The discussion of Anderson's text leads on to a final section which in many ways can be seen as the fourth stage in a progression from the idea of an integral self, a divided self, a pathological self, to what might be broadly termed a disintegrated self. This is one of the most striking features of the young writers' work, and is quite different from anything in the earlier texts by Braun and his generation. For some critics this change of emphasis signals the shift from a modernist to a postmodernist understanding of identity: to speak with Fredric Jameson, for example: 'alienation of the subject is displaced by fragmentation of the subject'.[99] There are two slightly different facets of this new self-understanding which it would be useful to distinguish: the loss of identity in the midst of media and (following on from the Anderson poem) in the gap between language and its referents.

The first of these is the influence of the media. For those in the GDR, television, radio, and film were the most important means of transcending their political and geographical horizons.[100] More important perhaps than the possibility of a window onto the West was the power television gave to enter into a virtual world, a world beyond the control of the authorities. In the text 'fernsinn' by Stefan Döring, for example, 'du hast die wahl | du sitzt am drücker | zwischen schwarz und weiß'.[101] However, that 'fernsinn' which enters the world of the lyric subject is often presented as suspect or threatening. A number of texts by Anderson and others are infiltrated by dislocated snippets of newspapers, literature, pop music, and advertising, distilled into disturbing caricatures of reality. This is particularly the case in Anderson's 'eNDe' cycle. In 'eNDe IV' for example, the snippets of TV political news, or even literary references, are ironically broken or dissolved into TV advertising: 'östwestlicher die wahn | machs gut mit spekulatius', or 'amnestie für die angebrochene | packung kekse marke favorit'.[102] Thomas Böhme's 'dem treuen medium' mixes (and diffuses) a vocabulary of menace with the smooth-talking flow of media hype.[103]

. . . ab

gekarteten talk-quarks. schon feuern die frage
kanonen blitzen die witze aus der pistole
geschossen ohne zunge vorm mund ohne transpiration.
sensationsbluff im bilde fakten beim namen ahnungen
bei der hand: handhabe für den spraydosen-akteur
wie für den leitartikler.

Another of the most common techniques in the poetry is to present an item of distant (and often terrible) news, or even a number of them, as they penetrate the closed domestic world of the lyric self.[104] In a 1989 article, tracing the reception of key elements of Brecht's poem 'An die Nachgeborenen' in GDR poetry, Silvia Schlenstedt points out how often Brecht's 'furchtbare Nachricht' is taken up, but still not received (or even forgotten) in recent poems.[105] The same gesture is true of the real pieces of news which are reported in the texts. Very often they remain unprocessed in the body of the text, fixed in a kind of collage or montage. As early as 1972 Heinz Czechowski (referring to texts like Volker Braun's 'Elendsquartier') had formulated the term 'positive Synchronität' to describe the montage of distant simultaneous events into a poetic text. Dealing with texts by the younger writers, however,

Schlenstedt is particularly critical of those poems which fail to move towards an aesthetic resolution of the material.[106] In her reading, the use of montage simply serves to reproduce the passivity and impotence of the lyric subject in the structure of the text.[107]

Schlenstedt's most interesting suggestion, although it is one which she does not follow up, is that the 'Flut' of Brecht's poem can now be interpreted as the 'die Überflutung des Individuums mit "furchtbaren Nachrichten" aus aller Welt [...] die Bilderflut des Fernsehens' (p. 89). As early as 1978 Günter Kunert had warned that his could be the last generation of writers, in the traditional understanding of the term: 'Nach uns kommt die Sintflut des Entertainments, der Sachinformation, der politischen Schaumschlägerei'.[108] For the young writers, in the accelerated 'hyper-realities' of global communication, that process is much further advanced.

In the final strophe of Böhme's 'dem treuem medium' (see above) the communications satellites make an ominous appearance, along with antennae, 'über uns heerscharen metallener | dachreiter', 'shitting' down their stream of information like pigeons. This links very closely, of course, with Anderson's own menacing 'Killer-satelliten', which appear in his collection involved in a seemingly independent circuit of communication with themselves.[109] Precisely the revolution in satellite technology has created an ontological landscape unprecedented in human history in its degree of pluralism. Today a rush of discontinuous images from different spaces can be experienced almost simultaneously, as they are collapsed nightly into a series of two-dimensional images on our television screen. A disrupted sense of spatiality, time, and narrative triumphs over any sense of integral coherence, identity, or perspective. This poses special problems for the writer. There are a number of possibilities in response. One can either assert a collective or personal identity, in part simply as an anchor, but also as a means of resisting the material. Alternatively one can attempt to process the material and make some kind of sense out of it. A third possibility is to embrace the discontinuity, to take it into the writing, without hope of a meaningful or aesthetic resolution.

The texts from the young writers in the GDR which address this issue are very often marked by a complete abandonment of identity. In Kolbe's 'Ich war dabei',[110] for example, the lyric subject blankly

attempts to assert itself, 'Ich war dabei. | Ich hatte Zeit', until it is
sucked into the babble of frequencies:

> Ich war dabei.
> Ich starb in Babel.
> Ich trat durch den Spiegel der Television.
> Ich hör mich noch sprechen.

The central lines of this poem, 'Aber die Sprache. | Warum spreche
ich?' signal the core of the dilemma. The sheer volume of the
endless degraded communication appears to render language and
meaning redundant.[111] For Hans Brinkmann it is precisely the
function of political poetry to offer the chance of asserting an
identity against the tide of the modern media. 'In diesem Sinne sehe
ich politische Gedichte als individualle Kommunikationsmittel, als
Emanzipationshilfe für den Einzeln im Rahmen der Massen-
kommunikation.' Hans-Eckardt Wenzel, on the other hand,
suggests an active effort to register the discontinuity, but to process
the material and create structures and meanings out of the
disjunction.[112]

> Wir suchten das Verbindungsstück
> Den ganzen Nachmittag. Außengewinde,
> Innengewinde, Versatz, Dichtungen und
> Wahrheiten, Engelshaar, Anschlüsse verfetten,
> Sieben Drehungen links, Bier
> In der Hand. Andere zur gleichen Zeit
> Verzweifelten oder warfen
> Bomben, schmierten
> Marmeladenbrote, Kosmonauten
> Scherzten in der Sauna, Fruchtbarkeitskult
> Afrikanischer Stämme,
> Werkzeugmaschinenexportplanerfüllung,
> Wie immer entgleiste ein Zug, ein Staatschef
> Schoß in sich . . .

In the centre of an ironic confusion of the banal and the historic
(even the grammatical structures break down), the lyric subject,
here significantly in the plural, works to make connections, to make
meaning out of the random simultaneity.[113]

Durs Grünbein takes the opposite approach, and creates a
compelling if unsettling poetry out of the polyphonic reality. In his
Grauzone morgens,[114] for example, his descriptions of Berlin and

Dresden are permeated with images of films and television, between which the lyric subject slips almost unnoticed:

> . . . Die Luft (sonst
> unverwundbar)
> war voller Szenen aus
> Chaplinfilmen, ein
> Wirbel grauer Pigmente davor, Tag und
> Nacht grauer Regen vom Kohlkraftwerk . . .

In a text, 'Zerebralis', from a more recent collection, *Schädelbasis-lektion*, that grey is the grey of the brain itself. Grünbein sets about exposing the brain clogged with media images and snatches of dialogue:

> »Die meisten hier, siehst du, sind süchtig
> Nach einer Wirklichkeit wie
> Aus 2ter Hand . . .«, sagte er.»Keiner
> Kann lassen
> Von dieser eiskalten Reizworthölle, den
> Massen zersplitterter Bilder
> am Morgen
> Unterwegs durch die Stadt, eingesperrt
>
> In überfüllte Straßenbahnen, gepanzert
> Auf engstem Raum (Hieß das nicht
> Entropie?) [. . .]«.

Yet, as the title of his collection suggests, in this poem Grünbein is not merely concerned with presenting this garbled reality, but much more with its dissection, both surgical and linguistic. In a masterly intercutting of images the precarious 'Schaltzentrale'—at once Berlin, the GDR, the subject, the human brain, and the system of language—is exposed as an unstable density threatened by 'holocaust'.[115]

The second aspect, that of the disintegration into language, is the most widely discussed aspect of the recent writing. In the critical anthology *Tendenz Freisprache*,[116] for example, 'der Abschied vom Ich' is identified as a fundamental paradigm shift of the 1980s in both Germanies, involving the raiding of textual 'IchEnklaven' and the dissolution of the speaking subject into 'Sprachmasse' (pp. 10 and 269). In the anthology *Punktzeit*,[117] Michael Braun speaks (in strikingly similar terms) of the site of the contemporary poet as 'ein soziales Vakuum' and the lyric subject as 'endgültig entthront, dezentriert'. He concludes: 'Das lyrische Subjekt, das hier spricht, wird von der Textbewegung gleichsam mitgerissen, treibt ab zu den Rändern [. . .] Ein multiples Ich beginnt als Relaisstation sich überlagernder Stimmen zu sprechen' (pp. 165 and 167–8). Peter Geist, in his ' "ich und die folgen"—eine Innensicht', part of the 'Nachwort' to his anthology of GDR poetry, *Ein Molotow-Cocktail auf fremder Bettkante*, also signals 'eine Krisenlage' (p. 385) in self-understanding and identifies the lyrical 'ich' in the work of some young poets as:

ein vielfach gebrochenes Ich, in wechselnden Masken und irrlichternd anwesend in den Differenzen und Rissen zwischen Wort und Bild, Bezeichnendem und Bezeichnetem. Es ist dergestalt zumindest Bewegungsmoment der Sprachmaterie, das sich unscharf in der fließenden Energetik, den ätherischen Grenzverwischungen der Sprachspiele verliert. (pp. 386–7).

I have cited these descriptions at some length for two reasons. First to demonstrate the remarkable consensus among observers, but also to make it clear that the interrogation of the notion of textual identity manifested in these texts should not be confused with the much crasser proposition (inherited from structuralism) of a simple 'death of the subject' which has been, in part at least, discussed above. This essentially postmodern identity is a much more subtle and orchestrated dramatization of subjects.

The writer Rainer Schedlinski, for example, confesses 'beim gedicht [. . .] gerate ich an einen punkt, wo es egal ist, ich zu sagen oder nicht'.[118] What he calls a calculated 'aufgabe neurotischer fiktionen zugunsten der wirklichkeit' (p. 163) forces the subject into a role as marginal presence in the texts. Discussing his own writing, and that of Prenzlauer Berg as a whole, Schedlinski continues: 'hier entstehen textuale formen, die den blick von der sache auf das zeichen wenden, die nicht ermitteln sondern vermitteln. die keine wahrheiten nahelegen, sondern mit wahrheitsgefügen brechen, die den blick verstellten, die nicht die dinge besprechen, sondern mit den dingen sprechen' (p. 163). Such a poetic practice, which has its roots in Saussurian linguistics and Foucault's discourse-theoretical essays, inevitably leads to a marginalization of the lyric subject. The illusion of 'reality' is perceived instead as a matrix of simulations:[119]

dann leuchten die stätten / im rouge
der geschichte / ordnen die leiber die
bilder / sekundenasyl auf den bühnen
simulieren die menschen / den menschen
und tun / als existierten sie wirklich

The reproductions begin to take over completely: 'maschinen erwachsen und produzieren das morgen- || grauen'.[120] This can be seen in relation to Baudrillard's theories of the simulacrum: modern society as a place where there is no longer a distinction between what might once have been understood as the unproblematically real, and media-generated simulations of the 'real'.[121] The texts register the over-stimulation of the individual by the competing simultaneous images, but at the same time use the denial of any kind of fixed centre in the texts as a deliberate strategy for exposing the ambivalences of reality. The first casualty is the lyric subject. A piece from Schedlinski's 1990 collection, for example, begins:

ich kam aus diesem zungenfilm
& der weg war eine folge
sich löschender zentren
im augenblick der erinnerung
(als hätte ich zu viel zu mir gesprochen)[122]

By the end of the text the self is almost completely dissolved and withdrawn:

am ende meines lateins
stand ich schlussendlich
vor dieser monitorwand
aber auch das war nur so
eine nutzlose wahrnehmung

Elsewhere, it is the buildings and structures of the city which assume responsibility for the coherence of the texts. In another text, for example, it is the 'namenlose treppenhäuser', 'fremde fenster', or 'ämtern, wänden, grünanlagen | mit werktätigen astern bestellt' which appear solid, while impressions of the subject shift and dissolve until they simply point to where a subject might have been.

ich erfand nerven aus draht, das radio
spielt nicht mehr für mich, im spiegel
all die scherben deiner kleider[123]

There is a problem with some of Schedlinski's work, in that sometimes the theorizing intrudes too blatantly and threatens to overload the poetry. In this text, however, the tension between a struggle for identity and the forces ranged against it is maintained poetically, so that the displacement of the 'ich' is at least registered in the poem as a loss.

This kind of laying bare of structures of self is taken to its most radical linguistic form in the work of Bert Papenfuß-Gorek. His 'Kwerdeutsch' at once exposes the roots of idiom and individual words, but also generates the alternative potentials of a word through the modulation of sound: '& siehe da; sinne soweit das auge trug, trügt & träumen wird'.[124] In the text 'innehalt' a crisis of identity is signalled within a matrix of linguistic oppositions, centring on closure and disclosure, content and redundancy.[125]

> hier droh ich zu versinken
> wenn ich mich versenke
> & mich mir verschenke
> ich muß mich abwenden
> hinwegheben von mir, oder
> innewerden & aushalten
> wie meine hochwichtigkeit
> in ausschließlichkeit schwindet

Here again, however, the loss of the subject is perceived as a threat, against which a struggle is enacted in the very language. I am not suggesting, as Habermas has done, that the new value placed on the transitory, the discontinuous and unstable, in fact discloses a nostalgia for 'an undefiled, immaculate and stable present', still less a straightforward and integral sense of self.[126] However, in these texts it should be noted that the loss of self runs alongside, and enmeshed with, an (in some instances also ironic) 'ausdrückliche klage aus der inneren immigration' (Papenfuß-Gorek).[127]

Conclusion

Although this final category—that of the (non)subject—is the one almost exclusively used to address the work of the young generation in recent criticism, it is clear that the textual 'ich' of these young writers is not simply one of ludic postmodernity, deprived of history, politics, and coherence. Many of the writers,

Ulrich Zieger, Jayne-Ann Igel, Gabriele Stötzer-Kachold, or flanzendörfer, for example, create an aesthetic which is a direct and often seemingly unmediated reflection of their biographical reality. As Peter Böthig points out in an editorial essay to the posthumous collection of flanzendörfer's work, *unmöglich es leben*, the poet was himself aware of his own lack of distance. Playing on the name of Bert Papenfuß, one of the most skilled of the young writers in linguistic sleight of hand, he described himself as 'papenbarfüssig'.[128] Indeed, even in the work of Papenfuß-Gorek himself, it is striking how often the cavalier pose becomes shrill and the texts enact an urgent search for correspondences, allegiances, and meaning: political and personal. Above I have sketched in some of the recognizably different approaches to the subject amongst the young writers. What can be said with some confidence about the generation as a whole is that the sense of a collective identity, such as it existed (and to some extent still exists) amongst the Braun generation, has made way, among the young writers, for expressions of identity more partial and singular. To quote Kerstin Hensel: 'Das große WIR der Dichter ist verflossen.'[129] It would certainly be wrong to understand self-conscious theoretical experimentation as the only gesture of the young writers' work. Nevertheless, it is also striking that the lyric subject of many of these young writers— whether it is one engaged in the militant search for utopian possibilities, or one which acquieses in the radical indifference of the postmodern—is more recklessly doubted, tested, and exposed to the contradictions of contemporary reality than perhaps ever before in the GDR.

4
'Traumhafter Ausflug': The Dimensions of History

Ein leerer Kirchturm, der erinnert
Ein alter Klang die Augen an die Ohren[1]

MARXISM, as a materialist refinement of the Enlightenment belief in progress, understood history as a rationally transparent, dynamic, and linear process, which would ultimately lead to the Communist goal. As Joachim Streisand says in *Deutsche Geschichte von den Anfängen bis zur Gegenwart. Eine marxistische Einführung*, Marx demonstrates: 'Der Weg der Menschheit von der Urgesellschaft über Gesellschaften, deren Geschichte durch Klassengegensatz und Klassenkampf geprägt ist, wie Sklaverei, den Feudalismus und den Kapitalismus, zur kommunistischen Gesellschaft.'[2] Although Streisand concedes that periods of 'Stagnation' and 'Rückschritte' might accompany this process, this does not temper the sense of historical inevitability, nor the view of history as a rising progression.

Just how important the acquisition of a sense of historical identity was thought to be for the legitimation of the socialist project can be seen in the intensive discussions about historical heritage after the War. The main object was to reclaim the sense of a German national historical identity, which had been so thoroughly appropriated by National Socialism. To this end historians insisted on the GDR's status as legitimate heir to all the revolutionary, progressive and humanist traditions of German history, especially the 'Arbeiterbewegung'. In literary terms this meant winning back the German humanist-idealist tradition, which had been arrogated and debased by the Third Reich. One upshot was prescribed 'Erbepflege' in the immediate post-war years and beyond, and the other was gradual appropriation of diverse aspects of literary history—founded, of course, on Lukács's predilection for Classicism and classical realism—as legitimating precursors of socialist culture.[3]

Volker Braun's essay 'Rimbaud. Ein Psalm der Aktualität' can be interpreted as a challenge, both to the understanding of socialist historical progress and to the prescribed literary canon. For Braun the narrative of history has degenerated into almost terminal stagnation: 'Geschichte auf dem Abstellgleis. Status quo. Was uns ersticken kann: aus der bewegten Zeit in eine stehende zu fallen'. It is not simply socialism which has become a historical 'Provinz'. The essay makes this clear: 'Wir haben an mehreren Welten zu würgen'.[4] However, the formula of 'das gebremste Leben' and the complaint about a historical immobility (also taken up in a number of poems in the collection *Langsamer knirschender Morgen*) clearly have a special meaning for those in a society governed by the sense of the 'locomotive' of historical progress.[5] The injunction to break the boundaries of that stagnant history is matched by the extension of the traditional GDR literary canon in the figure of Rimbaud and Braun's open (albeit qualified) support for those strands of an anti-realist literary tradition which might be broadly described as modernism.

An increasing sense of historical pessimism can be traced in the work of Braun and a number of other older writers from the mid-1970s on:[6] Kunert (perhaps the most extreme), Erich Arendt, Czechowski, Karl Mickel, and even Sarah Kirsch. However, it is in the works of the youngest generation, born into the historical standstill, that this feeling is most acute.

The sense of historical stagnation is evident in a large number of poems (cf. also Ch. 2). Hans Brinkmann's 'Narrenschiff', for example, presents a paradoxical picture of a crew and their ship stranded with a hand's breadth of dry land between them and the water: 'und die Flut, aus der wir gestiegen, | fällt nicht mehr und steigt auch nicht.'[7] The flood, clearly here again a reference to Brecht's 'An die Nachgeborenen', becomes the symbol of time stood still. With reference to quite different models, Wilhelm Bartsch's 'Höllenfahrt' presents the 'Verdammte dieser Erde', an allusion to Marx, trapped in the rings of a Dantesque Hell.[8]

The sense of being enclosed within circular structures (cf. also Ch. 2) finds a particular development in the images of an indifferent and grinding 'wheel of history' or 'wheel of fate' which appear in the poems. In Uwe Kolbe's 'Möglicher Bruch mit der Klage',[9] a 'Laufrad', on which humans run like mice or rats, drives inexorably on, sweeping together wars and revolutions, victims and oppressors in undifferentiated and aimless circles. The powerlessness and rage in Kolbe's poem is replaced by a feeling of resignation in another text, 'Déjà Vu', by Hans Brinkmann. Here the lyric subject imagines himself on a kind of treadmill of history.[10]

> Ich werd mich noch umgucken,
> wenn ich das alles schon kenn,
> was mein Los ist, geworfen
> ins Glücksrad der Geschichte:
> die Tretmühle. Dreh ich das Ding
> mit allen Tricks auch, gewiß
> bleibt nur, der mich rausreißt
> aus der philosophischen Spirale,
> aus der Fassung: der Tod.
> So werd ich mein Glück machen
> müssen in dieser rotierenden Welt,
> keine großen Sprünge, sondern
> Kreise ziehn und störn ist alles
> oder nichts, was dieses Los gewinnt.
> Daß wir uns aufreiben, heißlaufen,
> hat vielleicht einen Sinn außerhalb
> der Mühle. Und so treten wir an,
> trotten tagtäglich gegen den Trott los,
> geflochten auf dieses Rad, wie immer
> wirs nennen: das Leben—ein Strudel.
> Ich werd mich noch umgucken.

Brinkmann combines the sense of a kind of lottery ('Glücksrad') with the treadmill of everyday work and the wheel of torture. This is not a poetically convincing text: the alliteration is a little too forced and the bringing together of colloquial and philosophical registers appears contrived. However, it does signal the powerlessness of a lyric subject submitted to historical processes which appear meaningless.[11]

One of the particular manifestations of this sense of fatalistic absurdity is the prevalence of that most unholy of figures in the GDR mythical canon: Sisyphus. Sometimes, at least, this is not entirely a figure of negation. In Brinkmann's much more successful 'Sisyphos', the work of the mythological figure becomes a metaphor for the determination and perseverance needed to bring humanity closer to a Communist society.[12] He develops the poem out of an idea which, interestingly enough, also appears in Heiner Müller's *Traktor*: Sisyphus's labours are robbed of the stigma of futility by the fact the mountain is progressively worn down.[13] Brinkmann also exploits the Brechtian topos of the 'Mühen der Ebenen' and, in a number of arresting alliterations, many-layered references, and a confident colloquial language, makes it clear that Sisyphus's 'Mühen' are also those of the individual in his contemporary society.

> So ist das mit seinen Mühen
> der schiefen Ebene. Ja,
> sie ist uns geneigt, verdammt.
> Und einziger Ausblick: am Horizont scheint
> Himmel auf Erden zu sein. Er blinzelt,
> keine Hand frei, die Kräfte fehlen,
> flucht er, springt zur Seite, rast,
> rennt hinterher, sieht die Hoffnung zu Tal fahrn.
> Erst ganz unten hat er sie wieder,
> Kraft für ein Lächeln. Hier ist der Punkt,
> wo er weiß, er kommt übern Berg,
> er walzt ihn platt, der Verrückte
> nimmt Anlauf.

The text ends with a kind of determination, against all the odds. One must surely be intended to read 'der Verrückte' as an encouragement towards a kind of utopian absurdity. A similar kind of determination is found in the first of Uwe Kolbe's Sisyphus poems. Kolbe makes reference to one of Mattheuer's Sisyphus versions: 'den übermutigen', who gives the stone a kick.[14] Behind Sisyphus runs the lyric subject—writing.

> sisyphos, bergab
> gehst auch du andrer—
> seits ich bin hier hier hier
> ich bleibe bleib bleibe
> ich schreib schreib schreibe
> im ansatz klarer dann
> stockend nun rennend
> nach stoppuhr der klamotte nach
> tiefer gehts ja nicht mehr
> als anfang

Kolbe's comments in the anthology *Berührung ist nur eine Randerscheinung*, published only a few years later in 1985, reveal a profound shift of understanding. For him now Sisyphus, after

Camus's reinterpretation of the myth, has become the representation of the ultimate absurdity of the historical process: 'Camus'
Sisyphos als einzig wirkliche Aussage über die Welt.'[15]
This kind of disillusionment with a traditional Marxist understanding of historical progress has led a number of critics to
comment on the lack of historical awareness in the texts of the
young writers in general. More radically still, Anneli Hartmann has
identified the shift in the attitude towards history as one of the key
distinctions between older writers, like Braun, Czechowski, and
Mickel, and the young generation: 'Die jüngsten Autoren scheinen
die Solidarisierung mit dem geschichtlichen Prozeß gänzlich aus-
zuschließen.'[16] Hartmann's assertion is coloured by the choice she
makes in all her otherwise very interesting articles on the young
writers, which is to limit her conclusions to a very specific group of
poets, who are in many ways unrepresentative of what a great
many young writers thought they were doing.[17] However, as I hope
to demonstrate, even amongst the writers in whom she is
particularly interested, the situation is more complex. In two early
articles Ursula Heukenkamp made a more differentiated judgement. She claimed: 'daß man, unzufrieden mit einem abstrakten
und darum leicht selbstgefällig geratenden Geschichtsverständnis,
den Weg persönlicher Aneignung sucht', and that it was above all
'die vermittelte Erfahrung' which recent poetry appeared to
question.[18] This distinction offers a useful starting-point, from
which to discuss the historical understanding of the young writers.

History and the Subject

In interviews and essays one of the repeated complaints of the
young writers is the difficulty of coming to terms with a complex
historical reality, which has been reduced to a few set formulas.
There is no unmediated access to experience; theirs is instead
'Lernstoff'.[19] The young writers must look to second-hand
accounts of the historical battles of their parents and grandparents,
but also, perhaps more significantly, of the epoch-making struggles
taking place in the rest of the contemporary world. Texts by both
Grünbein and Drawert explicitly refer to their existence as a poor
second: 'aus zweiter Hand'.[20] Compare Elisabeth Wesuls:

Meine Generation ist in eine Gesellschaft hineingeboren worden, wo die
wesentlichen Dinge festgelegt sind. Es gibt viel Arbeit, aber in der täglichen

Erfahrung ist es die kleine und manchmal kleinliche Mühsal. Demgegen-
über stand für uns jedoch eine Erziehung, die geschichtemachende
Gestaltung, die Kämpfe und Siege in Aussicht gestellt hatte. Eine Ent-
Täuschung tat not, doch nach so großen Zielen konnte man die so klein
scheinenden Aufgaben kaum anerkennen.

Bernd Rump makes a similar point: 'Die mühsam errungenen
Erfahrungen einer hundertfünfzigjährigen Arbeiterbewegung, zu
wenigen Leitsätzen zusammengedrängt nehmen sich zum Beispiel
für manchen wie Klippschulweisheiten, wie Dinge, die man eben
lernen muß, die aber weitab scheinen von dem, was täglich
bewegt.'[21] The awareness that 'der große Stoff' (Kolbe) of history is
missing in their own lives, and has been replaced by a forced diet of
learnt facts, also marks the poetry of many young writers. A text by
Kolbe entitled 'Ich bin erzogen im Namen einer Weltanschauung'
starts 'Mit verklebten Augen blieb ich ein Gläubiger'.[22] Several
other writers focus specifically on the school environment, in order
to expose how belief was simply a question of taught truths,
unfiltered through critical awareness. In the poem 'Weihnachten in
Saßnitz' by Holger Teschke, the sense of disappointment which
Wesuls mentioned also becomes clear. The lyric subject goes back
to his home town and school, 'ein Totenhaus', where the children
were shown 'den Weg in die änderbare Welt hinaus'. Now, 'die
Märchen und die Wege sind vergessen', and the world, 'die
unbekannte schöne Welt', is 'fern wie der Kommunismus'. The
poem finishes:

> Wir gehn schlafen
> Und schlafen schlecht weil wir noch so viel Hoffnung haben
> Und Kraft genug all diese Hoffnung zu begraben[23]

Kurt Drawert also takes up the learnt version of reality, 'ein
Nachrichtenverstand. Ein | Schulbuchverstand', and confronts it
with the sudden nakedness of experience:[24]

> Die Worte gehörten mir nicht,
> kalt lagen sie mir unter der Zunge als
> nichtgemachte Erfahrung

Here what is interesting is the way experience (or lack of it)
becomes divorced from the language which is meant to define it and
leaves the words as random signs, 'kalt [. . .] unter der Zunge'. The

divorce of language and experience reinforces the lack of experience, to become a kind of double dispossession. Language and experience are doubly withheld.

A song written by Steffen Mensching when he was 16, entitled 'Lied für meine Freunde', also highlights the problematic relationship between learnt formulas and experienced realities.[25] The large words of mediated public experience—'Worte wie Frieden und Krieg'—do not respond to the reality of private experience.

> Wir stehn starr
> Und singen vom Frieden,
> Wir schreiben Gedichte
> Gegen den Krieg,
> Den wir nicht kennen [. . .]
> Ich kann euch nichts sagen
> Über Nächte in Kellern,
> Aber ich behaupte zu wissen,
> Was Stille ist und Regen
> Oder ein einfach mal so gesungenes Lied.
> Wir haben Augen Ohren Hände
> Und singen vom Frieden,
> Stehn starr.

In the 'wir' (one of the few places in his work where he borrows the collective lyric subject) Mensching sets out to speak for a generation born too late to witness those wartime experiences on which the rhetoric of socialism is built. It seems, however, perverse to see in the text the search for 'neue Möglichkeiten revolutionären geschichtsprägenden Handelns [. . .] im epochalen Zusammenhang der ganzen Welt', as Mathilde Dau claims to do.[26] It is about just the opposite: the awareness of lack, enforced enclosure, and conformity, and the discrepancy between the learnt and the real. The lyric subject can only link borrowed images and borrowed experiences with large epoch-making words like 'war' and 'peace': 'Wir glauben den Berichten der Alten | Gelesenen Büchern, gesehenen Filmen'. Against those he unapologetically asserts the integrity of quotidian experience: rain, warmth, girls, softness, grass, a simple song.

> Wir liegen im Gras
> Und denken an Wärme,
> Weichheit und Mädchen.
> Wir liegen auf Mädchen

Und denken an Wärme,
Weichheit und Gras

On the surface it might appear that he is setting in opposition the authenticity of private experience and the falsity of those public commitments which are required of him. And yet with the central lines, 'Unsere Gefühle sind gewöhnlich | Oder gekünstelt', and the slightly forced repetitions in the lines above, it becomes clear that Mensching realizes that the opposition is not as straightforward as it might seem. He is also questioning the way experience is mediated and expressed in literature. Here perhaps a double meaning of the line 'wir stehn starr' comes into play. It is undoubtedly meant to express the determination of the lyric subject and his comrades, but it also perhaps conjures up the serried ranks of the FDJ. In this way the song becomes a self-conscious reflection on the function and status of the political song of the FDJ.[27]

The fact that the feeling of alienation when faced with officially mediated versions of history was so widespread does not, however, mean that the poets also rejected the historical realities. Many of them demonstrate in their poetry a desire to render to their contemporary moment the dimensions of its historical past, to write, as Eliot put it, sensing 'not only the pastness of the past but its present'. 'Freilich brauche ich dazu eine Sensibilität für historische Prozesse, wenn ich nicht das Augenblickliche, das oberflächlich Erfahrbare als alles Bestimmendes begreifen will. Oberfläche ist auch Augenblick, Geschichtslosigkeit.'[28] However, theirs is a historical awareness which is based on a subjective acquisition of that past, with no acceptance of the ready-made narratives of official progress. Wenzel confirms this in a newspaper article of 1981, when he rejects the notion that his interest in history is inspired by the official promotion of a formally approved 'Kulturerbe':

nicht aus einer Ehrfurcht oder dem Gefühl der Schuldigkeit, es bewahren zu müssen, sondern aus den Problemen der eigenen Gegenwart, aus den Fragen nach Sinn und Unsinn der eigenen Handlungen, Motive, Haltungen. [. . .] Die paar Jahre, die wir erlebt haben, und die uns unmittelbar zur Verfügung standen, waren auf einmal zu wenig, um unsere Fragen überzeugend zu behandeln.[29]

This is not an attitude peculiar to the young writers. Heinz Czechowski emphasizes the role of a personal acquisition of history in an interview of 1982, when he speaks of poetry as 'ein Sich-

Wehren gegen die durch Ideologeme überwucherte Sicht auf Geschichte'. His writing becomes for him instead the instrument for a personal poetic 'Geschichtsschreibung', which is ultimately a gesture towards 'Vermenschlichung'.[30] However, the difference perhaps lies in the fact that, for some of the older writers, their personal history encompassed large and complex historical events—the War, the fall of the Third Reich, for example—but also then ran parallel with the development of the GDR. For the younger writers the timespan of lived history is shorter, and the sense of involvement in the evolution of national political history is more fractured. For them it is important first and foremost to articulate the excluded, silent histories that have not been recorded in the official narratives or, in some cases, to reinterpret the large historical events, so that they have a meaning for the poet's individual life.

It is noticeable that the desire to open the dimensions of the contemporary moment often begins on a very small scale, with an exploration of the lived history of the individual poet. In a poem 'genesis',[31] for example, Jörg Kowalski creates a montage of apparently randomly remembered episodes and fragments which left a great impression on the speaking subject: the 'Republikflucht' of the parents of a childhood friend, a confrontation with the authorities as an apprentice because of long hair, a Dürer book received as a present with texts from 1936 stuck into the pages, reports about Auschwitz, the alcoholic despair of a friend. The very act of recording these stages of his life allows the lyric subject to see them within the course of a historical development. He is at once writing his own history and creating his own identity. At the end of the text, as a kind of drawing together of his material, the lyric subject turns to direct speech.

> laßt die ausreden freunde
> wir leben im krebsgang
> weggealtert
> eh wir wissen
>   warum? [. . .]
> schlag um schlag
> wächst die klarheit:
> uns bleibt keine wahl
> als zu leben
> unnachgiebig.

Important in this 'Ortsbestimmung' (Adloff), as with those of a number of other poets, is the attempt to bring together the fragments of a personal history with broader historical events and to use them to create a sense of identity within a social context in the here and now.[32] It is striking with what a sense of responsibility this task is invested: 'laßt die ausreden freunde'. In interview Steffen Mensching confirms this: 'Was ich schreibe muß ich verantworten können vor mir und vor der Geschichte, die ich von mir nicht abtrennen kann.'[33] Similarly, in the long autobiographical poem 'Von mir aus', Mensching's lyric subject plays through the events of his youth in an ironic montage of experience, quotation, and news items, alive with the very contradictions within the lyric subject himself: Prague 1968, Marilyn Monroe, Yuri Gagarin, the English World Cup win, the 'seltsame Spannungen' in his trousers and the 'Entspannungspolitik in Europa'. By the end, however, a path has been fought through to a vindication of the authentic self in the present and before history: 'Da ist keiner mich aus meiner Pflicht | zu entlassen'.[34] The same sense of responsibility is expressed in Hans-Eckardt Wenzel's 'Amtliches Schuldbekenntnis'. Here the revolutionary dead, impatient at the stagnation of the present, exert their pressure on the souls of the living: 'Woyzeck | hat mir die Hand gedrückt | Ans Messer'. In, as it were, a reversal of Marx's image, Wenzel turns the sun into a desk lamp, which also becomes the spotlight of an interrogation, before which the subject must answer for himself: 'Gerichtet ist die Schriebtischlampe die Sonne | Zum Verhör: Alle schieben es auf mich.'[35] This very particular sense of responsibility penetrates, uncomfortably perhaps, into the most personal spheres of life. Wenzel translates Marx's 'Die Tradition aller toten Geschlechter lastet wie ein Alp auf dem Gehirne der Lebenden' into a striking concrete image:

> Einige Hundert Jahre drehn ihren Kopf
> Wenn ich den Kopf zu dir drehe,
>
> Und Millionen Tote liegen mit mir
> Auf deinem Bauch.[36]

This text furnishes a useful contrast with the image from the early Mensching poem (see above), where a naïve indulgence in the present was the reaction to the alienation from official versions of history: 'Wir liegen auf Mädchen | Und denken an Wärme, |

Weichheit und Gras'. Both the historical dimension of the Wenzel text, won through the submerged—internalized—quotation, and the confident personal engagement, indicated in the direct lyric voice, anchor that responsibility with great poetic conviction.

History in the Landscape

It is clear that the desire to seek a historical anchorage of sorts becomes more urgent if one perceives that the present (and with it, the past) is under threat. The tempo of change over the last decades, particularly manifested in technological progress, has threatened to overwhelm and even extinguish the fragile sense of human identity. As the influential GDR critic and thinker Wilhelm Girnus wrote in 1976:

Je rasanter die menschlichen Verkehrsformen sich entwickeln, je 'veloziferischer' ihr Tempo. Je massenhafter die Menschen als aktiv Mitwirkende in die Arena des öffentlichen Verkehrs treten, desto mehr bedarf es des Rückspiegels, um sich selbst im großen Strom der Geschichte richtig zu orten, sich nicht von der Vergangenheit überrollen zu lassen.[37]

The 1980s in particular, marked by historical cycles of ever-increasing velocity, and by revolutions in communications and computer technology, have brought with them an existential insecurity which can be perhaps best compared to the mood of the Expressionist writers and artists at the beginning of the century. It is no chance that Expressionism, particularly *Menschheits-dämmerung*, and even more particularly Jakob von Hoddis's 'Weltende', have found particular resonance amongst the young writers.[38]

One of the reasons that the historical sense of so many of the young writers became so urgent during the 1980s can surely be traced to the awareness of the all too real possibility of a 'Weltende' in nuclear or ecological annihilation. A sense of what one might, with Enzensberger, call 'Die Furie des Verschwindens' impinged on much of the literature of the decade in East and West.[39] But exactly there, that most bleakly determined of poetic chroniclers of the apocalypse, Günter Kunert, saw the small chance of poetry:

Das Gedicht bloß gewahrt
was hinter den Horizonten verschwindet
etwas wie wahres Lieben und Sterben[40]

This sense of poetry, as a realm in which that which is precious but under threat can be conserved, has a strong tradition in the GDR. This is manifested particularly in a second category of poetic engagement with history, which I want to discuss. Alongside, and bound up with the attempt to position the self in history, is the exploration of the historical dimensions of the landscape.

It is important to distinguish here between a poetic project which is simply 'conservative': the fossilization of the disappearing historical landscape 'im Bernstein der Balladen' (Biermann), and something which is more active, more exploratory in tone.[41] Certainly there has been a profound shift since the poetry of the early 1970s when the 'durchgearbeitete Landschaft' (Braun's programmatic title) served to represent the subjugation and exploitation of human, economic, and natural resources in the service of industry and rationalization, the power of new economics and new technologies.[42] The poetry of the 1970s and 1980s became more critical of such exploitation, but also more concerned to enact a personal excavation of sorts. The landscapes are invested with histories—personal memories, or the legacy of the many peoples and civilizations who have passed through them. Remembrance becomes the theme and the enterprise of the poetry. The GDR has a tradition of such poetic archaeology, especially in writers like Czechowski and Mickel, but also Kito Lorenc and Wulf Kirsten. Among the young writers, four in particular undertake a poetic archaeology of their landscape: Sascha Anderson, Uta Mauersberger, Róža Domašcyna and Wilhelm Bartsch.

I cannot discuss all these poets in detail here. At this point, I should simply like to mention Anderson's *totenreklame. eine reise*, because it is such an extraordinary project. Together with Ralf Kerbach, Anderson travelled 7,000 miles though the GDR, and the drawings and poetic texts which resulted are divided into sections and dedicated to different areas (Lausitz, Mecklenberg, Kyffhäuser, Frankenhausen, etc.). However, the journey is also one through history: literary history, ancient and modern—Petrarch, Heine ('eine harzreise', pp. 73–4), Mickel, and Erb (her poem 'der alte kaspar hauser' is quoted in full, p. 24), but also historical reality, from Thomas Münzer (p. 93) to National Socialism ('die monumente der macht', pp. 79–81).[43]

Mauersberger's project seems on the surface more limited. She concentrates on the 'Niederlausitz' and its history, as a history of the Sorbs and their struggle for identity. This is, however, a powerful poetic theme, for the Heidekreis Hoyerswerda, for example, as Mauersberger points out, was the meeting-point of the borders of Prussia and Saxony, where Germans and Sorbs shared villages, and where Protestant and Catholic faiths stood side by side.[44] The sense of that history is illustrated in the titles of her ballads: 'Ballade vom Jan Bok, der sich Ioannis Bocccatius nannte 1529–1621', 'Ballade vom Lohsaer Bauernaufstand 1794', 'Ballade vom Maler Heinrich Wehle 1778–1805'.[45] It is important to note that these histories are linked to the physical objects in the landscape that still bear the traces of the peoples which have passed through them: especially the woods, particular village houses and barns. In each of the poems the immediacy of the recalled history breaks out of the safety of the past to become part of the contemporary life of the lyric subject. Unfortunately Mauersberger does not often use the scope and range of the ballad form quite well enough, and the texts seem bland or, particularly in the rhymes, trite (this applies to the songs in the collection too).

A more interesting approach comes from Róža Domašcyna. Her collection *Zaungucker*, of 1992, conjures intensely concrete impressions of landscape from the same area. But she also explores the tension between those nationalities, histories, cultures, and languages, which are invested in them.[46] The notes to the collection quote a letter from the poet to Gerhard Wolf (the editor of Janus Press, where the collection appeared), in which she explains the strange quality of her texts: 'Vielleicht ist experimentell nur das Anderssein, die Empfindung hier zu Hause zu sein und sich doch weder als Sachse noch als Preuße zu fühlen.' The sense of being unhoused or split between identities is evident in a number of texts, such as the telling title poem 'Zaungucker' (p. 9) or 'Vom geteilten, dem doppelten leben' (p. 76), for example. The effort to forge a coherent sense of self is manifested in the effort to secure a sense of history in the local customs, legends, costumes, and, especially, in the landscape.

In the poem 'Budissin 89' (p. 10), a kind of historical palimpsest is laid bare.

> Da lugt er aus der esse: Augustin Guckindieluft
> setzt zeichen an zeichen jahrhundertlang in
> den wechselnden himmel. Unbeachtet. Auf der
> VIA REGIA strömen die menschen, verströmen

sich. Lassen Augustin sitzen auf seinem selbstge-
brauten sächsichen oder böhmischen bier.

The notes explain that Augustin is 'der graue Mann auf dem Dach' of the Bautzen 'Domstift', the deacon who in the 'Bierkrieg' of 1619 held the buildings through siege. But even he is set against the ninth-century trans-European trade route which stretched from Spain almost to China and passed through Verdun, Mainz, Frankfurt, Leipzig, Bautzen, and on to Krakow and Kiev. In Bautzen Domašcyna picks up the traces of where it ran, even along the tiny rundown local streets. In this case the enormous historical panorama is bitterly juxtaposed with the contemporary abandonment of that history and identity, in the streams of people rushing West in 1989. What is interesting here, and elsewhere in the collection, is the link between these historical identities and language. Here the opposition is set up between 'muttersprache' and 'reichs- | deutsch'. Elsewhere there are quotations from Sorbian hymns and poems (particularly Brězan) in Sorbian, fragments of old Sorbian sayings or particular customs. These are disinterred shards of language, memory, and personal history, which the poetry seeks to apprehend and to read aright. And, if it is the landscapes which impress on a first reading, one notices only afterwards how the poems insist on the very linguistic finding of those landscapes. In the longest poem in the collection, significantly entitled 'die heilung' (pp. 38–50), the search for family, linguistic, and sexual history are fixed against the landscape in the opposition between 'SCHÖNE LAUSITZ VATERHAUS' (the beginning of a Sorbian hymn), and 'ZA TEBJE, WOWKA' ('Für Dich, Groß-mutter').

As these poems make clear, the archaeology of a historical landscape is also in some senses the archaeology of the human and of the social consciousness. Applying the Freudian model of consciousness to the society as a whole, it is precisely that which has been repressed from the officially sanctioned view of the past which re-emerges as a belated psychosis. One of the most interesting aspects of the historical perception of the young writers is their interest in what Arendt called 'Geschichtsschreibung von der Leidseite, der Erleidenseite her'.[47] In particular it is noticeable that the period of National Socialism figures prominently in their work. The commitment to anti-fascism had played a central role in the legitimation of the young socialist state. In practice, however, this had meant transferring the guilt for the Third Reich onto the West and blocking out any sense of historical responsibility in the East for many years. The fact that the young authors take up this subject at all might appear surprising, given their age, but also the almost inescapable public commitment to setting up literary anti-fascist monuments. Brinkmann's 'Kino' gives a useful insight into the frustration at the enforced diet of anti-fascist rhetoric and the need to rehearse the required responses: 'Wir kennen den Krieg | vom Pflichtfilmsehen'.[48] In a collection of interviews, *Jenseits der Nation*, Heiner Müller even points specifically to this exaggerated honouring of the dead as one of the major factors contributing to the stagnation of the GDR. 'Die einzige Legitimation der DDR kam aus dem Antifaschismus, aus den Toten, aus den Opfern. Das war eine Zeitlang ehrbar, aber an einem gewissen Punkt fing es an, zu Lasten der Lebenden zu gehen. Es kam zu einer Diktatur der Toten über die Lebenden—mit allen ökonomischen Konsequenzen.'[49] Yet it is precisely out from under this weight of official bombast that the young authors write: searching out, for example in the landscape, the very real, the living, traces.

Hans-Eckardt Wenzel's cycle of 'Schmuggerower Elegien' trace the history of the Schmuggerow area through the centuries. One particular text, 'Drei-Dimensionales Bild einer Dorfkirche bei S.', illustrates in startling economy the giving of historical dimensions to the present, here with reference to the war years.[50]

> Eine Glocke, die einen schönen
> Klang schlägt, in einem Krieg unhörbar
>
> Eine Glocke, die einen schönen
> Klang schlägt und geopfert wird, für Krieg
>
> Ein leerer Kirchturm, der erinnert
> Ein alter Klang die Augen an die Ohren

Here the absence of the church bell, presumably melted down for the war effort, is a powerful reminder of all the other things—and people—which were lost. The very absence of the chime is itself a kind of call to remembrance. A two-dimensional country landscape painting suddenly becomes three-dimensional through stretched perspective. The absence is invested with history.

But the young writers also look for the human traces, the links—and the guilt—in their own family past: 'Großvater hatte eine Vergangenheit zu viel | er schweigt und da ist nichts still'

(Hensel).[51] Writing like this, without any direct involvement in the past, there is a danger that the young writers (and this is the case with a number of Hensel's poems) might appear precocious or overly judgemental, unlike Wolf's celebrated explorations of the Nazi past in *Kindheitsmuster*, for example, which gain their power, precisely because of personal involvement. However, a large number of these poems are very skilful in their attempt to make connections with the history. This is exemplified in Mensching's 'Amtliches Fernsprechbuch, Reichspostbezirk Berlin, 1941', in which the lyric subject tries to phone back through the past to the victims of the Nazi terror and to his parents-to-be.

> Eine Depesche
> An meine zukünftigen Eltern:
> dringend + ihr müßt euch bewahren + um beinah
> Jeden Preis + ich komme in 17 Jahren
> Aber niemand hebt den Hörer ab. Die einzige Verbindung
> Besteht in meinem Kopf.[52]

The poetic method that Mensching uses here, the notion of a dialogue with history, brings me to the final category of historical acquisition which I would like to discuss.

Historical Figures

In his 'Über den Begriff der Geschichte', Walter Benjamin spoke of: 'Eine geheime Verabredung zwischen den gewesenen Geschlechtern und unserem'.[53] I have already pointed out the particular interest among young writers to track the correspondences in their own personal history, in aspects of social and political history, and in the signs in the landscape. However, one of the most common practices is to seek solidarity with past figures in history. A number of critics have noted the prevalence among the young poets for portrait poems of sorts. In particular the volume *Lyriker im Zwiegespräch* is dedicated to discussing the relationship between GDR poets and their poetic traditions. Critics vary in their judgement of the phenomenon, from Ingrid Hähnel's approval for the confidence with which young writers in particular feel able to take up and examine their heritage, to the more critical stance of Stefan Stein, for example, to whom this kind of reception appeared often eclectic and superficial.[54]

The figures are varied and very wide-ranging. Silvia Schlenstedt lists Robespierre and Daumier in the work of Brinkmann, Hegel and Mayakowsky in Mensching, Blanqui, Baudelaire, and Munch in Teschke's poetry, and Hölderlin, Goethe, and Max Hoelz in Wenzel. One could extend this list many times over amongst a wide range of authors.[55] Here and elsewhere three common types of portrait poem are distinguished: firstly those where the historical figure is made into a kind of case study within his or her own context. The present disappears before the past, and the 'lessons' of history are presented. The possibilities open to this approach lie in striking a balance between establishing a convincing historical portrait and signalling the particular angle of interest.[56] A second approach brings the historical figure into an undefined present, where the contradictions found in the life of the historical individual can be explored, in a way which makes their significance for the present clear. The danger with this approach is that it can lead to a form of rather crude analogy. An interesting third approach, which Peter Geist signals as something quite new in GDR poetry, is the concrete dialogue between lyric and historical subjects in a temporal reality which belongs to neither of them. Geist continues: 'nicht Denkmäler werden errichtet, vielmehr "zwischenzeitliche" Beziehungen—in der Ratsuche, im Dialog, aber auch im Wider-Spruch organisiert'.[57] I would like to pursue the idea of this extra-temporal reality as an approach to the historical portrait poem, since it avoids the pitfalls of the 'tandem' approach to the temporal planes, and engages in innovative breaking of boundaries between the historical and contemporary reality.

One of the texts which is often quoted in this context is 'Die Deutsche Reichsbahn lädt zum revolutionären Ausflug' by Kathrin Schmidt, which can be read as an enactment of her political determination, 'Es liegt an uns, Überkommenes aufzubrechen'.[58]

> mal ein stück fahrn
> mit den vorwärtsbringern
> sie sitzen sich gut gegenüber:
> jeanne d'arc und engels
> (die mary die lizzy zur seite)
> der mohr mit dem sturmschwarzen schädel
> die stürmer und dränger aus vielerlei zeit

merkwürdig ist bloß die ruh
keiner sagt keiner fragt
geschweige denn fröhlich
selbst der schaffner schaut stumm verwundert
er wartet auf revolutionen
im fahrenden zug
(wo sie doch beisammen tun sitzen)
dann endlich
auf freiem feld
die kartoffeln sind gerade gerodet
da hält unser zug
etwas beginnt sich zu regen
die bauern laden ans feuer
jetzt hat auch der lokführer zeit
der heizer schmeißt den franzosen
heiße kartoffeln ins hemd
krupskaja flüstert mit martha
die füttert sonst schweine
da drüben im dorf
die gleisbauer packen ihr brot aus
viel brot
das ist die bewegung
lenin beginnt zu singen

For her fictive 'Ausflug' out of the constraints of temporal reality the poet selects the 'vorwärtsbringer' of history as companions. The 'stürmer und dränger aus vielerlei zeit', however, sit silent and inactive. Their revolutions, their historical moments are over, or yet to come, and they seem almost superfluous, discharged of their historical responsibility. The expectations of the 'schaffner', as a travelling representative of the ordinary individual, must remain disappointed. Without a concrete historical context, the impetus towards revolutionary change has little meaning. It is only in the context of an active meeting with reality, a reality geographically unspecific but reminiscent of Russia and of 1917, and, significantly, 'auf freiem feld' that 'bewegung' and communication ('laden ans feuer', 'flüstern', 'singen') is created. It takes revolutionary energy and the arrival in the historical moment to give the revolutionary progress of history any meaning. Although this poem is often praised (although, significantly perhaps, never interpreted), it is difficult to see quite where the innovation lies.[59] It is clearly intended to be read with some degree of humour, but the metaphorical use of the locomotive, and the meeting of the revolutionary leaders, good-hearted peasants, and stokers of revolution, all over communal bread, smack rather too much of early Socialist Realism and not quite enough of irony to be taken seriously. If, for Schmidt, the truth of revolutionary impetus is won only in the return to the concrete historical moment, there is another historical 'Ausflug' which comes to slightly different conclusions. Mensching's 'Traumhafter Ausflug mit Rosa L.' is one of the most discussed individual poems by any of the young authors during the 1980s.[60]

Weg sind wir, urplötzlich, für eine Liebe
Von den Kränzen und Märschen des Winters,
Aus den lautharten Straßen der Stadt
Mitten ins polnische Weizenfeld.
Und du, meine Freundin, bist so ganz anders
Als ichs gedacht.
Du wirfst deine Schuh, die so festen,
Leicht in den stinkenden Fluß.
Ich schmeiße dein Bild hinterher und sehe dich
Barfuß im Mohn stehn.—Der ist so rot wie die Fahne—
Ruf ich, dir zu gefallen, zum Himmel,
Der liegt, wie mein Blick, grau, als du fragst:
—Habt ihr denn noch keine anderen Augen,
Kindermund, Abendrot, Erdbeern?—
Ich greif dir einen Kranz aus Ähren ins Haar,
Keinen vergeßlichen Lorbeer aufs Grab.
Und trocken die Erde, die Kleider, die Haut,
Nur die Vögel erschrecken und fliehn.
—*Mein Innerstes Ich*—sagst du—*gehört mehr meinen Meisen
als den Genossen.*—Da rutscht mir der untere Kiefer
Zur Brust.—Nun wittre mal nicht gleich Verrat.
Ich sterbe bestimmt *auf dem Posten
in einer Straßenschlacht oder im Zuchthaus.*—
Und die Hand, die dich stumm macht,
Sind meine Lippen, wir schlagen zum Boden,
Wie Korn stürzt im Wind.
Nur irgendwo bellen Sirenen und Schüsse,
Und da läufst du schon fort
Hinkend und nackt, und ich ruf einen Gruß
Und hab Angst, daß du stirbst, und hab Angst,
daß du lebst und spring auf, und mein Fuß
Verfängt sich in Marmor, Schleifen und Lilien.

In this text Mensching forces collisions of opposites—ideal and reality, past and present, town and country, political and personal, empirical and subjective truth, male and female—all within the framework of an erotic encounter between the lyric subject and the revolutionary heroine Rosa Luxemburg. As Wenzel points out in an essay on this poem, Mensching is also confronting a poetic tradition, in the form of Becher's 'Hymne auf Rosa Luxemburg', written immediately after her death, and a late poem by Bobrowski, 'Rosa Luxemburg'.[61] Whereas Becher had used a kind of mystical Christian imagery, not without erotic intensity, to signal his grief and elevate the revolutionary into an untouchable Christ-like martyr, and Bobrowski had taken up an image out of one of the prison letters of the lark as the soul of the heroine, Mensching makes of her a very real and physical woman.

The 'Kränze und Märsche des Winters' (l. 2), the red flag, and the 'Lorbeer' (l. 15) place the start of the poem very firmly in the ceremonial demonstration in January of each year in Friedrichsfelde, where Luxemburg and Liebknecht were murdered in January 1919. Attendance at these demonstrations was compulsory for the schoolchildren and students in Berlin (Mensching wrote the poem when he was 20 years old), and the text is clearly set within the context of the large gestures of official remembrance. But the poem shifts abruptly and with a kind of cinematic sweep, 'Weg sind wir, urplötzlich' (l. 1), from the winter city to a summer landscape: Polish fields of corn covered in red poppies, presumably representing the region where Luxemburg grew up. There the lyric subject jettisons his unwieldy political expectations (he throws away his image of Luxemburg), just as she reveals herself, in a kind of sensual innocence, as a human being. The dialogue between them, however, demonstrates how far the present still falls short of revolutionary aspirations of the past. Luxemburg's innermost thoughts, related by quotations from the prison letters, are revealed to the lyric subject. They look forward to a projected age of naïvety, where there will be no distinction between the personal and political (this is emphasized by the marked assonance ll. 13–16) and where the colour red can be associated as much with 'Kindermund, Abendrot, Erdbeeren'. The lyric subject's inability to comprehend this, his unworthy suspicion of betrayal, and his final violent disappointment reveal the gap between the two.[62] The Daus understand the physical embrace of the lovers as the moment when the lyric subject realizes the full weight of the Luxemburg figure's political responsibility and her grisly fate. It is for them a moment of tenderness and communion (p. 261). However, the silencing force of his actions and the violence of the verbs ('zum Boden schlagen', 'stürzt'), are at best ambiguous in that they themselves also inevitably prefigure Luxemburg's fate. It is as if the only way the present can deal with the utopian ideal is by smothering it. The sense of an idyll is also threatened by the presence of the 'stinkenden Fluß', presumably flowing into the picture from the contemporary industrial city, which the lovers appeared to have left behind (and again prefiguring her end). Similarly the tryst is interrupted by the sounds of a call to arms, which Luxemburg follows without hesitation. The ideal flees the embrace of the present, naked, limping, and vulnerable: the lyric I runs off too, not after Luxemburg, but back into the useless commemorations of his own time, as represented by the images of the demonstration— 'Marmor, Schleifen und Lilien' (l. 32), with which the poem closes; symbols both of death and of the monumental status of the revolutionary heroine.

In an illuminating analysis of the poem Hans-Eckardt Wenzel explains: 'Das Ideal darf nicht der Wirklichkeit geopfert werden, die Wirklichkeit nicht dem Ideal'.[63] Neither ideal nor reality is diminished one in favour of the other; each pole of the contradiction retains its integrity, but the utopian moment in which these opposites are able to interact in productive dialogue is unstable, transitory, and threatened. What has been won, if one interprets the poem in this way, is an insight into the reality of a historical figure, mediated particularly through the prison letters, but also the bold personal access to a public cultural and historical commitment. The lyric subject also comes back to the present with a new understanding of his own time, and of historical responsibility. However, this is only half the story. The bitterness of that final verb, 'verfängt', signals the ease with which one is caught up in rituals of historical observance which do nothing to preserve the spirit which engendered them (it is, after all, 'vergeßlicher Lorbeer'). The curious lines 30–1 would also seem to make sense if interpreted in this light. The fear that Luxemburg will die belongs to the dream world, and signals the lyric subject's dismay that she will not see even the beginnings of her ideal realized in the contemporary GDR. The fear that she might live must surely belong to the real world outside the dream scenario once again, and signal instead despair that Luxemburg might actually see how little of that ideal has been realized. The 'Sirenen und Schüsse' (l. 27), which break into the dream world, confirm this. They do not belong to Luxemburg's particular historical moment; they are reminiscent of the continuing struggles and dangers of an altogether more modern world. They are the call of history itself.[64]

If the examples discussed above represent the subjects' attempt to secure meaning for themselves out of a dialogue with historical figures of primarily political importance, there is also a particular aspect of the portrait poem which is worth emphasizing in conclusion. This takes me back to my original point about Volker Braun's simultaneous challenge to history and to literary tradition in his Rimbaud essay. For one of the most important types of portrait poem written by the young writers during the 1980s concerned figures from literary, musical, or art history. This form of poem had a long history in the GDR from Becher and Bobrowski through to Czechowski, for example. However, in a review of the anthology *Vogelbühne*, Ursula Heukenkamp noted the prevalence of these poems in particular, but was concerned that they have become simply a rather self-indulgent fashion.[65] The most frequently cited of these historical figures and the one who offers the most interesting study is Hölderlin. I should like to conclude by offering a brief introduction to the ways in which history, and in particular literary history, are given a new dimension in the reception of Hölderlin amongst some of the young writers.

'Ins Feld, ins Feld mit Hölderlin'

The history of Hölderlin reception in both Germanys, and in the GDR in particular, is a vast and complex subject.[66] In particular, the reception of Hölderlin in poetry by young writers has scarcely been addressed.[67] One of the main points to make, however, is a general one. The poems which take up the historical or literary Hölderlin were already, in their very subject, manifesting a direct or implicit criticism of the traditional GDR literary canon. This had been fixed on the Classical heritage, and the demands for a representative national literature after the war and beyond had for a long time centred on the figure of Goethe. 'Sie haben aus Goethes Werk einen Werkhof gemacht für die schwer erziehbare Nation', complained Volker Braun in 1968.[68] The 'Erbedabatte' of the 1970s signalled an extension of the canon and encouraged a renewed interest in the historical reality of the life and times of the writers, particulary those more marginalized figures associated with Romanticism.[69] These were differentiated from the disinterested political accommodation of 'die klugen Ratgeber', Goethe and Schiller.[70] In particular the GDR writers focused on:

komplizierte Lebensläufe: persönliche Tragik, Einengung durch eine als verrottet erkannte Gesellschaft, immer aber konsequente Selbstbehauptung, viele 'Gescheiterte' (Grabbe, Lenz, Hölderlin usw.), ganz allgemein: Nicht-Etablierte, deren subjektiver Produktivitäts- und Veränderungswillen sehr groß, deren gesetzte objektive Möglichkeiten aber sehr gering waren.[71]

Such Romantic models were manifestly functioning as counterpoints to the GDR writers' own contemporary experience of marginalization, frustration, and a lack of future.[72] In some strands of reception this led to use of the stations of Hölderlin's life—particularly the tower—becoming simply symbols of timeless and existential repression.

It is worth taking three poems by writers from the so-called 'middle generation' which demonstrate the range of possibilities for a slightly more productive reception—one on which the reception of the 1980s clearly draws.

Czechowski's 'Goethe und Hölderlin'[73] takes up a series of antitheses: orderly care of the fields and madness, Weimar and Tübingen, Olympus and the Styx, near and far, the known and the unknown, and uses them to analyse the role of the poet in the divided Germany. Between the antithetical possibilities of the poem runs the ineluctable 'Grenze'. This is certainly a geographical and political divide, but also, it is suggested, something intrinsic to the nature of the poet himself.

> ...
> Hölderlin aber,
> Der dem Wahnsinn verfiel,
> Möchte ich sein.
> Ich weiß, Weimar und Tübingen
> Liegen dicht beieinander.
> Aber die Grenze, Freunde, die Grenze,
> Scheidet den Styx vom Olymp.

The themes of Volker Braun's 'An Friedrich Hölderlin' have been analysed many times in different contexts.[74] Here the historical-revolutionary ideals of Hölderlin are critically reappraised by the modern-day socialist Braun. He addresses Hölderlin directly and presents him at once as 'Bodenloser', and as the builder and owner of a shaded retreat. This 'retreat' refers, of course, to Hölderlin's 'freundlich Asyl' of the poem 'Mein Eigentum' (i. 306)—the realm of poetry. Braun's use of the words 'Eigentum' and 'Asyl', and the reference to the vines and trees, suggest the Hölderlin poem very strongly. Braun claims that this asylum has been realized and *positively* 'dispossessed' in the name of the GDR, with an emphatic assertion of the language of present-day politics: 'volkseigen'. In the second strophe he echoes the images, structure, and vocabulary of Hölderlin's 'Hälfte des Lebens'. He does not merely quote them, however, but assimilates them into his own contemporary under-standing and the language of the industrial sphere. Like all Braun's metaphors of production, the word 'eisern' has both literary and figurative meanings. The iron bands are the concrete products of labour, but also recall the 'eisernen Schlaf' of Hölderlin's 'Der Wanderer' (ii. 80–3). The people must be awakened from the benighted age to the hope of the ideal future. This awakening is associated with the spirit of revolution by the reference to Hölderlin's 'Der Rhein', where the poet idealized his revolutionary friend Sinclair. But in Braun's poem the revolutionary ideals come marching into the contemporary GDR, into the workplace, to bring the people to their natural rights.

> Bis doch zu eingeborenem Brauch
> Wird, was uns guttut, und
> Brust an Brust weitet sich so, daß sie aufsprengt diese eiserne
> Scheu voreinander!

The poem represents not so much a dialogue, as critics often claim, as a translation of Hölderlin's restless idealism into a modern idiom. What begins as a reassessment of Hölderlin gradually becomes a critical self-assessment, and an assessment of the present-day GDR.[75]

Wolf Biermann's song 'Das Hölderlin-Lied'[76] takes up the 'Scheltrede' from *Hyperion* in its motto and the repeated 'In diesem Lande leben wir wie Fremdlinge im eignen Haus' of the refrain. The word 'Fremdling' is the key here. Biermann's identification with the fierce social critic of *Hyperion* runs parallel to a personal affinity with the Hölderlin of the tower.[77] The complicity of the two alienated poets is established immediately. There is no dialogue; Biermann speaks with the voice of Hyperion. This has led some to some to see the poem simply as the expression of a personal affinity, and not as a political poem. Helen Fehervary, for example, charges Biermann with opportunism and a 'desperate kind of eclecticism' in his reception.[78] However, in the implicit comparison of the two societies, from which the poets feel themselves alienated, there is a fierce political comment. To take one example, the final arrival of peace in the poem is introduced with the word 'hereinbrechen', a verb more usually associated with menace or a storm. It is the 'peace' of enforced stasis and repression, which Biermann elsewhere in the collection (and with a passing reference to Heine's weavers) calls that 'dreimal verfluchten mörderischen Frieden | [. . .] der ein Frieden ist under dem Knüppel'.[79] This kind of peace, it is implied, has betrayed the revolutionary ideal. In the final repetition of lines 21–3 one can almost hear the hammering of the nails into the windows of the socialist house (tower), which might have opened onto a vision of change. Such a conclusion is the very opposite of the idealistic certainty of Braun's poem.

I have discussed these poems at length in order to demonstrate the dual impetus of subjective identification and criticism. All three poems focus on the personal affinity between the respective poets and Hölderlin, yet they are all concerned to maintain a contemporary critical awareness. The Braun poem is often seen as exclusively political and the Biermann poem as overtly self-indulgent. It seems important to me that, in fact, all three poets are careful to maintain a subjective approach with sharp critical edges.

The same cannot be said of much of the poetry by the younger poets which deals with the Hölderlin figure. Hölderlin has by now become a fashion in the GDR, but this is not a reception which makes any real attempt to engage with the person or the poetry. It is instead a wholesale exploitation of the symbolic value of his life, reducing it to pivotal images. In one sense it is deeply subjective. However, just as it is a wholesale use of images, so it is an undifferentiated lyric subject which is articulated. The poems pay lip-service to the historical contours of Hölderlin's life and to the present, but do not really exist in either; they hover somewhere between, busy with the creation of a new myth.[80]

On the other hand, not all of the young poets are quite so cavalier in their treatments. A rather more interesting case is Jörg Kowalski's 'Hölderlin kehrt aus Bordeaux zurück'.[81]

Garonne
der schöne fluß
ertrinkt im meer
Diotima ist tot.
(gewiss die hats nimmer ernst meinen können
des gatten capital circulierte vortrefflich)
mit ihr hab auch ich mich verloren.
was hält mich?
Deutschland
(der wohnliche kerker)
wo worte nichts mehr nützen
doch fern noch die zeit
zu beginnen was lang schon erträumt.
es ist als wäre losgelassen aus dem abgrund
alle finsternis.

This poem gives its title to the second section of the collection, in which historical themes are taken up (the Peasants' Revolt, the Paris Commune, and the Cuban Revolution). All of these touch on the disparity between the brevity of human life and the large scale of human history, so that points of communication between the two threaten to become disrupted. Kowalski's Hölderlin poem begins with the loss of beauty, when the concrete and individual is dissolved in the infinite: 'Garonne | der schöne fluß | ertrinkt im meer'. The Garonne, which Hölderlin treats in the poem 'Andenken', written after his return from Bordeaux, is not presented here as a symbol of the positive poetic journey to the source, but rather as a kind of death, a loss of its own individuality.[82] After the river flows into the limitlessness of the sea, the sense of movement, beauty, and all that was living for the lyric subject are lost. The bald and echoless despair of l. 5 is meant to signal Hölderlin's grief, after his return from Bordeaux and his first sight of the sea, on finding his beloved 'Diotima' dead, but it can also quite clearly be read as a more general lament for the loss of the ideal in the present. With the loss of 'Diotima' the lyric subject loses his sense of identity and threatens to go under in the limitlessness of despair and madness. The political weight of the poem depends on a reading of ll. 8–14. The question, 'was hält mich?', which suggests a continuation in the words 'am Leben' or 'davon ab, mich zu töten', is answered in the next line in the word 'Deutschland'. But here, as in Hölderlin's *Hyperion*, the 'fatherland' is seen in negative terms. Thoughts of the contemporary GDR cannot be far from the sense of the country as a prison, where the words of the poet are meaningless or silenced. In a discussion of this poem, Rüdiger Bernhardt indicates that the despair over the loss of the poet also encompasses a kind of hope that he will in fact remain, but in the poetry. In this reading he underplays the line 'wo worte nichts mehr nützen', and manages to understand the poem as a whole, however, as a confirmation that human values and human history can be preserved in poetry.[83] In fact, the loss of identity and communicative powers of the Hölderlin of the tower are clearly meant to signal the existential repression of the writer in the contemporary GDR. Equally, where he interprets the line 'fern noch die zeit | zu beginnen was lang schön erträumt' as a sign of revolutionary determination, it can also be interpreted as the bitter awareness that the ideals of the French Revolution have still not been truly realized in the contemporary socialist state.[84]

The dominant feature of a large number of texts is the tower, often further associated with images of darkness, shadow, and death. These poems can be understood as an exploration of the beleaguered poet figure *per se*. A particular facet of a large number of such texts is their imagery of stifled cries, the disintegration of language *in extremis*, and a final silence. In many of them, however, that silence is stated but not explored. A fitting summary of the thrust of these poems is Roland Erb's 'Auch steig zurück in den Turm'.[85]

Just the contrary injunction or invitation, 'Komm ins Offene, Freund' (ii. 84), lies at the heart of the Hölderlin-reception of a number of other writers.[86]

Hölderlin

Ha an der Fahne allein soll niemand unser künftig
Volk erkennen; es muß sich alles verjüngen, es muß
von Grund aus anders sein; voll Ernsts die Lust und
heiter alle Arbeit!

(*Hyperion*)

Holz und Tuch und Bänder.
Ich trage einen Baum, eine Fahne
Durch das kochende Stadion.
Ich komme, ich komme,
Ich grabe ein Loch
In der Mitte des Feldes,
Hier wollen wir tanzen.
Der kantige Himmel eckt ab
Und wird weich.
Die Tribünen klirren im Wind.
Tor! brüllen sie Tor!
Die Erde klebt mir am Fuß,
Ich bin doch kein Tor!
Was schießen die Ränge,
Die Fahnen, brecht doch
Die Standarten der Standarten.
Tor! wehen sie Tor!
Fahnenflüchtiger, flieh ich
Meiner einzigen Fahne zu.
Ein völlig anderes Tuch,
Eine selbst verbrennende Fahne.
Wieder und wieder und wieder.
Ich lache uns eine Lache Blut
Auf den grünen Rasen.
Toren! rufe ich Toren!
Richtet den Baum auf
Und ich richte mich hin.
Druckfahnen trage ich unter der Hirnhaut,
Fiebernde Korrekturen.
Ich ertrage meine Fahne noch
Falle ich lachend
Ins stumpfe Messer der Zeit,
Ins offene, Freunde, komm.

In a discussion of this poem Sture Packalén emphasizes it as an example of 'Selbst-Verständigung', 'Aussteigen aus der Gesellschaft', and 'vergebliche Hoffnungen'.[87] On a first reading there is something to support this: the images of death, the underlying menace of reprisal for 'Fahnenflucht', the echoes of Christ, and an identification with the persecuted Hölderlin. I will confine myself here to indicating a few things which defy such a reading and may serve to shift the weight of the interpretation. Hölderlin's 'Gang aufs Land' (ii. 84) becomes a rather more secular entry into a football stadium, presumably as part of a political rally. Once inside, the poem slips between past and present and sets up an opposition between the central poet figure, identified with Hölderlin by the modulation of a quotation from 'Hälfte des Lebens' (l. 10), and the jeering masses. As Hölderlin was misunderstood and marginalized in his own time, so the lyric subject stands remote from the symbols which legitimize his place in society, and at odds with the language of the crowd: the word 'Tor' slips in meaning from 'goal' to 'fool'. In the stadium, the poem revolves around the opposition of the accepted truths of society and the acquisition of authentic, subjective truth ('Standarten der Standarten', 'meiner einzigen Fahne'). The newly won flag is identified as a 'völlig anderes Tuch', 'eine sich verbrennende Fahne', terms which echo closely the quotations from *Hyperion* used as an epigraph for this poem. Packalén suggests that this flag is a symbol of martyrdom and reminiscent of the fate of Empedokles. A different interpretation might emphasize the connection with Marx, and his contention (quoted by both Mensching and Hans-Eckardt Wenzel in different contexts) that proletarian revolutions 'kritisieren sich selbst'. Against the stagnant standards which have been established, Mensching demonstrates a subjective, critical, but also fighting possibility. The poem is in no way static or complacent, but translates this potential into a communicative impetus—'Druckfahnen', and a collective momentum for change: 'ins offene, Freunde, komm' (l. 33).[88]

A very similar impetus underscores Kathrin Schmidt's 'Ins Feld, ins Feld mit Hölderlin'.[89] In many ways this poem can be seen as a direct dialogue with Mensching's text, taking up a range of the same images: a 'Tor' (but this time as gate), the flag, the Christian imagery, the quotations from the Hölderlin poem, and the sense of a split existence. In Hans-Eckardt Wenzel's reception of the poet there is also the sense of an inescapable dichotomy between 'Revolutionserfahrung', on the one hand, and 'Ansprüche, Ideale' on the other: 'Die Diskrepanz zwischen Prosa der Wirklichkeit und großem Entwurf, zwischen Antizipation und Konstruktion', which can become a productive and animating force.[90] In a sonnet by Barbara Köhler, such divisions and discrepancies are inscribed into the very text in the form of a linguistic dialogue.[91]

Endstelle

für Fritz

DIE MAUERN STEHN. Ich stehe an der Mauer
des Abrißhauses an der Haltestelle;
erinnre Lebens-Läufe, Todes-Fälle
vergesse, wem ich trau in meiner Trauer.

SPRACHLOS UND KALT: mein Herz schlägt gegen vieles
—nicht nur die Gitterstäbe in der Brust—
und überschlägt sich für ein bißchen Lust
und schlägt sich durch zum Ende dieses Spiels.

IM WINDE KLIRREN Wörter, Hoffnungsfetzen,
Nach-Ruf für die, die ausgestiegen sind
vor mir. Warum noch schrein. Es reißt der Wind

DIE FAHNEN ab. Was soll mich noch verletzen;
Verlust liegt hinter mir, vor mir die Schlacht-
Felder im Halblicht, zwischen Tat und Nacht.

The dedication 'für Fritz', can be read in conjunction with the extraordinary 'Innerdeutscher Dialog' from *schaden*, 1985–6.[92] This is a painful and poetic exchange of letters between Köhler and the GDR writer Fritz Hendrick Melle (who left for the West in 1985). Fritz was also, however, a name given to Hölderlin. References to Hölderlin, the split of worlds and the faithlessness of love and language run through the exchange. The poem focuses too on the experience of division made manifest in the political division of the German border. However, it is also a dialogue with another document of the division of life: Hölderlin's 'Hälfte des Lebens' (ii. 117). Hölderlin's question at the mid-point of life 'wo nehm' ich wenn | Es Winter ist . . .', is answered in Köhler's bitter 'Verlust liegt hinter mir, vor mir die Schlacht- | Felder im Halblicht, zwischen Tat und Nacht'. Köhler's 'Endstelle' could be read against the dark historical visions of Heiner Müller, for example, and his 'Endspiel'.[93] Behind the ruins of Europe, and the future promises only historical annihilation. Yet it is also an exploration of Hölderlin's 'half-life' of loss—the forty years in the tower, and a very personal and concrete loss. One of the most compelling aspects of the text is the density of its language. Each strophe explores a complex of language. In the first it is, after Hölderlin, 'Mauern', which become (via a pointed rhyme 'Mauer'/'Trauer') monuments to lost histories and death. In other strophes one can trace a modulation of 'schlagen', 'schreien' and 'rufen', and images of battle. The threat to language, which is so powerfully realized in Hölderlin's 'Sprachlos und kalt', and the 'klirrenden Wörter' of Köhler's adaptation, is the central preoccupation of the text— ironically, since Köhler testifies to the disabling of language in a sovereign mastery of that most integrative of forms, the sonnet. A clue to understanding this can be found in another of the several Hölderlin poems in the collection, 'Anrede zwo: Diotima an Bellarmin',[94] which veers between a desperate and unconvincing hope—'Ein Ende ist besser als gar kein Anfang'—and an utter despair—'die wahre Liebe verreckt, | Sprich nicht weiter'. It finishes, however, with a vindication of dialogue and language, and ultimately poetry:

> Sprache Ohneland. Deutsches Roulette endet mit Rien
> ne va plus.
> Sprich weiter. Woran sich halten.
> Aneinander nunja; wenig genug sind wir. Sogar dieser
> Plural eine Hypothese. Immerhin: in meiner Hand-
> schrift erkenne ich die Züge von anderen. Selbst Briefe
> tippe ich mit der Maschine: lesbar.
> Lebbar, das auch.
> Sprich weiter

The power of this injunction emerges precisely out of a sense of identity won in a negotiation with the past ('in meiner Hand-schrift . . .'). In this the text provides an interesting counterpoint to the Kowalski poem discussed above which takes up many of the same images. In particular, here and in the other texts, it comes out of an engagement with the thought and language of Hölderlin. The sense in Köhler of that impulse towards a better future which must be 'lesbar [. . .] lebbar' recalls Hölderlin's own insistence that the revolutionary ideal must be 'translated' into reality: 'Aus Gedanken die That | Leben die Bücher bald?' (i. 256).[95] In order to find 'Platz auf Erden' (iii. 96), it must, to borrow a phrase from David Constantine, 'fight for living space in the real world'.[96]

These three texts by Kowalski, Mensching, and Köhler can be read against the background of the texts, mentioned earlier, by Biermann, Braun, and Czechowski. Tentatively at least one could interpret them as continuations of strands of reception already established in the GDR: Biermann and Kowalski—the alienation and silence of Hölderlin; Braun, and Mensching—the revolutionary dialogue; and Czechowski and Köhler (along with Wenzel)—the awareness of division.[97] In general one could point out three differences, however. The texts of the young writers are founded on a very personal, sometimes idiosyncratic, access to the life and thought of Hölderlin, even where that relationship ultimately takes on a broader and more representative function. They are as a rule more agonized than those of their forebears; it seems as if the whole field of reception has shifted further towards the 'Leidensgeschichte' (Arendt) of Hölderlin, even when underpinned by the most positive political energies (Mensching). But the texts are also more reflective in their reception. The sense of spontaneous identification has largely given way to a more self-conscious (sometimes ironic) appropriation of the language and material concerned. It is no chance that all these texts are also about the function and possibilities of poetry.

My final example, however, is something quite new amongst the approaches to Hölderlin (and to literary history) in the GDR, precisely in its insistence on the materiality of the language and in its apparent distance from that material. Papenfuß-Gorek's 'süßer odin' cannot perhaps be discussed in terms of conventional categories of Hölderlin reception at all. Indeed I would have hesitated to offer a reading of this text without the illuminating interpretation offered by Erik Grimm, to which I am indebted. Nevertheless it is an important example of the fractured relationship with history manifested by a number of the young writers in the GDR.[98]

der du hangest
im antlitz des windes
& ausspuktest
in's flüstern
abgebogenen liebesgenusses
wie du da rumhingst
inne kaschemme
voller todfeinde & vorfreude
& mitte dritte zunge
die häuser der großen stürztest
befestigte städte niederrissest
salbad & labsal mengtest
& viel volk zerstreutest

> mitte hucke voll liebe
> bezüglich des aktus jedoch
> ist ungeschminktheit weiß gott
> nicht schon ehrlichkeit
> geschweige reinen herzens
> streutest du ein
> schwerlich
> ändert sich der mensch
> doch dann
> befällt der himmel sein haupt
> & er zerstreut sich selbst

The title of the poem encompasses the archaic 'süßer odem' and the nordic god Odin, whilst at the same time suggesting the classical form of the ode. This distillation of antiquity is brought into brutal and absurdist confrontation with modernity in the dedication 'in memoriam samuel beckett'.

The text can be read as an exploration of 'liebesgenuss' (l. 5) on the one hand, and the possibilities of talking about it freely on the other. In the play on words 'salbad & labsal' (l. 12), Papenfuß-Gorek demonstrates his disapproval of the pious hypocrisy of the carefully contrived linguistic deceit. Grimm, however, suggests that further references to revolutionary aspirations, fulfilment of love, and social isolation indicate that this text can be read against the work and the life of Hölderlin. He understands the text as a parody of the classical concern to clothe sexuality in the rhetoric of the hymn. However, as he points out, it is also contrasted with the apparent openness of revolutionary progressive thought. He concludes: 'Das märtyrenhafte Bild Hölderlins als Revolutionär steht nach Papenfuß-Goreks Auffassung in scharfem Kontrast zu dessen Ausdrucksvermögen für das Sexuelle' (p. 13), and he quotes from Hölderlin's 'Heimkunft' (ii. 96–9):

> . . . Unschikliches liebet ein Gott nicht,
> Ihn zu fassen, ist fast unsere Freude zu klein.
> Schweigen müssen wir oft; es fehlen die heiligen Nahmen,
> Herzen schlagen und doch bleibet die Rede zurük?

Certainly much of Papenfuß-Gorek's poetry centres on the theme of love as a form of self-realization (but also torture), and on sexuality as a form of provocative moral and linguistic taboo-breaking. It is equally clear that Papenfuß-Gorek's work is a vast reservoir of literary and historical references from Classical German literature, modern rock music, French medieval saga, Celtic myth, and a bewildering array of individual thinkers and writers. Some of the references are traceable (the poet often provides detailed notes), but others are submerged into the text, or manipulated, in a way which makes tracing their origins very difficult. It is clear that the interest of the poet lies not so much in the historical perspective which these fragments of the past might offer, but rather in their function as material for his contemporary text.

Grimm offers a large number of ways of undertaking such a reading, from a discussion of Odin as god of poetry and romantic adventure (along with his martyr-like end in Scandinavian myth, which might tie in with Hölderlin's themes) to a list of lines which could be read as paraphrases or 'memories' of Hölderlin. The last line can thus be read against 'Menons Klagen an Diotima' (ii. 75–7), which runs: 'Ach! und nichtig und leer, wie Gefängißwände, der Himmel | Eine beugende Last über dem Haupte mir hängt!'. Papenfuß-Gorek's variation on 'od-' formulations ('odin', 'öde' and 'alleröd' come into a number of poems) can also be linked, according to Grimm, with the 'Heilige Othem', and 'Aber das Haus ist öde mir nun' of the same poem. In the motif of the arrival of the saviour and the disintegration of the city, Grimm makes connections particularly with Hölderlin's 'Stimme des Volks' (ii. 49) and the second version of his 'Versöhnender der du nimmergeglaubt' (ii. 133–5). However, although the asserted connections look convincing on the page, when one goes to the originals the link is less clear. There are certain connections which can be established, particularly in theme: the longed-for coming of grace in the form of a hero figure, the religious aura, and the link with love as a realization of harmony. Papenfuß-Gorek is also clearly cultivating a 'Hölderlin-tone': in the inversion of word order, the rhythms, and vocabulary—'hangest', 'antlitz', 'reinen herzens' (Grimm points to specific texts where they occur in relation to a Christ figure or love, but this is probably less important than the self-conscious tone for itself).

The 'insgeheime Affinität' between the young Berlin poet and the Swabian precursor (Grimm, p. 12) is reminiscent of the interest of many of the other young poets. What is fundamentally different is the understanding of literary history as 'material' to be raided, parodied, or borrowed and re-installed in the text perhaps simply as a trace of its original context. The same sense governs Papenfuß-Gorek's approach to political history, as I discuss later. While his texts are clearly not unhistorical, confined to the emphatic postmodern 'Jetzt', as some critics have claimed,[99] the access to history is fragmented and more distanced still than that of the other writers already discussed. There are two conclusions which one can draw from the texts like this, by the writers associated with Prenzlauer Berg. Firstly, that the historical figure of Hölderlin is not of central importance to them as a counterpoint for their own experience, in the way he had been for many older writers. Instead, fragments of his work are taken up, or rather remembered, but these are dislocated from their historical context. More generally, it should be noted that Romanticism, the centre of interest for the older generations, has been replaced here with Expressionism, Modernism, but also Surrealism, Concrete poetry, or even Mannerism, and the linguistic and post-structualist philosophers of the contemporary French scene.[100] If there is a constant at all, it lies in the rejection of what might be called Classicism, and classical realism. However, the young writers appear to 'sample' historical traditions, without allegiance or investment.

The second point to be made is that this approach to literary heritage is symptomatic of a shift in historical thinking more generally. This is evident amongst the older writers too, as I have already pointed out. Perhaps nowhere more so than in Braun's 'Burghammer', for example, in which quotations and self-quotations, political 'Losungen', and historical and literary references are disinterred from their historical contexts and presented in brutal juxtaposition. Phrases are torn apart, struck out on the page and dislocated, in an attack on the very notion of continuity or coherence:

> Ich stehe BETRETEN auf der Böschung VERBOTEN
> Archaische Landschaft mit Losungen
> Das Getöse in meinem Kopf[101]

But where Braun's text is at the same time also an active excavation of that 'archaeological landscape', many of the younger writers embrace discontinuity as an existential given. They understand themselves as 'born into' that ruined postmodern landscape where the overarching structures of meaning, historical progress, and identity can now only be approached through the dismantled fragments of such structures. This access to history can either be understood as the symptom of a crisis of meaning and coherence, or as a deliberate and sometimes playful strategy for deconstructing large structures of thought. Fragments of history are picked up, removed from their context, copied, paraphrased, parodied, or discarded at will.

This understanding of history marks a fundamental turning-point for the cultural and political identity of the GDR. For if the historical and political identity of the GDR was founded on the internalization of the teleology of the Marxist revolutionary progress and a tradition of rationalism rooted in the Enlightenment, such blatant gestures of despair, indifference, or deliberate subversion are surely symptons of the demise of the historical identity of the GDR. A particularly resonant text in this respect is Durs Grünbein's 'Du, allein'.[102]

> Du, allein mit der Geschichte im
> Rücken, ›Zukunft‹ ist
> schon zuviel gesagt, ein paar Wochen
> im voraus (es gibt
> keine Leere), dazwischen die
> Augenblicke von Einssein mit dir
> und den andern, die
> seltsame Komik von Emigranten-
> träumen in einer Zeit des
> ›alles erlaubt‹

The transition from the schemes of history, ('Geschichte im | Rücken', echoing Heiner Müller's *Hamletmaschine*) into a postmodern present of 'anything goes' is documented here in a personal context. The poem might also be understood, on another level, as a representation for the most extreme positions in the work of the young writers. The 'end of history' is a given, and one is exiled alone into a radically emancipated but ultimately one-dimensional present. Simultaneous exhilaration and anxiety mark such an ending. It is worth pointing out that the collection from which the Papenfuß-Gorek text is taken was written largely in the last year of the GDR and is called *tiské*, that is: 'é-k-s-i-t', or 'exist'.[103]

5
'wortschritt um schritt': Poetology, Language, and Form

'GEGEN die Selbstherrlichkeit der Macht gab es nur den Kampf im Untergrund: im Text.'[1] In the analysis of GDR literature, criticism (from East and West) has often neglected the struggles played out at that most fundamental of textual levels, the language. In literary histories, often motivated by ideological considerations, the sort of textual analysis which can lead to aesthetic evaluation has come a very poor second. And yet questions of form are ideological questions too. The young authors may well have extended or subverted traditional GDR understandings of the subject and history, but it is perhaps in their experimentation with language that they have most left their mark on the history of GDR poetry.

The dominant aesthetic in the GDR was founded on an outmoded Socialist Realism, borrowed from the Soviet Union and refined through a retrospective reworking of the controversies of the 'Realismusdebatte' of the 1930s and 1940s. Although successive cultural liberalizations brought with them a gradual broadening of aesthetic criteria, the establishment understanding of literature remained dependent on a confidence in mimesis, representation, and the referentiality of language.[2] The revolt of the young writers against accepted forms of literary expression was then, in part, a deliberate response to the heavy-handed definitions imposed by cultural politics. However, that revolt also contained a more fundamental protest against the wholesale degradation of language in the public sphere. 'Leben ist außerhalb der staatlichen Sprache', claimed Uwe Kolbe.[3] Both their theoretical work and their poetry testify to an acute awareness of the complex interrelationship between ideology, language, and power. In interview, for example, Stefan Döring warns against the manipulative power of the dominant discourse, 'Durch Sprache wird Person erzogen, hat man die Sprache gefressen, dann auch die Ordnung', and Bert Papenfuß-Gorek's experimental cycle 'krampf–kampf–tanz–saga' is a poetic exploration of the central dilemma: 'wer das wort hat, hat die macht'.[4] The dominant ideology has permeated all forms of linguistic expression, they claim, until it has become, to take up a formulation from Uwe Kolbe, 'eine Grammatik des Denkens'. This 'grammar', which Kolbe describes as the 'Sprache der Sprachregelung, die Kollektivlüge der herrschenden Sprache', dominates to such an extent that the language of the individual is in danger of becoming entirely eclipsed.[5] As Sascha Anderson complains in an early text:

> und manchmal nicht wissen wessen
> sprache wir denken
> das kleinhirn des riesen
> das grosshirn des zwerges[6]

A similar threat to linguistic identity is to be found in Kolbe, 'Mit Sätzen die ausgesprochen sich selbst | Nicht mehr kennen'.[7]

A sensitivity to the invasion by an ideologically determined language is not, of course, something exclusive to the young writers. One of the most concrete descriptions of the threat to the embattled linguistic sensitivity of the individual writer is given by Kito Lorenc. Reflecting on a change in his own poetry, 'ein Gefühl-nicht-mehr-so-schreiben-zu-können wie noch in den sechziger Jahren', he cites as causes both the pressure of the language of the mass media and 'die vorherrschenden öffentlichen "Sprachreglungen" '. It is the second of these which, according to Lorenc, has had the most insidious effect. He goes on to create a four-point catalogue of the abuses of language, ranging from 'Grandiosität', which he defines as 'Repräsentation, Feierlichkeit, Ausführlichkeit bei Amtsaufzählungen, offizielle Stilfärbung, Pleonasmen, aufgeblähte Formulierung, Dingwortkrankheit usw.', to an excessive tendency to large generalizations, enforced linearity, and the overuse of rhetorical cliché. Perhaps his final category is worth citing here in full.

4. *Übergreifende Wirkungen* (sprachliche 'Umweltbelastung', Einordnungsdruck auf andere Formen des gesellschaftlichen Bewußtseins, Infizierung, Amputation, und Selbstamputation des unmittelbar-individuellen Ausdrucks, Aushöhlung von Vorstellungsgehalten und -werten, Vordringen funktionsloser Strukturelemente, auswuchernde Verwendung des anonymen Kommuniqué-Stils, verbale 'Vergegenständlichung' des Menschen zum Prozeßbegleiter, Wortfetischismus und -entfremdung).[8]

It is against this almost total ideological infiltration of language that he and other writers in the GDR mobilize their poetry. For his own part, Lorenc notes a growing tendency to engage in a kind of linguistic ('sprachkritisch') parody of the regulated language of the State.[9] Other writers, of course, have other strategies, from the urgent exploratory cycles of Elke Erb, for example, to the scurrilous satires of Adolf Endler or the linguistic excavations of Volker Braun.

Amongst the younger writers, this poetic mobilization may also take many different forms. Some writers turn to parody, as Lorenc observes; others try to counter the linguistic obfuscations of the State with a more creative use of metaphor; others again take up parts of the public rhetoric and test them against the reality of experience. There is, however, a still more radical response too, one which goes beyond the sense of critical engagement with the dominant language inherent in all the other strategies mentioned above. It is a controversial move which has been claimed on behalf of a number of writers, particularly those associated with Prenzlauer Berg: namely, the complete withdrawal from all dialogue.

> ich habe euch nichts zu sagen
> ihr habt mir nichts zu sagen
> ihr macht was ihr wollt
> ich mache was ich will[10]

However, the linguistic initiatives of the young writers were not directed only against the ideological determination of language from above, nor even just against the linguistic impoverishments and restrictions I have adumbrated. They were defined also against the textual strategies of their literary forbears.

It is notable that, in an interview with Elke Erb, Kolbe explicitly sets himself against, not simply the 'Metasprache' of the State, but also its critical opposite, 'das Negativbild der Metasprache'.[11] To engage with the language of power, albeit critically, is, as it were, already to be infected by it, to be compromised, he claims. The linguistic forms which the older writers cultivated for their critical or subversive potential—parable, mythological and historical scenarios, or ambivalent metaphor, for example—were thus seen as, at best, forms of 'Sklavensprache', and, at worst, as a fundamental complicity in the discourses of power. The point is made quite neatly in an essay written in 1989 by Sascha Anderson.

He cites subversion as a fundamental poetological principle, but identifies the scope for it only outside the boundaries of the officially recognized language.[12]

den künstlern in den sogenannten undergrounds der 80er jahre in der ddr wurde oft aus den eigenen reihen vorgeworfen, ihre texte seien apolitisch, unverständlich, separierend und und und. dieser vorwurf resultierte aus dem mißverständnis, kunst sei waffe. waffe gegen waffe, maschinengewehr gegen bajonett. dies aber ist ebenfalls eine psychologische problematik und leitet sich her aus der sehnsucht, am ort der wirklichen auseinandersetzung zu sein. sie berührt das konventionell dialektisch-marxistische denken und dichten.

Anderson's answer, like Braun's ('der Kampf im Untergrund: im Text'), is textual; it entails, however, not a 'struggle' against the official discourse, but rather a move outside it: 'wir haben nicht ihre sprache (und damit natürlich auch nicht die sprache des inneren widerstands) gesprochen' (p. 98). The 'mündigkeit' (p. 98), which he claims that he and the other Prenzlauer Berg writers achieved, was generated outside the 'battle' of officialdom and dissent, and the textual forms in which such a battle must be enacted. From the perspective of 1993, of course, and particularly since the revelations from the *Stasi* files, such claims need to be re-evaluated. I discuss this issue in some detail in Chapter 7. First, however, the strategy should be examined in its original context.

Some critics have understood the radical retreat from official discourses on the part of some of these poets as a symptom of a fundamental 'Sprachskepsis'—akin to that most readily associated with Hoffmansthal's 'Chandos Brief', but here precipitated by the claims of modern linguistics and semiotics.[13] At one extreme it has been interpreted as a retreat from a referential understanding of language altogether. For Anneli Hartmann, for example, the poetry of the young generation is marked by 'den Verlust weltanschaulicher Gewißheiten und künstlerischer Naivität', which is then in turn manifested 'in der Absage an Mimesis, in Diskontinuität und Alogik'.[14] Elsewhere, Hartmann, and a number of other critics, go further still, and identify a fundamental 'Sinnkrise' among the young writers, of which the crisis in language is simply one acute manifestation.[15] The loss of faith in rationalism, historical progress, and utopian aspirations has created a vacuum, it is claimed, which the young writers are not willing to fill with new surrogate systems: 'Glauben ersetz ich nicht | durch weiteren Glauben'.[16] In her introduction to the anthology *Berührung ist nur eine Rander-scheinung*, Elke Erb interprets this in a positive light, claiming that the young poets will no longer allow themselves to become dependent on official panaceas. The new literature has, she claims, released itself from the discourses of Enlightenment rationalism.

> Sie läßt sich nicht mehr infantilisiern von ihren utopischen Gehalten und widersteht ihre Kompromisse [. . .]. So ist sie auch nicht verführt zu einer folgenlosen Kritik und überhaupt über konfrontativen Positionen hinaus. Dieses neue Selbstbewußtsein läßt sich nicht bestimmen und begrenzen von dem System, dessen Erbe es antritt. Seine soziale Reife ist die Konsequenz des Austritts aus dem autoritären System, der Entlassung aus der Vormundschaft eines übergeordneten Sinns.[17]

In fact, many of the texts in this anthology (and in the collections and underground magazines which have since become available), are involved in an abrasive and confrontative shredding of meaning in a manner perhaps most reminiscent of Dada. The fundamental question is whether the poetry exhausts itself in such gestures of negation—'non-sense', or whether, in decamping outside the boundaries of conventional 'sense', it actually manages to generate a kind of 'new sense'.

If the commentators noted above have interpreted the new language poetry as the symptom of a crisis, or a negation of meaning, there is another quite different interpretation which could be offered. At its most exuberant and creative, as in the work of Bert Papenfuß-Gorek, for example, the language poetry is not simply a reaction to the degradation of language in the public sphere. It moves closer to becoming an animating force, one perhaps almost capable of generating an alternative and autonomous realm of poetic language.

> Wort-Anschauung für Weltanschauung
> Wortbeachtung für Beobachtung
> Wortsinn statt Weltsinn
> Wort-Welt an die Stelle von Mord-Welt[18]

The key term here is autonomy. Since Adorno, if not before, the notion of aesthetic autonomy has become a complex philosophical issue loaded with an almost insuperable historical ballast. In the debates surrounding the young writers, before and after the *Stasi* revelations, any attempt to arrive at a clear understanding of the implications of the term has been made more complex by the lack of consensus as to what, precisely, it means. Perhaps this is inevitable, given that the many theoretical and poetological statements collected in *ariadnefabrik* or in the *liane* 'Poetikheft', for example, were the work of many different writers or editorial groups. Nevertheless, the notion of an autonomous poetic realm and an autonomous discourse generated from within it appears to lie at the root of the self-understanding of many of the individual writers, and particularly of that group which has become known as 'Prenzlauer Berg'. Literary criticism has often colluded in the lack of clarity surrounding these claims, by taking up the notion of autonomy quite unproblematically. Very often it has been crudely defined as lack of political engagement. There is no doubt that the young authors made a radical break with power by setting up their own publishing network, thus freeing themselves from the constraints of censorship, and self-censorship, which were endemic to the official publishing industry. However, the relationship between the language of their poetry, social and political reality, and the discourses of State was (even before the *Stasi* revelations) a much more complex issue.

There is a final point to be made before I discuss some of the poetry in more detail. There has been a tendency in recent criticism to use a kind of multi-purpose formula to refer to the experimentation with language which went on during a decade of GDR writing: 'Sprachkritik'. The terminology is difficult. However, this particular label is misleading in three important ways. First, it serves to conflate several very different poetic initiatives which came out of the young writers' work. It also posits from the beginning a negative stance; the poetry is defined in terms of the language which it is attempting to criticize or subvert. However, most importantly, it also defuses the very political aims and effects which some of this writing had. Where one might begin, and where the writers appear united, is in a 'Haß auf die "Sprache der Sprachreglung" '.[19] This is what is raised over and over again in the large number of poetological texts these authors produced, some of which are considered below. Their responses, however, are many and varied. It would be a mistake even to associate any one particular author exclusively with a single poetic strategy, and taken together it is even more difficult to identify patterns. Nevertheless, it is possible to distinguish a number of distinct linguistic initiatives, which might be considered broadly typical.[20]

'*Klüger als der Autor*': Metaphor[21]

In his programmatic address, 'Probleme der Lyrik', J. R. Becher warned against the cultivation of metaphor as 'ein Fluchtversuch, eine Art Vision und ein Mangel an Treue'. In an aesthetic climate governed by the notion of a loyalty to the concrete, metaphor, with its inherent ambivalence, its ungoverned connections, was long considered risky, if not subversive.[22] In a recent essay Peter Geist has traced the important shifts in the understanding of metaphor in the GDR.[23] In the early 1960s, when the then young generation of poets were under attack from the authorities, Georg Maurer had gone to their defence, praising their poetry for its 'Genauigkeit der Benennungen'.[24] In 1967, in a tribute to his former teacher, Rainer Kirsch had signalled a similar commitment to the value of concrete reality: 'nach Zeiten der Abstraktion Wirkliches als Wirkliches ins Gedicht zu bringen'. For him that reality was to stand for itself, and was not intended simply to serve as a 'Symbol für dunkel Erahnbares, noch als verschleiernde Metapher fur Banales, das damit literaturfähig gemacht werden soll'.[25] In the 1970s a similar kind of insistence on everyday things can be traced, although there it can be understood as the reaction to very different cultural circumstances. Writers sought to assert the immediacy and 'authenticity' of an individually lived reality, against the instrumentalization of the public sphere. In the discussion reprinted in her *Der Faden der Geduld*, for example, Elke Erb speaks of 'eine Art Würdigung durch das Hinstellen'.[26]

However, in the late 1970s in particular, Geist detects a shift.[27] The emphasis on the authentic experience of reality was now often perceived as a limitation on the imaginative potential of the lyric subject. In an interview of 1976 Richard Pietraß pleads for the emancipatory and animating force of metaphor:

Ich sehe in der metaphorischen Konstruktion eine Möglichkeit zur Erweiterung des Vorstellungs- und Sprachraumes und damit des Bewußtseins. Sie ist Ausdruck schöpferischer Wahrnehmung, Spurhund verborgener Wirklichkeitsbeziehungen. Nicht genug, daß Phantasie so Realität entdeckt und schaffen hilft: In Gestalt der Metapher verbindet sie diese Erweiterungsfunktion zugleich mit einer sprachlichen Verdichtung und Verschichtung. Sie ist der Wassertropfen, der Welt spiegelt; je nach Situation in verdunkelnder oder erhellender, jedoch stets in überraschender Optik.[28]

Pietraß here claims a uniquely creative function for metaphor. It is a way of both sensing and articulating the secret 'correspondences' in the world, but also of anticipating that which lies beyond the reach of a traditionally mimetic language. During the late 1970s, the understanding, expressed so vividly here by Pietraß, became widespread, as the emphasis on an imaginative extension of reality grew. Metaphor was favoured less for its mimetic than for its creative potential. Geist concludes: 'Das, was die Metapher vermag, wird als menschliches Vermögen herausgestellt: Zwischen Wirklichkeit und Wunschbarem, Ich und Welt, Einzelnem und Allgemeinem blitzartig zwingend und konnotationsreich so zu vermitteln, daß im Moment der Überraschung eine Ahnung gesteigerten/intensivern/anderen Lebens sinnlich erfahrbar wird' (p. 67).

It is precisely this force which Volker Braun attributes to Rimbaud's work in his 'Rimbaud. Ein Psalm der Aktualität'. Focusing on the Rimbaud of the *Illuminations*, and the 'Lettres du Voyant', Braun fixes on Rimbaud as a poetic seer. 'Je dis qu'il faut être *voyant*, se faire *voyant*. Le Poète se fait *voyant* par un long, immense et raisonné *dérèglement* de *tous les sens*.'[29] Braun emphasizes that Rimbaud's visionary expeditions into the unknown are the result both of his radical engagement with a sensuous reality, and also of his writing, his literary 'Entgrenzung'. Writing, for Braun, cannot simply be a confirmation of reality, it must venture into a dimension beyond: 'er kritzelte wütend über den Rand: ein schöpferischer Akt' (p. 982). Braun locates this creative potential in the very structure and texture of the writing:

Poesie sieht durch in die Schrecken/Freuden der Verwandlung. Sie ist nicht zu brauchen, wo man die *vortrefflichen Verhältnisse* nicht ändern will. Nicht die Einsamkeit des Rasierspiegels: das Brennglas der sozialen Erfahrungen. Die Metaphern werden sie nicht beschönigen oder schmücken für den jeweils 'Gegenwärtigen Parnaß', sie decken nicht zu: sie klären auf. Die decouvrierende, die sehende Metapher, die Metapher als Auge. Die Widersprüche am/im Werke. Die Struktur, die den Kampf austrägt. Nicht der Reiz der Erscheinungen: das Wortwesen, im Augenblick der Versprengung durch das *Neue*. (p. 986)

The very specific sense of writing as a metaphorical 'seeing through', and an antidote to the 'Betriebsblindheit der Ideologie' (p. 986), runs through Braun's essay. It leads him to condemn even

Trakl's poetry, which, he claims, got caught up in the superficial reality of the everyday. 'Lyrik der Ablaß des Tages; er blieb darin in "den so unendlich banalen Banalen", er sah nicht durch seine Verhältnisse durch. Und formulierte das Bleiben; es ist, so erschütternd sie immer empfunden sind, ein Bleiben bei den alten Bildern' (p. 995). Braun's understanding of the new creative poetry in the spirit of Rimbaud's work is complex. In one sense at least it is a radical reformulation of Rimbaud's poetic impetus, in that the vision won is existential, but also poetological and social. However, Braun goes further, insisting on a poetry which is simultaneously an aesthetic and a political emancipation. This second demand explains his otherwise curious reading of Trakl.

A very similar sense of an emancipatory 'Durchblick' (p. 989) and an understanding of poetry as an instrument of metaphorical insight is the basis of a number of texts by the young authors. It is noticeable how often young writers complain that the mechanics of day-to-day life in existing socialism have become petrified, largely impenetrable to those seeking change, and 'zu einem beträchtlichen Teile überhaupt nicht mehr in umittelbarer Weise durch- und überschaubar'.[30] Marxist philosophy does not offer an adequate instrument to penetrate and apprehend the social ills. The writers turn instead to poetry. Poems like those of Hans-Eckardt Wenzel, Thomas Böhme, Kurt Drawert, Uwe Kolbe, Kerstin Hensel, Kathrin Schmidt and, surprisingly perhaps, Rainer Schedlinski, different as they are, are governed by pictures of an often sensual and concrete reality. But this is not to say that they simply reproduce reality in the manner of a photograph. Theirs is 'eine Art utopischer Realismus'.[31] They seek to see through to suppressed levels of existence, and to rehabilitate what has been obscured from view.

A programmatic example is Steffen Mensching's 'Erinnerung an eine Milchglasscheibe'.[32]

> Der Januar war schneeig.
> Ich hatte eine Scheibe.
> Ich wußte, wenn ich reibe,
> Verwelkt der blinde Frost.
> Ich drückte mit der Stirne
> Und küßte lang das weiße Glas.
> Einer fragte, siehst du was.
> Durch sagt ich seh ich.

The lyric subject begins with confidence in conventional wisdom and his own actions: 'ich wußte, wenn ich reibe, | Verwelkt der blinde Frost'. However, his actions on the glass have been rendered futile by a higher instance. It is 'eine Milchglasscheibe', frosted glass, which necessarily has as its function to be impermeable to the gaze. By the end of the text the reader is faced with a dilemma. Has the concentrated subjective engagment, here with the forehead and a kiss, in fact allowed some kind of new vision, despite the apparent impossibility? Unsurprisingly, GDR critics have generally taken this line, and the text has been understood as a model of Maurer's 'arbeitende Subjectivität'.[33] However, unless the term 'Milchglasscheibe' in the title is itself being used metaphorically, no amount of human scrubbing, however determined, will change it. Another way of reading the poem would be to conclude that in becoming aware of the futility of his efforts, the lyric subject is able to 'see' his situation clearly for the first time. In either case, the final lines, 'Einer fragte, siehst du was. | Durch sagt ich seh ich', indicate that some kind of sight has been won. The lyric subject does not identify anything outside the window, however; it is the principle of 'seeing through' which is paramount, as indicated by the emphatic and disruptive inversion at the beginning of the last line. The double meaning of 'ich hatte eine Scheibe', answered in the 'durch seh ich', fixes the moment in the concrete reality of everyday speech and the subject's own personal confusions. However, the text also has a political and a poetological dimension. This sight is a combative and concrete response to the impenetrable nature of socialist reality attested to so frequently in contemporary GDR writing, and it perhaps echoes the metaphorical rhetoric of the Cold War, 'Tauwetter', 'Frost', 'Kälte', etc. However, it is also poetological. Alexander von Bormann interprets the final line as follows: 'Das "sagt ich" geht dem "seh ich" voraus. Damit wird Wörtlichkeit vor Bildlichkeit gestellt. Das Sagen betont den Anspruch, der in der lyrischen Rede gelegen ist, den Anspruch auf eine Durchsicht, die die Verhältnisse eigentlich nicht mehr erlauben.'[34] On one level there is something to support this: the metaphorical intensity of l. 4, which opened a dimension into the natural world ('verwelken'), is replaced by a concrete and unpoetic language. However, Bormann is too eager to trace a line between what he sees as a failure of poetic vision, 'die Grenzen des Sehens', and the turn to rhetorical devices, to poetic 'Wörtlichkeit' (p. 113). Here the two verbs, 'sagt ich' and 'seh ich', cannot be divided quite so neatly. It is in the saying that the sight is truly won. The fact that the memory is selected as an experience worth communicating at all indicates its programmatic nature (for the collection also). In working on (and telling) a past experience the lyric subject gains 'insight'. With work at the poem, the reader too can see through the surface of the text to its metaphorical dimensions. In short, it is a metaphorical exploration of the metaphorical power of poetry. The 'Durchsicht' and 'Bildlichkeit' proper to poetry, which Bormann judges lacking here, in fact underpin the poem and the collection as a whole. The text enacts its own poetic.[35]

A confidence in such insight by way of metaphor can be found in a number of texts. In Kerstin Hensel's 'Grenzen', for example, the lyric subject enjoins a 'du' to see beyond the boundaries placed on their lives, and to 'see to it' that this sight is not lost. The final lines, 'auch wenn der Schnee zuzieht | auch wenn ers über uns | tut, sehen wir zu, sagen wir', are strikingly reminiscent of the Mensching poem.[36] A text by Uwe Kolbe, however, 'Entschieden frühes Jahr' (1980), which again takes up a very similar range of images to those in the Mensching poem, points to a rather different poetic understanding.[37] It begins with a polite acceptance of the impermeability of the glass: 'Mild sei, behaupten die Ohren, der Milchton | des Glases'. However, faced with the impossibility of seeing through, the lyric subject expresses a bitterly ironic resignation.

> Vernünftig, sprech ich es mehrmals nach,
> streiken die wählenden Augen beständig,
> steht das Verständnis in mir
> auch blutig dagegen, das Ahnen, die Sprache.

The eyes 'strike', because there is no choice.[38] Instead the subject can rely only on the inner revolt of language. In this text, language also fails. The poem ends with the lines, 'Ich kann keine Heimat benennen. | Mein Haus ist die Zeit, da leb also zweifle ich an.' What is new here is Kolbe's scepticism at the power of any such insight, and ultimately at the power of poetry to 'see through' at all. As Kolbe puts it elsewhere in the collection: 'leben | ohne die Notdurft zum Gleichnis'.[39]

In his analysis of rhetoric in modern GDR poetry Alexander von Bormann traces a line from the loss of 'Bildlichkeit' to a new

'Buchstäblichkeit', especially amongst the young poets.[40] Although he does not do justice to the metaphorical intensity of some of the poetry, he is, I think, right to signal a shift in the poetic understanding of some of the young poets in the GDR. In the poem 'Bilder', Heiner Müller comments:

> Bilder bedeuten alles im Anfang. Sind haltbar. Geräumig.
> Aber die Träume gerinnen, werden Gestalt und Enttäuschung.
> Schon den Himmel hält kein Bild mehr.[41]

Amongst the younger poets, what has been diagnosed as a 'Krise des metaphorischen Gebrauchs von Sprache' is the result of a similar mistrust in the reliability or rather the capacity of images. It is particularly noticeable in the work of Sascha Anderson and Andreas Koziol.[42] Anderson's metaphoric constructions often turn in on themselves and withdraw from reality completely. Koziol, on the other hand, takes commonly used metaphors literally, and exposes their absurdities. In his 'realindex der drastischen poesie', for example:[43]

> ein käfig der von losen vögeln eingeschlossen
> ein könig der dem lieblingshund das wasser reicht
> ein narr dem seine rüstung passt wie angegossen
> ein stabsmatrose der die segel mit dem anker streicht

What results is 'ein letterleuchten', which illuminates the faulty connections and undermines the metaphorical 'seeing through'. In another text, from a poetological cycle in his *mehr über rauten und türme*, Koziol mocks 'den gang der metaphorischen psychose | aus meiner unentschlossenheit ein schloß zu zimmern'.[44] And another text begins with an elusive possibility of communication only to deny it:

> es liegt mir auf der zunge, das will heißen
> noch kann es zünden, eh ichs ganz vergesse
> ich weiß nicht was, ein etwas heißes eisen
> glimmt auf im fast erloschenen interesse

By the end, however, the attempts metaphorically to 'illuminate' his idea dissolve into darkness: 'der rote faden, ist er endlich abgebrannt? | wer lichtet jetzt die gräserne umnachtung?'. The poem closes as follows:

> es liegt nur an der zunge, soll das heißen
> es mündet eben dort, wo's auch entspringt?

> vielleicht läßt sich die sonne nicht begreifen
> vielleicht ist es der herzschlag der uns linkt[45]

The attempt to apprehend (and comprehend) the sun in the metaphorical structures of language breaks down. It is noticeable that where poets like Koziol and Schedlinski, for example, allow metaphorical structures to stand in their poetry, it is with a certain mistrust. This can partly be explained by the conventional function of metaphor itself. In illuminating a temporary correspondence between two quite separate objects or words, the metaphor depends on the solidity of the mediating instance, the lyric subject. As soon as that mediating vision is put in doubt, the temporary linguistic contract which has been created becomes unstable and threatens to collapse. A crisis in the understanding of metaphor amongst the young poets can be interpreted as a symptom of a much greater crisis in language itself: to quote the title of a poem by Stefan Döring, 'mit den worten sterben die bilder'.[46]

'Buchstäblichkeit': Language at its Word

This poem by Döring is programmatic for his undertaking to strip language to its basics and expose its workings on the surface of the text. In this sonnet of sorts, the three quatrains explore the speechlessness of the lyric subject, before arriving at the point (pointe) of articulation.

> spruch:
> natürlich fühle ich mich sprachlos
> selbstverständlich überrede ich mich
> es zu sagen wie ich mich fühle
> ohne zweifel drücke ich mich falsch aus
>
> anspruch:
> immerhin wer nicht hinhört versteht mich
> schliesslich ist der witz nur dahergesagt
> gefühle stecken sowieso unter einer decke
> worte zumindest haben hier nichts zu sagen
>
> einspruch:
> aber dennoch, einbildungen führen mich an
> gesichte bereden, visionen besprechen mich
> spots preisen an, vorstellungen überzeugen
> alle bilder werden wörtlich genommen

ausspruch:
zwar sind die kaum was sehn verständnisvoll
doch wems die sprache verschlägt kann zusehn

The key to the text is l. 12, 'alle bilder werden wörtlich genommen'. In taking the images ('gesichte', 'visionen', etc.) at their word, the text moves from a monologic 'spruch', through the modulations 'anspruch' and 'einspruch', to a final act of communication, or at least self-expression: 'ausspruch'. The struggle for language is apprehended in language itself. It is obvious that this is not an attempt to articulate the curve of a particular experience, but rather to create a formal linguistic construct, which itself shapes a perception of the world. The ironic aside, 'worte zumindest haben hier nichts zu sagen' (l. 8), is both true and false. Words are denied their referentiality, and yet they nevertheless generate a visible way out of the silence—a 'saying' of sorts. Döring's own last line must (inevitably) have the final word: 'doch wems die sprache verschlägt [vers-schlägt?] kann zusehn'.

A text like this begins from a completely different premise from a text like the one by Mensching analysed above. Bearing in mind the 'Milchglasscheibe' poem for a moment, a comment by the American poet Steve McCaffery will serve to pinpoint the distinction.[47] McCaffery controversially refers to the poet's task as to 'demystify the referential fallacy of language', and he adds, 'Reference, I take it, is that kind of blindness a window makes of the pane it is.'[48] Blindness can here be understood in the sense that a window-pane, being transparent, is not 'seen' at all by the viewer who looks through at the reality on the other side. McCaffery argues instead for a language in which the direct, empirical experience of a grapheme might replace what the signifier in a word will always try to discharge: its referential responsibility. In other words, McCaffery, and with him, I would argue, the young writers of Prenzlauer Berg, set about producing a text which demands to be read 'on', rather than read 'through'. It is this concentration on language which underpins the second category of poetry I should like to discuss. Once again, the tendency manifests itself in a number of distinct ways. I would like to take up four which could be broadly placed under the categories of parody, repetition, automatic writing and hermeticism.

The first of these is a kind of linguistic humour, ranging from irony, the introduction of the grotesque, parody, subversive rhymes, right through to cabaret.[49] Some critics associate the cultivation of a kind of 'Lachkultur' primarily with the older writers. They are often more adept in manipulating traditional forms with parodistic intent, but also they are the most ready to engage with the language of the State, to take it into their writing. However, in a text from 1982, Uwe Kolbe offers a rousing injunction to reclaim the subversive power of parody: 'Wir sollten uns diesen Höllenspaß erlauben [...] | Wir sollten jene Sprache wieder erlernen'.

> Ich bin nur einer der Boten.
> Kommt, laßt uns lästern die Prediger des Wassers.
> Wir lachen sie kaputt.[50]

Although Kolbe's own work is not particularly noted for a playful experimentation with language, examples can nevertheless be found in the work of a number of the young writers.[51] Jan Faktor, whom Endler dubs 'der Schalksnarr, der Schwejk' of the GDR poetic landscape, explicitly points to humour as one of his poetic methods.[52] In his 'Manifeste der Trivialpoesie', themselves amusing parodies of the manifestos of Dada and Surrealism, Faktor claims: 'Zu dieser Kunst gehört etwas, das man ungefähr mit dem Wort Humor bezeichnen könnte (...) Humor als Resultat der Selbstreflexion (...) Humor, zu dem Aggressivität gehört (...) die Aggressivität der Relation.'[53] The humour in these 'hypertrophierte Fragmente einer bastardierten Poetik, unsaubere Mysifikationen— inkonsequente Parodien' (p. 91) is generated, as in many of Faktor's more poetic texts, through exuberant repetition, an arch self-consciousness, and the juxtaposition of banality, seriousness, and sudden bitterness.[54] Faktor's texts are sometimes difficult to read on the page because of their enormous length and often fatiguing repetitions. But both Endler and Wolf point to the Faktor's own perfomance of the texts, 'nach Art mancher Zirkus Clowns', as an integral part of the experience.[55]

A quite different kind of linguistic pastische is to be found in a number of texts by Sascha Anderson. His 'eNDe' cycle parody in their title the SED Party newspaper *Neues Deutschland*.[56] In three of these texts Anderson expresses his alienation in the face of the ideological jargon of the newspaper, by mixing it with a garbled version of familiar literary quotations, especially from Goethe.[57] In a number of the other texts from the series Anderson eavesdrops on snatches of everyday chatter. The petit-bourgois tone of the conversational titbits functions as a counterpoint to the ideologically retouched reports of the Party newspaper.[58] One of the most straightforward of these texts mirrors the language of a chief from a military academy.

> ich will mal sagen
> natürlich gibt es menschen di
> e anders denken mit diesen menschen
> muss man geduldi
>
> g arbeiten mit denen muss man
> diskutiern und das wissen di
> e vielleicht auch die stärksten argumente
> sind auf unserer seite i
>
> ch zum beispiel bin chef
> der mili
> täraka
> demie
>
> friedrich
> engels der ddr[59]

The text involves a kind of mimicry. Here the shrill repeated 'i' sounds and the abrupt breaking of words across lines both suggest the automatic, clipped rhythms, as the orders are barked out, and also underline the hollowness of the claims.[60] Other writers again, like Papenfuß-Gorek or Schedlinki, no longer so much parody the language of officaldom as dislocate and subvert it to form a 'wustsein im unterwolz'.[61]

A second aspect of the linguistic poetry is a concentration on repetition, which Thulin, with reference to Jan Faktor, calls a 'Recycling-art-Verfahren'.[62] Faktor, who works as a computer programmer, programmes his texts with the precision of a mathematical, or at least grammatical, exercise (some of his texts are translated into German from his native Czech). Indeed, it is precisely the forms of grammar books or dictionaries which he takes up into his texts in order to explore the language.[63] A particularly striking example of this is his 'Georgs Sorgen um die Zukunft'. The text printed in his first collection is a shortened version, 'Ein Text zum Durchblättern', but is nevertheless almost thirty pages long (with five pages of notes). It consists almost completely of the repetition of a single grammatical structure: a comparative which takes on ever more negative dimensions.

> das Zukünftige wird immer zukünftiger
> das Sorgende immer sorgender
> und
> das Hiesige immer hiesiger
> das Dortige immer dortiger
> das Zerbrechliche immer zerbrechlicher
> das Langweilige immer langweiliger
> das Irreparable immer irreparabeler
> das Sinnlose immer sinnloser
> das Ratlose immer ratloser
> das Böse immer böser [. . .] (p. 37)

One should certainly read this in ironic counterpoint to the steady diet of official optimism in the newspapers: the notion that socialism is constantly moving closer to its goal, industry becoming more productive, standards higher, etc. One might expect Faktor's negative version of this to isolate a similar movement, simply on a downward slope, rather than ever onwards and upwards. In part this does happen. The list is interrupted every so often by short phrases, such as 'wohin wird das alles führen', 'was soll man zu alledem noch sagen', 'mein Name ist Georg und ich habe Angst vor der Zukunft', 'das Aufschreiben meiner Ängste hilft mir ein bißchen'. However, the sheer monotony of the text in fact seems to evoke a kind of absurd standstill. At the beginning the text performs according to grammatical rules, but very soon it is itself like a machine, able to swallow up all kinds of words and process them.

> der Rainer immer Rainer
> das Durcheinander immer durcheinander
> das Wieder immer wieder wieder
> die Dichter immer dichter
> das Immer immer immer (p. 42)

Every so often the text seems to come to rest, with a shift of direction, an interruption, or a change of font size. Occasionally even, the text seems to hold its own against the grinding process of decay:

> aber das Wasser bleibt immer Wasser
> die Oper immer Oper
> die Trauer immer Trauer
> der Heizer immer Heizer
> der Körper immer Körper
> der Oktober immer Oktober (p. 42)

However, then the process moves blindly and inexorably on, revealing even these pauses as false hopes:

> der Härter bleibt immer härter
> der Schlächter immer Schlächter
> und die Propaganda immer Propagander
> das Sofa immer Sofer
> die Paranoia immer Paranoier
> das Dogma immer Dogmer
> der Opa immer Oper (p. 42–3)

The text is to be understood as a kind of personal apocalypse ('Georgs Sorgen um die Zukunft'), and the ironic—and exasperating—nature of 'Georg's' interruptions are part of its humour: 'und—ich Georg—sage euch | das sind lange noch nicht alle meine Sorgen um die Zukunft'.[64] However, in the way that words are manipulated and forced into a preformulated scheme, Faktor manages to point up the degradation of language in the GDR. In these kinds of text, the experimental poetry of the GDR comes closest to the Concrete poetry of the 1950s, and is most in danger of appearing simply a gag or a rather pale imitation. Once the gesture of Faktor's recycling has been understood, apart from the occasional clever linguistic effect, there seems, on the page at least, little more to be gained. It has been suggested that the force of the text stems from the reader's knowlege of its origins,[65] but whether the text will outlast the demise of its context is another question.

It was Frank-Wolf Matthies who commented of himself and his generation, 'Hineingeboren in eine surrealistische Umwelt werden wir fast zwangsläufig Surrealisten.'[66] The traces of Surrealism, particularly its anarchic sensuality, striking imagery, and interest in the subconscious, are to be found in the work of a number of poets. However, the most interesting facet of the writing in this respect is the way that what Anderson calls 'die surrealistische bewegungsform dieser gesellschaft', is echoed in the very movement of their texts.[67] In texts by Gabriele Kachold and Johannes Jansen, for example, one could almost speak of an 'automatic writing'.

In the notes to her *zügel los* Kachold makes this point herself. Language, as an immediate and unchecked expression of repressed emotions, is understood as a personal, sexual, and political emancipation.

ich habe die wut
ich habe die wut
auf das verfluchte
auf die verfluchten
auf mich verfluchte
(damit ich die kraft habe über alle grenzen zu gehen und in ein
anderes land)[68]

Sometimes it is the very sounds and associations of the words
themselves which create their own dynamic and leave sense behind:

ich bin das wort
ich bin schau kann sun gewesen
running over mund grützenpfeffer
ich bin das wort tschak tram fuschsch issopi rassuntra esso
ich bin das wort
ich fliege gehe renne schreite hoble turne drehe winde scheide
sinne nach (p. 136)

In the case of Johannes Jansen's 'haltlose wortketten', a
disturbing mixture of linguistic association and suddenly naked
fear makes the texts even more arresting. They are at once a form of
linguistic play, splicing together the language of fairy-tales,
advertising, and ideology, for example, and also an expression of
impotence. This tension creates the interest of the texts. One is
called 'lauf masche' and asks in an epigraph, 'was soll ich
durchschauen, wenn die erfahrungen das gelernte widerlegen.' The
response is in the movement of the text:[69]

in meiner hilf losigkeit
die zeit betreffend in zeit not
mache ich tag täglich text

This urgency transmits itself into his 'gangart' poems too, which
snatch an apparently unmediated sequence of impressions from the
'fragmentbaukasten' of reality through which the speaking subject
progresses.[70]

fort sind die schritte die bilder die ein bahnhof waren von fuß zu fuß
den fortschritt einverleibt gehe ich durch einen darm als ginge ich
durch einen darm und es geht gut fuß vor fuß und es geht ein
schärfer wind in den offenen rachen des redners der auf mich zutritt
heraus aus dem schatten der pulte und bühnen der zeigefinger
wankt und fällt zwischen mich und straßenbahnschienen
endstelle bornholmer straße

und es ist ein flüstern da eine brücke
voller lichter die stadt ein sandhaufen voller augen die ich zu
kennen glaube und wieder die tür hinter mir schließe ohne den
käfig zu verlassen
              von fuß zu fuß
                   durch den
darm
     nördlich
         gehe ich
            neben der straße
                    (bornholmer straße)

Jansen explains what he calls his 'neologische sprache', which sets
fragments of language next to each other without obvious causal or
syntactical connections, as a kind of dream language: 'mit
machbaren worten wird man dem traum kaum gerecht in einem
land wo jeder eine traumlandschaft verinnerlicht hat um das land
nicht als ausrede benutzen zu müssen.' In 1987 he formulated a
poetology of the open text, 'text als prozeß':

> der text ist nicht der ausdruck einer scheinbar konkreten idee sondern die
> dokumentation des lebensabschnitts in dem er entstand. er ist es in der
> wahl der worte ihrer reihung und der daraus enstehenden struktur die in
> jeder beziehung ein bild ist das weitertreibt durch die täuschungsmanöver
> der mit ihm verbundenen erinnerung [. . .][71]

Jansen's texts make few allowances for the reader. Sometimes
one feels overcome with the velocity of the pieces and the sheer bulk
of material; sometimes the texts seem random and lack tension. In
the best texts there is something frantic about the independence and
force with which the language runs on. On occasion the cause for
this panic becomes clear. Jansen's texts are attempts 'dem wrack zu
entsteigen', in a political but also, and primarily, in a linguistic
sense. Each attempt, however, is constantly threatened by reabsorb-
tion, by death and silence.[72]

The threat of silence, which is frenetically, and often precariously,
overcome by Jansen's linguistic exuberance, is something sensed by
other writers too. For some, the ideological bombast and the
authoritarian structures of official language themselves threaten the
individual's language to the point where it may congeal entirely.
'Die Angst vorm Schweigen fordert immer wieder Ausstieg', writes
Uwe Kolbe.[73] However, that 'Ausstieg' can bring with it a silence of
its own, one born either of resistance, or of despair.[74]

In the case of Durs Grünbein, the tone is one of ironic resignation.

> Eine Stimme läuft über vom Denken und verirrt sich tief in der Sprache im Dickicht des Nicht-Ich. Was erwartet sie dort, wo das Kommen und Gehen der Worte, dieser Schmeißfliegenschwarm um das alte Metapherntier, alle Befürchtungen übertrifft. Eine neue Elektro-Komik? Eine alberne Neuro-Melancholie? Ein verwegenes An-den-Quanten-Scheitern? Wirklich, es fragt sich, was in aller Welt sie dort will. Denn außer Peinlichkeit und Vergeblichkeit handelt der Eigensinn sich nichts ein. Gegen die Ordnungen [. . .] beweist sie nichts.[75]

The ambivalences of Grünbein's attempt to develop a kind of 'anatomical' poetry, both as a form of resistance to official language and as a form of self-expression are very clearly expressed in his second collection, *Schädelbasislektion*.[76]

> Wie denkt ein sauber abgetrennter Kopf?
> Was sucht ein Irrtum auf der flachen Hand,
> Ein roter Pfeil entlang der Wirbelsäule?
> Wen hintergeht Vergangenheit, ein *slang*
> Aus Anekdoten, Interieurs . . . Die Körper?
> Vom Hörensagen bleibt kein Ohr verschont.
> Die beste Zuflucht—ein geschlossener Mund.
> Im Hals die Zunge, den geköpften Aal.

Whereas Grünbein's texts articulate the threat, and then go on to try and subvert it, the language of other poets seizes up into a kind of unintelligibility or a deliberate hermeticism. A number of critics have already pointed to the dark and closed metaphors of Sascha Anderson's work, for example. Before 1991, this 'Sprachverdunklung' was often understood as a kind of protection from the authorities. Since the revelations from the *Stasi* files it has been seen as a deliberate attempt to obscure the traces of his double life.[77] However, Anderson is not the only young poet to build into his work a deliberate gesture of non-communication. A number of texts in *Berührung ist nur eine Randerscheinung*, for example, are wilful in their disregard for the reader. Some of the language-based textual experiments of Lanzendörfer, Holst, and Jansen are filled with private allusions, or are so dislocated from normal linguistic usage that the reader can glean from them little more than the gesture of negation. Whereas sometimes their energy to express outruns the structures of language available and issues into a rich and potentially productive babble, (too) often the strained self-consciousness degenerates into pre-linguistic gibberish.

Looking back at the writing of Prenzlauer Berg, Jan Faktor insists that the idea that they were writing simply for themselves is 'nicht nur ein hilfloses Klischee, sondern mehr schon eine Lüge'.[78] On the other hand, in an article entitled 'Wem schreibe ich', Manfred Jäger confirms the impression of a poetry which has often turned in on itself and away from any sense of communication with the reader.[79] This must be partly due to the conditions under which it was conceived and composed: little chance of publication, and every chance of harassment from the authorities. Quite often the work which has come out of this scene is so dense, or allusive, or fragmented, as to appear (at least to the uninitiated) unintelligible, 'monologic', and close to silence. Here, in a sense, is the low point in any analysis of the young writers' work. The attempt to retreat from a regulated linguistic sphere, and to move outside orthodox notions of 'Sinn', to make linguistic forays over the borders of the articulate, can result in nonsense, or, ultimately, silence.[80]

'wortschritt um schritt':[81] *Movement*

There is, however, yet a further initiative in the poetry. For some of the poets, as I have already hinted, the urge to criticize existing language is superseded by the desire to generate a language of their own. Theirs is not simply a rejection of the dominant 'Sinn', and a crossing over to the other side, into 'Unsinn'. That would leave the limitations intact. Rather, their language asserts itself at, and beyond, the margins of the dialectic, beyond the limitations which have been placed on language. Such playful and creative speaking on the boundaries of sense is well illustrated in the work of Bert Papenfuß-Gorek.

Papenfuß-Gorek's work is perhaps best read with an eye to Lyotard's descriptions of his postmodern 'language games'. The disruption and expansion of the limits of language allow for a corresponding expansion of what can be thought. A constant 'misuse' of language permits, and encourages, the subversion of dominant thought patterns. As Lyotard sums up: 'invention is always born of dissension'.[82]

Papenfuß-Gorek has been the subject of more critical attention than perhaps any other of the Prenzlauer Berg language poets, and there are already a number of very perceptive articles about his protean and vast body of work.[83] That is not to say that all of his work will necessarily bear such scrutiny. Martin Kane is one of the few critics open enough to confess that:

> As one [. . .] sits half-mesmerised, half-perplexed over particularly inaccessible parts of *dreihzehntanz* [Papenfuß-Gorek's first collection in the GDR] the wicked thought occasionally occurs that perhaps the socio-literary observation and analysis of the phenomenon might at times be a good deal more beguiling than the thing itself.[84]

Wolf Biermann, of course, recently went so far as to denounce Papenfuß-Gorek's work as 'gequirlter Stumpfsinn'.[85] Especially in the early collection *harm*, the experimentation often appears self-indulgent or simply derivative. Here I want to concentrate on those more positive aspects which might really seem to break linguistic boundaries and generate new possibilities for language.

Whereas Döring or Koziol often work to subvert idioms or phrases, Papenfuß-Gorek is inclined to concentrate on individual words. One of the most obvious strategies in his early collections is the break with orthographical conventions and the cultivation of a private orthography. This is not a particularly hermetic strategy, however. The shifts are fairly transparent, and the poet even describes them, in the text 'schriftbruch', from his *SoJa*:[86]

nach ueberstandener
seh-krankheit
erkennen
erweiterte augen die
riffgelaufnen
stabenschiffe
'ix' als 'ka-es' &
'zet' als 'te-es'

aus innigen
zwingenden
dringenden
gruenden werden sie
flott gemacht zu
'ch' & 'sch'

As well as these shifts, he often substitutes 'kk' for 'ck', 'f' for 'v', 'kw' for 'q', 'y' for 'i', and so on. Although one fairly quickly reads one's way into these changes, they still produce the occasional surprises; and, most importantly, the materiality and 'change-ability' of the language are foregrounded. Achim Trebeß has identified a number of distinct ways in which Papenfuß-Gorek then sets about subverting individual words: splitting them to restore what has been lost, or to discover new dimensions ('ver-lust', 'vers-pott'); leaving letters out to suggest unorthodox connections ('errorismus', 'ortschritt'); 'mixing up' letters to parody the original meaning ('wahrheftigkeit', 'weltschmelz'), or introducing 'errors' ('achtaben', 'introllektuelle'); and, finally, emphasizing different parts of words to create further meanings ('potenZierung').[87] Karl Mickel once wrote of the mass of simultaneous meanings generated around individual words in Papenfuß's texts. The reader is faced with an enormous task to follow up even some of these and hold them in mind. As Gerhard Wolf comments, this is a poetry 'nicht für Leser sondern für Partner, die sich beteiligen wollen, für Produzenten'.[88] One has constantly to slow down and test one's reactions, watching alternative meanings and associations as they emerge from under the surface of the text.

Papenfuß-Gorek also makes his writing porous to a vast store of sources and traditions, from Shelley to Schwitters, Dada to the Grateful Dead, Johann Fischart, ancient Celtic mythology, and contemporary punk.[89] Equally, he mobilizes fragments from a wide range of languages and registers: quotations from the classics, 'Rotwelsch', snippets of English written phonetically, chants from Zen. But this is not simply a form of academic eclecticism. It is at once more playful and more violent. The fragments of sense and non-sense are compelled into a 'dance' of aggressive and exuberant sensuality.

> das wort soll lodern [. . .]
> in aller beweglichkeit einhergehen
> aus sinnlosigkeit in alle sinne.[90]

In addition, Papenfuß-Gorek is out to break taboos with the explicit and casual sexuality in his texts. He is not far wrong when he claims, 'meine gedichte wimmeln von pimmeln, strotzen von votzen', and especially in the more recent collections he mixes sex and politics in provocative play: 'soziolinguistik aus meinem fickwinkel'.[91] One fascinating aspect of his work, which has been neglected in criticism so far, is his preoccupation with love and sexuality, from the deliberate undermining of the traditional discourses of love with the language of politics, 'schübe sozialen engagements in's bessere bett', to the exploration of the courtly love of Chrétien de Troyes's *Lancelot*, in his cycle 'Karrendichtung'.[92] Papenfuß-Gorek's 'zmetter-lingue'[93] is a promiscuous amalgam of competing discourses, yet it would be wrong to see it simply as a postmodern indifference. Papenfuß himself comments: 'der Aspekt der Attacke gegen Konventionen ist mir ebenso wichtig wie der Aspekt der Tiefe des Verwurzeltseins'. His attitude leads him, on the one hand, to an etymological fascination with individual words, and, on the other, to a militant engagement in the politics of language.[94] It is striking how often the texts engage in explorations of explicitly political vocabulary, concepts such as 'vaterland', 'freiheit', and 'revolution', even 'wahrheit'.[95] His insistence on 'fielfalt anstatt einfalt' is not simply directionless plurality, but rather a kind of linguistic resistance to the deformations of thought and language in the GDR: 'widerstand im widerspruch [. . .] bewegung, d. h. bewegung'.[96] Yet, at the same time, that very plurality and openness generates an energy which breaks down barriers. In his 'SOndern' this is expressed in very visual terms.

> schrei gegen die wand
> schreib es an die wand
> schreite durch die wand[97]

To conclude, it is perhaps worth citing 'wortflug', a text in which Papenfuß-Gorek demonstrates the commitment to a radical kind of regeneration in some of the ways I have described:[98]

> meine umwelt gebrichts
> an geschlechtlichkeit
> & noch solchen wortschaetzen
> so ich schaetz aller leute
> noch solcher wortschaetze
> gegen ferfestigungen
> ferfestigter zungen
> & bekwehmlichkeiten
> trott zu beschreiten
> dergestalt gleichgeschalt
> ist selbst in blutgeflut
> strammstand noch der anstand
> so wortschritt um schritt
> flugs ich wortflog
> eingesehens

unfersehens
schrifttriftig
m e i n e haupttracht
der sinntracht trachtet
spiel ich sinntrachtwegen
wortspare durch blosses
auslassen ein, also :
liegen worte
wenn ihr ruhe wollt
                brach
sitzen worte
wenn ihr daran wollt
                bereit
stehen worte
wenn ihr gedicht wollt
                dikk da
gehen worte
wenn ihr weiter wollt
                noch weiter
laufen worte
wenn ihr dorthin wollt
                wort —
flugs um bestimmten
forkommnissen zuforzukommen
    for ort beim wort
        dass kommunismus
            kommen muss

This headlong pursuit of language is the poet's response to the monolithic forms of officialdom: 'ferfestigungen | ferfestigter zungen'. Words are dislocated, subverted, and forced out of their habitual contexts and meanings in order to discover a new autonomy. Movement is a central theme for several of the language poets. It is, however, Papenfuß-Gorek who articulates that most radically, and demonstrates that movement most visibly in the texture of the language. If some of the young writers used poetry as a way breaking the boundaries of their reality, of 'seeing through' into dimensions which had been suppressed, this poem is itself, to borrow Anneli Hartmann's phrase, 'die transparent gemachte Entgrenzung'.[99]

'opas metrik': A Return to Form

The experimental strategies associated with writers like Papenfuß-Gorek, Döring, or Jansen which I have outlined above were never the only literary responses to the young writers' reality, they were simply the most radical in formal terms. Alongside these initiatives were others which worked much more within the constraints of traditional forms and languages. It is interesting to note, for example, the marked interest in traditional forms among a number of writers: the use of rhyme in general, but also of rondo forms, ritornellos, and, especially, the sonnet.

At first sight this tendency might seem a curious pendant to a discussion of *Entgrenzung* among the work of the generation. In the chapter 'Hineingeboren und Aussteigen. Lebens- und Schreibweisen junger Autoren' of his *Kleine Literaturgeschichte der DDR*, Wolfgang Emmerich sums up the achievements of the generation by concentrating on the innovations of the Prenzlauer poets, and leaving their contemporaries in the background. He concludes: 'Diese Autoren zersprengen die überlieferte Sprache night, sie halten an vertrauten Formen des gesellschaftlichen Engagements fest, sie suchen die große Öffentlichkeit' (p. 438). However, it is at least worth pointing to the potential of language which stays within the recognizable and accepted forms, and yet challenges and undermines accepted understandings as it does so. Indeed Andreas Koziol's ironic 'die moritat von opas metrik', in which he ironically bemoans the restrictions of rhyme and work-play like ('mache nicht gleich wieder ein sonett | —stotter erst die wortspielschulden ab'), is itself an example of his virtuoso command of rhyme, rhythm, form and its subversive innuendo: 'taktgefühl', 'bodenlosigkeiten', and 'doppelsinn'.[100] This line of argument is perhaps obvious, so I do not want to labour it here. One might even understand it as the essential job of poetry to extend the boundaries of the sayable. There is a danger, however, that this sort of gesture is overlooked. Two brief examples.

Rondeau Allemagne[101]

Ich harre aus im Land und geh, ihm fremd,
Mit einer Liebe, die mich über Grenzen treibt,

Zwischen den Himmeln. Sehe jeder, wo er bleibt;
Ich harre aus im Land und geh ihm fremd.

Mit einer Liebe, die mich über Grenzen treibt,
will ich die Übereinkünfte verletzen
Und lachen, reiß ich mir das Herz in Fetzen
Mit jener Liebe, die mich über Grenzen treibt.

Zwischen den Himmeln sehe jeder, wo er bleibt:
Ein blutig Lappen wird gehißt, das Luftschiff fällt.
Kein Land in Sicht; vielleicht ein Seil, das hält
Zwischen den Himmeln. Sehe jeder, wo er bleibt.

This is an extraordinary poem, which moves once again within a topography of emancipation and restraint. The restrictions of land are set against the possibility of flight and the open sea. These gain a political significance in the light of the title, but also a sexual one in the mention of 'Liebe' and the slippage of 'geh, ihm fremd' to 'geh ihm fremd' between ll. 1 and 4. Emancipatory gestures— 'fremd gehen', 'über Grenzen treiben'—are checked by the undertow of stasis or imprisonment: 'ausharren', 'bleiben', 'fallen', 'halten'. The use of the traditional form underlines the tension in the enclosing repetitions, and the encroachingly compact end stops of the rhyme. And yet just as the metaphorical implications slide, so does the syntax. In reading for sense, one is forced break through those meanings imposed by the form and the rhyme scheme, and new possibilities are generated. Language, form, and interpretive gesture are teased and thwarted in a poetic *tour de force* which might truly be said to enact the promise of poetry at its best: 'Übereinkünfte verletzen'.

But it is the quite widespread use of the sonnet form itself which is perhaps the most interesting case, and most worthy of investigation. This is, after all, a form more usually associated with the resolution of dissonances, rather than their exploitation. In the GDR this aspect was given a particular ideological colouring by a tradition of sonnet-writing which stretches back to J. R. Becher, and to his own theory of the sonnet as an aesthetic manifestation of Hegelian synthesis.[102] It is exactly this problematic ambivalence which is developed in a text by Kurt Drawert, simply entitled, like one of Becher's poems from the 1930s, 'Das Sonett'. Here Drawert complains about the 'List und Leim und Schleim und Schlamm' which is needed to cement together the disparate material of life. The sonnet form he sees as an aesthetic sleight of hand:

> Ach all die Regeln, all die Norm,
> die baun zur Harmonie den Müll,
> Der letztlich niemals passen will
> Und doch sich biegen läßt zur Form
> Durch den Betrug von höhrer Art
> Als ließe sich die Welt verwalten
> Als ganzes in den Händen halten.
> Ein Spiel, ein Trick, die Form Verrat,
> Denn alles Leben will sich spalten
> Will Brüche, Löcher, Kanten, Falten.[103]

Of course the force of Drawert's complaint is ironically undermined by the form of his own text. It is not particularly innovative in itself, although the deliberately colloquial tone of some of the language and the sly political implications are played off against a certain pathos and the solemnity of the form. And yet he does, I think, diagnose precisely that nostalgia for wholeness ('als ließe sich die Welt verwalten | Als Ganzes in den Händen halten'), which has contributed to something of a renaissance of traditional forms. It is noteworthy that two of the young poets, Kerstin Hensel and Kathrin Schmidt, have even written 'Sonettkränze', one of the most demanding of poetic forms, and that in each of them the form is used as kind of injunction against the collapse of identity, shifting narratives, and a disintegrating world. Each of these cycles deserves detailed attention in itself, but the 'Meistersonett' of Hensel's 'Märchen-Land' gives a good sense of what is at stake.[104]

> Jetzt da es wohnlich wird in unserem Haus,
> die dürre Hexe durch den Schornstein geht
> und süßer Kuchen an den Fenstern klebt,
> da laden wir gemächlich bilder aus
>
> der alten Kutsche die leichter lenkt
> wenn unbelastet sie durchs Tor geführt.
> Am Kreuzweg sind die Pappeln festgeschnürt.
> Das Brot im Moor, worauf wir treten, senkt
>
> sich tief, bis wir uns vor dem Spiegel sehn
> verwunschen und mit braunem Blut im Haar
> und weil wirs doch nicht sind, erschrecken gar
>
> vor der Erlösung, der wir nicht entgehen.
> Ich sitz im Gold das ich zu Stroh verspinn
> und dreimal darfst du raten wer ich bin.

It is tempting to conclude that it is primarily the women of the young generation who work with traditional forms. Although this is by no means exclusively the case, it might suggest that the dissolution of identity and language is the prerogative of those who feel that both are secure to start with. That the opposite is the case with many of the women on the borders of the young GDR subculture—Heike Willingham, Gabriele Stotzer-Kachold, Róža Domašcyna as well as Köhler, Hensel, and Schmidt—has been demonstrated by Birgit Dahlke.[105] Although this will certainly be an interesting field for academic work in the future, one should not push the division too far. The contradictory and ambivalent nature of the literary scene is perhaps best illustrated by the fact that some of those 'Prenzlauer-Prinzen' most celebrated for their disregard for conventions have also experimented with that most traditional of forms: Sascha Anderson, Bert Papenfuß-Gorek, and Stefan Döring combined to publish a book of 'Fünfzehn deutsche Sonette' under the title *ich fühle mich in grenzen wohl*.[106]

Conclusion

One of the most frequently posed and most pressing questions about the young writers' poetry is whether, in retrospect especially, it can be truly understood as a breaking of boundaries. This question can be asked on a number of levels, and has perhaps different answers depending on where one places the emphasis. Generally, there have been large claims made for the texts of the young writers, especially the Prenzlauer poets, by a number of influential critics. Often these claims elide various forms emancipation and regeneration, be they political, metaphorical, historical, or aesthetic. Emmerich speaks of a 'Schwinden der ästhetischen Doktrinen', Böthig of a 'Prozeß der Entautorisierung der ideologischen Mächte', Geist of 'Grenzüberschreitungen in Richtung einer radikalen Moderne'.[107] Here I would like, briefly, to raise some of the problems in making such a judgement.

Hans Magnus Enzensberger, reviewing the poetry of the 1980s in the *Frankfurter Allgemeine Zeiting*, described it provocatively as 'einen kleinen Schwächeanfall in der langen Geschichte der Phantasie'. Clearly growing impatient with what he called the 'betäubende Harmlosigkiet' of the younger generation of writing, he voiced the suspicion that most of them contented themselves 'mit der Wiederaufbereitung ausgebrannten Materials [. . .] und daß dieses lyrische Recycling alle Standards der Vorlagen unterbietet'.[108] One of the most common questions raised about the young GDR writers in particular is whether they are not simply, and belatedly, working off a historical deficit of sorts. Volker Braun was perhaps over-aggressive in his Rimbaud essay when he dismissed the poetry of the young writers as 'die Wiederholung des geistlosen Handbetriebs der Avantgarde'.[109] All the same, there are indeed aspects of the work, both conceptual and formal, which could be seen as simply taking up those strands of Modernism which had been marginalized in the literary canon of the GDR.[110] Enzensberger has long been sceptical about the claims of any modern literature dubbing itself 'avant-garde': 'Jede heutige Avantgarde ist Wiederholung, Betrug oder Selbstbetrug. [. . .] Ihre Bewegung ist Regression. Avantgarde ist zu ihrem Gegenteil, ist zum Anachronismus geworden.'[111] And in the 'realismus-geschädigten DDR' the danger of such repetition and anachronism is perhaps particularly acute.[112] There is no doubt that part of the radical gesture of the young writers was their appropriation of the forms and traditions which had previously been taboo; their occupation with Modernism stands alongside their interest in drug culture, punk music, and modern French theory. Already in giving voice to these different cultures and traditions they were breaking boundaries in the GDR. But was that all?

A number of critics have drawn out more specific similarities between the young writers' work and various 'avant-garde' experiments of the twentieth century: particularly the young generation of German Expressionists, Dada, and even the radical Concrete poetry of the 1950s and 1960s in the West. There is no doubt that there are elements of congruence and even imitation, but the best of the young writers' work taps into these traditions and makes the poetic energies it finds there its own. Where the work of the young poetry differs from those earlier avant-garde experiments is partly in its level of self-consciousness. There is very little of the ecstatic confidence, nor the intemperate pessimism, of Expressionist poetry, for example. The exuberant anarchy of Dada has been replaced in these writers by a more controlled destruction and disintegration. And the naïvety and irresponsibility of some Concrete poetry has given way to a much more purposeful manipulation of language. The young writers in the GDR write with a knowledge of all these traditions, but their access to them is filtered through their own historical and political reality, a reality which poses quite different problems and demands quite different responses. Theirs is, then, a calculated political experiment: 'vers aus der retorte'.[113]

All the same, from the vantage point of 1993, and the West, quite a number of the texts may indeed appear dated. Some of the work was always going to be more important for its gesture than for its achievement. It remains as a fascinating historical document. But one should also remember that any avant-garde is in part determined by the particular social and political reality to which it responds. From outside it is sometimes difficult to rediscover the power which any one text may have had in its own particular context. It is also in the nature of any avant-garde to be short-lived. Its ineluctable fate is to be reintegrated into the structures and institutions from which it was trying to escape.[114] This was already most palpably the case with the work of the young writers when it was taken up by the official publishing houses, which had so long ignored and suppressed it. The development was noted within the underground itself. As early as 1987 the artist A. R. Penck wrote an essay describing 'Das Ende des Untergrunds', and in the run-up to 1989 a number of writers, including Papenfuß-Gorek, Faktor, and Anderson, remarked that the potential of many of those aesthetic and political gestures which had originally appeared subversive or provocative was now exhausted: 'unumstößlich klingt sie aus, die ära des aktiven wortspiels'.[115] In a piece of intriguing acrobatics Peter Böthig suggests one might understand their aesthetic instead as a 'Post-Avantgarde-Konzept'; one which might already anticipate its own political demise. It is a moot point whether political prescience has any bearing on literary value, however.[116]

This brings me on to the second question which must be raised here: the interrelation of political commitment and poetic autonomy for the young writers. For some there is no problem. They always understood their work as part of a broadly socialist extension of the Enlightenment tradition, engaged at a profound and explicitly political level in critical dialogue with their society.[117] Even, perhaps especially, for those writers who worked in strict opposition to the regime, political commitment and the function of literature were not in doubt. It is, however, a commonplace of the secondary literature to make a link between the supposedly apolitical stance of some of the writers and an innovative aesthetic autonomy of sorts. As I have demonstrated above, a great deal of the poetry was either directly political, or set about illuminating, apprehending, and deconstructing the structures of political thought in language. An absolute division between politics and aesthetic is surely a false one. Sascha Anderson, for a long time considered as one of the least directly political of the writers, spoke, for example, of an 'ästhetische Politisierung' in the work of Prenzlauer Berg.[118] The notion of autonomy is, consequently, also a vexed one. It would be possible to understand it either as the creation of a retreat entirely outside the constraints of political and instrumentalized reality, or else as an independent position from which those constraints could, at last, be effectively criticized. The poetry itself shows signs of both of these movements, in an unstable dialectic. It attempts to remove itself from degraded forms of official language, but also to unmask them and expose their ideological content. Such an ambitious project courts the possibility of spectacular failure. It can easily lead to the sort of political and, significantly, aesthetic stalemate which Adorno condemns in his essay on 'Engagement'. He warns against the dangers which beset any work of art in its attempt to achieve an autonomous status:

Sie gerät an den Rand von Gleichgültigkeit, degeneriert unvermerkt zur Bastelei, zum in anderen Kunstgattungen durchschauten Wiederholungs-spiel mit Formeln, zur Tapetenmuster. Das leibt oft der groben Forderung nach dem Engagement im Recht. Gebilde, welche die verlogene Posivität von Sinn herausfordern, münden leicht in Sinnleere anderer Art, die positivistische Veranstaltung, das eitele Herumwürfeln mit Elementen. Dadurch verfallen sie der Sphäre, von der sie sich abstoßen.[119]

When cultural theorists talk of autonomy their language usually implies absolute claims of difference and separation. Perhaps it is more appropriate here to recall the vocabulary of political geography, in which 'autonomy' is almost invariably something granted from above, in some carefully circumscribed form (say to a 'homeland' in South Africa). In political reality, Prenzlauer Berg was not, of course, an autonomous enclave in the GDR. The recent revelations have demonstrated that even the most heretical of literary experiments carried out there were to some extent permitted, even sponsored, by those authoritarian structures they were designed to escape. On the other hand, however, the writers' textual gestures towards an aesthetic autonomy are not necessarily quite so easily recuperated by the political realities. Peter Bürger has understood the essential position of the 'avant-garde' to be a constant dialectic of emancipation and reintegration. Perhaps this is a useful model to shed light too on the linguistic experimentation of Prenzlauer Berg and of the generation as a whole. It can be understood as a vigorous gesture of emancipation constantly checked by its own project, premise, and circumstance. This in a positive and in a negative sense. For it is this dialectic which gives the language its unstable energy, its urgency, and, oddly perhaps, its dignity. As Sascha Anderson concluded: 'ich habe ausser meiner sprache keine | mittel meine sprache zu verlassen'.[120]

PART III

Was bleibt: Literature after the Wall

Introduction

'WAS bleibt' is the title of a semi-autobiographical text by Christa Wolf written in 1979, revised after November 1989 and published in 1990.[1] In the post-unification *feuilleton* debates it became one of the most aggressively reiterated formulas for dismantling forty years of cultural history from the GDR. Under the sign of left-wing melancholy,[2] it has also become the starting-point for a nostalgic salvage operation. And while Wolf's text itself does not carry a question mark, the debates which it generated in the summer of 1990 and beyond, and the recent revelations concerning the involvement of writers with the *Staatssicherheit* (including Heiner Müller and Wolf herself) have initiated a large-scale interrogation of the very values upon which our understanding of the cultural history of both German states has been based.[3] Not only the shortcomings of post-war *Vergangenheitsbewältigung* in East and West have come under fire, but also the tragic 'error' of Utopian thinking in East and West, the crimes committed in the service of the 'Epochenillusion' of really existing Socialism,[4] and the 'Failure of the German Intellectuals'.[5]

Two key focuses of attention during the excavation of GDR literature occasioned by the 'Was bleibt' debate and the subsequent *Stasi* debate have been the integrity and self-understanding of the writer on the one hand, and the role of memory on the other. The discussion of the role of the writer has become fixed on the often uneasy compromises made by intellectuals in their negotiations between 'Geist' and 'Macht': a discussion which was brought into sharp relief by the revelations of covert involvement with the *Stasi*. The discussion of memory has focused on the possibility of coming to terms with the political and personal histories which were dissolved and discredited in 1989, and from 1991 onwards this gained new impetus from the apparent amnesia of certain writers regarding the truth of their relationship with power. Both of these can be seen as an extension, albeit fraught and partial, of the long process of German 'Trauerarbeit'. In his personal and philosophical chronicle of the demise of the GDR, *Volk ohne Trauer* (1992), Rolf Schneider identifies in the current arguments elements of that same 'Unfähigkeit zu trauern' which Alexander and Margarete

Mitscherlich had examined in 1967. He concludes by reproaching intellectuals (himself included) for their failure in this respect, and wondering if, once more, it will take twenty years and the revolt of a young generation to cease cheating history and begin the process of revision.[6]

A process of revision has, in some senses, already begun. As is clear from the references to the larger question of post-war *Vergangenheitsbewältigung* (references which have played an increasingly large part in the recent polemic about the *Stasi* files), this is an extraordinarily complex enterprise. Here I want to focus quite simply on the start which has been made since 1989, with special reference to the young GDR writers who are my central concern. There are two aspects to explore. First, the recent work in which the writers themselves have attempted to come to terms with their own history. Secondly, the recent attempts which critics (and writers) have made to reassess the place of this generation in recent literary history. Here it is appropriate to talk of 'generations' once again, for the urgency of the issues up for discussion has often encouraged the most categorical and damaging of generalizations. It is as a generation almost lost that the young writers were rescued and celebrated after the fall of the Wall, and it is as a 'generation' that they are in danger of being lost once again as a result of the accusations of complicity with the *Staatssicherheit* levelled against them. However, in focusing on the young writers from these two angles, it is necessary to sketch in the background to the debates which have so dominated German intellectual discussion since 1990. There are two reasons for this. It is important to establish in the first place the differences between the process of literary 'Trauerarbeit' initiated by the young writers and their older predecessors. In addition, although the young writers themselves were often only marginal to the central discussions in the immediate post-1989 years, it is the course of these arguments which have determined the way they are now received in the new Germany. I make no apologies for starting, at the beginning, with Wolf's *Was bleibt*.

6

'Was bleibt': Revisions from the New Germany

I HAVE argued that memory and the crisis of the intellectual are the two central issues of the recent German literary debates. Both of these are central to a reading of the two most discussed poems of the post-*Wende* period: Heiner Müller's 'Selbstkritik', and Volker Braun's 'Das Eigentum' (see Introduction). However these issues are also inscribed in Wolf's own text, *Was bleibt*. Whatever else the story is about, however ill-timed its publication, and however it is relativized by the recent revelations from her own past, Wolf's text is an extraordinarily subtle exploration of the relationship between the writer and the mechanisms of power. This is signalled in the title itself, which refers to the famous last lines of Hölderlin's hymn 'Andenken'. A number of critics have recognized the quotation, but without signalling quite how central it is to the current debates.[1]

The figure of Hölderlin, as I have argued, was central to the appropriation of Romanticism by GDR writers, particularly in the 1970s. Gerhard and Christa Wolf in particular used their pre-occupation with Hölderlin as a way of exploring their own dilemmas as writers in the GDR.[2] As the title suggests, Hölderlin's poem is about memory; it is, in part, a celebration of his time in Bordeaux. In larger terms it is also a tribute to memory itself, which Hölderlin understands not simply as backward-looking nostalgia, but as an animating and redemptive force set against the killing amnesia of 'slumber' (l. 29).[3] However, the poem also returns to another of Hölderlin's other central themes, the role of the poet. In the image of the outgoing mariners and the reference to Bellarmin (l. 37) Hölderlin is setting up an opposition between the active and contemplative 'journey' to the source. The final lines represent one of Hölderlin's most confident claims for the project of the imagination—the project of the writer.

> . . . Es nehmet aber
> Und giebt Gedächtniß die See,
> Und die Lieb' auch heftet fleißig die Augen,
> Was bleibet aber, stiften die Dichter.

What remains, what is lasting beyond the contingencies of the pragmatic, is founded by the writer. The poet has power to establish something which will abide. However, between the triumphant (if momentary) confidence of Hölderlin's poem and the title of Wolf's text, the emphasis has shifted dramatically. For Wolf does not complete the quotation, not even along the bleak lines of Heiner Müller's ready cynicism 'Was bleibet aber stiften die Bomben'.[4] The quotation is fractured; the syntax ambivalent. What remains is absence. An absence, which I would suggest, reflects Wolf's profound scepticism as to the power of memory and the project of the writer in the GDR.

This is borne out by an analysis of the narrator figure and the many submerged literary quotations which run through the text. The book might be 'eine Geschichte des schlechten Gewissens' (p. 30), as the narrator claims, and as commentators have not failed to underline in the light of Wolf's own 'bad conscience'.[5] However, it is openly so. The narrator is laid low not primarily by the external attentions of the *Stasi*, but by the realization that their mechanisms of repression have already taken hold within her. Hence the various refractions of that 'innerer Begleiter' (p. 60), who polices her thoughts more reliably even than the young men in the Wartburg. In a sense the whole work is an act of memory, an attempt to discover when it was that the State was not outside but inside her, when it was that she went to meet the installations of the totalitarian State half-way (pp. 61–2). This is made clear in the narrator's two central projections of her writing-self in the characters of the menacing Jürgen M. and of the young writer who has just been released from prison and comes almost immediately, bringing new texts. Jürgen M. becomes for the narrator the nightmare vision of someone who has sold out to the *Stasi* ('Sie hatten ihn in der Hand', p. 48). He twice explicitly warns her that he is not alone in this and names the price that a writer has to pay for his/her privileged position in the GDR: 'wenn man sich als Wissender über die Masse der Unwissenden erheben wolle, dann müsse man seine Seele verkaufen, wie eh und je' (p. 48).[6] Even if opportunism does not corrupt the writer, it seems that fear (a key motif in the work) will. This is made explicit as the narrator walks through the dystopian cityscape and reflects on her own compromise: 'Mir hatten sie nicht einmal die Instrumente gezeigt' (p. 30), before noticing a placard advertising a production of

Brecht's *Galileo* by the Berliner Ensemble. In a broad sweep she makes the link between Brecht and then Galileo himself ('listig und furchtsam', p. 52) fighting through fear and compromise towards his belief in truth, to a conclusion which has echoes of Büchner's analysis of the human character.

Eine reine Charakterfrage also, ob er gegen die Lüge antrat. Wir angstvoll doch auch, dazu noch ungläubig, treten immer gegen uns selber an, denn es log und katzbuckelte und geiferte und verleumdete aus uns heraus, und es gierte nach Unterwerfung und nach Genuß. Nur: Die einen wußten es, und die anderen wußten es nicht. (p. 32)

This is a damning condemnation of the writer herself and the 'wir' with whom she identifies. It is clear that, far from being the naïve attempt at self-exculpation which some critics have made it out to be, let alone an attempt at cynical apology, this text is a ruthless self-examination. The narrator knows. Even at the end of the text, she offers little hope for herself: the work with memory failed to engender a new perspective, and the 'neue Sprache' (p. 107) which the writer has hoped to find is still missing.

The young woman writer, on the other hand (the source for whom has since been identified as Gabi Kachold), along with the young poet who sends the narrator his poems, represent the individual's potential autonomy, at once precarious and utopian. It is here that the myth-making starts. The presentation of both writers is schematic and largely representative in function. Yet it is the narrator's reaction to them which is particularly interesting. Startled by the uncompromising nature of the manuscript sheets which the girl gives to her to comment upon, the narrator replies: 'ich sagte, was sie da geschrieben habe, sei gut. Es stimme. Jeder Satz sei wahr. Sie solle es niemandem zeigen. Diese paar Seiten könnten sie wieder ins Gefängnis bringen. [. . .]

Ich dachte: es ist so weit. Die Jungen schreiben es auf' (p. 76). This writer and the young poet are presented as naïve perhaps, but also fearless, endangered but also uncompromising: 'sie rannten ins Messer' (p. 56). It is noteworthy that in both cases the narrator extends her impressions of individuals to represent a plural; she clearly has a generation in mind ('*sie* rannten ins Messer', '*Die Jungen* schreiben es auf' [my emphasis]). It is in them, the narrator concludes, that the chance of building a better future resides. They are without the shackles of bad conscience which inhibit the narrator. They are a generation who have paid for their authenticity with prison. 'Das Mädchen, dachte ich, ist nicht zu halten. Wir können sie nicht retten, nicht verderben. Sie soll tun, was sie muß, und uns unsrem Gewissen überlassen' (p. 78). Apart from the key concept of compromise, one other important aspect distinguishes the girl and her fellows from the narrator: her attitude to memory and to what would remain. 'Das Mädchen fragte nicht krämerisch: Was bleibt. Es fragte auch nicht danach, woran es sich erinnern würde, wenn es einst alt wäre' (p. 79). The narrator does not spare herself, nor her generation, in the examination she imposes, although it can, of course, be argued that Wolf spared herself only too much by leaving out her own experience of active complicity. However, the naïvety with which she views the possibilities of the youngest generation is extraordinary. It seems odd in retrospect that Wolf should have presented the young writers as unproblematically autonomous, authentic, free, and should have so completely failed to recognize that the pressures of complicity, the complexities of memory, and the schizophrenia of living within a dictatorship, which she was so acutely aware of in her own experience, might weigh on them too.

There are perhaps two main reasons for Wolf's attitude. Many of her works and interviews testify to what she saw as the unique deformation of character suffered by the generation, her generation, who had been tainted by Fascism and had then come under the spell of new Stalinist fathers. The young writers appeared to be free from that peculiar burden of memory. They also appeared to be free of the utopian aspirations for socialism, from which many of the older writers had taken so long to free themselves and which had made them so long tolerant of (blind to?) the failings of GDR reality. However, more important is the fact that the narrator celebrates the young writers for having found their way out of the stranglehold of a compromised language towards that perceived 'neue Sprache' ('Die Jungen schreiben es auf'), which she herself is unable to reach. In doing this, Wolf has found a way of salvaging some vestige at least of the particular utopian project of the writer. Clearly it is tentative and embattled, deferred for the narrator herself, and transferred into the project of the young, but it is nevertheless there. This is perhaps the greatest 'blind spot' of Wolf's text. Her inability even in 1989 to give up her faith in the special role of the writers in the GDR, and her desperate contribution to a myth of the young.

Before I move on to examine exactly how the myths around the young writers were generated and how they—the myths, the writers, and now their work—are being dispatched, it is necessary to set out the terms of the discussion which followed the publication of Wolf's text.

'Was bleibt': The Debate

There have already been several useful commentaries on the debates immediately set in motion by the publication of *Was bleibt*.[7] There were three stages of debate. Particularly important in this context is the turn that the debate took after the Frankfurt book fair of autumn 1990. However, it is worth isolating here several significant factors from the early part of the debate, in order to illuminate the reception of the young writers in the new Germany.

The first stage of the debate, initiated by articles of Ulrich Greiner and Volker Hage in *Die Zeit* and by Frank Schirrmacher in the *Frankfurter Allgemeine Zeitung*, moved very quickly from disagreement about the aesthetic quality of the text itself— 'sentimental und unglaubwürdig bis an die Grenze des Kitsches' (Schirrmacher), 'kunstvolle Prosa' (Hage)—to an examination of the writer herself.[8] While Hage claimed that Wolf had become a 'moral instance' by virtue of the beauty and honesty of her prose, and could thus be 'accused of nothing' (p. 71), Greiner claimed that Wolf's decision to publish the text when she did had not only shown a 'lack of sensitivity' but also a moral blindness and opportunism. She was a 'Staatsdichterin' (p. 67) acting now out of a mixture of fear and calculation, her text was the attempt to exculpate herself: 'das Gejammer einer Heuchlerin für Heuchler' (Serke).[9] But, as a comment by Wolf Biermann which came to furnish the title of Thomas Anz's anthology suggests, the debate was not primarily about Christa Wolf.[10]

Frank Schirrmacher's article was more subtle and far-reaching than Greiner's. He did not accuse Wolf of being identical with the SED regime, of opportunism, or even of awkward timing. He argued instead that Wolf's career was paradigmatic of an entire generation of GDR writers who had been raised under the shadow of National Socialism. The resistance of Wolf and her compatriots to Fascism, he argued, had led to a blind identification with the State. The writers had exchanged one belief, one world view for a new belief, a new totalizing and closed system, this time Marxism.[11] His psychoanalytical vocabulary translates their acceptance of the new authority of a socialist world view into 'familial' terms, that is an obedient acceptance of their new socialist fathers: 'Christa Wolf hat wie viele andere Intellektuelle ihrer Generation ein familiäres, fast intimes Verhältnis zu ihrem Staat und seinen Institutionen aufgebaut' (p. 80). Schirrmacher was not the first to put forward such a hypothesis; this uncomfortably intimate relationship with power is something which Wolf herself had often commented upon in her work, notably in *Kindheitsmuster*. A comment made in 1987 takes up this theme and underlines the differences between her generation and the younger writers, in very similar terms to *Was bleibt*.

Meine Generation hat früh eine Ideologie gegen eine andere ausgetauscht, sie ist spät, zögernd, teilweise gar nicht erwachsen geworden, will sagen, reif, autonom. Daher kommen ihre—unsere Schwierigkeiten mit den Jüngeren. Da ist eine große Unsicherheit, weil die eigene Ablösung von ideologischen Setzungen, intensiven Bindungen an festgelegte Strukturen so wenig gelungen ist, die Jungen so wenig selbstständiges Denken und Handeln sehen und daher keine Leitfiguren finden, auf die sie sich verlassen können. So holt uns, im Verhältnis zu den Jungen, unsere nicht genügend verarbeitete Kindheit wieder ein.[12]

Uwe Wittstock's contention that a necessary moral and historical debate had been displaced into the literary arena is, in part at least, true: 'Es geht *nicht* um die Literatur, sondern um eine exemplarische Abrechnung mit exemplarischen Lebensläufen. Die Schriftsteller sind Stellvertreter'.[13] In some senses the 'reckoning' with the GDR writers can be seen simply as part of the West's triumphalist dismantling of the East and of socialism as a whole.[14] The writers, because they had a high profile, were being judged as representatives of all the compromises of morality and integrity made by a nation, and for all the crimes perpetrated in the name of the socialist dream. On another level, I would argue that the writers were standing in for an entire generation and being called to account for their mistakes, in much the same way as a generation had judged their 'fathers' some thirty years earlier. The importance of this question is worth emphasizing here, as it became a significant factor in catapulting the young writers into prominence in the autumn of 1990. Yet it would be wrong to understand the writers simply as scapegoats, as Wittstock implies. The complex of issues addressed—morality, integrity, the relationship with power—was also a specifically literary one.

Writers in the GDR had a unique duty: they were the only access that the majority of people had to the public political arena. Their failure to speak out radically enough, early enough, led to charges that they and their literature had contributed to prolonging a corrupt system which might have been toppled earlier but for them. There are two closely allied points here. First, that their failure to offer fundamental criticism of the State had made them 'fellow travellers' of the regime.[15] Secondly, it was argued that the minor criticism they did make of the State had the effect of a kind of 'Droge für Unterdrückte, [ein] quietistisches Labsal', lulling the people with the illusion of hope, and, inadvertently perhaps, stabilizing the social order.[16] This impression of deep-seated complicity on the part of leading cultural figures was accentuated when, in the autumn of 1989, after the fall of the Wall, many of the older writers were left stranded among the ruins of the SED State, still calling for the citizens to support revolutionary renewal, a democratic socialism, a third way, rather than capitalist 'annexation', when such possibilities had already been overtaken by the popular tide of change.[17] It became clear that whereas, under the pressure of a closed society, literature had functioned as a proxy for those who had no voice or who had been forced into silence, as soon as their political will could be expressed directly, the *Ersatzfunktion* of literature was redundant. In apparently finding their own political voice (as can be seen in the modulation of Wolf's 'Wir sind das Volk', to the perhaps inevitable response 'Wir sind ein Volk') the people, in one moment, rescinded their contract with writers as advocates and moral representatives. Instead, they felt resentment: a 'Künstlerfeindlichkeit',[18] based on long years of deprivation, while writers and other intellectuals enjoyed special privileges. The real gulf between the writers and those whom they believed they could represent was revealed by the horror, but also the condescension, with which writers like Stefan Heym deplored the crowds poring 'with cannibalistic lust' over the glitzy trash of Western consumerism.[19] What Kunert compellingly termed the 'Sturz vom Sockel'[20] of the writers began the shock waves which have destabilized our most fundamental assumptions about the role of literature in society, not only under a dictatorship.

It is easy to understand that the new sobriety of judgement led to a reversal of what has been termed the 'Dissidenten-Bonus', according to which ideological applause for the apparently dissident had long dominated Western criticism of the GDR literary scene. To borrow a phrase from Günter Grass: 'Die Zeit der Nachsicht ist vorbei. Vom Bonus zum Malus'.[21] This quickly led to the perception of a concerted media campaign against intellectuals— one which pointed to a sinister conservative restoration. Volker Braun warned of a 'große Treibjagd' against critical intellectuals, instituted in order to divert attention from the real problems of unification; a number of critics placed this in the context of a long-standing hostility towards intellectuals in Germany, and Heiner Müller spoke out bluntly against the 'Stalinism of the West'.[22]

Whether the main thrust of this criticism was 'necessary' or simply the demonstrative 'execution' of major GDR writers is open to debate.[23] Certainly many observers were outraged by what appeared to be a personalized witch-hunt against Wolf.[24] However, the wider discussion about the whole complex of morality, writing, (self-)censorship and the State was not merely necessary but, in some senses, long-overdue. Both Schirrmacher and Greiner placed the relationship of Wolf and her fellow writers and the State firmly within a long and sorry German intellectual history.[25] In particular, the subtitle of Schirrmacher's essay clearly points to the study of the 'authoritarian personality' written by Adorno in exile, and the essay goes on to establish the SED state as the 'zweiter totalitärer Sündenfall' of German intellectuals in the twentieth century.[26] Even if not explicitly stated, the comparison between Stalinism and Fascism ghosts through many of the essays and contributions to the debate, and nowhere more than in the rhetoric. The accusations against writers like Wolf obviously recall the post-war debates about 'inner emigration'.[27] Even the responses to such charges were also clearly conditioned by the truncated debates of the 1940s and 1950s. Walter Jens pleaded against the 'Preisgabe der DDR Kultur' and drew parallels with the 'Spruchkammer-Denken' of post-war denazification;[28] Stefan Heym recalled the techniques of 'Meinungsterror' used by US forces in Germany after the war;[29] and the German PEN bluntly condemned what they saw as 'postmodern McCarthyism'.[30] A specifically German nerve has been touched here. Both the dangerously inflated rhetoric of the discussions and the sometimes sinister political manoeuvring visible behind the scenes point to the fact that this debate is a long-suppressed spasm of the post-war 'Trauerarbeit'.

The extent to which the discussion was also a reckoning with post-war history more generally was evident in the second phase of the debate, which, in general terms, signalled a shift in the argument from morality to aesthetics. It began with an article by Frank Schirrmacher, which coincided with the Frankfurt book fair of autumn 1990, and which proclaimed the end of the literature of the Federal Republic.[31] There are three strands of argument in his polemic, which take up elements of his earlier attack on the older authors, but indicate a new tack. First he argues that the literary history of West Germany had long since stagnated into ritualistic forms and themes, fixated on providing the (delayed) moral response to Fascism. He continues by exploring how this literature exhausted itself in the service of social and political causes, providing the legitimation for a society that had lost its moral identity after 1945. Finally, he suggests that these preoccupations have divorced German literature from the mainstream of European literary Modernism, and have denied it its proper concern with a progressive and autonomous aesthetic. On one level this is clearly still an issue of generations.[32] The literature generated by those authors associated with the impetus of the 'Gruppe 47' (Grass, Böll, Fried, Walser, Johnson) had inflicted a stranglehold on the German literary scene up until the 1990s, he claimed. It was a 'Stillhalte-literatur',[33] which had so choked the imaginative enterprise in Germany that the old generation of writers had, as it were, killed off the younger generations who should have succeeded them. Schirrmacher's polemic against the veterans of the 1960s and the dearth of literary innovation is in part legitimate. But this is mixed up with a more suspect analysis of the deformations of literature in the service of the 'Gründungsmythos' of German identity. He argues that literature in the 1960s was primarily concerned with demonstrating to a cowed people how to 'mourn', and thus providing them with social and national legitimation. Literature functioned 'als gleichsam sozialpsychologisches Organ, als Instrument und Spiegel des kollektiven Bewußtseins, als Produk-tionsstelle der westdeutschen Identität'. In this it is close, he continues, to literature of the former GDR: 'Nicht nur die Literatur der DDR sollte eine Gesellschaft legitimieren und ihr neue Traditionen zuweisen; auch die Literatur der Bundesrepublik empfand diesen Auftrag und führte ihn gewissenhaft aus.'

As he begins to examine this 'identity', Schirrmacher's theoretical provenance becomes clear. For it is with a subterranean reference to Baudrillard's postmodern critique of identity that he continues: 'Die Literatur und mit ihr das kulturelle Milieu simulieren ein Ich, das es längst nicht mehr gibt und an dem sie doch verzweifelt festhalten.' The concern with 'simulating' the illusion of a stable and autonomous identity (one, he implies, which is anyway impossible) is the cause of the aesthetic conservatism of post-war literature. Its unhealthy preoccupation with the past has produced a dinosaur in aesthetic terms, which now he proclaims dead. The direction he supposes literature must take after his definitively proclaimed 'Nullpunkt' is less clearly formulated. Later, in his reviews of the poetry of the young writers, it becomes clearer. But at this point he contents himself with invoking isolated character-istics: 'das radikale Ich' and a 'pure' aesthetic, one which is uncoupled from social identities and political responsibility. These he justifies with a passing reference to Paul Celan and Thomas Bernhard, authors, he claims, of a literature which 'steht nur für sich selbst', a literature which cannot be pressed into service for the legitimation of a society or a state.[34]

In *Die Zeit* Ulrich Greiner responded to this aspect of Schirrmacher's argument with a provocative and pointed formula-tion: 'die deutsche Gesinnungsästhetik'.[35] This he uses to attack the 'marriage of convenience' (p. 209), as he calls it, between morality and literature in forty-five years of German literary history, and to inveigh against the 'burden' of extra-literary themes, such as class consciousness, failures of justice and the dangers of ecological collapse, which have distorted the true vocation of literature (p. 213). At the root of his argument is a challenge to no less than two hundred years of German literary history: the ideal humanist marriage of the good, the true and the beautiful at the heart of Weimar Classicism.

At this point in the debate, a number of critics have noted (with varying degrees of paranoia) the influence of Karl Heinz Bohrer. Although he has a broader historical approach and deals less with the differences between individual generations than the other critics, he is worth mentioning here, partly because of his influence, and partly because his comments crystallize neatly the major implications of the debate so far.[36] The anniversary issue of his journal *Merkur* carried an essay by him celebrating 'die Ästhetik am Ausgang ihrer Unmündigkeit'.[37] It is impossible to do justice to Bohrer's detailed historical critique here. Two important points can be made, however.

Bohrer condemns the post-war moral policing of the literary tradition, which, he argues, has brought the German people to the point of repressing entire categories of the cultural tradition, because these categories supposedly helped prepare the consciousness that made Fascism possible. Instead he pleads for a 'normalization' of the aesthetic as the only worthy criterion for judging a work of art.

With this claim it is clear why some critics have seen in the 'Literaturstreit' a reprise of the 'Historikerstreit' of four years earlier. Both debates were concerned in essence with the end of the German 'Sonderweg' and what might be called a 'normalization' of post-war German consciousness (in historical and literary terms respectively). Both sprang in part at least from precisely the same questions of frozen German history, collective guilt, and the left-wing liberal consensus which had appeared to dominate the exploration of the German conscience.[38]

In insisting on the uniqueness of the aesthetic phenomenon Bohrer upholds for literature, in an enlightened and secularized society, only the exigencies of the sublime, rather than those of moral and social responsibility. In this he bases his arguments on Adorno's *Ästhetische Theorie* (ironically, for Adorno insisted on literature's inevitable social character) and claims the ultimate autonomy and amorality of the aesthetic imagination.[39]

But it would be wrong to allow the ostensible concern with the past, which has dominated the terms of the debate, to obscure the extent to which it is also a debate about the future. The very phrase 'was bleibt' (especially recalling the sense in the Hölderlin text) is Janus-faced. In arguing about what does and should remain, critics are clearly also setting about defining the new German literature to come.[40] In some senses the 'Was bleibt' affair marked the *end* of a literary and critical paradigm—a kind of 'Nullpunkt'. But out of it had also emerged the demand for a *new* literature, a literature uncoupled from social identity and responsibility, one that had cut itself loose from morality, and had extricated itself from the demands of politics, history and remembrance.

'Was bleibt': The Generation

It was precisely in these terms that the work of the young writers was celebrated after the fall of the Wall. In an attempt to rescue something from the wreck of the socialist project, and at the same time to set a mark for the literature of the new Germany, it is perhaps unsurprising that critics turned their attention to 'die neuen Nix-Künstler' from the GDR.[41] These were writers who, by virtue of their very youth, could not be implicated in what had by now become a grotesque rerun of the immediate post-war recriminations. Moreover, they had apparently refused to 'collaborate' with the structures of power in the GDR and had instead fallen victim to its repressive measures: 'die Generation, die nicht zu sich kommen durfte', the 'lost generation' of the GDR.[42] In 1991, for example, in his article analysing what would remain after the collapse of the utopian ideal, Wolfgang Emmerich immediately pointed towards the experimental texts of the 'jungen Wilden', as he called them:

Und ein Drittes wird bleiben: Der Impuls einer *alternativen literarischen Kultur* der Jungen, nach 1950 Geborenen, die nicht erst mühsam aus dem 'Eisenwagen' des Resozismus auszusteigen brauchten, weil sie in ihn gar nicht eingestiegen waren. Diesen Autoren sind vielleicht noch nicht die ganz großen Werke gelungen, aber ihr bleibendes Verdienst ist der Ausbruch aus der Selbstfesselung an das System, von der sich die Autoren der vorhergehenden Generationen nie ganz hatten freimachen können.[43]

Important here is the idea that the young writers have founded an autonomous literary realm, outside the ideological structures of complicity or dissidence. Emmerich emphasizes here and elsewhere that this was an achievement peculiar to the young writers.[44] Even those older writers like Biermann, he argues, who were steadfastly in 'opposition', were enmeshed in the very structures and discourses that they were trying to oppose. It is interesting to note that Biermann himself recognizes this and expresses the dilemma in a 'familial' vocabulary similar to Wolf's:

Wir waren verfitzt, verfilzt und hochverschwägert mit unseren Widersachern. [. . .] Die tiefen familiären Kontakte zu unseren Todfeinden brachen nie ab, weil wir den Widerspruch in uns selber trugen. [. . .] Und so redeten wir miteinander, ja wir waren Familie, bis aufs Blut zerstritten, aber Familie. Und aller Haß, das Gift, die Galle kamen aus dieser familiären Verklammerung mit unseren Unterdrückern.[45]

Writers like Biermann and Wolf were all, to borrow Uwe Kolbe's phrase, 'Stichwortlieferanten der Herrschenden'.[46] The same point was made in an influential article of 1990 by the young GDR poet Kurt Drawert. He took up the notion of an older generation preoccupied with the historical legacy of Fascism, and all its attendant moral baggage, but claimed that developments in the GDR had seen a literature which moved beyond the antagonistic deadlock of ideological dictates, on the one hand, and a morally entrenched opposition on the other. In its experiments in form and language, its espousal of play and irony, he claimed, the work of the young writers was a reaction against monological thought and against the words and meanings colonized by a corrupt ideological monopoly. In short: this was a literature which had resisted the pressure to reproduce the structures of power aesthetically, and had insisted on its autonomy, a 'third discourse' from the GDR.[47] It took little time for this 'unofficial', 'third', '*other* literature of the GDR'[48] to be swiftly re-packaged as *the* literature of the new Germany, and raised up in *Die Zeit* as 'Dichterhoffnung der Nation'.[49]

This claim demanded a very particular reading of the young writers and their work. And, in accordance with this, critics set about their documentation and analysis of the young writers' work with very specific assumptions.

The first of these is the notion of generations. The rhetoric of generations had accompanied the discussions from the very beginning. It is inscribed in Wolf's text itself; it governed that part of the 'Literaturstreit' which addressed the deficiencies of German 'Trauerarbeit' and the links between the deformations of Fascism and Stalinism; it is clearly part of Schirrmacher's agenda; and, to point forward for a moment, it has characterized the clashes in the recent *Stasi* debates.[50] However, although it was as a 'generation' that these writers were salvaged over into the new Germany, critics almost always confined their attention to what Adolf Endler called 'die eigentlichen ihrer Generation',[51] that is: the writers associated with 'Prenzlauer Berg'.

The second problem was the new theoretical understanding which came to dominate the reception of the work. Not only had the 'Was bleibt' affair called into question the distortions of literature in the service of politics and morality ('Gesinnungs-ästhetik'), but also in the service of large-scale models of 'meaning' ('Sinngebung').[52] The spectacular fall of the writer as moral instance also threatened the central pillars of Enlightenment thinking, which had long guaranteed our understanding of literature and literary history. This collapse was signalled in the calls for new critical paradigms and for a rewriting of GDR literary history. The process of revision which had been set in motion coincided with (and was quickened by) the widespread German discussion about the theories of the postmodern.[53] In East and West one of the most contentious facets of young GDR writing had long been its association with post-structuralist theory. Some of the writers themselves, and a large number of (mainly young) critics (notably those featured in Gerhard Wolf's *Die andere Sprache*, but also, for example, increasingly, Emmerich) have also argued from positions heavily footnoted to Foucault, Lacan, Lyotard, and Baudrillard. I have argued that a more differentiated understanding of the reception of these writers is necessary. Nevertheless, in the climate after 1989, it is little surprise that the 'neudeutsche Literaturkritik', which came (well versed in the litany) to set about the writing of the new literary history, allowed virtually no reading of the work of the young writers other than as the realization of a radical postmodern aesthetic.

Despite the prevailing tone of the critics, however, there is another strand to the reception of the young writers, which can also be identified. The attacks levelled at Wolf were largely to do with dismantling her status as a moral instance. That is also true of the re-evaluation of her texts, which, before 1989, had been to a great extent judged as moral projections of their author. It is exactly this subordination of the aesthetic to the moral that Bohrer and the others condemn in their critique. However, it is noticeable that the celebration of the young writers after 1989 was also governed by a form of the same moral and political judgement. Wolf's *Was bleibt* was dependent on creating a myth of the young writers as heroes. But Wolf's claims for them—their autonomy, their relationship with power, their freedom from the past, and their status as heroes—were amplified and exaggerated by writers, critics, and press in East and West after the fall of the Wall. Exactly because the young writers appeared to have resisted the intervention of the

State in their lives and in their work, in a way that the older writers had not, they could now be represented as the morally unimpeachable hope for the new German literature.[54] A Western readership, 'auf das Dissidentische scharf',[55] could now claim them, and even their apparently apolitical autonomy, as a kind of heroic opposition to the State. The question of politics in Prenzlauer Berg in particular is complex and does allow for a reading of the aesthetic developed there as political. However, the reception of the young writers after 1989 was often fuelled by that very same kind of uncritical 'dissident bonus', which the discussions of the 'Literaturstreit' had exposed and undermined.[56] This attitude has become most evident (ironically) now that some of the leading figures from the underground scene have been implicated in the operations of the GDR *Staatssicherheit* and can no longer be celebrated as heroes of cultural autonomy—or of dissidence. For it is as a generation of fallen 'heroes' that the young writers have been discredited.[57]

7

'Rechnungen': Literature and *Staatssicherheit*

es sind die selben worte, mit denen wir lügen[1]

IF the function of the 'Literaturstreit' of 1990 was to define what remained of the literature of the GDR, the revelations from the archives of the *Staatssicherheit*[2] make the question more pertinent than ever.[3] The crisis signalled by the 'Literaturstreit', however important it may have been in exposing our entrenched assumptions about literature, integrity, and literary criticism, did little to elucidate the work of the young writers. After the fall of the Wall the literature from 'Prenzlauer Berg' was celebrated for its postmodern aloofness, for refusing to accept the deadlock of collaboration and dissidence, and for founding an autonomous realm beyond official discourses. Critics seized upon the vast store of previously suppressed work from those young writers who had been unable to publish in official journals or publishing houses, particularly as many of the older GDR writers seemed to have very little which had been 'written for the drawer'.[4] But critics were also fascinated by the fates of the young writers, for their symbolic worth. This created a paradox. On the one hand, much stress was laid on the way the work had emancipated itself from the 'deformations' of ideological responsibility and could not be pressed into service for the legitimation of political or moral identities. On the other hand, the lives of the young writers functioned as guarantors of the moral conscience of the nation. In the wake of the revelations about the role of the *Staatssicherheit* in the underground scene, the tables were turned. Prenzlauer Berg has been discredited in three very different ways. Those many 'wahrheits- und heldensüchtige Leser', who, even if they did not appreciate the poetry of the underground scene had nevertheless understood its simple existence as a gesture of defiance to the State, felt that they had been betrayed.[5] Equally, those very critics who, during the 'Literaturstreit', had condemned the political 'corruption' of literature in post-war Germany and argued instead for a new aesthetic avant-garde without allegiances, were quick to abandon Prenzlauer Berg as a whole, rather than revise their cherished ideals of amorality and aesthetic autonomy. Finally, those who anyway despised the underground scene and its supposedly postmodern aesthetic as worthless saw their chance to discredit two unwanted phenomena with one stone—Postmodernism and Prenzlauer Berg.

In 1990 the call for a rewriting of German literary history came first from the *feuilleton* sections of the conservative German press and then, in a more measured tone, from critics and academics. The revelations, which have initiated what one critic at least has dubbed 'der neue Literaturstreit', accelerated the discussions and raised the stakes. After the initial bombast of *Der Spiegel*: 'Die Geschichte der DDR-Literatur muß neu geschrieben werden. Bisherigen Interpretationen fehlte der exakte Stasi-Kontext',[6] it is now noticeable that the same demands have been endorsed, and often exceeded, by writers themselves. Lutz Rathenow, one of the most vociferous of the young writers to publish extracts from his files and to pursue publicly those who, he claims, have betrayed him, wrote in an article entitled 'Die Vergangenheit beginnt gerade erst': 'Die Geschichte der Literatur in der DDR muß wohl ohnehin erst geschrieben werden, besonders die der 70er und 80er Jahre. Der Einfluß der Staatssicherheit als spezieller Teil des Machtapparatus dürfte ein eigenes Kapitel ergeben'.[7] To return for a moment to the question which sparked off the first literary debate, it is impossible to say what will ultimately remain of GDR literature as a whole, or indeed of its most celebrated representatives.[8] However, since Wolf Biermann's first public accusations against Sascha Anderson in October 1991, it is already possible to trace the early process of revision which the notion of 'Prenzlauer Berg' has undergone. For example, Kurt Drawert's open letter to Rainer Schedlinski, 'Es gibt keine Entschuldigung', is a difficult and painful piece of writing. The broken syntax and the clumsy repetitions make it read very much like a personal reckoning with a former friend, which has somehow strayed into a newspaper by mistake. However, the letter also indicates how much more is at stake: 'Mit Dir wird etwas in die Tiefe gezogen, die unser gemeinsames trauriges Herkunftsland für nicht wenige Lebensläufe bereitgehalten hat, was durch keine nachgereichte Erklärung wieder hergestellt werden kann: die Glaubwürdigkeit der Literatur—gerade auch die unserer

Generation.'[9] In referring to his generation, Drawert is first and foremost thinking of Prenzlauer Berg. However, as with the controversies surrounding Wolf's text, this literary scandal goes far beyond complaints about individual writers or individual texts. The charges against Anderson and Schedlinski have now influenced the perception of 'Prenzlauer Berg', of a generation of writers, of a body of literature, and ultimately of an aesthetic.

It is important to acknowledge, right at the outset, that even (or especially) as an outsider, writing about Prenzlauer Berg and the *Stasi* is not easy. The sheer weight of information which has come to light since the first accusations were made exerts its own morbid fascination.[10] The attempt to make sense of what happened there is inevitably mixed up with strong feelings of disappointment and personal betrayal, along with nostalgia for what the place might have represented. It is unnerving to be writing as a literary critic about the wrecks of people's lives. As Péter Nádas points out in his essay 'Armer Sascha Anderson': 'Solange ich nicht in einer solchen Situation gewesen bin, kann ich nicht sagen, wer ich bin.'[11] Most disturbing, however, is the question of finding an 'Ethik des Sprechens' (Michael Braun) and recognizing the ease with which the vocabulary of literary analysis can also become the vocabulary of moral judgement.[12] Here I want to concentrate on three very specific questions: what remains of the writers, the texts, and the notion of Prenzlauer Berg. However, in order to ask these questions it is necessary to sketch briefly the larger context to which they belong.

Literature and Staatssicherheit: The Debate

The central question, as it concerns this book, is an almost embarrassingly fundamental one: the relationship between literature, aesthetics, and morality.[13] It is noticeable that this question has often been only marginal to the broader *Stasi* debate. Perhaps this is inevitable, given that it is only a small (if emotive part) of a much more extensive reckoning: 'Ein ganzes Volk geht in die Archive, um seiner Vergangenheit zu begegnen.'[14] In some senses, the intellectuals are in the spotlight of a debate which must be carried out on behalf of those many thousands of people whose silent resistance meant that they will never be recognized as 'victims'. As Kurt Drawert puts it:

Der zweite Maßstab wird von denen gesetzt, die sich verweigerten, die auf Karrieren verzichtet und Vereinnahmungen entsagt haben. In der Dunkelheit der Fabriken und in den Finsternissen der Geschichte sind sie zu finden, für die es niemals eine Gelegenheit gab, das Licht der Öffentlichkeit zu sehen, in dem die Intellektuellen sich selbstgerecht spiegeln.[15]

In a broader sense, however, it is clear that this 'neudeutsche Literaturstreit' (the continuities with the 'Literaturstreit' of 1990 are striking and inevitable) is an 'old trauma' in only a slightly new guise.[16] It is at once a debate about the legacy of the socialist experiment and a reckoning with 'die doppelte Vergangenheit' of Germany, in particular the 'old trauma' of German Fascism.[17] The actions of Anderson, Schedlinski, and others have been drawn into the centre of a hailstorm of rhetoric, in which the words 'Stalinism' and 'Fascism' have at times become almost interchangeable.[18] Once again reference has been made to the German inability to mourn and to the truncated post-war denazification programmes. This dimension of the debate has been underscored by the register of language which has become the norm. A rhetoric which implies a comparison between the horrors of the Nazi past and revelations of the *Staatssicherheit* is commonplace but nevertheless disturbing. For example, Jürgen Fuchs notoriously described the imminent confrontation with the truth of secret files as an 'Auschwitz in den Seelen'.[19] Even if not specifically linked with Fascism, a rhetoric of extremes has filtered into almost all aspects of the debate. Discussions have become hinged on emotive terms like 'Verrat'. Detlef Opitz's thoughtful and much more cautious analysis of the resonances of the word concludes: 'Verrat—wie stolz das klingt. Man setzt sich der Lächerlichkeit aus will man erklären, was Verrat ist. Man kann ihn nur illustrieren.' He then goes on to catalogue the grim detail of the 'betrayals' of his friend Rainer Schedlinski (Inoffizielle Mitarbeiter (IM) 'Gerhard').[20] At other times discussions have polarized around moral absolutes such as 'Opfer' and 'Täter': words used at times as if there could be no ground between them.[21] The absurdity of such co-ordinates is highlighted when one remembers that the much trumpeted 'Fakten in den Akten' have also been exposed as unreliable.[22]

Some of the difficulties in this respect are practical. Many of the files of reports written by those 'Inoffizielle Mitarbeiter' who were most valued, were destroyed by the 'Ministerium für Staatssicherheit' (MfS) before the Normannenstraße central archives in

Berlin were stormed on 15 Jan. 1990.[23] This means that in some cases, although researchers have the card with the code name ('Deckname') and registration number of an IM in the 'Hauptabteilung XX' (the literary division active in Prenzlauer Berg), they must wait until they can match this with the same number and real name ('Klarname') of the individual from their own observation file (that is, their file as the object of an 'Operative Personenkontrolle' (OPK), or a more active 'Operativer Vorgang' (OV)), before establishing the IM's identity beyond doubt.[24] In other cases, the crucial 'Verpflichtungserklärung' (with a signature acknowledging the status of IM) is missing, although it has been argued again that in certain cases, the MfS would waive such an obligation, in favour of an oral undertaking. In the absence of such evidence researchers are forced to piece together information from the reports of those 'victims' who have been granted permission to read their files.[25] This complex procedure means that accusations have been made (notably by Biermann and Fuchs from their platform in the *Spiegel*), before concrete evidence has been available to the general public. Files have also appeared on the black market or been leaked to newspapers and television.[26] Both of these facts have led to an extensive debate about the role of the media in the 'outing' of agents and the dissemination of information, which has at times threatened to obscure the more important issues.[27] The practical confusion is compounded by evidence that certain people were exploited as 'Inoffizielle Mitarbeiter' apparently without their knowledge, and that the information in other files was deliberately forged by members of the *Staatssicherheit*, in order to destabilize the underground or, more mundanely, in order to produce impressive statistics for their superiors.[28] All these essentially non-literary discussions converge on one essential question. They are attempts to illuminate what. the *Stasi* was. The rhetoric has swung between extravagant demonization—'das monströse Hirn eines Staates, dessen innerste Motivation Angst, Bosheit, und ungeheure Anmaßung waren' (Schirrmacher) and a naïve (or cynical?) playing-down of the facts—'verkalkte Greise, die man betrügen, belügen, ausnutzen, hintergehen und verlachen konnte; eine debile Macht' (Schedlinski).[29] For the time being, the only thing which has emerged beyond all doubt is the catalogue of fears, compromises, ambitions, and deceits of very ordinary people.

If these broad questions—the comparison with the Fascist past, the inflated rhetoric, the influence of the media, the unreliable status of the *Stasi* files, and the phenomenon of the MfS itself—are all questions which have determined the course of the debate, there are also a number of issues which are more directly related to Prenzlauer Berg in particular.

The key issue which has dominated the discussion about Prenzlauer Berg is the attempt to elucidate the extent and the exact nature of *Stasi* activity in the underground scene. It appears that Prenzlauer Berg, this niche of autonomy, was the area most densely infiltrated by the *Stasi* in the whole of the GDR.[30] Lutz Rathenow has discovered that there were fifty-three IMs informing on him, for example. In part, such a density of surveillance is in step with Prenzlauer Berg's status as a centre of political opposition. But it also has serious implications for an understanding of the activities which went on there.

The very individual histories of Anderson and Schedlinski have generated very different responses. Anderson at first denied the charges against him as absurd, before beginning a slow process of partial admissions, obfuscations, and apparent losses of memory, until documentation was produced in the media which demonstrated that he had knowingly informed on his friends for at least fifteen years, including the three years (after 1986) in the West.[31] Since then, he has remained obstinate that he was not an informer and yet, paradoxically, he has also admitted his 'guilt', and accepted that he told the *Stasi* everything he knew. As Gabriele Dietze points out, the lack of an adequate response is important; Anderson has become a 'blank screen' onto which others have projected their own explanations and condemnations, as part of the struggle for the power to define a new literary canon. She concludes: 'Wer jetzt Geschichte schreibt, der bleibt. Den anderen droht historische Verurteilung oder das Vergessen.'[32] During the controversy about Anderson, Schedlinski remained silent about his own involvement with the *Stasi*, until he was exposed early in 1992. At this point he almost immediately gave interviews and wrote a long factual account for the *Frankfurter Allgemeine Zeitung*, in which he detailed the history of his dealings with the *Stasi* (a history of blackmail, psychological pressure, the relentless undermining of his will and his identity, nervous breakdown, and attempts at suicide). 'Dem Druck, immer mehr sagen zu sollen', he concludes, 'hielt ich nicht stand.'[33] In June of the same year *Neue deutsche Literatur* published a rather more controversial essay in which, in quite a different tone, he analysed the relationship between the underground scene and the *Staatssicherheit* in theoretical terms. His essay 'Die Unzuständigkeit der Macht' is a fascinating examination of the function of the *Staatssicherheit*, and its relation to the underground. It moves between very sophisticated and persuasive analysis and crude attempts at moral self-justification, and provoked an immediate and heated response.[34]

Since it is has been made clear that both writers did deliver oral and written reports to the *Stasi*, the debate has moved around two central issues. A number of writers from Prenzlauer Berg and beyond have insisted that there is an absolute division between those who talked to the *Stasi* and those who did not, and that crossing this line was, to borrow a phrase from Uwe Kolbe, 'the only taboo'.[35] Others have taken rather different approaches; some claiming that everybody 'talked' to the *Stasi* and that the line between 'talking' and 'informing' is difficult to define in retrospect. This hinges for many on the question of whether the reports were delivered in secret, that is, whether the relationship was 'konspirativ' or not. Schedlinski and Gabriele Eckart have, for example, both claimed that they told several of their companions about their links with the *Staatssicherheit* in order to make themselves useless to it. Others again have argued that the *Stasi* was not an issue in Prenzlauer Berg, and that everything was openly discussed by everyone. Klaus Michael, for example, explains: 'Die Stasi ist kein Thema mehr. Das heißt, es war uns egal, ob die Stasi davon wußte, was wir machen. Im Gegenteil. Sie sollte sogar Kenntnis davon erhalten. Man gab Namen und Adressen bekannt. Damit hörte das vorsichtige Lavieren und Taktieren in der Halblegalität auf.' This appears less than convincing when one considers how many of the writers (including Michael) used pseudonyms. More convincing is Detlef Opitz's explanation that the 'Stasi ist kein Thema mehr' response was a way of banishing fear and creating a psychological space to write.[36] Schedlinski, responding to an open letter from Uwe Kolbe, takes the most extreme position by arguing that it was an act of 'Zivilcourage' to deal with the *Stasi* (and to try to influence it) rather than simply remaining silent and thereby acquiescing in the regime.[37] On the other hand the volume *MachtSpiele* offers a number of accounts by writers who managed to dissociate themselves from the *Stasi*, after having at first 'talked', or 'co-operated' (especially when they were very young), which go to illuminate the extreme difficulties in arriving at definitions, let alone moral judgements in this matter.[38] Heartening in quite a different way is the discovery, made by Wolf Biermann in his files, that a number of those IMs who were set onto him and his friends in order to infiltrate their activities became 'dienstuntauglich' to the *Staatssicherheit* because of their growing association with Biermann and his ideas.[39]

Arising from this, already complex, issue of whether and how writers might have 'talked' to the *Stasi* is a second question: that is, whether the reports were in any way harmful to those who featured in them. On the one hand Anderson and Schedlinski have both argued that their reports gave them a chance to influence the authorities (especially in aesthetic, theoretical, and political matters), but also to filter the information or even lie, thereby in effect benefiting their fellow writers.[40] Unlikely as a such a possibility might seem, the extracts from reports written by IMB 'David Menzer' (Sascha Anderson) offer detailed character sketches of the poets in Prenzlauer Berg, along with speculation about their political attitudes, but also a large amount of literary analysis and a certain number of recommendations concerning the cultural politics of the GDR, especially in relation to Prenzlauer Berg.[41]

Schedlinski and others have also claimed that the information which they passed on was harmless because it was all generally available; they gave away no secrets.[42] The response to these claims has been threefold. The claim that any of the 'Inoffizielle Mitarbeiter' were able to influence the *Stasi* has generally been thought absurd.[43] Several writers have responded further that any information given to the *Stasi* was harmful, in that it confirmed and legitimized what might have been otherwise suspicion, and often became important if the MfS had initiated a process of 'Bearbeitung' and 'Zersetzung' against any individual.[44] Finally, in recent extracts published from his files, Lutz Rathenow appears to have demonstrated that Schedlinski did pass on information that, in itself, could have resulted in a prison sentence for the subject of his report.[45] These are the general discussions against the background of which more specifically literary issues have come into focus.

Literature and Staatssicherheit: Prenzlauer Berg

The mounting scale of the attacks against the writers associated with Prenzlauer Berg reveals that, as with the 'Literaturstreit' of 1990, it is not simply individual writers who are being targeted, but rather a whole aesthetic understanding. Wolf Biermann's Büchner Prize speech confronting 'der unbegabte Schwätzer Sascha Arschloch . . . der Stasispitzel, der immer noch cool den Musensohn spielt', was primarily aimed at discrediting Anderson as an individual.[46] However, Anderson's status as 'guru' of the alternative scene in the GDR also provoked writers and critics to disqualify the GDR underground as a whole as '*Stasi*-sponsored'. In his later Mörike Prize speech Biermann makes this explicit:

Jetzt erfahren wir, daß die bunte Kulturszene am Prenzlauer Berg ein blühender Schrebergarten der Stasi war. Jedes Radieschen numeriert an seinem Platz. Spätdadaistische Gartenzwerge mit Bleistift und Pinsel. Die angestrengt unpolitische Pose am Prenzelberg war eine Flucht vor der Wirklichkeit, sie war eine Stasizüchtigung aus den Gewächshäusern der Hauptabteilungen HA-XX/9 und HA-XX/7.[47]

It was not only Biermann. Frank Schirrmacher, one of the former champions of Prenzlauer Berg, and the critic who, during the 'Literaturstreit', had led the campaign against bringing moral criteria to bear in the judgement of literature, took up—although in language less colourful than Biermann's—the same line of argument.

Wenn Anderson für die Stasi gearbeitet hat, dann wäre nicht nur [. . .] der Lyriker und Liedermacher sondern auch der Mythos Prenzlauer Berg erledigt. All die subversiven Mappen, Texte und Aktionen, die von dort ausgehend, die ganze DDR erfaßten, wären dann kaum etwas anderes als eine perfide Simulation der Stasi.[48]

More significant, perhaps, than attacks like these from outside are the comments from young writers formerly associated with Prenzlauer Berg. They take up two particular issues. Firstly there is the amount of money which Schedlinski and Anderson put into the production of magazines, and which now appears to have come directly or indirectly from the MfS. Schedlinski, for example, justifies the fact that he passed on copies of *ariadnefabrik*, the magazine he edited, to the secret police by the fact that he asked inflated sums for them. The suggestions of financial dependency also implicate the publishing house Galrev, of which Anderson and Schedlinski were two of the founders.[49] Secondly there is Anderson's much talked about status as 'Integrationsfigur' in Prenzlauer Berg—his central role as editor and manager.[50] In some senses Anderson's simple presence within Prenzlauer Berg served, as it were, to 'earth' the fear and sense of menace which otherwise might have paralysed the young writers. Whatever his personal motivation, his activities did create a climate where literature could be written. His presence might even have served as a kind of protection.[51] For Leonhard Lorek, however, his status as 'selbstinstallierte Epizentrum' of Prenzlauer Berg casts doubt on the way the whole scene functioned. The same point is taken up by Faktor: 'Die Fäden führten alle zu ihm, und bei ihm verschwanden sie dann irgendwo in dem Keller, den keiner kannte. Auch die noch echten Impulse und Regungen mußten in dem Loch verschwinden. [. . .] Anderson hat durch sein "integratives Dasein" andere, authentischere Beziehungen verhindert.' Biermann pushes it to a more extreme conclusion: 'Sascha Anderson war die coole Cultfigur der letzten Jahre, er war der Geist dieses geistlosen Künstlervölkchens. Er bestimmte auch selbstherrlich, wer und was in den achtziger Jahren "illegal" gedruckt wurde: Also die Staatssicherheit bestimmte in dieser Farce.'[52] Both of these matters, despite the eloquent anger of Frank-Wolf Matthies or the bluntness of Rathenow, strike at the very heart of Prenzlauer Berg.[53] According to Foucault, on whose writings many of the Prenzlauer Berg poets drew, the primary strategies of power do not lie in repression, exclusion, or secrecy, but rather in processes of integration and transformation. Prenzlauer Berg had sought to situate itself outside the integrative strategies of power, and had based its very identity on the autonomy which that appeared to generate. The fact that this autonomy was an illusion, that the 'freedom' of Prenzlauer Berg was in the gift of the very structures of power it had sought to ignore, undermines the notion of Prenzlauer Berg, more than any individual act of betrayal.[54] In asking 'what remains' of 'Prenzlauer Berg', Peter Böthig, one of the most important editors and critics of the underground scene, concedes the bankruptcy of its self-understanding. 'Was bleibt—? Das Konzept politischer und ästhetischer Autonomie ist durch die Arbeit der IM genauso lächerlich zusammengebrochen wie die ganze Realität des Landes. [. . .] Autonomes Handeln, das man sich von der Stasi genehmigen ließ, ist absurd. Handlungsfreiheiten mit der Denunziation anderer zu erkaufen bleibt Verrat.' With the revelation that, although it set up camp outside the structures and discourses of the State, it was nevertheless not beyond their reach, the 'myth' of Prenzlauer Berg has been destroyed. Böthig continues: 'Die kulturelle Identität des "Prenzlauer Bergs" ist eingestürzt. Der Verrat von Freunden betrifft die Substanz des Selbstverständnisses. Der konkrete Kontext "Prenzlauer Berg" wird verblassen, die Metapher ist entleert.'[55]

And yet beyond the individual writers and beyond the myth, there is the literature. 'Was kann eine Literatur wert sein, die unter dem Judaszeichen, unter der repressiven Toleranz der Staatssicherheit aufs Papier kam?' asks Thomas Assheuer in reviewing Anderson's poetry.[56] The moral weighting of the question is indicative of the attitude which has dominated such enquiries among the critics. Significant, however, is the fact that the same slant is evident in the response of young writers formerly associated with Prenzlauer Berg. Jan Faktor explicitly refuses to draw a distinction between the morality and the work of writers like Anderson, but also dismisses much of the work which was produced under his influence.[57] Kurt Drawert goes furthest, dismissing the literature of Prenzlauer Berg as a whole: 'Jetzt kann nur noch Skepsis die Texte begleiten, deren Bestes Ende die Ignoranz wäre.'[58] Later I will return to possibilities and difficulties inherent in reading such texts. At this stage it is important to notice that the target of such as Biermann is larger than one strain of literary production.

The sight of Biermann and Anderson locked in their grim battle is like nothing so much as Goya's picture of the giant duellers, knee-deep in the landscape, from the series 'Pinturas Negras'.[59] What is on one level a personal duel has also been variously interpreted as a gargantuan struggle between charismatic heroes jealous of each other's status,[60] between 'Emigranten und Dagebliebenen', and ultimately between generations.[61] All of these interpretations are of some value; the generation aspect is one I will come back to. However, they are only fragments of something far larger and far more important. Beyond accusing an individual poet of deception, Biermann's real aim is to boycott an entire poetic project. This is made clear in the open letter to Lew Kopelew published in January 1992, where Biermann's scorn for Papenfuß-Gorek's work ('gequirlter Stumpfsinn') is then extended to become an (entirely undifferentiated) attack on Dada, the Concrete poetry of the 1950s, and the language-centred work of the 1980s GDR: 'Originale Prenzlpoesie—seichte Wortspielereien, an denen gemessen der Blödl-Jandl in Wien ein Poet mit tiefsinnigem Witz ist.'[62] Biermann's contention is that experimental or Concrete poetry was consciously introduced by the *Stasi* and encouraged by Anderson, to undermine the more threatening and potentially subversive poetry of other writers—writers presumably more like himself. The 'angestrengt unpolitische Pose' which he attributes to Prenzlauer Berg was, he claims, a 'Flucht vor der Wirklichkeit', engineered by strategists of the MfS.[63] In both the Büchner and Mörike Prize speeches, he pleads for a realist aesthetic anchored in morality and political opposition. Biermann wears his allegiances on his sleeve, and this makes moving reading, but it should not blind us to the fact that a short-circuit has been made from a loss of individual integrity to loss of artistic integrity, and hence to the wholesale disqualification of a 'corrupt' aesthetic. At least two of the young writers have recognized the real target of Biermann's aim. Detlef Opitz discerns the contours of 'eine alte Fehde' between a literature based on '*bekennenden* Widerspruch' and one affiliated to an avant-garde aesthetic. He concludes: 'Es wird heute nicht über die u. a. hier am Prenzlauer Berg entstandene Literatur befunden, ich sagte es bereits, es gilt als fesch, sie gar nicht erst zu lesen. Jetzt wird Rache genommen an einer Haltung des *anderen* Widerstands.'[64] Durs Grünbein accuses Biermann of out and out aesthetic 'Stalinism' and the creation of a new kind of literary censorship.[65] Despite Grünbein's deliberately provocative rhetoric, the core of his thinking is right. If the 'Literaturstreit' had apparently dismissed the post-war legacy of a morally and politically inspired literature, the new German 'Literaturstreit', was about reversing the process and discrediting the notion of an aesthetic avant-garde.[66] This kind of attitude has, of course, a considerable history. No ruling ideology, whether on the right or the left, has shown itself comfortable with a literature of reflexivity, ironic play, and self-conscious formal experimentation. In Germany the Fascists decried it as 'entartet' and the Stalinists as 'dekadent'. This time it was to be discredited on the back of the young generation and their supposedly post-structuralist theory.

Biermann scathingly sweeps aside post-structuralism as an

attempt 'moralentsäuerte Ware auf dem Markt der Ideen zu bringen'.[67] Elsewhere he emotionally denounces the 'postmoderne Gemütlichkeit' of the contemporary climate, for what he sees as a cynical reversal of values: 'Die Opfer haben sich endgültig als die wahren Täter entpuppt. Sie vergiften die postmoderne Gemütlichkeit mit einer rigoristischen Moral der Wahrhaftigkeit, mediengeil vermarkten sie ihre eingebildeten Stasi-Wunden. Verdrehte Welt. Im Kopf halte ich es grad noch aus, aber nicht im Herzen.' His line of attack is taken up by other critics.[68] Their hostility undoubtedly springs, in part at least, from Anderson's clumsily expressed claims in the earliest interviews after Biermann's accusations that he and the other writers in Prenzlauer Berg understood the *Stasi* as an 'eine Informationsstruktur [. . .] unter vielen Strukturen'. The arguments here are confused, but broadly he sets his own suspicion of systems—'das System der politischen Lyrik', 'das System der Opposition'—against Biermann's 'einfache von ihm Dialektik genannte Dogmatik'.[69] However, on the other side of the debate, Biermann's condemnation of the influence of post-structuralism in Prenzlauer Berg is hardly a considered critique ('Die Musenjünglinge von Prenzelberg haben offenbar eine Neigung zum Strukturalismus oder sogar zum Post-Strukturalismus. Kritzekratze-Fritzefratze'), and it is noticeable that other critics also content themselves with sneering at 'French theory' or, equally vaguely, 'the postmodern'. Where they concur is in dismissing the young writers as fashion victims, and following Biermann's line that the introduction of these theoretical texts was a calculated strategy on the part of the *Staatssicherheit*: 'Denn lieber ein Umsturz des Signifikanten als ein Umsturz des Systems.'[70] It is left to Frank Schirrmacher to offer a (fairly scrappy) reading of Baudrillard's theories of simulation (a theme he also took up in the 'Was bleibt' affair, see Chapter 6 above), but this time to claim that the same 'radical indifference' which Baudrillard saw as the only form of resistance, and which Schirrmacher himself had previously promoted, was encouraged and sponsored by the MfS.[71] None of the critics engage in a serious critique of the theories or the poetry.

There *is* an important issue at stake here; it is simply that the critics do not address it. A *Stasi* report exists, for example, of a meeting with IM 'Gerhard' (Schedlinski) in which he is explicitly encouraged to concentrate on his theoretical texts and to bring them to the attention of the underground scene.[72] This would support the suspicion that post-stucturalist theories were welcolmed by the *Staatssicherheit* for the reason that they distracted the writers from more threatening issues like, for example, political opposition. Explored in detail, it would cast an interesting practical light on the political interpretations of the postmodern. Instead, however, in attacking Prenzlauer Berg in far cruder terms, critics seize their chance to discredit what they see as a cynical erasure of truth, meaning, and identity, a wholesale abandonment of critique or allegiance and a philistine anti-historicism. They see postmodernism as the aesthetic and moral precondition for the 'duplicity' of Anderson and Schedlinski: the betrayal of their poetry and their friends—to borrow a phrase from Lutz Rathenow, 'die Ästhetik des Verrats'.[73]

Literature and Staatssicherheit: The Texts

There is a general consensus among the writers that both the theory and some of the poetry at least will survive these attacks.[74] One cannot save Sascha Anderson with his poetry, but equally, one cannot destroy the poetry with the details of his biography.[75] If the poetry is still to be read, however, it must be read in a new light.

The calls for a rewriting of literary history which went out from the *Spiegel* signalled that previous interpretations of literary works were lacking 'der exakte Stasi-Kontext' (see above). Attempts to fill in that missing *Stasi* context have led to several texts by writers associated with Prenzlauer Berg being subjected to rereading with the aid of what Hajo Steinert has called 'die dreidimensionale Stasi-Lesebrille'.[76] Indeed there is quite an industry in such rereadings. There are two main types. Jan Faktor, for example, points to Anderson's first collection, *Jeder Satellit hat einen Killersatelliten* (1982), and claims, especially in the title poem, to discover explicit confessional revelations about Anderson's 'bedrohliche Stellung zwischen den Fronten'.[77] Dorothea von Törne produces a list of such references to a schizophrenic existence from the same collection.[78] Other critics have begun 'decoding' texts by authors not accused of *Stasi* complicity as explicit references to the presence of the *Stasi* in the underground.[79] There are problems with this. As Steinert also points out, although the 'Stasi-Lesebrille' might be 'ein verführerisches Werkzeug', it can also lead to a narrowness of focus, and even blindness. Many of the writers included references to the atmosphere of distrust created by the *Stasi* in their supposedly unpolitical work—that does not make them IMs—and the motif of a schizophrenic existence has, in Germany and elsewhere, a long literary history. As Steinert concludes: 'literarische Texte sind kein juristisches Beweismaterial'.[80] Schedlinski goes further in dismissing such 'Gesinnungsschnüffelei':

Auch die Exegese von Gedichten auf der Suche nach Stasi-Hinweisen ähnelt jenem Interpretationswahn der Stasi fatal, von dem aus sich schließlich alles erklärt: die einen verstehen nun, warum ich so unpolitische Gedichte schrieb, und die anderen, warum gerade ich so kritische Gedichte in der DDR habe veröffentlichen dürfen.[81]

It is clear that deciphering the texts merely in biographical terms entails reinstalling a very blunt equation of 'real' life and text. It constitutes a reversal of the kind of criticism that saw in Prenzlauer Berg only a sophisticated and indifferent abandonment of referentiality. All the same, it is an unhappy antidote. This is made especially clear by an analysis of a text by Rainer Schedlinski.[82]

I

nun ist das bleiben ein standhafter weg
so weit wie es geht, der wohlstand steigt
und niemand verbraucht seine zeit, das ist die
moral
der geschichte, das ständige denkmal
mit dem charme des verrats DU
KANNST ES WIE DER DACHDECKER HALTEN
mit doppeltem boden
DIE EINZIGEN DIE NICHT BEI DER STASI SIND
SIND DIE DIE DABEI SIND,
das ministerium ohne fenster hat untergänge
stock für stock in die erde gepflanzt, das land
unterkellert
in nächster nähe der geräuschlosen sender
welch unerforschlicher nachrichtendienst

At first glance this appears to be a poem relating to the *Staatssicherheit*, one which might easily find itself a candidate for a reductive biographical interpretation. Schedlinski even appears to makes it easy for the reader by highlighting two significant statements in upper-case, at the central axis of the poem. Graphically caught between them, however, and this should make the reader wary, is an enclosed space, the void between the layers of the roof and of meaning, which becomes the theme of the text. I do not want to interpret the poem here, rather simply to show how this strategy can be understood as paradigmatic of the poetic enterprise. The text works by setting an architectural vocabulary ('dach', 'boden' 'fenster', 'untergänge', 'stock', 'keller') alongside snatches of familiar phrases ('der wohlstand steigt', 'die moral der geschichte', and, perhaps implied, 'der boden der tatsachen'). Yet all these are linguistically 'undermined', and exploited to reveal another layer of reference. Almost the entire text plays on ambiguities. For example 'die moral der geschichte' is linked with 'das ständige denkmal', but so is 'der charme des verrats'. These notions do not merely contradict each other ('moral', 'verrat'), but each of them is ambiguous ('doppelbödig') in itself. History is, after all, amoral, and betrayal is not charming. Equally, the apparent solidity of the repeated 'stand' in the first four lines ('ständig', 'standhaft', 'wohlstand'), is soon dissolved into ambiguously intercut levels of physical and moral meaning. They also, one critic points out, stand in the way of the possible movement of the text: 'weg', 'geht', 'zeit'. Such play can be infectious, as demonstrated by Charitas Jenny-Ebeling: 'Das "ständige denkmal" ist, als ein stumm Dastehendes, nicht ge-ständig, aber es kann, als imperatives "denk mal", auf ein einständiges Denken verweisen und damit etwas in Bewegung setzen.'[83] Even if one does not follow the suggestion of reading the 'monument' also as an 'injunction', the grammar does allow for a reading of the upper-case lines not simply as an example of 'Verrat', but rather of a distilled 'Rat': 'DU | KANNST ES WIE DER DACHDECKER HALTEN'. It would then follow that the only ones who are not with the *Stasi* are those, 'DIE DABEI SIND', that is, those who are engaged playing exactly this double game. It would be wrong to understand this as advice to seek refuge in a kind of schizophrenic double morality. Rather, it should also be understood as an explicit poetic strategy. The poet is to undermine the structures of reference, which emanate from the unseen 'sender' below the 'boden der tatsachen'. Moreover, this is a text which enacts its own poetic, it is a rhetorical *tour de force*. The poet exploits that gap between layers of meaning, between the signifier and signified, in order to survive.[84]

Bearing in mind the notion of the 'doppelter boden' of the poetic text, I would like to illustrate just what the difficulties of rereading the poetry of Prenzlauer Berg are, by examining Sascha Anderson's text 'RECHNUNGEN' in greater detail.[85]

RECHNUNGEN

im anfang war die stunde auf dem stuhl, dem leeren,
rotberührten beins. der rest war sitzen, darauf
hoffen, glaube an und fraß, in mich hinein. was ich auch
    berührte
schlief ein. als der stuhl zerbrach, und sie mich fragten,
ob ich den finger auf den knoten legen könnte, als sie
mich zum zeugen in eigner sache aufriefen, alle dinge
schliefen. löwenthal, du weißt, was ich mein'.
KONZENTRIERE DICH AUF DIE FARBEN. DAS IST IHR WUNDER
PUNKT. NICHT, WAS IHRE ZEICHNUNGEN SAGEN, IHRE FARBEN
    VERRATEN DEN GRUND.

Michael Braun in an analysis of this text understands 'die stunde auf dem stuhl' as a direct reference to Anderson's experiences of interrogation.[86] In this text, it is claimed, Anderson has, to borrow a phrase, 'den Versen den Verrat verraten'.[87] Compared with much of Anderson's work, this appears to be an unusually frank text, in that the pointers to outside experience have not been obliterated and the lyric subject has not been totally dissolved in the piece. The questioning and the need to bear witness 'in eigner sache' in the face of a threatening and anonymous 'sie' brings the lyric subject (in Braun's reading 'das Double des Autors') to a crisis point. Here he recalls or calls to 'löwenthal', identified elsewhere in the collection as Anderson's artist friend Nicolaus Löwenthal, who died in 1979. The subject then appears to escape into another realm, a realm governed by the dictates of art, not real moral dilemmas, which Braun links on another level with the attitude of Prenzlauer Berg as a whole: 'Zusammen mit seinem poetischen Double taucht der Autor ab in eine hermetische Kunstsphäre, wo nur wenige Eingeweihte Zutritt erhalten.'

The biographical reading is seductive. The text appears in a cycle dedicated to Löwenthal and shot through with the vocabulary of imprisonment: 'zeuge', 'verraten', 'aufrufen', 'glühbirnen', 'zelle'. The notes in the collection make reference to the 'knast lukkau' and also point to the 'story' of Löwenthal in one of the much more open and brutal prose pieces dealing with prison experiences in one of Anderson's earlier collections.[88] In addition, Anderson's own descriptions of his interrogations, given in interviews after the allegations made by Biermann, bear a striking resemblance in tone.[89]

A reading which sought to move away from the restrictions of biography might start by recognizing how much more elusive this text can be than might appear on such a first reading. The poem offers gestures towards a syntax of organization, but in fact thwarts a sustained reading. The piece is marked by dissolution—especially a dissolution of self. In other texts in the cycle this is done more mechanically, referring to the subject as 'ein lächerliches denkmal. cut up', and consistently highlighting the artificiality of the construction—'requisitenwerkstatt', 'bühne', 'problem der übersetzung'.[90] In this poem the 'ich' is largely edged out; in the first lines it is 'die stunde', 'der rest', 'darauf hoffen' 'glaube an' or 'fraß' which form a precarious and grammatically ambivalent subject. However, the subject is also eroded by structures of repeated negation. The introduction of the chair is countered by the revelation that it is in fact empty, the link with a substantial world ('was ich auch berührte' (l. 3), the only active mode of a verb associated with the lyric subject, is severed, and the call to bear witness implicitly fails. The extraordinary losing touch with the world through touching is emphasized by prominent repetition and inverted word order (ll. 6–7). However, the significance of the 'rotberührten beins' linking the important concept of colour and touching is difficult. Does it belong to a subject or the chair? Red has clear resonances, and Anderson uses colours precisely in his texts, yet the link with the colour of the last lines remains unclear. One is reminded of earlier texts of Anderson's which are governed by a similar sense of bleak loss, and a very similar use of colour.[91]

> wenn ich über grün spreche
> stirbt grün
> wenn ich über rot spreche
> stirbt die leuchtschrift über
> dem bahnhof
> wenn ich über mich spreche
> stirbst du
> doppelpunkt

In this text the surroundings are dissolved and the notion of self is (albeit ambiguously) destroyed. Similarly, in the poem 'RECHNUNGEN', everywhere one would seek to find a centre to the text ('die stunde auf dem stuhl', 'knoten', 'eigne sache', 'FARBEN', 'GRUND') it is denied, betrayed, emptied, broken, or eliminated in sleep.[92]

These ambivalences are compounded by the foregrounding of the linguistic ambivalence of the piece. This is done on two levels. Firstly, a mood of grammatical indeterminacy is created. The dislocating punctuation of 'fraß, in mich hinein' sets up a tension between readings which would understand 'fraß' as a verb or as a noun. The 'darauf' at the line-break also throws up parallel possibilities of reading. Particular problems are posed by the upper-case lines. It is unclear both who is speaking and to whom, and how the 'IHR' relates to the various possible subjects. The implication of strength is pivoted on the line-break and revealed as hurt (called up by the thwarted rhyme 'WUND/GRUND'), vulnerability or weakness: 'DAS IST IHR WUNDER | PUNKT'. Even the last line could be interpreted as 'to give away the cause', 'to betray the foundation', or, linking with the other references to art, 'to reveal the background'. But the text also urges a shift to another level of meaning. There is an opposition between the implied 'wort' ('im anfang war das . . .' l. 1) and the implied 'schweigen' ('der rest war . . .' l. 2). This links with 'zeichnungen', 'farben', 'sagen', 'zeugen', and the implied 'deuten' of l. 6 to set up a matrix of problems of translation (a key term in the cycle) and representation. The very form of the last lines suggests that they provide a key of some sort: a code which would enable the subject to come to terms with what has gone before ('Rechnungen') and, on another level, one which would enable the reader to make 'sense' of the text. In fact they serve to highlight the fallibility of meaning—and of a system of language which has become divorced from the 'dinge' and the experiences it is meant to signify.[93] One might ultimately see the text as a dialogue between a political and poetological exploration of the phrase 'Farbe bekennen'.

Nevertheless, it is important to hold such readings in tandem. An explanation of the text in terms only of a decentred subject and a crisis of representation would ignore the emotive political vocabulary and specific history of the text, which is an important strand of the collection as a whole. Equally, a reading which insisted on a naïve confessional subject would not do justice to the tortured self-reflexivity of the piece.[94] Such a reading would imply that the apparent hermeticism of the text was simply a form of cover, and that once the key is given (i.e. the knowledge of Anderson's activities as an IM) the text could be read as a straightforward account of experience. A number of critics have taken up this point and used it to discredit the metaphorical intensity in Anderson's and Schedlinski's texts. What was once praised as a linguistic strategy to take the texts beyond the comprehension of the authorities is now interpreted as cowardice or duplicity.[95] Read like this, the metaphors and ambiguities of the text function as a kind of 'Sklavensprache', cynically employed to conceal the 'truth' of the text—not this time from the authorities, but from the poet's fellow writers.[96] Both these lines of argument fail to do justice to the texts as literature. Schedlinski explicitly counters what he calls a fundamental misunderstanding of the nature of Prenzlauer Berg:

nämlich die Annahme, daß die neuere Literatur des Prenzlauer Bergs nur deshalb irgendwie verschlüsselt geschrieben sei, um von der Macht unbemerkt ihre konträre Gesinnung durchzuschmuggeln. Ich habe immer versucht zu erklären, daß jene und auch meine Texte mitnichten chiffriert sind, sondern genau das sagen wollen, was da geschrieben steht, und wer anders in ihnen liest, betreibt nichts anders als die Stasi, und setzt, von welcher Position aus auch immer, deren Gesinnungsschnüffelei fort.[97]

Although Schedlinski's argument is unconvincing in the specific context in which it is adduced (as a reponse to an attack by Kurt Drawert based on earlier theoretical assertions by Schedlinski himself), he touches on a central point. Such a reading is reductive. It ignores the sustained tension between the various levels of meaning in the texts. The only productive way to deal with texts like these is to recognize the different levels of meaning, and to negotiate out of the space (that 'doppelter Boden') between them.

Much emphasis has been placed on the fact that, however one might choose to read the poetic texts of the underground scene, they must now be set alongside that 'other' literature of Prenzlauer Berg: the hundreds of kilometres of files in the *Stasi* archives. Frank Schirrmacher concludes with an almost breathtaking boldness: 'Auch die subversive Literatur war eine Literatur der

Staatssicherheit—so wie die einhundert Kilometer Akten in Berlin.'[98] On the surface this might appear exaggerated; and yet, there is a very serious argument here. Is it possible to take seriously the literary fine-tuning of Anderson's poetry, when one reads the cynical, scrupulous prose he wrote for the *Staatssicherheit?* Biermann raises the same question in more colourful form, refusing to allow postmodern indifference or a schizophrenic self-awareness serve 'als Persilschein für ordinäre Stasiagenten, die morgens inhaltsleere, muffige Gedachte [*sic*] in verdeckter Sklavensprache husten, die sie Gedichte nennen, und die dann abends prallgefüllte realsozialistische Spitzelberichte in kader-welscher Prosa verfassen'.[99] The published extracts of his reports are marked by that precise and chilling rhetoric of *Stasi* officialdom, which Biermann has compared to a 'Sprache des Vierten Reichs'.[100] In Wolfgang Hilbig's 1993 novel '*Ich*', a poet 'W.' is simultaneously the IM 'C.', and is operating on a 'Vorgang "Reader" ', in a context which is clearly identifiable as Prenzlauer Berg. The schizophrenia of the underground poet in the pay of the *Stasi* is fixed in a striking image of his desk: 'Auf der einen Seite der Platte, links, lagen die wild bekritzelten Zettel mit den Entwürfen für seine Gedichte, auf der anderen Seite, sauber geschichtet, das Schreibmaschinenpapier, das für seine Berichte bestimmt war.'[101] Hilbig's novel offers no opportunity of separating the selves or their 'work'. On arriving in the freedom of the West, the writer discovers that now—perhaps more than ever—'er' is simultaneously and inextricably inscribed within 'ich'. Perhaps the notion of such a separation is only something which one can contemplate from the outside. Hilbig certainly appears to indicate that schizophrenia is endemic to identity in a postmodern world. The painter A. R. Penck, whom the *Stasi* wanted to discredit with the help of his friend Anderson, has suggested that the figure of Anderson, 'Sascha als Untergrundheld und Stasi-Spitzel in einer Person', should enter the history books as a synonym for the irreconcilable schizophrenia of life in the GDR.[102] This is not the same thing as the very specific and pseudo-medical exploration of *ad personam* schizophrenia ('unkontrollierte Schizophrenie', Christine Cosentino calls it), which a number of critics have begun to practise.[103] At its most extreme this becomes crude pscychology for which literature simply supplies the occasion. Instead one could argue that the texts (poetic and otherwise) of Anderson and Schedlinski are unique historical documents. Inscribed within them, and between them, is the ambiguity of an entire existence. One could go further and argue that these texts make explicit the schizophrenia at the heart of, but so often suppressed by, forty years of GDR literature. As documents they represent, if anything perhaps, an 'authentic' legacy of the GDR.

Conclusion: 'es wird wieder landkarten geben'[1]

I STARTED working on the poetry of these young writers because I thought it was something quite new and important on the German literary scene. Only a few years on, the status of that poetry and our ways of reading it have fundamentally altered. This body of work has had to face the test of history more quickly than almost any other. The context of which it was a product and a reflection has disappeared almost as fast as the street names and sentry-boxes. It is hardly surprising, then, that some of the poetry, which depended entirely on that context, has been overtaken and stranded by history. Some of it seems unconvincing, or simply dated. Part of the interest of the work was, after all, its experimental nature. One had the feeling that one was witnessing work in progress. The writers were determined to explode boundaries at all costs, to challenge taboos and dominant aesthetic understandings. Looking back now, at least some of the texts seem to exhaust themselves in that gesture for its own sake. This does not mean that this category of the work is unimportant, simply that its primary interest is now as much historical as aesthetic. Other texts, on the other hand, have withstood even that most brutal of historical scene changes: 'STASI-LICHT HARTE WÄHRUNG EUROPACK'.[2] It is possible to recognize in these texts the beginnings of the poetic programmes which will now dominate the literary scene in the new Germany. However, if the status of the texts has shifted, so too has our perception of the writers themselves. Until the mid-1980s very few of them had been heard of outside the literary circles of Berlin; now they are at the centre of one of the most pressing literary debates since 1945. Already we read and judge with very different perceptions. If the *Stasi* debate has served to clarify anything, it is the extent to which any judgement of the poetry up until 1989 was coloured by its political context, perhaps more than many critics would have been prepared to admit. The opportunity that the complete change of historical and literary context has given us for reflection on our own motives and criteria for literary judgement will be decisive in the rewriting of German literary history. The place that these young writers and their work will occupy in future histories will depend on the honesty and thoroughness of that reappraisal.

In 1979 a new generation of authors was officially acknowledged in the GDR. Today they must be recognized as unique: the first, and last, generation to have been 'born into' the established socialist state. In 1980, writing the epilogue for the collection which was to become so closely identified with the young generation, Uwe Kolbe's *Hineingeboren*, Franz Fühmann explained how much he envied the 'homogeneity' of the young writers' experience. Compared with the disparate and traumatic histories of his own contemporaries, he claimed, the lives of the young writers would be uniform and secure. For they were the first generation to be raised from the start within the new order, the first generation whose successes, disappointments, and aspirations would be entirely those of the socialist state.[3] Fühmann, of course, was speaking primarily, if not exclusively, about those authors who could be published and acknowledged officially in the GDR. The subsequent emergence of the huge body of literature which had been forced out of the public sphere, and which documents often very different experiences and develops often very different ways of dealing with them, has initiated a widespread reappraisal of the understanding of that literary generation. By 1985, on the other hand, some Western commentators were already claiming that the definitive characteristic of many of the same writers was their radical difference, their heterogeneity. 'Das Gemeinsame liegt in der je persönlichen Abwehr von kollektiver Vereinnahmung ... So paradox es auch klingen mag: An der Stelle der Gemeinsamkeit der Gruppe ist die Gemeinsamkeit von "Einzelgängern" oder "Vereinzelten" getreten.'[4] But in this respect too, one should be cautious. Despite enormous differences in the poetic and political aspirations of individuals involved, it now seems that comparisons can be made and that broader patterns within the work can begin to emerge. It is these which I have also attempted to indicate here.

After the fall of the Wall the perceptions of the young writers themselves as well as the outside perception of them and their literature underwent significant changes. Exposed to the atomized and market-controlled literary environment of the West, they were forced to come to terms with their past, but also to negotiate a new political and literary identity.[5]

In some ways, much of their work in the new Germany has

continued and developed the same themes, forms, and strategies as it pursued in the days of the former GDR. These have, however, been quickened by the acute need to reflect and work through the events of 1989. Striking, for example, is the topos of 'unhousedness'. This finds expression most positively in the many travel poems which have appeared in recent collections by the young writers. But set against this is the darker topos of an existential dispossession: 'ich bin die frau aus einem land | das es nicht mehr gibt | und gehe durch länder | die es für mich nie gab' (Stötzer-Kachold), 'ich habe mein Land verloren' (Kolbe), 'Und heimatlos sind wir doch alle' (Drawert).[6] This finds powerful expression in one of the key poems of the *Wendezeit*, Volker Braun's 'Nachruf', which mourns a lost past, lost identity, and lost ideals: 'Was ich niemals besaß, wird mir entrissen. | Was ich nicht lebte, werd ich ewig missen'. The ambivalence of the losses and gains of 1989 are made plain in a large number of the poems of the young writers. Annett Gröschner's 'Verlust und Gewinn' is characteristic in this respect, and reads almost like a response to Braun.[7]

> Was mir nicht gehörte
> wird mir genommen im Namen
> Deutschland ist gründlich
> am Grund der Bodensatz Toter
> stinkt nicht flüstert kaum noch
> GERMANIA eine Erfindung der Männer
> ist wieder
> keine Frau nur ein Held
> Kein Wort mir von Heimat
> es war mir
> ein heimeliges Gefängnis
> ohne Licht zur billigen Miete
> ein zu enger Schuh
> und nun ist da nichts mehr
> außer den Wänden
> gegen die ich jetzt treten darf

It is noticeable that, as in the Braun poem, many of the writers turn to Hölderlin as a reference point in this loss.[8] The bewildering acceleration of time during the events of 1989, which turned the so-called *Wendezeit* into a kind of 'Zeitwende', finds its way into the texts as a collapse of any form of comprehensible linear historical narrative. Instead the images of the self, of the events of 1989, and of the German reality which succeeded them are appropriated and displaced into a simulated reality of the television or video screen.

DIE ERDE IST EINE SCHEIBE: Erfahrung der Zweidimensionalität. Die Mauer war auch nur eine vertikale Ebene, genau wie die Mattscheibe des TV, die Leinwand im Kino, die Seiten der Bücher. So sind Welt-Bilder entstanden, Vorstellungen, die keinen Raum haben. Auf glatten Flächen, nicht einmal Blindenschrift.
Wer soll das BEGREIFEN.[9]

In two collections since the fall of the Wall Durs Grünbein has offered acute visions of the self as an instance generated at the intersection of 'Niemands Land Stimmen'. The implications are clearly also political, as in the long text, 'In Tunneln der U-Bahn'.[10]

> Vielleicht war diese Stille nichts
> > als die Halbwertzeit
> > > einzelner Wörter
> > In mir,
> > und wer war ich:
> > > ein genehmigtes Ich,
> > Blinder Fleck oder bloßer Silbenrest...(-ich),
> > zersplittert und wiedervereinigt

This is perhaps not so extraordinary a topos in Grünbein's work, since a very similar perception of reality marked his work even before 1989. However, it is interesting to note a similar development in texts by Steffen Mensching, for example. In 'Simulis, simulis', or 'La vie ou la vite' published in 1992, he presents snatches of reality which are suspended in the flashbacks and simultaneities of a synthetic medium.[11]

> Der Penner am Kuhdamm tanzt mit *Madonna*
> Vor zwanzig Fernsehapparaten,
>
> Epochenschrott säumt die *Allee*
> *Der Kosmonauten. Welcome*
>
> *To the machines* im Radio. Schnellste Gegenwart
> Der Weltgeschichte. Ein *Pin-up-girl*
>
> mit ausrasierten Achselhöhlen, blond
> Und geschmacksneutral wie ein Drei-Minuten-Menü
>
> Aus der Mikrowelle. Sternschnuppen
> Über dem *Nürnberger Todesdreieck.*

Zerbeulte Leitplanken. Tempo 130. Richtung
Atlantik. In der Radarfalle
Im Zykloton. Im Schnellkochtopf,
time is money, honey, totsein können wir
Noch lange genug...

Mensching here quite clearly casts a critical eye over the materialism
of the West, in which all becomes a commodity. Others of the
poets have also polemicized in their work against the values of
the new German reality, to borrow Kerstin Hensel's words:
'Großtäuschland voran'. In a poem dedicated to Volker Braun, and
taking up a number of quotations from his own past texts, she
expresses bitter disillusionment:

Noch rot hinter den Ohrn und aufgefressen!
Die Kluft im Nischel; Freisein oder Fressen.
Es rollt sich aus in was wir nimmer wollten.
Die Räder stehn. Es strampeln die Revolten.
Denn hier ist keine Heimat—Jeder treibt
Und festgeflochten in das Lenkrad Zeit
Dem Ziele zu das sich verramelt, so
kriecht unser Troß dem Nichtigen entgegen

The final lines offer a touching gesture of solidarity with the older
poet: 'Komm, laufen wir, als ob uns nichts mehr hält. | *Denn jede
Straße führt ans End der Welt*'.[12] But elsewhere it is an almost
unalleviated picture of degradation, commodification, and a
bulimic sense of glut which is presented. In a series of scornful and
explicitly political texts by Bert Papenfuß-Gorek, a lyric subject is
seen trying to locate a place for itself in the sexist commodified
excesses of the 'soziale marktmonarchie', but ends up alienated and
unsure: 'hier will ich ja bleiben: aber wo', or later, 'fortschreiten
möchte man | & zwar möglichst fort'.[13] In a series of texts written
since 1989 Papenfuß-Gorek takes apart the rhetoric of the old and
the new German reality and undermines the institutions which lie
behind them:[14]

die diktatur der mißverständnisse,   mischverhältnisse, die
durchdrücken
das feenreich der wortgewalt   im vorfeld einer wahnsinnigen
sinngebung
wort für wort wühlte ich mich durch,   nagte buchstäblich am
monopole

These examples of the way young writers have begun to deal with the new reality of which they are a part is matched by a reassessment of the role of literature and of the poet in their work. In the new Germany both the experience of the poets and the language in which it can move is radically different from that which they were used to. The audience too, bombarded by the verbiage of the market, is not attuned in the same way to the finely wrought mechanisms of a poetry developed under censorship. More important, the status of the poetry as language has changed. Without the 'Klandestinität' which, in a sense, all critical poetry suffered and enjoyed in the GDR, its purchase on reality is very different.[15]

In his 'Rede über Lyrik und Gesellschaft' Adorno identified the poetic voice as one articulating different concerns from the dominant, ideologically determined discourse: 'Kunstwerke jedoch haben ihre Größe einzig darin, daß sie sprechen lassen, was die Ideologie verbirgt.'[16] Writers in the GDR had long understood poetry as a voice of 'opposition'—as an arena in which they could articulate political and personal aspirations which would otherwise have remained unvoiced in the highly regulated public sphere.[17] Volker Braun gave voice to this understanding in his essay 'Rimbaud. Ein Psalm der Aktualität', where he spoke of poetry as an antidote to the 'Betriebsblindheit der Ideologie', whose essential 'contra-diction' existed in both its project and its structure. He summed it up perhaps most cogently: 'Poesie ist eine Gegensprache'.[18] Rainer Schedlinski warned very early on, in terms which echo Braun's, that it would be exactly this form of 'speaking against' which would disappear in the new German state. 'Verschwinden wird mithin [. . .] jene notorisch verweigernde Literatur, jene Sprache *gegen* die öffentliche Sprache, denn wo alles öffentlich ist, kann man sich dieser öffentlichen Gewalt schwerlich entziehen.' In the West, he claimed, the particular voice of the GDR poet would not survive without compromise. It would simply be re-institutionalized, swallowed in the throng of pluralism.[19] However, although the understanding of the identity and function of literature has inevitably changed for the young writers from the former GDR, the possibilities of poetry to reject the dominant ideology, to become what Enzensberger has called 'Antiware schlechthin' must surely remain.[20] Shortly after the fall of the Wall Bert Papenfuß-Gorek made that shift of perspective and language the subject of texts like 'dichter zerfallen' or 'die zuheit der vergangenkunft', in which he claimed:[21]

> aus des widerstands geborgenheit
> der ich so lang verlegen war
> muss ich mich schön schreiben

It is interesting to note that his very recent texts have not been written in the peculiar and personal orthography which he had developed for himself in the GDR.

From the perspective of the present, there is almost no trace left of the national identity, the political and geographical boundaries and the historical understanding which were to have forged the secure and homogeneous existence which Fühmann so envied in the young writers' lives and their work. The young writers live dispersed in the new Germany and beyond. Some have successfully made the move to the big Western publishing houses, the new German Schriftstellerverband, and the talk-show circuit. Many more are scratching out a living with journalism and looking for somewhere they can afford to live. Others again have become the political and moral 'untouchables' of the new German conscience. All of them are engaged in a very individual search for meaning in their past and in their present. And yet, paradoxically, at a point when it is perhaps most difficult to speak meaningfully of these writers as a group, it is again as a 'generation' that they are in danger of being written out of literary history altogether.

The revelations of the *Stasi* files have destroyed more than the reputation of individual writers. In the eyes of many, when Sascha Anderson fell he not only took Prenzlauer Berg, but the credibility of a whole literary generation with him. In fact, there were many good reasons why the myth of 'Prenzlauer Berg' and those associated with it should have been deconstructed. Jan Faktor, along with other 'insiders', Kurt Drawert and Adolf Endler, had criticized the complacent 'provincialism' of the underground scene and the attendant mediocrity of much that had been produced there, long before the *Stasi* accusations came to light. In a long essay of 1992 Jan Faktor noted that the reckoning with Prenzlauer Berg was, in some senses, a justified response to the uncritical exaggeration of its worth in the years preceding: 'Die Rache für die furchtbare Überheblichkeit [...] der Szene', 'die Rache für die Unreife und infantilen Trotz', and ultimately for 'viele leere

Worte'.[22] But the scale and intensity of that particular reckoning with the past has threatened to obscure, or even replace, a more cautious and differentiated review of the literature of the 1980s, and of the generation as a whole. Powered by the justified anger of the victims and the crusading outrage of the *Feuilletonisten*, the media-machine grinds on. Of course, there is no doubt that the complex relationship between the intellectual élite of the GDR and the mechanisms of state must be examined and debated openly, and that the need for that debate is perhaps nowhere more pressing than among the youngest generation of writers. However, the spectacle of 'IM-Outing' appears to have gained a momentum all its own, and, when the moral and legal stakes are so high, it is perhaps inevitable that questions of literary value are scarcely taken into account.

It is certain that the revelations from the *Stasi* files will fundamentally alter our understanding of the literary history of the GDR. At the moment it is too early to tell what place the youngest generation of writers will have in that history. Anyone writing now is inevitably too close to the material and too involved in that shift of perspective to see clearly. It might be, as some critics suggest, that the generation as a whole will become identified with the fate of 'Prenzlauer Berg' and will enter literary history marked with the stigma of *Stasi* involvement. A far more likely scenario is that individual writers will fall away, while others are taken up into the literary history of the new Germany, leaving the notion of a literary 'generation' open again to new definitions and interpretations. It is probably indicative of things to come that, very soon after unification, reviewers, literary journals and even large-scale anthologies of German poetry, began to draw out the connections between writers like Papenfuß-Gorek, Döring, Grünbein, Köhler, Hensel, and Jansen and those most interesting writers of the same age from West Germany, Austria, Switzerland, and German-speaking Romania: Peter Waterhouse, Brigitte Oleschinski, Gerd Bolaender, Albert Ostermeier, Thomas Kling, and Werner Söllner.[23] With this is mind, it is perhaps all the more necessary to ask how meaningful the notion of a literary generation has been in categorizing the work of the young GDR writers up until now. By the same token, the conclusions drawn now might shed light on the usefulness of the approach for identifying the work of young writers to come.

Certain things are clear, even after a fairly superficial survey of the young writers' lives and work. The notion of 'Generationser-fahrung', which has been questioned by a number of writers but most notably by Faktor and Hensel, is a category which should be approached with care. Even in a state like the GDR, where the extremes in life-styles which we are used to in the West were evened out to some degree, there is a great deal of difference between the experience of a poet who has published three collections with Aufbau, is supported by the Writers' Union, and has been allowed to read in the West (Kolbe), and one who has been unable to publish or perform officially in the GDR for over a decade (Papenfuß-Gorek). Equally, as a mother of four children and a trained psychiatric nurse, it is not surprising that Kathrin Schmidt has a different outlook from the writers at the centre of the punk, drug, and café culture at the heart of Prenzlauer Berg. As a number of critics have emphasized recently, the self-understanding of writers isolated in the provincial GDR was also very different from that of those in the thick of the publishing network in Berlin.[24]

The sense of a common identity amongst the young writers was in part created by external political pressure from the authorities. This created a common bond between many of the writers which Barbara Köhler has identified, in a resonant phrase, as a 'ein kleiner Plural der Vergewisserung'.[25] But for those who were excluded from the official publishing industry, it was especially important. The euphoria of finding a realm in which they could communicate freely generated a special dynamic, which led, in the early years at least, to a period of extraordinary productivity and experimenta-tion, as well as to a number of intense collaborative projects. However, that it was the appearance of solidarity and consensus which was necessary in order for the young writers to assert themselves against the authoritarian structures of state, rather than the reality, has been suggested recently by a number of the writers. In interview, Papenfuß-Gorek confirms the impression that, after a while, an appearance was all that remained, a 'synthetische Solidarität', as he calls it. Although based on a broadly oppositional consensus, it in fact served to repress power struggles among the writers which have since come to the fore.[26] He takes up the same theme in a recent poem.

die solidarität unter unseruneiner
ist die wohlan nie gewesen, aberaber
aus irgendgenau beuterischem beweggrunde
mußten wir waswohlwementgegen jahraus so tun
als seien wir durch & gesotten
solidarisch, & zwar soldatisch
genossen, jetzt, da dieser zwang
wegfällt, fällt auch der rest weg...[27]

But Papenfuß-Gorek and others make it clear that it was not simply personal power struggles or even political differences which were submerged in the common front. Anderson, for example, was thought of as unpolitical, Lutz Rathenow was associated with the *Bürgerbewegung*, and Papenfuß-Gorek understood himself at that time as an anarchist. There were also fundamental aesthetic differences. Papenfuß-Gorek even goes so far as to suggest that the vehemence of the *Stasi* debate amongst the young writers is in part due to the aesthetic disputes which could never take place. For him, Rathenow and others already belonged to the 'Hochkultur': they had Western publishers, and money, and a more conventional aesthetic.[28]

These differences—political, theoretical, geographical, and poetological—are clearly manifested in the work of the young writers. The readings of the treatment of the subject, history, and language in the young writers' work which I have offered above are intended to demonstrate those differences, as well as suggesting broader tendencies and possibilities for discussing the young writers' work. But if the differences between the writers manifest themselves so clearly on all these levels, what is to be gained by discussing them as a group, as a generation?

Recent criticism has tended to distinguish absolutely between writers like Böhme, Hensel, Mensching, Wenzel, Rathenow, Drawert, and Schmidt on the one hand, and those writers like Papenfuß-Gorek, Anderson, Schedlinski, Döring, and Faktor, on the other, who are more readily associated with the experimental impetus of 'Prenzlauer Berg'. Other writers again, particularly Jansen, Köhler, and Grünbein, have, from the beginning, been considered more as individuals (it is no doubt significant that they are amongst the youngest of the writers). Especially since 1989, it is the second group of writers, those who are at the centre of what has become known as Prenzlauer Berg, who have been understood almost exclusively as the representatives of the generation. In dissolving these divisions and reintegrating these distinct strands of this literature, or at least setting them side by side, to consider the sweep of the 'generation' once again, a number of new perspectives are opened up.

First, the picture of the generation as a whole is radically altered. Different emphases can be made and different distinctions drawn. The most important shift of perspective is probably the move away from the dominant idea of this generation as completely alienated, anti-utopian, anti-historical, and fundamentally unpolitical. This final point was in any case always a misapprehension even with regard to the Prenzlauer poets. However, there are also a number of more specific shifts of emphasis which suggest themselves when one looks at all the poets together. A fruitful line of analysis might be to compare the radical mixing of discourses of politics and love in Papenfuß-Gorek, Mensching, Köhler, and Schmidt, for example, something quite distinctive in the German poetry scene. Another might be to examine the presentation of the city in the work of the young writers generally. These writers have produced a efflorescence of 'poetry of the city', unseen in German literature since Expressionism, which is at once a continuation, and also a fascinating redefinition of traditional approaches (I have only been able to give a very brief introduction to this topos here). Finally, an analysis of the notable re-emergence of traditional forms, particularly the sonnet form, in the work of Kolbe, Schmidt, Hensel, Köhler, Döring, and Koziol, for example, might produce a new critical line on the relationship between language and identity in the young writers' work.

These examples also point towards a second but related shift of perspective. Since the late 1980s it has become the norm of criticism to concentrate almost exclusively on analysing facets of linguistic experiment in the young writers' work, and to explore these through the prism of post-structuralist theory. This is in part the result of the dominance of the Prenzlauer poets in recent surveys. However, it also stems from the pressure placed on GDR critics and academics to 'catch up' with the theoretical discourses of the West, and to take on Foucault, Baudrillard *et al.* (if only to secure themselves a future and a job). A third reason is simply that a new generation of critics is coming to prominence, critics in Germany and abroad who are contemporaries of the poets themselves. They have been schooled in the same theories, shared some of the same experiences, and have similar misgivings about those theoretical and political models which older writers and critics alike may doubt but are often reluctant to abandon completely. There have already been, for example, some very fine analyses of the relationship between the poetry of the young writers and the theories which have informed them—particularly by Peter Böthig, Klaus Michael, and Peter Geist. There is doubtless still a great deal to be done on this aspect of the work, as there is on the experimentation with language. However, this cannot be the only approach, not even to the poetry most readily associated with these experiments and theories. I have argued elsewhere that the importance of post-structuralist theory in Prenzlauer Berg has been exaggerated.[29] It is one of a number of different discourses which the young writers take up as material into their work, and it should not be invested with the significance of a single and universal key to their poetry. However, there is a further problem inherent in this approach to the writing. Suspicious of referentiality, and curiously embarrassed by emotion, a number of critics focus exclusively on footnoting the textual disarray in the work. There is a danger that this serves to neutralize what is most extraordinary in the best writing from the young generation: the struggle to create a language, fully self-conscious and yet adequate to express the precarious aspirations and disappointments of a very specific moment in history.

The third advantage of bringing the different writers together like this is, paradoxically perhaps, that one can recognize all the more clearly those writers who are truly original and important. The study of the whole generation is worthwhile for many reasons, which I explore in more detail below. However, there are only very few writers who go beyond the general concerns and techniques of their compatriots, and create genuinely new ways of seeing and saying. In the future, criticism will surely focus on these. I would like to mention four of them here. Papenfuß-Gorek is already considered something of a classic (he has many imitators), and he has inspired some of the keenest interest and the best critical analysis of any of the young writers. Durs Grünbein is one of the current darlings of the *Frankfurter Allgemeine Zeitung*, and has been described by Gerhard Wolf (paradoxically perhaps) as the Volker Braun of his generation.[30] Although he shares none of the idealism and energy of the early Braun, his fixing of a *Generationserfahrung* in poetry has brought him to the forefront of recent discussions. His *Schädelbasislektion* will surely become thought of as one of the most important collections since German unification. Steffen Mensching has devoted himself since unification to prose works, film, music, and particularly cabaret projects. There is a danger that his explicit political commitment and his cabaret work with Wenzel may leave him marginalized in the poetic scene of the new Germany (in the Gerhard Wolf interview mentioned above he is dismissed almost without comment as a 'Komödiant'). Barbara Köhler has published only one collection, *Deutsches Roulette*, and is in some ways the most traditional of the four, but for me she is the most convincing poetic talent of the generation. All of these writers have won important literary prizes since 1989, and all will undoubtedly merit critical attention in their own right.

However, more important than the obvious differences between the writers, and beyond those smaller groupings which can be drawn out under certain aspects of enquiry—love poetry, the city, the sonnet, etc.—there are, I believe, compelling reasons for continuing to understand these writers as a generation. A number of critics have tried to assess these, and it is worth surveying their conclusions briefly here.

One of the most common ways in which critics set about identifying this young generation of writers is to claim that they were the first generation who invested nothing in the utopian ideals of the socialist state. They were not, it is claimed, infected with what Uwe Kolbe called 'der *Fluch* der Hoffnung'.[31] As a general observation about the generation as a whole, however, this goes too far. It is clear from the writing of Barbara Köhler, Uwe Kolbe, Kerstin Hensel, Steffen Mensching, or Hans Brinkmann, for example, that they too were motivated by a utopian aspiration, which was also political in nature. Peter Geist puts it most strikingly, when he says of some of these writers: '[sie] haben in den fortschrittseuphorischen Jahren ihrer Kindheit noch genügend Utopiesplitter ins Auge eingepflanzt bekommen'.[32] That is seen by the mixture of nostalgia and bitterness with which they have left behind the aspirations of the old to confront the realities of the new.

ROT HAT VERLOREN. DIE BANK
Räumt ab. Jetzt setzt man
Auf Schwarz. Faites votre jeu.
Die Kugel rollt weiter.
Nichts gilt mehr, Genossen, *adieu.*

This poem by Mensching bears striking resemblances to the matrix of gambling vocabulary in Barbara Köhler's *Deutsches Roulette*, and both in turn echo the terms and sentiments of older writers such as Braun, for example.[33] The difference between these younger writers and some of their older compatriots, however, is that their hopes did not blind them to the reality of the GDR as it was. For them it was never a case of having their aspirations 'eaten away' at by reality; they lived from the beginning with the discrepancies.[34]

A second approach, which is related to the first but entails a significant shift of emphasis, is to identify the end of GDR literature with this generation of writers. This is a notion which has been under discussion for some time, in the form of the various 'convergence' theories which have been posited for the two German literatures. Laurel Cohen-Pfister has claimed, for example, that the end of GDR literature correlates, not to an arbitrary date made famous by the historical union of East and West, but rather to the subversive literary process set in motion by this generation of writers long before that. For her, they represent the essential shift between a 'socialist literature' and simply 'a literature within socialism'.[35] Such an understanding is reiterated in Keith Bullivant's 1994 text *The Future of German Literature*, where he also claims that the writing of the younger generation constitutes 'a separate category outside what can be called GDR literature, precisely because of its rejection of the fundamental ideology of the state'.[36] There are elements of truth in this assertion. As I pointed out when discussing the understanding of history in the young writers' work, there were indications very early on that the foundations upon which the historical identity of the GDR had been built were being eroded, or at least playfully undermined. And yet many of the young writers have also very clearly engaged with those traditions, often critically, sometimes ironically, but always working in order to generate meaning for the here and now. It would perhaps be more useful to move away from the conviction of a single state-sponsored literature of the GDR (along with its critical extension) and instead to understand the work of these writers as one of many contemporary and competing literatures of the GDR.

The importance of that sense of historical and political identity for some of the young writers has been expressed most forcefully now that it has all but disappeared. A 1991 poem by Hans-Eckardt Wenzel mourns the loss with dismal passivity:

UNLUST UND SCHWERMUT
Begreifen mich beim Lesen
Der Annoncen

Die Aufbrüche euphorischer Art
Im Glauben ans Wunder

Wie hilflos vollstreckt sich
Der Untergang, wie nebenbei

Ich weiß jetzt, wie es sein wird
Genauso wird es sein.

Elsewhere, in an essay he confronts the 'Untergang' more explicity:

Der Traum, aus der keine bisherige Klasse in der Geschichte wieder erwacht ist, der Traum von sich selbst oder von einer *historischen Mission*, der Traum, der sich an den Spiegelsplittern der Vergangenheit wiederzuer-kennen glaubte, mit denen Licht in die dunkle Zukunft reflektiert werden sollte—dieser Traum ist in Gefahr, in eine Agonie überzugehen, ein Delirium, das den Träumenden den Maschinen gleich entmündigt und ent-träumt.[37]

Wenzel's striking evocation of the individual's dispossession and impotence, as structures of history, identity, and meaning collapse all around, points to an unease which I would suggest is fundamental to an understanding of this generation of writers. Of course, Wenzel's essay is written partly in response to that extraordinary historical acceleration which swept away some very particular structures. On the other hand, however, a very similar sense of vulnerability and exposure in the face of collapsing structures has underpinned much of the young writers' work since the mid-1980s.[38]

One of the most powerful texts to have emerged from the history of GDR literature is Heiner Müller's *Hamletmaschine*. Müller's Hamlet figure, standing with the ruins of European civilization behind him, and the ruined fragments of European literary history buried within his speech, has become one of the central images to define an age.[39] For the young writers this image has a special significance. They are the generation who were born into that historical 'waste land'. They stand with the ruins of ideology, history, truth, and all the 'meta-narratives' of Enlightenment thinking behind them, while before them stretches the void of 'post-history'. This is the experience that distinguishes these young writers from their forebears, and marks their work at the most fundamental level. It is these writers who straddle a modernist apprehension of wholeness and a postmodern delight in disintegration. It is not simply that they have lived through the very particular collapse of a state, a political system, and a unique historical experiment. The scope of that collapse is greater. In his *Zaungäste*, for example, Reinhard Mohr describes a very similar fate for the same generation on the other side of the border:

Es ist das kontingente Merkmal dieser Generation, daß sie biographisch mit einem Bein in der Geschichte und mit einem anderen in einer vermeintlichen zukunftslosen Gegenwart steht, deren 'Hyperrealitäten' sämtliche Ursachen und Wirkungen chaotisch durcheinanderwirbeln. Mit dem historischen Einbruch des europäischen Realsozialismus im Jahre 1989 ist diese Konstellation nur noch deutlicher geworden: Weder gibt es ein Zurück zur progressiv-utopischen Geschichtsphilosophie, noch hat sich der postmoderne Diskurs vom 'Ende der Geschichte' als plausibel erwiesen.[40]

Naturally, one must be cautious about how far such broad cultural analyses can play a part when it comes to examining individual texts. They are clearly fashionable at the moment—as the publication of a number of texts defining the new generation in East and West has recently demonstrated.[41] I would argue that the arrival of these writers on the literary scene marked neither the end of socialist literature, as some critics claim, nor part of a new postmodern literature in Germany, as others have done. What is most interesting about the body of work as a whole is the tension between forces of disintegration—of self, of history, of language—and the very different attempts of very different individual poets to create structures of meaning for themselves, however temporary or fragile.

I pointed out earlier that it was perhaps still too early to be certain how this generation of young writers would be represented in the new literary histories of the GDR which are already being written. In Germany at least there are few hopeful signs. The revelations about the *Stasi* involvement of so many writers and artists have created a climate in which only very particular brands of literary history appear to be called for, or acceptable. When, in February 1993, the influential critic Ulrich Greiner called in *Die Zeit* for an end to the *Stasi* debate, he did not do so in order to check the unseemly scramble on the part of Western newspapers to discredit everything from the GDR that had once been respected. His motivation was rather a sense of frustration that so many people were still unwilling to concede that such a dismantling process was necessary.

Das Feuilleton hat Fragen gestellt. Die Befragten sahen darin einen Angriff. Sie parierten ihn mit der Verteidigung des Mythos. Über den Mythos aber läßt sich nicht diskutieren. Man kann ihn nur zur Kenntnis nehmen. Deshalb ist die Debatte über die Vergangenheit der DDR gescheitert. [. . .] Sie könnte nur dann halbwegs gelingen, wenn Übereinkunft herrschte über zwei Voraussetzungen: daß erstens der Sozialismus verdientermaßen gescheitert ist, und daß zweitens die reale DDR nichts war, dem man ein längeres Leben hätte wünschen dürfen. Dieser Konsens herrscht weder unter den Intellektuellen des Westens noch unter denen des Ostens und schon gar nicht zwischen Ost und West.[42]

Greiner is certainly right to remark on a growing tendency amongst left-wing intellectuals in Germany and elsewhere to see the GDR in a nostalgic light: to see only what might have been.[43] However, in his article it becomes clear that Greiner is actually demanding a form of public penance from those intellectuals who remained in the GDR until the end, or who now still feel that something important has been lost with its demise. In an account of the *Stasi* debate Karl Deiritz summed up the mood of the historical moment with a provocative formulation: 'Die sogenannte Literaturdebatte ist eine Anti-Sozialismus-Debatte. Es geht um das Bekenntnis zum Westen. Geführt wird sie aber nicht als politische sondern als moralische Debatte.'

In part he is right. The involvement of so many GDR writers and academics (and, it seems now, Western intellectuals, journalists, and academics) with the *Staatssicherheit* has provided a useful weapon in the hands of those who see it as their duty to school the political conscience of the nation. Yet this is only half the story. The article by Fritz Raddatz in September 1993, in which he claimed that Christa Wolf and Heiner Müller had done irreparable damage to literature through their 'betrayal', was not simply one of the many attempts to dismantle the GDR past under the cover of a phoney moral rhetoric. The article is clearly written out of anguish and incomprehension.[44] Raddatz's view, and that of a number of other writers and commentators, is that the complicity of GDR writers in the mechanisms of State has fundamentally changed the way writers and literature can be perceived in the new Germany. For example, Kurt Drawert: 'Die verlorene Glaubwürdigkeit der literarischen wie pragmatischen Aussage, dadurch daß ihr Verfasser praktisch gegen sie verfuhr, hat der Literatur irreparable Schäden zugefügt.' For him the complicity of GDR writers, should not, however, be condemned as a unique historical failure, but rather as an exemplary demonstration of a process which is universal, but often obscured, especially in Western democracies: 'die Unausweichlichkeit, Macht zu berühren und von ihr berührt zu sein.'[45] For Drawert, the only thing which has been won out of the recent debates is a new sense of urgency in the attempts to restate the moral categories at the heart of literary production and analysis. He continues: 'Wo moralische Kriterien aus den ästhetischen Diskursen zu verschwinden beginnen, gilt es sie zu behaupten. Andernfalls verlieren die Produkte, die literarischen zumal, ihre Spuren an Sinn, lösen sich in wohlgefällige Spielerei auf und fügen sich ein ins Ensemble der Entbehrlichkeiten.' Although these various approaches to defining an understanding of literature in the new Germany begin from entirely different premises, they unite to create one very particular effect. The left is on the run in Germany, and with it the perception of literature as something intrinsically political—an understanding which has formed the basis of literary criticism in both Germanies since 1945. In some senses it does promise a new freedom for literature. No longer forced into the role of documentary substitute in the East or political conscience in the West, it can go back to its 'real' job, as Heiner Müller put it: 'die Wirklichkeit, so wie sie ist, unmöglich zu machen'.[46]

In practice, however, the effects of this new spirit are well illustrated in some of the most recent attempts to take on the difficult task of rewriting GDR literary history. Wolfgang Emmerich's call for a new reading of GDR literature which would move away from ideological determinants to aesthetic ones may signal a useful shift of emphasis.[47] In practice, however, it is rarely straightforward to separate the two. A number of examples would perhaps be useful to illustrate the dangers and the confusions which have resulted.

An early, but much cited, article by Thomas Rietzschel, in which he declared that: 'Gedichte aus der DDR verlieren ihren Reiz', fixed the dilemma quite neatly.[48] Seeking to counter a tendency towards reading GDR texts between the lines as a kind of 'Sklavensprache', he instead hoped to impose new, 'aesthetic', criteria for judgement. Only now in texts by Brigitte Struzyk and others he discovers none of the 'aufrührerische[n] Tiefsinn', he would have previously judged appropriate, and dismisses the texts instead as banal. In the course of his polemic, however, he reveals to what extent his previous reading of poetic texts was reductive. His former delight '[sie] als Zeichen des Widerstands zu goutieren' has now transformed into an aggressive wholesale denial of any worth. This kind of gesture has became all too familiar in the last few years. In another article reviewing the poetry of the GDR, Gerd Labroisse errs at the other end of the political scale. He credits GDR literature as a whole with value in the new Germany despite the collapse of the SED state and of the GDR's socialist society because, he claims, 'the literature of the GDR is a genuinely political literature' with 'a social function', what is more, 'a social "enlightening" function'. He does not reflect on the way our understanding of that function has been affected by the revelations about the system it outlived, nor does he ever explore the suspect negotiations between ideology and aesthetics upon which that literature relied.[49] Keith Bullivant's attempts to formulate 'the future of German literature' by sketching out an alternative canon represents a worrying departure in a different ideological direction again. Having run through the history of the 'Literaturstreit', and quoted the recent calls for more differentiated accounts of literary histories, he nevertheless fails to subject his own selection criteria to rigorous examination. His project is noticeably marked by the convergence theories of the 1970s and 1980s, in that he claims for the literary canon of the new Germany only those GDR texts which, apparently, transcend their GDR background. Some works then fall short, because, for him, they are 'very little without the oppositional context' or because they demand 'familiarity with that society'. Against another he contends instead that it 'does not really add to our knowledge of the latter days of the GDR, on which it is vague in the extreme'. Applied to literature of any age these critical standards would seem inadequate. Applied now, however, so soon after the ideological assumptions which they reveal have been so thoroughly exposed and discredited, they are particularly inappropriate.[50] These examples which hail from writers and critics in the West (Germany, Amsterdam, and California) are inevitably different from the internal reappraisals which have been conducted within the GDR. One of the most important is entitled *Verrat an der Kunst?*.[51] The defensive tone is unmistakable in the title and characterizes the volume as a whole. One or two critics attempt to stand their ground: Peter Geist begins his survey of the 'Kulturbiotop in Wildostberlin', for example, with a characteristically combative flourish: 'Nein nicht noch ein Nachruf, noch ein Bleibt-was-Gedönse, das je nach Interessenlage trotzig, melancholisch oder gehässig ausfällt.'[52] Rather more often, however, the agonized rereading of literary texts from the former GDR is overtaken by the attempts of individual critics to make sense of, and justify, their own former beliefs and positions.[53] There is nothing wrong with this in itself. Such efforts to come to terms with the collapse of the socialist state are themselves fascinating historical documents. Nevertheless, one of the most damaging results of this strand of *Vergangenheitsbewältigung* is the assumption that a text from the former GDR might only pass through the strait gate into the new German literary history by largely abandoning any claim to political significance.[54] A similar salvage operation under the sign of the apolitical has also been performed on Heiner Müller in the *Frankfurter Rundschau*. This strategy is, however, fatefully reminiscent of the attempts by critics like Ulrich Greiner to see off forty-five years of political literature in both Germanies in 1990. Although with very different goals in mind, a 'Gesinnungsästhetik' of sorts is still being played off against the notion of some truth of art which is essentially sublime, unpolitical, and autonomous. To set these up as a straightforward literary opposition is crass. That attempts to divide them are undesirable, and possibly even dangerous, has been clearly demonstrated by the fate of the young generation of writers in the GDR since 1989.

This leads me to a final set of considerations. I have argued that the study of the texts, individual writers, and even the 'generation' of young poets as a whole can offer a number of useful insights into a decade of literature in the GDR and beyond. Perhaps now especially, in the current climate of political purism, they will provide usefully complex moral and political dilemmas to confound the over-simplified arguments which appear to be gaining ground. However, as a body of work this poetry can also shed light on certain much broader issues, much closer to home. Some of the most important are mentioned below.

The poetry of the young writers, particularly those of them associated with Prenzlauer Berg, can be considered as a case study of sorts which exposes the ambiguities at the heart of a postmodern aesthetic. The fate of Prenzlauer Berg translates the much discussed subversive potential of the postmodern, but also its knowing complicity, into disturbingly real terms.[55] It is difficult to speculate with enthusiasm about the possibilities of schizophrenia as an aesthetic when one has seen it played out in its most cynical and damaging reality.

In the same light, the revelations about those writers who became embroiled with the *Staatssicherheit* shed an interesting light on our habits of reading and judging literature. Despite the much publicized 'death of the author' back in the heyday of structuralism, it is instructive to see how quickly such hygienic theories break down when confronted with the messiness and urgency of historical reality. The author might have been ripped up, de-centred, or killed off completely for twenty years now, but at moments like these it is possible to see just how much we still invest in the notion of an autonomous, integral subject and the textual subject which becomes its insignia.

Another way to look at much the same problem is to shift our attention from the mechanics of the betrayal to examine, instead, our own reactions to it. Put simply: instead of asking how exactly the writers were involved with the *Stasi*, it might be equally productive at least to ask why it matters to us so much that they were. In an interview in May 1993 Heiner Müller claimed 'ein Menschenrecht auf Feigheit', on the one hand, but went on to assert: 'Ich habe nicht das Recht, rein zu bleiben in einer schmutzigen Welt.'[56] The constellation is intriguing. The reception of GDR literature since the facts about the *Stasi* have come to light has demonstrated how little of the 'right to cowardice' critics have been prepared to accord the writers of the GDR, yet conversely how unwilling they were to acknowledge the dirty world in which such writers were living. The events since the fall of the Wall have made obvious just how much our understanding of GDR literature as a whole has been dependent on the notion of the writer as morally unimpeachable, a representative of the conscience of the nation. One might also say that the GDR writers contributed themselves to the creation of that myth, and thus prepared the way for their fall. In truth none of the writers from the GDR were 'heroes' in the way that Havel, or a number of other writers from the Soviet bloc are now seen. But what reader, with the privilege of clean hands, can presume to demand heroic action as the standard? In 1993 Günter Kunert described the 'fall' of the writer in very moving terms in his 'Gedicht für Dichter':[57]

> Gefallene Engel: Wir
> unseres unerwählten Metiers halber
> das sich dunkel bekundet
> als luziferisches Unglücksspiel.
> Aus allen Himmel gestürzt
> unter der Last bleierner Schriftzeichen

But perhaps the pathos of this text, painful as it is, already seems uncomfortably anachronistic, reminiscent more of a Romantic poet than one of the late twentieth century. Now writers must come to terms with working in a climate where they have no privileged position, where they must fight to be heard amidst the din of the market and the media. And as readers, a nation must come to terms with the fact that the writers in whom they invested so much were not 'heroes', but simply writers, with the same very ordinary fears and weaknesses as their readers.[58] To borrow a sentiment from Brecht's *Leben des Galilei*: 'Unglücklich das Land, das keine Helden hat!' [. . .] 'Nein. Unglücklich das Land, das Helden nötig hat'.[59]

But, as readers also engaged in the business of writing literary history, academics and critics have very special questions to ask themselves as they survey this body of writing. In an article of 1991 Jan Faktor asks what light recent revelations cast on those many commentators who did not recognize that something was rotten at the centre of Prenzlauer Berg.[60] Faktor's formulation is extreme, but it raises a valid point. In the reception of these young writers we have a case study in the failures, blindnesses, and complicities of Western criticism as a whole, the lessons of which must be learned before new literary histories are set in print. But exactly there lies a particular opportunity for 'Auslandsgermanistik'. The current literary disputes in Germany are intrinsically bound up with questions of German national identity and forty years of political and geographical division. They are also manifestly part of a much larger process of delayed 'Trauerarbeit' which is, again, part of a uniquely German history. A number of critics have taken up Wolfgang Thierse's call for Germans from East and West to exchange their histories and biographies with one another.[61] This is one of the great strengths of their access to recent literary history, but also one of their greatest blind spots. In these discussions a degree of distance from those historically loaded exchanges can afford new perspectives and quite different evaluations.

In the confusion surrounding the calls for new schemes of literary history, it is perhaps inevitable that commentators should favour large distinctions and bold historical strokes. Much of the commentary in the years after unification, and after the *Stasi* revelations, has revolved around crude binary oppositions: 'collaboration' and 'dissidence', 'ideology' and 'aesthetic', 'commitment' and 'autonomy', 'morality' and 'betrayal'. However, as always after a fundamental rupture, the continuities and interconnections will gradually begin to reassert themselves. A picture of a literary landscape will emerge, which will acknowledge the successes and failures of the 'literatures' of the GDR and record the extent to which they were able to break boundaries, but also the extent to which they bound themselves within them.

In 1990, in a moving speech in Nuremberg, Hans Mayer reflected on the opportunities which had been lost with the final demise of the GDR:

Einen kurzen geschichtlichen Augenblick lang, unvergeßbar trotzdem für uns alle, hatte es auf deutschem Boden den Anschein, als seien die Gedanken der großen bürgerlichen Aufklärung [. . .] wieder einmal durch die heutigen Denker und Schriftsteller und Künstler unmittelbar weitergegeben an das Volk. [. . .] Einen kurzen, unvergessenen Augenblick lang durften wir alle hoffen, daß der tiefe Wunsch aller großen Deutschen, das Ernstnehmen deutscher Denker und Dichter, des Geistes, [. . .] nicht nur von der jeweiligen Macht anerkannt werden würde, sondern daß der Geist selbst zur Macht werden konnte.[62]

The notion of an intimate and equal relationship between 'Geist' and 'Macht' has always been the stuff of utopias. Set against this, the very real attempts to marry them under the sign of a totalitarian ideology has led to some of the most sorry chapters in German literary history. In the current climate in Germany it appears that the hopes of the Enlightenment, and with them any thought of bringing 'Geist' and 'Macht' together into some kind of union, have little hope of being fulfilled. Some would argue, in any case, that these are aspirations inappropriate for the (post-)modern age. In practice, literature has once again been left on the outside, while the ideological, economic, and moral disputes are played out in another arena. But perhaps this is where literature functions best: on the margins, where it can work at redressing those aspirations which might otherwise be extinguished, and subverting those structures which might otherwise succeed in extinguishing them.

The final word should go to the poets themselves. The last poem in Bert Papenfuß-Gorek's collection *tiské* is marked by the savage energy of someone who has seen his political and poetic aspirations thwarted. Nevertheless the poet mobilizes the power of the poem as a determined 'speaking against': an obstinate redress to an obscene political reality.

> gründet ihr erstmal euer scheißvolk
> & ich dann den untergrunduntergrund.
> in einem wahlweisen untergrundstaat
> der mir noch den kopf zerbricht
> dieser text ist ein gedicht
> das für die vorantrift der bastadisierung
> sprich polackisierung, sprich regionalisierung
> sprich krautkrauterei spricht
> & zwar sprechend, sprich...[63]

In an extraordinary essay of 1989, on the other hand, Durs Grünbein celebrates the radical estrangement of the young poet of the late twentieth century who stands with the 'wreck of history' behind him. He sets out a long list of deformations which poetry has suffered:

Eine Poesie langzeit mit Botschaften beladen, von allerlei Idealismen vergewaltigt, mit Rauschmitteln vollgepumpt, später versachlicht nach besten Kräften, in hermetische Engen getrieben, nüchtern in Laboren zerlegt, dem Zufall wiedergeschenkt, aller Repräsentanzen beraubt, endlich als Müllcontainer herumgeschoben, zum Alltag befreit . . . kommt morgen vielleicht schon mit Gesten eines tierhaften Charmes daher.

But in the exhilaration and anxiety of that new freedom he looks forward to the possibility of a poetry of heretical emancipation: 'unzitierbar für die Kulturhüter und Rhetorikzwerge an allen Auf- und Abbaufronten'.[64]

In a poem dated January 1991 Barbara Köhler presents the precarious vision of the landlocked city at last shifted to within 'sight of the sea'. In the final lines it becomes clear that the lyric subject's absurd and hopeful vision against the odds also represents that of poetry itself.

> —es ist ja nur die Versuchung der Liebe
> zu Orten, sie sich ans Meer zu wünschen
> die sonderbare Gewohnheit der Böhmen
> mit Ahoi zu grüßen
> und ein Gedicht.[65]

All three attribute to poetry a fundamental power to break boundaries, to undo our landscapes of reality, and to create new topographies of the imagination. If Papenfuß-Gorek locates that power in poetry's awkward and peculiar ability to undermine the limitations of immediate reality, Köhler finds it rather in its power to transcend them, 'Meer in Sicht', and Grünbein, in a sudden and illuminating departure for the unknown 'Inseln des Imaginären'.[66]

Notes

1. 'Pegasus an der Stasi-Leine', *Der Spiegel*, 18 Nov. 1991, 276–80.
2. Also the title of one of the first volumes to assess the literary consequences of the end of the GDR: *Geist und Macht: Writers and the State in the GDR*, ed. Axel Goodbody and Dennis Tate, German Monitor, 29 (Amsterdam: Rodopi, 1992).
3. The title of a polemical critical work: *Dichter im Dienst: Der sozialistische Realismus in der deutschen Literatur*, ed. Lothar von Balluseck (Wiesbaden: Limes Verlag, 1956).
4. First published in *Neues Deutschland*, 4–5 Aug. 1990; repr. in *Grenzfallgedichte: Eine deutsche Anthologie*, ed. Anna Chiarloni and Helga Pankoke (Berlin and Weimar: Aufbau, 1991), 109.
5. Chiarloni and Pankoke, *Grenzfallgedichte*, 55. Müller first read this during the performance of his *Quartett* in the 'Theater im Palast' on 2 Oct. 1989. It appears as part of a considerably extended text in Heiner Müller, *Gedichte* (Berlin: Alexander Verlag, 1992), 94–6.
6. The later title of the poem, 'Das Eigentum' also underlines its poetological significance. It is taken up under this title in Volker Braun, *Die Zickzackbrücke: Ein Abrißkalender* (Halle: Mitteldeutscher Verlag, 1992), 84. Braun's 'An Friedrich Hölderlin' takes up the same Hölderlin reference (see Ch. 4).
7. Cf. Jürgen Rennert, 'Mein Land ist mir zerfallen', ibid. 108, Günter Kunert, 'Biographie', ibid. 98, Annerose Kirchner, 'Zwischen den Ufern', ibid. 97; and see Conclusion.
8. Günter Kunert, *Der Sturz vom Sockel: Feststellungen und Widersprüche* (Munich: Hanser, 1992), 12.
9. Wolfgang Emmerich, *Kleine Literaturgeschichte der DDR 1945–1988* extended and rev. edn. (Frankfurt/M.: Luchterhand, 1989) and Emmerich, 'Für eine andere Wahrnehmung der DDR-Literatur: Neue Kontexte, neue Paradigmen, ein neuer Kanon', in Goodbody and Tate, *Geist und Macht*, 7–22.
10. Emmerich, 'Wahrnehmung', 10, 16, 13–15.
11. Ibid. 13 and 14. Emmerich's approach is derived in part from a reading of Uwe Japp, *Beziehungssinn. Ein Konzept der Literaturgeschichte* (Frankfurt/M.: Europäische Verlagsanstalt, 1980) and Bernhard Greiner, 'DDR-Literatur als Problem der Wissenschaft', *Jahrbuch zur Literatur in der DDR 3* (Bonn: Bouvier, 1983), 233–54, and is broadly in line with the form of reappraisal suggested by various GDR critics in 'Umfrage zur Situation der Literatur-, Kunst- und Kulturwissenschaften', in *WB 1* (1991), 9–54 and 'Fortsetzung', 2 (1991), 234–84. See particularly Ursula Heukenkamp's call: 'die Geschichte, an der wir beteiligt waren, neu [zu] buchstabieren', 25.
12. Cf. Emmerich, 'Wahrnehmung', 13 and 19–20, where he speculates on

future comparisons between writers such as Eva Strittmatter and Ulla
Hahn, 'um ein abschreckendes Beispiel zu nennen', or between Bert
Papenfuß-Gorek and Thomas Kling.

13. Ibid. 12 and 14. Cf. Heukenkamp, *WB* 1 (1991), 25.
14. The title of a poetry collection by the writer Uwe Kolbe (b. 1957),
    Hineingeboren: Gedichte 1975–1979 (Berlin and Weimar: Aufbau,
    1980).
15. Cf. *Tendenz Freisprache: Texte zu einer Poetik der achtziger Jahre*, ed.
    Ulrich Janetzki and Wolfgang Rath (Frankfurt/M.: Suhrkamp, 1992),
    268.
16. Reinhard Mohr, *Zaungäste: Die Generation, die nach der Revolution
    kam* (Frankfurt/M.: Fischer, 1992), 10.
17. Cf. Janetzki and Rath, *Tendenz Freisprache*, 1–13 and 268–72.
18. Erik Grimm, 'Der Tod der Ostmoderne oder Die BRDigung des DDR-
    Untergrunds: Zur Lyrik Bert Papenfuß-Goreks', *ZfG*, 1 (1991), 9–20.
19. Christine Cosentino, ' "ich habe ausser meiner sprache keine | mittel
    meine sprache zu verlassen": Überlegungen zur Lyrik Sascha Andersons',
    in *DDR-Lyrik im Kontext*, ed. Christine Cosentino, Wolfgang Ertl, and
    Gerd Labroisse, ABznG 26 (Amsterdam: Rodopi, 1988), 195–221 (196).
20. *Die andere Sprache. Neue DDR-Literatur der 80er Jahre*, ed. Heinz
    Ludwig Arnold in collaboration with Gerhard Wolf, Sonderband *Text
    + Kritik* (Munich: text + kritik, 1990).
21. Wolfgang Emmerich, 'Status melancholicus: Zur Transformation der
    Utopie in der DDR-Literatur' *Literatur in der DDR: Rückblicke*, ed.
    Heinz Ludwig Arnold and Frauke Meyer-Gosau, Sonderband *Text +
    Kritik* (Munich: text + kritik, 1991), 232–45 (243).
22. The shift in attitude is made clear in *Vom gegenwärtigen Zustand der
    deutschen Literatur*, ed. Heinz Ludwig Arnold, *Text + Kritik*, 113
    (Munich: text + kritik, 1992).
23. Frank Schirrmacher, 'Verdacht und Verrat: Die Stasi-Vergangenheit
    verändert die literarische Szene', *FAZ* 5 Nov. 1991.
24. Kunert, see n. 8 above.
25. Martin Meyer (ed.), *Intellektuellendämmerung? Beiträge zur neuesten
    Zeit des Geistes* (Munich: Hanser, 1992). Cf. Wolf Lepenies, *Aufstieg
    und Fall der Intellektuellen in Europa* (Frankfurt/M.: Suhrkamp, 1992).
26. Adolf Endler, ' "Alles ist im untergrund obenauf; einmannfrei" . . .
    Anläßlich einer Anthologie', a review of the anthology of interviews and
    text *Sprache & Antwort* (see Bibliography), first published in *ariadne-
    fabrik*, 4 (1988), repr. and rev. in Endler, *Den Tiger reiten: Aufsätze,
    Polemiken und Notizen zur Lyrik der DDR*, ed. Manfred Behn
    (Frankfurt/M.: Luchterhand, 1990), 40–65 (46).
27. Ingrid and Klaus-Dieter Hähnel, 'Junge Lyrik am Ende der siebziger
    Jahre', *WB* 9 (1981), 126–54 (129).
28. Daniela Dahn, *Kunst und Kohle: die 'Szene' am Prenzlauer Berg*
    (Frankfurt/M.: Luchterhand, 1987), 226.
29. A conference held in London 12–13 Nov. 1993 was entitled 'Prenzlauer
    Berg: Bohemia in East Berlin?'. Cf. Dahn, *Kunst und Kohle* and *VEB
    Nachwuchs: Jugend in der DDR*, ed. Norbert Haase, Lothar Reese and
    Peter Wensierski (Reinbek bei Hamburg: Rowohlt, 1983).
30. 'Sogar aus Frankreich und den USA flogen sensationshungrige Feuille-
    tonisten und Germanistikstudenten auf der Suche nach einem Thema für

ihre Diplomarbeit ein, und sie saugten dankbar aus jeder Plastikblume des Ostens ihren Kunsthonig.' Biermann, 'Ein öffentliches Geschwür', *Der Spiegel*, 13 Jan. 1992, 158–67 (160).

31. ' "Dableiben? Weggehen? Weiterschreiben", Tagung in Zusammenarbeit mit dem Internationalen Arbeitskreis Literatur und Politik in Deutschland', Karl Arnold Stiftung, Bonn-Bad Godesberg 12–14 June 1992.

32. I have borrowed this term from Steve McCaffery's 1976 essay 'The Death of the Subject: The Implications of Counter-Communication in Recent Language-Centred Writing', in $L=A=N=G=U=A=G=E$, 1 (1980).
McCaffery is one of the central theorists of the influential American poetry of the 1980s, dubbed 'Language Poetry'. It bears many hallmarks of the phenomenon in the GDR. Cf. the anthology *The $L=A=N=G=U=A=G=E$ Book*, ed. Bruce Andrews and Charles Bernstein (Carbondale and Edwardsville: Southern Illinois University Press, 1984).

33. Janetzki and Rath, *Tendenz Freisprache*, 257.

34. The controversy surrounding Sascha Anderson meant that some publishing houses and authors insisted on the removal of texts by him, before critical volumes or anthologies could go to press. In *Tendenz Freisprache*, for example, this has the bizarre result that his contribution has been replaced with a note to this effect (p. 14), while he and his work are discussed in the 'Foreword' and 'Epilogue' without mention of the recent events. A similar debate surrounded the publication of *vogel oder käfig sein: Kunst und Literatur aus unabhängigen Zeitschriften in der DDR 1979–1989*, ed. Klaus Michael and Thomas Wohlfahrt (Berlin: Galrev, 1992), although this is hardly indicated in the evasive and tight-lipped note (p. 12). The publishing history of the volume *MachtSpiele: Literatur und Staatssicherheit im Fokus Prenzlauer Berg* (Leipzig: Reclam, 1993), ed. Peter Böthig and Klaus Michael, also bears traces of disputes: see esp. 15–16 and Anderson's letter, 197–200.

35. See esp. Peter Bürger, *Theorie der Avantgarde* (Frankfurt/M.: Suhrkamp, 1974) and *Postmoderne: Alltag, Allegorie und Avantgarde*, ed. Christa and Peter Bürger (Frankfurt/M.: Suhrkamp, 1988).

36. *Zensur in der DDR. Geschichte, Praxis und 'Ästhetik' einer Behinderung der Literatur*, ed. Ernest Wichner and Herbert Wiesner (Berlin: Literaturhaus Berlin, 1991).

37. *D1980D1989R Künstlerbücher und Originalgrafische Zeitschriften im Eigenverlag: Eine Bibliographie*, ed. Jens Henkel and Sabine Russ (Gifkendorf: Merlin, 1991). Cf. also *Zellinnendruck*, ed. Egmont Hesse and Christoph Tannert (Leipzig: Katalog der Galerie EIGEN+ART, 1990). The magazines and folders which I have consulted in archives are listed in the Bibliography.

38. Jan Faktor, *Georgs Versuche an einem Gedicht und andere positive Texte aus dem Dichtergarten des Grauens* (Berlin and Weimar: Aufbau—Außer der Reihe, 1989), 9. Cf. Bibliography for further genre descriptions of collections by Jansen, Kachold, and Papenfuß.

39. Durs Grünbein, 'Transit Berlin', *Zwischen den Zeilen*, 2 (1992), 21; Michael Braun, 'Entfesselungsversuche: *zügel los*: Das Prosadebüt von Gabi Kachold aus der Ex-DDR', *Basler Zeitung*, 2 Nov. 1990.

40. Gerrit-Jan Berendse, *Die 'Sächsische Dichterschule': Lyrik in der DDR der sechziger und siebziger Jahre* (Frankfurt/M.: Peter Lang, 1990). For

the ironic Prenzlauer Berg label see Gerhard Wolf, *Sprachblätter Wortwechsel: Im Dialog mit Dichtern* (Leipzig: Reclam, 1992), 156.

41. Adolf Endler, 'DDR Lyrik Mitte der Siebziger. Fragment einer Rezension', *ABznG* 7 (1987), 67–95 (73).

42. Cf. the terms used of them: 'Plejade', 'Ensemble', 'team-work Attitüde' 'Dichterschule', all discussed in Berendse, esp. pp. ix–xv and 131–47.

43. Anneli Hartmann, 'Der Generationswechsel—ein ästhetischer Wechsel? Schreibweisen und Traditionsbezüge in der jüngsten DDR-Lyrik', in *Jahrbuch zur Literatur in der DDR* 4, ed. Paul Gerhard Klussmann and Heinrich Mohr (Bonn: Bouvier, 1985), 109–34 (111).

44. See esp. pp. xiv–xv and 1–22.

45. Peter Geist, 'Gedicht-Schreiben in der DDR zwischen Mitte der siebziger und Anfang der achtziger Jahre: Positionen—Probleme—Tendenzen' (unpublished dissertation, Karl-Marx-Universität, Leipzig, 1987), 96.

46. *Schöne Aussichten: Neue Prosa aus der DDR*, ed. Christian Döring and Hajo Steinert (Frankfurt/M.: Suhrkamp, 1990), 8.

47. Hans Mayer, *Der Turm von Babel: Erinnerung an eine Deutsche Demokratische Republik* (Frankfurt/M.: Suhrkamp, 1991), 17.

48. Anthonya Visser's 1994 dissertation, now published as *'Blumen im Eis': Lyrische und literaturkritische Innovationen in der DDR. Zum kommunikativen Spannungsfeld ab Mitte der 60er Jahre*, Amsterdamer Publikationen zur Sprache und Literatur, 107 (Amsterdam: Rodopi, 1994), also explicitly responds to Emmerich's article in its aim to observe and record the dynamic of communicative strategies over two decades of poetry in the GDR.

49. See Jean-François Lyotard, *The Postmodern Condition: A Report on Knowledge*, tr. Geoff Bennington and Brian Massumi, Theory and History of Literature, 10 (Manchester: Manchester University Press, 1984; 5th edn. 1991). Cf. Christopher Norris, *What's Wrong with Postmodernism: Critical Theory and the Ends of Philosophy* (New York, London: Harvester Wheatsheaf, 1990), and for the opposite view, see Linda Hutcheon's persuasive *The Politics of Postmodernism* (London: Routledge, 1989).

50. See Persicke Meinhard, 'Tendenzen der Lyrik von Jugendlichen der 70er Jahre in der DDR 1973–1980' (unpublished dissertation, Pädagogische Hochschule, Dresden, 1984), and Katrin Hagemann, 'Die Analyze von Wertvorstellungen und Lebensorientierungen in der jungen Lyrik der DDR' (unpublished dissertation, Akademie für Gesellschaftswissenschaften beim ZK der SED. Institut für marxistisch-leninistische Kultur und Kunstwissenschaften, Berlin, 1985), 15–19. Geist, 'Gedicht-Schreiben', is an exception.

51. Certain GDR libraries were far-sighted enough to start collecting magazines in the mid-1980s and now hold examples available for public consultation: notably the 'Deutsche Buch- und Schriftmuseum der Deutschen Bücherei', Leipzig, and now also the 'Deutsches Literaturarchiv' at Marbach am Neckar.

52. The section 'Debatten' in *vogel oder käfig sein* goes some way to repairing this lack; it includes polemical essays by a number of writers including Faktor's essay 'Was ist neu an der Literatur der 80er Jahre', 367–89, from which the quotation is taken (387).

53. Since the completion of my dissertation two further dissertations have

been produced by young GDR academics which deal with particular aspects of the unofficial writing of the GDR: Peter Böthig, 'Differenz und Revolte: Literatur aus der DDR in den 80er Jahren. Untersuchungen an den Rändern eines Diskurses', (unpublished dissertation, Humboldt Universität, Berlin, 1993) and Birgit Dahlke, ' "Die romantischen Bilder blättern ab". Produktionsbedingungen, Schreibweisen und Traditionen von Autorinnen in inoffiziell publizierten Zeitschriften der DDR 1979–90' (unpublished dissertation, Freie Universität, Berlin, 1994). Although I have been unable to consider these dissertations in any detail, both authors have produced a number of important articles which are included in the Bibliography.

54. *Ein Molotow-Cocktail auf fremder Bettkante: Lyrik der siebziger/ achtziger Jahre von Dichtern aus der DDR—Ein Lesebuch*, ed. Peter Geist (Leipzig: Reclam, 1991).

CHAPTER 1

1. Siegfried Rönisch, *WB* 7 (1979), 7–10 (7).
2. Kolbe, *Hineingeboren: Gedichte 1975–1979*.
3. Leonhard Lorek, 'Ciao! Von der Anspruchslosigkeit der Kapitulationen', in Böthig and Michael, *MachtSpiele*, 112–25 (113). A similar understanding is signalled in Ulf Christian Hasenfelder's 'Die Generation, die nicht zu sich kommen durfte: Junge Avantgarde der ehemaligen DDR', *Der Literat*, 4 Apr. 1991, 18–20, and Thomas Günther also celebrates the 'lost generation' of the GDR in his 'Die subkulturellen Zeitschriften in der DDR und ihre kulturgeschichtliche Bedeutung', in 'Aus Politik und Zeitgeschichte', *Das Parlament*, 8 May 1992, 27–36 (36).
4. Cf. ' "Eine eigene Sprache finden": Walfried and Christel Hartinger sowie Peter Geist im Gespräch mit den Lyrikern Thomas Böhme, Kurt Drawert, Kerstin Hensel, Dieter Kerschek, Bert Papenfuß-Gorek und Kathrin Schmidt', *WB* 4 (1990), 580–616. This discussion was originally held in 1988 but could not be published because of the political nature of some of the comments. See also the comments by Böhme, Drawert, and Papenfuß-Gorek, esp. pp. 598–602.
5. 'Eine eigene Sprache finden', 598. Cf. Hensel, in interview in 1991: 'Was ist Generation? Was ist Generationsgefühl? Ich kann nicht sagen, daß ich das Gefühl meiner Generation kenne.' Klaus Hammer, 'Gespräch mit Kerstin Hensel', *WB* 1 (1991), 93–110 (96).
6. Faktor, 'Was ist neu an der jungen Literatur der achtziger Jahre', *vogel oder käfig sein*, 369.
7. 'Mein Lieblingspreis wäre der Franz-Jung-Preis: Gespräch mit dem Dichterwerker Bert Papenfuß-Gorek', *Freitag*, 7 June 1991; Detlef Opitz, 'Literatur in diesen Zeiten: Staatssicherheit und Prenzlauer Berg', *Freitag*, 7 Feb. 1992, and Barbara Köhler, 'A la Recherche de la révolution perdue: Ein innerdeutscher Monolog', in *Women and the Wende: Social Effects and Cultural Reflections of the German Unification Process*, ed. Elizabeth Boa and Janet Wharton, German Monitor, 31 (Amsterdam: Rodropi, 1994), 1–5 (2).
8. Sascha Anderson 'Die Generation nach uns ist freier. Gespräch mit Sascha Anderson', *Der Spiegel*, 1 Sept. 1986, 74–8. Bert Papenfuß-Gorek

makes the same point, in 'Eine eigene Sprache finden', 603. In his *Generationen Temperamente Schreibweisen. DDR Literatur in neuer Sicht* (Leipzig: Mitteldeutscher Verlag, 1986), Hans Richter concludes: 'Die Jüngeren unterscheiden sich schon fast von Jahrgang zu Jahrgang' (14).

9. Johannes Jansen, *prost neuland: spottklagen und wegzeug* (Berlin and Weimar: Aufbau, 1990), 66. See also Alexander von Bormann, 'Wege aus der Ordnung', in *Jenseits der Staatskultur: Traditionen autonomer Kunst in der DDR*, ed. Gabriele Muschter and Rüdiger Thomas (Munich: Hanser, 1992), 83–107 (101).

10. With particular reference to the GDR cf. Günter Erbe, 'Schriftsteller in der DDR: Eine soziologische Untersuchung der Herkunft, der Karrierewege und der Selbsteinschätzung der literarischen Intelligenz im Generationsvergleich', *Deutschland Archiv*, 11 (1987), 1162–79.

11. Kurt Drawert, *Spiegelland: Ein deutscher Monolog* (Frankfurt/M.: Suhrkamp, 1992), 156.

12. Uwe Kolbe, 'Rundfunk Essay', originally *Bizarre Städte* 4 (1989), repr. in *vogel oder käfig sein*, 391–2 (392). In the cycle 'Gedichte eines alten Mannes aus Prag' Faktor in a sense agrees: 'jede neue Generation bringt in die Welt das Gefühl der Normalität zurück'. Faktor, *Georgs Versuche an einem Gedicht*, 11–22 (22).

13. For the metaphors see *Geschichte der deutschen Literatur von den Anfängen bis zur Gegenwart*, xi. *Literatur der DDR*, ed. Horst Haase *et al.* (Berlin: Verlag Volk und Wissen, 1976). The quotation comes from Alexander Demandt, *Metaphern für Geschichte: Sprachbilder und Gleichnisse im historisch-politischen Denken* (Munich: Beck, 1978), 227.

14. Wolfgang Emmerich, 'Gleichzeitigkeit. Vormoderne, Moderne und Postmoderne in der Literatur der DDR', in *Bestandsaufnahme Gegenwartsliteratur*, ed. Heinz Ludwig Arnold, Sonderband *Text + Kritik* (Munich: text + kritik, 1988), 193–211 (194).

15. Hans Richter, 'Zum Thema Generation(en): Thesen und Gedanken, vorgetragen in der Werkstatt Junge Kunst II der Akademie der Künste der DDR, 20 März 1988', *Temperamente*, 1 (1989), 66–73 (66).

16. See Christel and Walfried Hartinger, 'Unterwegs in der Erfahrung. Zeitgenossenschaft und lyrische Subjektivität', in *Ansichten: Aufsätze zur Literatur der DDR* ed. Klaus Walther *et al.* (Halle/S.: Mitteldeutscher Verlag, 1976), 340–469 (343) or *Selbsterfahrung als Welterfahrung: DDR Literatur in den siebziger Jahren* ed. Horst Nalewski and Klaus Schuhmann (Berlin and Weimar: Aufbau, 1981).

17. Emmerich, *Kleine Literaturgeschichte der DDR*, 216–32; John Flores, *Poetry in East Germany: Adjustments, Visions, and Provocations, 1945–1970* (New Haven: Yale University Press, 1971), 275–316; Harald Hartung, *Deutsche Lyrik seit 1965. Tendenzen Beispiele Porträts* (Munich: Piper, 1985), 98–139.

18. Kurt Hager, 'Parteilichkeit und Volksverbundenheit unserer Literatur und Kunst', quoted in Fritz J. Raddatz, *Marxismus und Literatur: Eine Dokumentation in drei Bänden*, iii (Reinbek bei Hamburg: Rowohlt, 1963), 248.

19. Günther Deicke, 'Auftritt einer neuen Generation', in *Liebes- und andere Erklärungen: Schriftsteller über Schriftsteller*, ed. Annie Voigtländer (Berlin and Weimar: Aufbau, 1972), 36–7 (37).

20. Cf. Konrad Franke, *Die Literatur der Deutschen Demokratischen Republik* (Munich: Kindler Verlag, 1971); Werner Brettschneider, *Zwischen literarischer Autonomie und Staatsdienst: Die Literatur in der DDR* (Berlin/W.: Erich Schmidt Verlag, 1972; 2nd edn. 1974); and Emmerich, *Kleine Literaturgeschichte der DDR*, first pub. 1981.

21. Cf. also Wolfgang Emmerich's similar analysis: 'Im Zeichen der Wiedervereinigung: die zweite Spaltung der deutschen Literatur', in *Kultur und Macht: Deutsche Literatur 1949–1989*, ed. Sekretariat für kulturelle Zusammenarbeit nichttheatertragender Städte und Gemeinden in Nordrhein-Westfalen, Gütersloh (Bielefeld: Aisthesis, 1992), 26–40.

22. Uwe Wittstock, *Von der Stalinallee zum Prenzlauer Berg: Wege der DDR-Literatur 1949–1989* (Munich: Piper, 1989). Rüdiger Thomas, 'Selbst-Behauptung', in Muschter and Thomas, *Jenseits der Staatskultur*, 11–42 (11).

23. Sascha Anderson, 'das ist sicher ein traum', *Jeder Satellit hat einen Killersatelliten* (Berlin/W.: Rotbuch, 1982), 52–3.

24. The following articles were particularly significant in initiating the discussion: Mathilde Dau, ' "Mit meinen Augen": Junge Lyrik beim Entdecken neuer Wirklichkeit', *Temperamente*, 3 (1979), 90–106; Mathilde and Rudolf Dau, 'Noch einmal: Junge Lyrik am Ende der siebziger Jahre', *WB* 3 (1982), 152–6; Ingrid and Klaus-Dieter Hähnel, 'Junge Lyrik am Ende der siebziger Jahre', *WB* 9 (1981), 126–54; Walfried Hartinger, 'DDR-Debüts in der Reihe "Poesiealbum" ', *Temperamente*, 3 (1980), 148–53; Ursula Heukenkamp, 'Das Ungenügen an der Idylle', *SuF* 5 (1981), 1120–30, and 'Funktion und Ausdruck: Gedanken zu einer Anthologie neuer Lyrik', in *DDR-Literatur '83 im Gespräch*, ed. Siegfried Rönisch (Berlin and Weimar: Aufbau, 1984), 295–302; Hans Kaufmann, 'Veränderte Literaturlandschaft', *WB* 1 (1981), 27–53; Heinz Plavius, 'Positionsbestimmung', *WB* 6 (1980), 136–47.

25. There is, of course, no entirely standard framework for identifying generations. Contrast the schemes proposed by Emmerich, *Kleine Literaturgeschichte der DDR*, 406–10; Brettschneider, *Zwischen literarischer Autonomie und Staatsdienst*, 48–59; Erbe, 'Schriftsteller in der DDR'. The Hähnels were the first to distinguish the 'Zwischengeneration': 'Junge Lyrik', 128. Since 1981 virtually all the critics have followed their example, setting apart the writers born between 1945 and 1950 (Emmerich, *Kleine Literaturgeschichte der DDR*, 407 and 438). The most important writers involved are Thomas Brasch (b. 1945), Christiane Grosz (b. 1944), Richard Pietraß (b. 1946), Andreas Reimann (b. 1946), Thomas Rosenlöcher (b. 1947), Bernd Rump (b. 1947), Brigitte Struzyk (b. 1946), Bettina Wegner (b. 1947), and Bernd Wagner (b. 1948). Erbe, 'Schriftsteller in der DDR', uses the term 'Zwischengeneration' to refer to the writers born between 1940 and 1945 (p. 1175).

26. This term was used by Biermann to characterize Jürgen Fuchs: 'Fuchs ist ein unvermischtes DDR-Produkt. Den Westen kennt er nicht.' Wolf Biermann, 'Zwei Portraits', in Jürgen Fuchs, *Gedächtnisprotokolle: mit Liedern von Gerulf Pannach und einem Vorwort von Wolf Biermann* (Reinbek bei Hamburg: Rowohlt, 1977, 7–10 (7).

27. Cf. Müller on Brasch's poetry: 'Prag nicht als Trauma, sondern als Ende eines Traumas. Ein Ende, mit dem der Beginn eines anderen gesetzt war,

das nicht mehr im Bewußtsein angesiedelt ist, sondern in die Existenz greift'. Müller, 'Wie es bleibt, ist es nicht. Zu Thomas Braschs "Kargo" ', *Der Spiegel*, 12 Sept. 1977, repr. in Heiner Müller, *Rotwelsch* (Berlin/W.: Merve Verlag, 1982), 150–5 (154–5).

28. Uwe Kolbe, 'Frau Wolf, warum lächeln Sie nicht?', in Muschter and Thomas, *Jenseits der Staatskultur*, 250–8 (250).

29. Günter Kunert, 'Fünf Jahre nach Biermann', repr. in *Der Sturz vom Sockel*, 136. Michael Meinicke also speaks of 'Vor-und-nach-Biermann' as an accepted literary understanding in Meinicke, *Junge Autoren in der DDR 1975–1980*, (Düsseldorf: drei-ECK Verlag, [n.d.]), 129.

30. Cf. Ian Wallace, 'The Failure of GDR Cultural Policy under Honecker', in *The German Revolution of 1989: Causes and Consequences*, ed. Gert-Joachim Glaeßner and Ian Wallace (Oxford: Berg, 1992), 100–23.

31. Christa Wolf, *Die Dimension des Autors: Essays und Aufsätze, Reden und Gespräche 1959–1985* (Berlin and Weimar: Aufbau, 1986), ii. 422 and 424. See also 424: '1976 war ein Einschnitt in der kulturpolitischen Entwicklung bei uns: [. . .] eine Gruppe von Autoren wurde sich klar darüber, daß ihre direkte Mitarbeit in dem Sinne, wie sie sie selbst verantworten konnte und für richtig hielt, nicht mehr gebraucht wurde.'

32. Cf. Thomas, 38. It is also worth noting the profound effect that Hans Mayer's *Außenseiter* (Frankfurt/M.: Suhrkamp, 1975) had on writers at this time. It begins with the premise that the bourgeois Enlightenment, including its revolutionary extension in Marxism, has failed.

33. Kunert left the GDR in 1979 under pressure from the security services. His increasing pessimism (ecological and poetological) has also marked his collections in the West, especially *Abtötungsverfahren* (1980), *Stilleben* (1983), and *Fremd daheim* (1990). Wolfgang Hilbig's, 'der poet und die wüste' (1978), reprinted in Hilbig, *die versprengung: gedichte* (Frankfurt/M.: Fischer, 1986), 46–7, is a direct response to Eliot's 'The Waste Land'. Heiner Müller's *Hamletmaschine*, reprinted in *Mauser*, (Berlin/W.: Rotbuch, 1980), 89–97, again explicitly takes up Eliot's text. For a general discussion of the motif of apocalypse in German poetry at this time see Hermann Korte, *Geschichte der deutschen Lyrik seit 1945*, (Stuttgart: Metzler, 1989), 166–207.

34. Günter Kunert, *Vor der Sintflut: Das Gedicht als Arche Noah* (Munich: Hanser, 1985), 51. Ernst Bloch's *Das Prinzip Hoffnung*, the first two volumes of which were published in the GDR in 1955, had a marked influence on a large number of writers, the effects of which lasted during the 1960s and into the 1970s.

35. Anderson, 'Die Generation nach uns ist freier', 74, Rüdiger Rosenthal, 'Hintergrund und Widerstand: die Parallelkultur in Berlin-Ost', in *'Freiheit ist immer Freiheit . . .': Die Andersdenkenden in der DDR*, ed. Ferdinand Kroh (Berlin: Ullstein, 1989), 141–54 (145), *Jansen, prost neuland*, 7.

36. Müller, 'Wie es bleibt, ist es nicht'. Zu Thomas Braschs "Kargo" ', *Rotwelsch*, 154. This review, unsurprisingly, caused Müller problems with the authorities, see Heiner Müller, *Krieg ohne Schlacht: Leben in zwei Diktaturen* (Cologne: Kiepenheuer & Witsch, 1992), 213–14.

37. Fritz Hendrick Melle, in *Berührung ist nur eine Randerscheinung: Neue Literatur aus der DDR*, ed. Sascha Anderson and Elke Erb (Cologne: Kiepenheuer & Witsch, 1985), 147.

38. Cf. Petra Boden, 'Strukturen der Lenkung von Literatur. Das Gesetz zum Schutz der Berufsbezeichnung Schriftsteller', in Böthig and Michael, *MachtSpiele*, 217–27.
39. Karl-Wilhelm Schmidt, 'Grenzüberschreitungen: Über Leben und Literatur ehemaliger DDR-Autoren in der Bundesrepublik. Eine Bestandsaufnahme kulturpolitischer Folgen der Biermann-Ausbürgerung', in *Pluralismus und Postmodernismus: Zur Literatur- und Kulturgeschichte der achtziger Jahre*, ed. Helmut Kreuzer, 2nd edn., rev. and expanded (Frankfurt/M.: Peter Lang, 1991), 149–89 (155). For example, Frank-Wolf Matthies (1981); Bettina Wegner (1983); Katja Lange-Müller, Christa Moog, Volker Palma, Michael Rom, Cornelia Schleime (1984); Fritz Hendrik Melle, Bernd Wagner, Wolfgang Hilbig, (1985); Raja Lubinetski, Sascha Anderson (1986); Gabriele Eckart, Rüdiger Rosenthal (1987); Ulrich Zieger, Uwe Kolbe (1988).
40. Meinicke talks of the 'Sogwirkung' of the exodus of older writers in his *Junge Autoren in der DDR 1975–1980*, 7.
41. Cf. Bernd Wagner, 'Tod der Intelligenz: Das Jahrzehnt nach der Biermann Ausbürgerung', *Frankfurter Rundschau*, 20 Dec. 1986, repr. (slightly revised) in Wagner, *Der Griff ins Leere. 11 Versuche* (Berlin: TRANSIT, 1988), 107–20 (110–11). Rüdiger Rosenthal, on the other hand, saw the protests at the *Ausbürgerung* as a beginning of a unique (if brief) period of cultural solidarity in the GDR, 'Hintergrund und Widerstand', 149.
42. Wagner, *Der Griff ins Leere*, 111. Emmerich makes a direct connection with the beginnings of a postmodern aesthetic, 'Gleichzeitigkeit', 209.
43. Emmerich, 'Gleichzeitigkeit', 208. For an analysis of the career path of the older writers see especially Günter Erbe, 'Schriftsteller in der DDR'.
44. Heukenkamp, 'Funktion und Ausdruck', 297. Cf. the comments in interview by Uwe Kolbe and Thomas Rosenlöcher, in *DDR-Schriftsteller sprechen in der Zeit: Eine Dokumentation*, ed. Gerd Labroisse and Ian Wallace, German Monitor, 27 (Amsterdam: Rodopi, 1991), esp. 211 and 301–3.
45. Cf. 'Die Generation nach uns ist freier. Gespräch mit Sascha Anderson', 75. Meinicke discusses the influence of the 'Singebewegung' and the Schwerin seminars in *Junge Autoren in der DDR: 1975–1980*, 15–21.
46. The biographical notes provided in the anthologies *Vogelbühne* (1983), *Berührung ist nur eine Randerscheinung* (1985), and Geist, *Ein Molotow-Cocktail auf fremder Bettkante* (1990), illustrate the point very clearly. A detailed and insightful study of the social conditions is given in Antonia Grunenberg, *Aufbruch der inneren Mauer: Politik und Kultur in der DDR 1971–1990* (Bremen: Edition Temmen, 1990), esp. ch. 3, 'Bewußtsein von Jugendlichen im Sozialismus—zwischen Resignation und Rebellion', 81–138.
47. Ingrid and Klaus-Dieter Hähnel, 'Junge Lyrik am Ende der siebziger Jahre', 128. 'Die Generation nach uns ist freier. Gespräch mit Sascha Anderson', 75, and Bert Papenfuß-Gorek, *harm. arkdichtung 77* (Berlin/W.: KULTuhr, 1985), 83.
48. Cf. e.g. most recently and comprehensively, Laurel Cohen-Pfister,

'Defining the End of GDR Literature: Making the Case for Young Literature', *Germanic Review*, Theme Issue: 'The End of GDR Literature (Conclusion)', 4 (Fall 1992), 151–8.

49. Henkenkamp, 'Funktion und Ausdruck', 302.
50. Cf. the round-table discussions in *WB* 7 (1979): 'Vorbild—Leitbild' 11–22; 'Zwischen Text und Szene' 23–40, and esp. 'Ohne den Leser geht es nicht', 41–52. For the reactions, see Petra Boden, in Böthig and Michael, *MachtSpiele*, 217–27.
51. 'Vorbild—Leitbild', 18.
52. 'Ohne den Leser', 46. That it was a calculatedly shocking gesture is indicated by the more detailed comments made by Kolbe in 1982. See ' "Ein Nein ist keine Lebenshaltung": Vier Gespräche mit Uwe Kolbe' (geführt von Ellen Barthels), in *Absage—Ansage*, Schriftenreihe DDR-Kultur, 2, ed. Siegfried Radlach (Berlin/W.: Paul-Löbe-Institut, 1982), 17–35. That it succeeded is demonstrated by the number of times Heinz Plavius alludes to it in this 'Positionsbestimmung', 136–47. The problems caused for *Weimarer Beiträge* on account of this comment are described in a second round-table interview some ten years later; see 'Eine eigene Sprache finden', 582.
53. 'Ohne den Leser', 41–2 and 49–50.
54. Hartinger, 'DDR-Debüts', 53; Dau, 'Mit meinen Augen' 94; Hähnels, 'Junge Lyrik', 130.
55. 'Ohne den Leser', 47.
56. Dau, 'Mit meiner Augen' 91, Rönisch, 'Notizen', 7. See also 'Vorbild—Leitbild', 10 and 48.
57. This was esp. true of the prose writers. Cf. Cohen-Pfister, 'Defining the End of GDR Literature', 156.
58. 'Ohne den Leser', 46.
59. 'Vorbild—Leitbild', 17.
60. Ibid. 189.
61. Dau, 'Mit meinen Augen', 106.
62. Ibid. 106 and Hartinger, 'DDR-Debüts' 149.
63. See Hähnels, 'Junge Lyrik', 129–34, and finally 134.
64. Mathilde and Rudolf Dau, 'Noch einmal: Junge Lyrik am Ende der siebziger Jahre', *WB* 3 (1982), 152–6. This is a long-standing dispute between critics of GDR poetry. It is, however, worth pointing out that several controversial, and some excellent, poets had their beginnings in the FDJ or in Schwerin: for example, Hans-Eckardt Wenzel, Steffen Mensching, Gabriele Eckart, Kathrin Schmidt, Sascha Anderson, Stefan Döring, Johannes Jansen, and Frank Lanzendörfer.
65. Heukenkamp, 'Funktion und Ausdruck', 297.
66. Ibid. 299. Compare Cohen-Pfister, 'Defining the End of GDR Literature', 157.
67. Hähnels, 'Junge Lyrik', esp. 150–2. The Hähnels also discuss Uwe Kolbe, another writer who was to encounter problems with the authorities.
68. Erbe, 'Zum Selbstverständnis junger Lyriker in der DDR', 184, and Plavius, 'Positionsbestimmung', 141.
69. Jurij Brězan, 'Über Widerspiegel, das kleine und das große Erleiden und die Würde des Schriftstellers', *NdL* 4 (1982), 5–15. Inge von Wangenheim, 'Genosse Jemand und die Klassik', *NdL* 3 (1981), 99–119. Although Wangenheim's idiosyncratic article begins as the quoted

discussion of the pitfalls of 'Generationswechsel' (p. 104), it moves on to a become a tirade against the evils of science fiction.

70. Quoted in Uwe Kolbe, 'Brief in gestriger Sprache', in Haase, Reese, and Wensierski, *VEB Nachwuchs: Jugend in der DDR*, 80. From the distance of the West, however, Michael Jäger dismisses such metaphors of continuity, and the whole ethos behind them: 'Mittlerweile macht sich eher lächerlich, wer die harmonisierende Metapher weiter gebraucht. Die jungen Leute finden sich entweder nicht auf dem Übergabeplatz ein, oder sie versäumen es, im rechten Augenblick, die Hand auszustrecken. Es lohnt sich nicht, das dürr gewordene Stück Holz, das dar feierlich angeboten wird, zu ergreifen und in die angeblich vom Geschichtsprozeß vorgegebene Richtung weiterzulaufen.' Quoted in Emmerich, *Kleine Literaturgeschichte der DDR*, 425.

71. Kolbe notoriously fell foul of the authorities after publishing a coded attack on the State in a poem 'Kern meines Romans'. See *Bestandsaufnahme 2. Debütanten 1967–1980*, ed. Brigitte Böttcher (Halle–Leipzig: Mitteldeutscher Verlag, 1981), 82–3. Mensching and Wenzel were often prevented from performing their satirical cabaret and were barred from performing at all in certain towns and districts.

72. Bert Papenfuß-Gorek is a useful example. The first of his texts to be published in the GDR were a selection from his manuscript volume 'naif'. They appeared in a magazine in the FDJ publishing house 'Verlag Neues Leben': *Temperamente*, 2 (1977), 117–25, with an introductory note ('Handreichung'), by the poet Richard Pietraß, in which he asked: 'Was geschähe, erschienen die folgenden, gewiß nicht gewöhnlichen Gedichte ohne die Protektion dieses Kommentars?' (p. 116). A smaller selection appeared in *Auswahl 78. Neue Lyrik—neue Namen*, ed. Richard Pietraß, Holger J. Schubert, and Wolfgang Trampe (Berlin: Verlag Neues Leben, 1978), 103–5, although certain texts were censored out even at the proof stage. Cf. Wichner and Wiesner, *Zensur in der DDR*, 183. One text under cover of a commentary by Karl Mickel, 'Das Einfache das selten gelingt', was published in *NDL* 8 (1980), 68–71, but by 1983 Papenfuß-Gorek was notably absent from the anthology *Vogelbühne*, ed. Dorothea von Törne. It was not until Gerhard Wolf initiated the 'Außer der Reihe' series with Aufbau in 1989 that a full length collection by Papenfuß-Gorek could appear in the GDR.

73. Endler, *Den Tiger reiten*, 46.

74. In an article first written in 1985 for a radio broadcast in the West, he comments: 'Die Literaturkritiker/Literaturwissenschaftler der DDR pflegen in solchen Fällen Mann für Mann und Frau für Frau ohne Ausnahme zu parieren! Papenfuß gibt es nicht mehr—und ganz so als hätte es ihn nie gegeben!'. Ibid. 21.

75. Emmerich, *Kleine Literaturgeschichte der DDR*, 428, and Klaus Michael, 'Papierboote', in Muschter and Thomas, *Jenseits der Staatskultur*, 62–82 (71). Compare: *Mikado oder Der Kaiser ist nackt. Selbstverlegte Literatur in der DRR*, ed. Uwe Kolbe, Lothar Trolle, and Bernd Wagner (Darmstadt: Luchterhand, 1988); *Sprache & Antwort. Stimmen und Texte einer anderen Literatur aus der DDR*, ed. Egmont Hesse (Frankfurt/M.: Fischer, 1988); *abriss der ariadnefabrik*, ed. Andreas Koziol and Rainer Schedlinski (Berlin, Galrev, 1990); *Die andere Sprache. Neue DDR-Literatur der 80er Jahre*; *Zellinnendruck*; 'Alles ist

*im untergrund obenauf; einmannfrei ...': ausgewählte beiträge aus der
zeitschrift* KONTEXT *1–7,* ed. Torsten Metelka (Berlin: KONTEXTverlag,
1990); *vogel order käfig sein.*

76. Useful general accounts of a history of the underground scene are given
    variously in *Zellinnendruck, Die andere Sprache, vogel oder käfig sein,*
    and most recently, in Böthig and Michael, *MachtSpiele.*
77. Uwe Kolbe, *Vaterlandkanal: Ein Fahrtenbuch* (Frankfurt/M.: Suhrkamp,
    1990), 49.
78. The motif of the precarious existence as artist is common. Cf. Hans-
    Eckardt Wenzel's melancholy reflection on the jester/poet in 'Abschmink-
    Lied', Wenzel, *Lied vom wilden Mohn* (Halle–Leipzig: Mitteldeutscher
    Verlag, 1984), 67, which concludes: 'Meine Narrenfreiheit freilich | ist
    ein lächerliches Stück'. See also Sascha Anderson, 'ich bin kein artist', in
    Jeder Satellit hat einen Killersatelliten, 26. These make an interesting
    contrast to the confidence of Volker Braun's 'Meine Damen und Herrn',
    Provokation für mich, 4th edn. (Halle: Mitteldeutscher Verlag, 1973),
    35.
79. This poem is one of number from the 'Bornholm' manuscript which fell
    victim to the censor. The collection was eventually published as
    Bornholm II: Gedichte (Berlin and Weimar: Aufbau 1986), the 'II'
    signalling its altered state. 'Das Kabarett—kostenlose, limitierte Beilage
    des Autors zu Bornholm II' was circulated privately in the same year and
    dedicated to the 'Verlagslektor' who had been instrumental in preventing
    publication. Part of it is reprinted in *Vaterlandkanal,* 39–53.
80. For an overview of the subversive poetic strategies developed by the older
    writers in the GDR see Karl Heinz Wüst, *Sklavensprache: Subversive
    Schreibweisen in der Lyrik der DDR 1961–1976,* Europäische Hoch-
    schulschriften Reihe 1, Deutsche Sprache und Literatur 1129, (Frankfurt/
    M.: Peter Lang, 1989).
81. From 'flexitus vitalis', in 'pest sowohl als strom. ein personensubkult für
    cerstin', quoted in Michael, 'Papierboote', 68. Cf. also Lutz Eiffert (i.e.
    Uwe Kolbe), 'Vater und Sohn', in *Mikado oder Der Kaiser ist nackt,*
    56–7.
82. Apart from informative essays on rock, art, theatre, and photography in
    Muschter and Thomas, *Jenseits der Staatskultur,* there are useful surveys
    of music, theatre, and art in Antonia Grunenberg, 'Musikkultur und
    "Szene" ', in *Aufbruch der inneren Mauer,* 125–9, Detlef Böhnki, DADA-
    Rezeption in der DDR-Literatur, Kunstwissenschaften in der Blauen
    Eule, 4 (Essen: Verlag Die Blaue Eule, 1989), and *Kunstkombinat DDR:
    Daten und Zitate zur Kunst und Kunstpolitik der DDR 1945–1990,* ed.
    Günter Feist in collaboration with Eckhart Gillen and the Museums-
    pädagogischen Dienst, Berlin (Berlin: Verlag Dirk Nishen, 1990).
83. Gerd Poppe gives an account of the readings in 'Der Staatsfeind im
    Wohnzimmer. Aktenfunde zum Kampf gegen Dichterlesungen', in Böthig
    and Michael, *MachtSpiele,* 228–41, as does Sascha Anderson, under the
    name 'David Menzer', in his report for the *Staatssicherheit,* in Böthig and
    Michael, *MachtSpiele,* 250–74.
84. Peter Böthig, 'die verlassenen worte—eine skizze (literatur in den 80ern)',
    SitZ, 112 (Dec. 1989), 262–5 (263).
85. Christiane Grosz, *Blatt vor dem Mund* (Berlin and Weimar: Aufbau,
    1983).

86. Anderson speaks of it as 'dialog': Anderson, 'jeder, der spricht, stirbt', in *Sprache & Antwort*, 58. The other quotations are from 'MIKADO—Statement der Herausgeber' [Uwe Kolbe, Lothar Trolle, Bernd Wagner], *Mikado oder Der Kaiser ist nackt*, 8, and Michael Thulin and Egmont Hesse, 'sprachabbruch und umbruch des sprechens: zur situation der zeitschriften SCHADEN und VERWENDUNG', originally *liane*, 5 (Poetik-Materialheft, 1; 1989), repr. in *Zellinnendruck*, 16–20 (16).

87. 'Wortlaut', *Sprache & Antwort*, 220.

88. Geist, ' "Mit würde holzkekse kauen"—neue Lyrik der jüngeren Generation nebst Seiten- und Rückblicken', *NdL* 2 (1993), 131–53, esp. 138–9.

89. ' "Es gibt nichts Schlimmeres, als recht zu haben": Gespräch mit den DDR-SchriftstellerInnen Elke Erb und Rainer Schedlinski', *Volkszeitung*, 18 May 1990.

90. Cf. Sascha Anderson's explanation in interview, reprinted in Böhnki, *DADA-Rezeption in der DDR-Literatur*, 169–78.

91. Cf. Michael Thulin [i.e. Klaus Michael], 'Das Unikat-Syndrom', *vogel oder käfig sein*, 295–8.

92. Birgit Dahlke, ' "Die Chancen haben sich verschanzt": Die inoffizielle Literatur-Szene der DDR', *Mauer Show: das Ende der DDR, die deutsche Einheit und die Medien*, ed. Rainer Bohn, Knut Hickethier, Eggo Müller, sigma medienwissenschaft, 11 (Berlin: edition sigma Rainer Bohn Verlag, 1992), 227–42 (229). The other quotations come from Peter Böthig, 'Aufbrüche in die Vielfalt', *Zellinnendruck*, 10, Michael Thulin and Egmont Hesse, 'sprachabbruch und umbruch des sprechens', *Zellinnendruck*, 19, and 'MIKADO—Statement der Herausgeber', *Mikado oder Der Kaiser ist nackt*, 9.

93. Dahlke settles eventually on 'unabhängige Literatur', 229, Alexander von Bormann, in his 'Wege aus der Ordnung', in Muschter and Thomas, *Jenseits der Staatskultur*, on 'nicht-offiziell', 82–3. Kolbe's comment comes from his editor's statement for the first issue of *Der Kaiser ist nackt* (May 1981), quoted in Endler, ' "alles ist im untergrund obenauf; einmannfrei . . .": Anläßlich einer Anthologie', in Endler, *Den Tiger reiten*, 40–68 (43). Endler examines the political interpretations of the notion of an 'other' literature, pp. 40–6.

94. Schedlinski, 'an das literaturinstitut der akademie der wissenschaften', *ariadnefabrik*, 5 (1988), repr. in *abriss der ariadnefabrik*, 203–4 (203).

95. Cf. 'Sascha Andersons letzter Freund': Bert Papenfuß-Gorek zu Sascha Anderson, Rainer Schedlinski und der "Ortsbestimmung" von Literatur zwischen Häresie und Staatssicherheit', von Ute Scheub und Bascha Mika, *die tageszeitung*, 29 Jan. 1992, 11, or Rosenthal, 'Hintergrund und Widerstand', 148.

96. Compare Dahlke, 'Die Chancen haben sich verschanzt'; Thomas Günther, 'Die subkulturellen Zeitschriften in der DDR', 27–36; Gerhard Wolf, 'POE SIE ALL BUM bis POE SIE ALL PENG: Texte auf der FLUCHT NACH VORN', in Wolf, *Sprachblätter Wortwechsel*, 178–90; Peter Böthig, 'Möglichkeitsräume: Selbstverlegte Originalgrafisch-Literarische Zeitschriften in der DDR', in Henkel and Russ, *D1980D1989R*, 95–100; and Klaus Michael, 'Papierboote', in Muschter and Thomas, *Jenseits der Staatskultur*, 62–82.

97. Jan Faktor, 'Was ist neu an der Literatur der achtziger Jahre', *vogel oder käfig sein*, 367–90 (384). A. R. Penck (Ralf Winkler), was the star of the

art underground in Dresden until he was forced to leave for the Federal Republic in 1980. He became extraordinarily successful, particularly in New York, and contributed widely to illegal 'Lyrik-Mappen' of the 1980s, which, partly because of his originals, became valuable collectors' pieces. He supported the foundation of Druckhaus Galrev and his angular stick figures or abstract designs are a prominent feature of many Galrev texts.

98. Kachold's poem 'das gesetz der szene' is a bitter deconstruction of the brutal promiscuity and betrayal of the scene, written in 1988 and published in Gabriele Stötzer-Kachold, *grenzen los fremd gehen* (Berlin: Janus Press, BasisDruck, 1992), 133–8. See also ' "Denn wir haben uns nur bekämpft und verletzt" ' Gespräch mit Gabriele Stötzer-Kachold', in *Freitag*, 3 Jan. 1992, and Cornelia Sachse, 'Vage Zagenvragen' and 'Die Orange Leben: ein abwesender Essay über die Abwesenheit der abwesenden Autorinnen', in *vogel oder käfig sein*, 401–2 and 402–4 respectively.

99. The magazine *liane*, 'Poetikheft 1', documents the major contributions to the 'Zersammlung' held in Lychener Straße 6 (Berlin, Prenzlauer Berg) from 5 to 11 Mar. 1984. Faktor describes it as 'Erster inoffizielle Schriftstellerkongreß der DDR'. 'Was ist neu an der jungen Literatur der achtziger Jahre', p. 367. See also Papenfuß-Gorek in 'Sascha Andersons letzter Freund'.

100. Brian Keith-Smith, 'Little Magazines from the Former German Democratic Republic—A Survey', *German Monitor*, 26 (1992), 64–93.

101. Faktor, 'Was ist neu an der jungen Literatur der achtziger Jahre?', *vogel oder käfig sein*, 373.

102. Jan Faktor, 'Das, wozu die Berliner Szene geworden ist', first in *ariadnefabrik* 4 (1987), repr. in *vogel oder käfig sein*, 399–400.

103. Faktor, 'Sechzehn Punkte zur Prenzlauer-Berg-Szene', in Böthig and Michael, *MachtSpiele*, 91–111. Rosenthal also makes the point that privileges and punishments were distributed by the *Staatssicherheit* in order to destabilize the solidarity of the underground scene, 'Hintergrund und Widerstand', 149, as does Klaus Michael, discussing Sascha Anderson's *Stasi* reports: 'Einige junge Lyriker dezentralisieren: Sascha Anderson: Machtspiele und Freundesverrat in der Ostberliner Literatenszene', *Focus*, 4 (1993), 80.

104. Compare the fascinating details in Klaus Michael, 'Eine verschollene Anthologie: Zentralkomitee, Staatssicherheit und die Geschichte eines Buches', in Böthig and Michael, *MachtSpiele*, 202–16.

105. See 'Zum Vorgehen in der Angelegenheit der Anthologie "Leila Anastasia" ' in Wichner and Wieser, *Zensur in der DDR*, 188–9.

106. Hartung, originally in Hans-Jürgen Schmitt (ed.) *Die Literatur der DDR*, Hansers Sozialgeschichte der deutschen Literatur xi (Munich: Hanser, 1983), 263, reiterated in *Die Deutsche Lyrik seit 1965*, 100. Emmerich, *Kleine Literaturgeschichte der DDR*, 3rd rev. edn. (Frankfurt/M.: Luchterhand, 1985), esp. 176 and 188. The only references to the younger writers are to Lutz Rathenow and Frank-Wolf Matthies, and these chiefly concern their particular difficulties with the authorities.

107. Compare the reviews of the anthology: Konrad Franke, 'Glauben ersetz' ich nicht durch weiteren Glauben. Neue Literatur aus der DDR in vier Anthologien', *Süddeutsche Zeitung*, 25–7 May 1985; Roland Mischke, ' "Diese tierische Menschheit". Eine Anthologie mit "Neuer Literatur aus

der DDR" ', *FAZ* 24 Sept. 1985; Beatrice von Matt, 'Generationswechsel in der Literatur der DDR', *Neue Zürcher Zeitung*, 18 Apr. 1986; and Anneli Hartmann, 'Berührung ist nur eine Randerscheinung', in *Colloquia Germanica*, 21 (1988), 94–5. The interest had undoubtedly also been stimulated by Uwe Wittstock's much publicized 'discovery' of Sascha Anderson: compare 'Ohne Mauer im Kopf. Der DDR-Schriftsteller Sascha Anderson', *FAZ* 23 June 1983, repr. in a slightly different form in Wittstock, *Von der Stalinallee zum Prenzlauer Berg*, 258–64.

108. See esp. Günter Erbe, 'Zum Selbstverständnis junger Lyriker in der DDR: Kolbe, Anderson, Eckart', *Studies in GDR Culture and Society 4*, ed. Margy Gerber *et al.* (Lanham, MD: University Press of America, 1984), 171–85; Anneli Hartmann, 'Neuere Tendenzen in der DDR-Lyrik' *Deutsche Studien*, 85 (1984), 5–29, and 'Der Generationswechsel—ein ästhetischer Wechsel? Schreibweisen und Traditionsbezüge in der jüngsten DDR-Lyrik', in Klussmann and Mohr, *Jahrbuch zur Literatur der DDR 4*, 104–35, and 'Schreiben in der Tradition der Avantgarde. Neue Lyrik in der DDR', in Cosentino, Labroisse, and Ertl, *DDR-Lyrik im Kontext*, 1–37; Gerd Labroisse, 'Neue Positionen in der DDR-Lyrik der 80er Jahre?', in *The GDR in the 1980s*, ed. Ian Wallace, GDR Monitor Special Series, 4 (Dundee: [n. pub.], 1984), 101–19; Gerrit-Jan Berendse, 'Outcast in Berlin: Opposition durch Entziehung bei der jüngeren Generation', in *Zfg*, 1 (1991), 21–7.

109. Cosentino, 'ich habe ausser meiner sprache', 216; Berendse, 'Outcast in Berlin', 20; Cohen-Pfister, 'Defining the End of GDR Literature', 153; Hartmann, 'Berührung ist nur eine Randerscheinung', 95.

110. Wolf Biermann, ' "Laß, o Welt, o laß mich sein": Rede zum Eduard-Mörike-Preis', *Die Zeit*, 15 Nov. 1991, 73–4, repr. in *Der Sturz des Dädalus, oder Eizes für die Eingeborenen der Fidschi-Inseln über den IM Judas Ischariot und den Kuddelmuddel in Deutschland seit der Golfkrieg* (Cologne: Kiepenheuer & Witsch, 1992), 64–79 (esp. 71 and 72).

111. Faktor, 'Was ist neu an der jungen Literatur der achtziger Jahre', 379. Endler, *Den Tiger reiten*, 46. Similar open confrontations, although with variously shifting fronts, have occurred between Kolbe and Mensching, between Kolbe and Frank-Wolf Matthies, and between Kolbe and 'die Dilettanten der Linguistik'. See Frank-Wolf Matthies, 'Offener Brief', *Frankfurter Rundschau*, 11 May 1992, Kolbe's response, 'Ein Nein ist keine Lebenshaltung', pp. 18–19, and Kolbe's assault on the experimental poetry in 'Rundfunk Essay', first published in *Bizarre Städte*, Sonderband 4 (1989), repr. in *vogel oder käfig sein*, 391–2 (391).

112. Papenfuß-Gorek, 'under uns gesagt, aber behalt es für dich', *ariadnefabrik*, 4 (1986), repr. in *Sprache & Antwort*, 199.

113. Emmerich, *Kleine Literaturgeschichte der DDR*, 411 and Hartmann, 'Der Generationswechsel—ein ästhetischer Wechsel?', 119–25.

114. Cf. Emmerich's 'Status melancholicus', 243, and *Kleine Literaturgeschichte*, 438.

115. *Berührung ist nur eine Randerscheinung*, 147. See also Ingrid Pergande, ' "Volker Braun?—Da kann ich nur sagen, der Junge quält sich . . .": New Voices in the GDR Lyric of the 1980s', in *Socialism and the Literary Imagination*, ed. Martin Kane (Oxford: Berg, 1991), 229–45.

116. Volker Braun, 'Rimbaud. Ein Psalm der Aktualität', originally presented

in Mainz in 1984 and subsequently printed as an essay in *SuF* 5 (1985), 978–98. I take this up in more detail below. See also 'Die Generation nach uns ist freier. Gespräch mit Sascha Anderson', 75.

117. For two very specific but fascinating explorations of the links between the generations see Peter Geist, 'Gruß, Gerade, Grat—Anmerkungen zur Mickel-Rezeption bei jüngeren Lyrikern aus der DDR, *Diskussion Deutsch*, 12 (1991), 619–37, and Gerrit-Jan Berendse, 'Zu neuen Ufern: Lyrik der "Sächsischen Dichterschule" im Spiegel der Elbe', in *Studies in GDR Culture and Society 10*, ed. Margy Gerber *et al.* (Lanham, MD: University Press of America, 1991), 197–212.

118. Müller, the Wolfs, Franz Fühmann, Adolf Endler, Karl Mickel, and Elke Erb were all active in supporting younger writers with opportunities to publish or with financial help, or by protecting them from the authorities. Volker Braun, for all the apparent antagonism between them, was Sascha Anderson's support in applying for membership of the Writers' Union. He wrote simply, 'Sascha Anderson ist ein großer Dichter'. Cf. Braun, 'Monströse Banalität', *Die Zeit*, 22 Nov. 1991.

119. Cf. the Hähnels, 'Junge Lyrik'; Heukenkamp, 'Funktion und Ausdruck'; and Hartung, 'Ziemlich zahme Vögel: Eine Rezension als Nachsatz', in Hartung, *Die deutsche lyrik seit 1965*, as well as articles by Hartmann and Krippendorf (see Bibliography), who all use this as a framework to some extent.

CHAPTER 2

1. Stefan Döring, 'ich fühle mich in grenzen wohl', *Heutmorgestern: gedichte* (Berlin and Weimar: Aufbau—Außer der Reihe, 1989), 15.
2. Müller, *Krieg ohne Schlacht*, 288–9.
3. 'Ohne den Leser', 46.
4. Kolbe, *Vaterlandkanal*, 46. Ironic also because it comes from a text which was censored out of his Bornholm manuscript, precisely because of its provocative contemporary subject matter: the brutality of the state during the Polish dock strikes.
5. Heukenkamp, in 'Ohne den Leser', 49, Rönisch, 'Notizen', 9, and Michael Franz, ' "Offene Fenster"—Schülergedichte zwischen 1967–1977', *WB* 7 (1979), 149–53 (150). The same point is made by Western critics: see Hartmann, 'Berührung ist nur eine Randerscheinung', 95, or Harald Hartung: 'Wieviel Lebensstoff—aber wie wenig davon ging in die Gedichte dieser Anthologie [*Vogelbühne*] ein', in Hartung, *Deutsche Lyrik seit 1965*, 136.
6. Kolbe, 'Rundfunk-Essay', *vogel oder käfig sein*, 392.
7. Rönisch, 'Notizen', 7. For a discussion of the 'großen Gegenstand' see Adolf Endler, 'Czechowski und andere: Heinz Czechowski, ' "Nachmittag eines Liebespaares" ', *NdL* 11 (1963), 137–45 (140).
8. Drawert, 'Zweite Inventur', in *Zweite Inventur* (Berlin and Weimar: Aufbau, 1987), 69–70.
9. Günter Eich, 'Inventur', in Eich, *Gesammelte Werke*, ed. Suhrkamp Verlag in collaboration with Ilse Aichinger and others (Frankfurt/M.: Suhrkamp, 1973), i. *Die Gedichte*, ed. Horst Ohde, 35.
10. Cf. Drawert in interview: ' "... Die Tür ist zu, das ist alles": Robert

Stauffer im Gespräch mit Kurt Drawert 19. 12. 1988', in Drawert, *Fraktur: Lyrik, Prosa, Essay* (Leipzig: Reclam, 1994), 230–41 (234–5).

11. 'Zu sagen die wenigen Dinge', in Drawert, *Privateigentum* (Frankfurt/M.: Suhrkamp, 1989), 30.

12. See Kolbe, *Hineingeboren*, 33, and Jansen, *Poesiealbum*, 248 (Berlin: Verlag Neues Leben, 1988), 10. For the Schmidt see Charitas Jenny-Ebeling, ' "Jeder Text ist ein Wortbruch": *Neue Zürcher Zeitung*, 30 Mar. 1993, and cf. Durs Grünbein's *Grauzone morgens* (Frankfurt/M.: Suhrkamp, 1988), 88: 'Sieh genau hin, ehe sie dich | für blöd verkaufen'.

13. Braun's 'Material' texts are taken up into his *Training des aufrechten Gangs* (Halle–Leipzig: Mitteldeutscher Verlag, 1979), and *Langsamer knirschender Morgen* (Frankfurt/M.: Suhrkamp, 1987).

14. Kolbe, *Vaterlandkanal*, 50; Hensel, *Gewitterfront: Lyrik* (Leipzig: Mitteldeutscher Verlag, 1991), 67. Hensel is playing on the story of 'Aschenputtel', and evokes those who attempt by self-mutilation to fit a slipper made for someone else: Compare Grimms' *Kinder- und Hausmärchen* (Stuttgart: Reclam, 1980), 143. Grünbein, 'An diesem Morgen. . .', *Grauzone morgens*, 16–17.

15. Kolbe, 'Kontext', *Vaterlandkanal*, 66–7.

16. Sascha Anderson, *Jeder Satellit hat einen Killersatelliten*, 26, and Gröschner, from 'Meiner fortgelaufenen freundin', in Gröschner, *Herzdame Knochensammler* (Berlin: KONTEXTverlag, 1993), n.p.

17. Kolbe, *Hineingeboren*, 46.

18. For a discussion of Kolbe's debt to Expressionism see Anthonya Visser's 'Überlegungen zur Lyrik Uwe Kolbes', in Cosentino, Ertl, and Labroisse, *DDR-Lyrik im Kontext*, 297–334.

19. In Grünbein's 'Gesehen ganz wie. . .' the lyric subject is brought to a standstill by the sight of a jammed transport of animals patiently on their way to slaughter, and inevitably thinks of himself, *Grauzone morgens*, 21. See also, from the same collection, 'Fast ein Gesang', 68–70, and 'was alles klar wird', 22–3.

20. In *Berührung ist nur eine Randerscheinung*, 82.

21. Gerhard Wolf, *Sprachblätter Wortwechsel*, 51–2.

22. A more extreme form of the same kind of thing occurs in Richard Pietraß's, 'Generation', *Freiheitsmuseum* (Berlin and Weimar: Aufbau, 1982), 26, which is dedicated to Khlebnikow.

23. Lutz Rathenow, *Zangengeburt: Gedichte* (Munich: Piper, orig. 1982, here 1987), 61.

24. Quoted in Christine Cosentino, 'Lutz Rathenows Lyrikband *Zangengeburt*: Eine Stimme von Prenzlauer Berg', in *Studies in GDR Culture and Society 5*, ed. Margy Gerber *et al.* (Lanham, MD: University Press of America, 1985), 141–51 (143).

25. Frank Lanzendörfer, who wrote under the pseudonym flanzendörfer, left only fragments of his extraordinarily wide-ranging artistic output after his suicide in 1988. These have been collected and documented in flanzendörfer, *unmöglich es leben*, ed. Peter Böthig and Klaus Michael (Berlin: Janus press BasisDruck, 1992). 'Garuna ich bin' (pp. 1–25) is a cycle of texts, photographs, film-stills, and sketches. Parts of it have also been published in various versions in *Bizarre Städte*, Sonderheft 3 (1989) and *Die andere Sprache*, 140–3. The quotation comes from the posthumous edn. of flanzendörfer's work, 186.

26. Grünbein, *Schädelbasislektion* (Frankfurt/M.: Suhrkamp, 1991), 111.
27. Lanzendorfer 'ich knüpfe an', *unmöglich es leben*, 41. Cf. also: Wüstefeld's 'für Uwe Kolbe' (as above) which concludes 'Geborensein wie totleben'; Anderson's 'wie immer am morgen', where he presents the ' "totenreklame" atem | derer die noch tot sind', in Sascha Anderson and Ralf Kerbach, *totenreklame. eine reise: texte und zeichnungen* (Berlin/W.: Rotbuch, 1983), 9; Gabriele Stötzer-Kachold's 'heimchen ddr', *grenzen los fremd gehen*, 150–2; Tohm di Roes, 'ICHS APOKALYPTUS: eine autobiographische Weltgeschichte', *Berührung ist nur eine Randerscheinung*, 209–18; or Jayne-Ann Igel, 'ich trank es. . .', which carries the motto 'ich habe das Gift | getrunken, ich trank, | eingebunden in meine Zeit', in Igel [Bernd], *Das Geschlecht der Häuser gebar mir fremde Orte* (Frankfurt/M.: Fischer, 1989), 34.
28. Bert Papenfuß-Gorek, *vorwärts im zorn &sw. gedichte* (Berlin and Weimar: Aufbau, 1990), 65.
29. Ulrich Zieger, *neunzehnhundertfünfundsechzig* (Berlin: Edition qwert zui opü, 1990), 27.
30. Hensel, *Stilleben mit Zukunft: Gedichte*, (Halle–Leipzig: Mitteldeutscher Verlag, 1988), 19.
31. Marianne and Ursula Heukenkamp, 'Fragen zwischen den Generationen: Kerstin Hensel: "Stilleben mit Zukunft" ', *NdL* 6 (1989), 132–6, (134–5). Cf. also Mathilde Dau, 'Selbstporträt einer Generation: Zu "Stilleben mit Zukunft" von Kerstin Hensel', *Temperamente*, 3 (1988), 145–8. It is interesting to note that this is very different from Braun's positive understanding of the 'Larvenzustand', *Training des aufrechten Ganges* (Halle–Leipzig: Mitteldeutscher Verlag, 1979; 4th edn. 1987), 62–5.
32. Anderson, *Jeder Satellit hat einen Killersatelliten*, 52–3. This is the same poem in which he seeks a formula for his generation (see also above). Cf. also Thomas Böhme, 'vom lebensrythmus der eintagsfliege', *stoff der piloten* (Berlin and Weimar: Aufbau, 1988), 82, and 'Elegie', *vogel oder käfig sein*, 31. A variation on the birth as death theme appears in Hans Brinkmann, 'zoo', *Wasserstände und Tauchtiefen* (Berlin: Verlag Neues Leben, 1985), 63.
33. Kachold, *zügel los*, 79–81 (79). See also Drawert, 'Zu spät Gekommen' *Zweite Inventur*, 47, and 'Vorwärts, Rückwärts', 73, and Hensel's 'Lamento in medias res', *Stilleben mit Zukunft*, 32.
34. Ralph Grüneberger, *Frühstück im Stehen: Gedichte* (Halle–Leipzig: Mitteldeutscher Verlag, 1986), 32–3.
35. See Kerstin Hensel, 'Lyrik im Stehen: Zu Ralph Grüneberger "Frühstück im Stehen" ', *Temperamente*, 2 (1987), 148–9 (148), and the defensive response of the editors of *Temperamente*, which examines the question of generations: Regina Scheer and Thomas Wieke, 'Senden auf verschiedenen Frequenzen: Notiert zu Kerstin Hensel und Ralph Grüneberger', *Temperamente*, 2 (1987), 149–53.
36. Kachold, *zügel los*, 81.
37. Drawert, *Zweite Inventur*, 9–15 (12). Cf. also Steffen Mensching's dense and witty autobiography of the lyric subject and his search for a place in history: 'Von mir aus', in Mensching, *Tuchfühling: Gedichte* (Halle–Leipzig: Mitteldeutscher Verlag, 1986), 35–59.
38. Hensel, *Stilleben mit Zukunft*, 26, Schleime, *liane* 5 (1989), 27.

39. Bernd Wagner, *Zweite Erkenntnis* (Berlin and Weimar: Aufbau, 1978), 85. Kolbe, 'Brief an Lothar Walsdorf', *Abschiede und andere Liebesgedichte*, (Berlin and Weimar: Aufbau, 1981; here Frankfurt/M.: Suhrkamp, 1983), 79–82. Cf. also Hans Brinkmann, 'Frühling', *Wasserstände und Tauchtiefen*, 19.

40. Harold Bloom, *The Anxiety of Influence* (Oxford: OUP, 1973).

41. Mohr, *Zaungäste* 9.

42. Volker Braun, 'Allgemeine Erwartung', *Gegen die symmetrische Welt* (Halle: Mitteldeutscher Verlag, 1974), 55–9. Peter Geist also takes up Braun's text as paradigmatic in his 'Gedicht-Schreiben in der DDR', 5–12.

43. Bernd Rump, 'Kann das schon alles sein?', *Poesiealbum*, 141 (Berlin: Verlag Neues Leben, 1979), 11.

44. See Müller, *Rotwelsch*, 51; Braun, *Langsamer knirschender Morgen*, 45–6, and the contemporaneously written 'Rimbaud. Ein Psalm der Aktualität', 993: Steffen Mensching, *Erinnerung an eine Milchglasscheibe* (Halle–Leipzig: Mitteldeutscher Verlag, 1984), 17.

45. This is clearly manifested in Braun's 'Eisenwagen', which functions as a symbol for the 'locomotive of history' and is a grinding, destructive tank—a bleak parody of socialist aspirations. See *Langsamer knirschender Morgen*, 52–7. Emmerich takes it as the key poetic representation of the failure of really existing socialism, *Kleine Literaturgeschichte der DDR*, 422–3. But it also finds strong echoes in a very large number of texts from young writers, where 'historischen Autos' (Mensching) of one sort or another long to scorch the asphalt, but are forced onto 'der gleiche bremsweg' (Döring). Compare Mensching, 'Vollgas', *Erinnerung an eine Milchglasscheibe*, 7; Döring, 'halt' quoted in Gerhard Wolf, *Sprachblätter Wortwechsel*, 57; Grüneberger 'Jungstraum Manchmal', *Frühstück im Stehen*, 12; Grünbein, 'Kursiv', *Grauzone morgens*, 67.

46. See Dieter Schlenstedt, 'Entwicklungstendenzen der neueren Literatur in der DDR', in *Die Literatur der DDR 1976–1986*, ed. Anna Chiarloni, Gemma Sartori, and Fabrizio Cambi, 29–54, esp. 39–44. One might compare Mohr's description of the young generation in the West as 'Zaungäste der Geschichte [. . .] auf dem gesellschaftlichen Abstellgleis', *Zaungäste*, 9.

47. Wenzel, *Lied vom wilden Mohn*, 89–108 (91). I take up the idea of the split self in Ch. 3.

48. This text appears on Wenzel's *Reisebilder* Amiga VEB Schallplatten 8 45 357 (1988), with a whimsical but repetitive accompaniment and the sound of a fairground organ suggesting endlessly circling rides. In interview Wenzel related 'Wartung eines Landes' particularly to the reticence of the GDR authorities in the face of Gorbachev's *glasnost*. Cf. NDR radio programme 'Zeitfragen—Streitfragen', broadcast 25 Dec. 1987, where Wenzel also performed it as a spoken text.

49. Cf. also Wenzel's 'Ich bin die ganze Zeit nur hier', and 'Tage von so große Dauer', *Antrag auf Verlängerung des Monats August: Gedichte* (Halle–Leipzig, Mitteldeutscher Verlag, 1986), 16 and 76–7; Gabriele Eckart, 'Das Warten', in *Sturzacker: Gedichte* (Berlin, Buchverlag der Morgen, 1985), 81; Kolbe, 'Warten', *Bornholm II*, 96.

50. Samuel Beckett, *Waiting for Godot* in Beckett, *The Complete Dramatic Works* (London: Faber, 1986), 7–88 (72).

51. Peter Geist makes the connection between 'solche "Warte"-Situationen und das Gefühl im Kreis zu gehen, nicht recht vorwärts zu kommen' ('Gedicht-Schreiben', 9). Compare the striking circle motif in: Böhme, 'agonie' and 'beautiful morning', *stoff der piloten*, 86–7 and 92; Lothar Walsdorf, 'Jährliches '85', in his *Über die Berge kam ich: Gedichte* (Berlin and Weimar: Aufbau, 1987), 9; Drawert, 'Theater', and 'Spiel', *Zweite Inventur*, 39 and 117; Kolbe, 'die dunkle Musik', *Bornholm II*, 26–7. One could go further and point to the controversial Sisyphus motif in the work. Cf. below, Ch. 4.

52. Döring explores this theme in a number of texts, *Heutmorgestern: gedichte* (Berlin and Weimar: Aufbau—Außer der Reihe, 1989). See especially 'der gegenwert der gegenwart', 12, the poetic dialogue 'ein stück zeit: gespräch mit einer pause', 53–66, and the section of texts from 1985–1988, 'weilen', 69–105.

53. For very different treatments of this almost ubiquitous theme see: Barbara Köhler, *Deutsches Roulette: Gedichte* (Frankfurt/M.: Suhrkamp, 1991); Hensel, *Stilleben mit Zukunft*, esp. the central 'Fünf Gesänge', 46–57; Wenzel, 'Grenzen', *Lied vom wilden Mohn*, 52–8; or the section 'Grenzstrasse', in Michael Wüstefeld's *Stadtplan* (Berlin and Weimar: Aufbau, 1990), 99–119.

54. 'sprachabbruch und umbruch des sprechens', in *Zellinnendruck*, 19.

55. It is striking that poetry about the natural landscape, which is such an overworked part of the GDR tradition (from *Aufbau* to 'Öko'), esp. among those writers of the 'middle generation' (Braun, Czechowski, Kirsten, Mickel), and those even a little older (Wolfgang Hilbig), is almost completely absent from this generation of writing. An exception of sorts is Hans-Eckardt Wenzel's beautiful cycle of 'Schmuggerower Elegien'. However, they too are 'city' elegies and clearly stand in a tradition with Kunert's 'Bucher Elegien', Biermann's 'Buckower Balladen' and are, ultimately, a homage to Brecht.

56. *Unreal City: Urban Experience in Modern European Literature and Art*, ed. Edward Timms and David Kelly (Manchester: Manchester University Press, 1985). Since 1945 Berlin, especially, has featured centrally in German literature, whether as symbol of urban corruption, 'socialist metropolis', or palimpsest of historical change. Cf. *Berlin: Literary Images of a city. Eine Großstadt im Spiegel der Literatur*, ed. Derek Glass, Dietmar Rösler, and John J. White, Publications of the Institute of Germanic Studies 42 (Berlin: Erich Schmidt Verlag, 1989).

57. In the work of Günter Kunert (probably the most important recent poetic chronicler of the city), Berlin is often poetically merged with other lost cities: Pompeii, Babylon, Mycenae, Vineta, or Troy. Brinkmann's photographic and poetical collages of Cologne, London and New York, *Westwärts 1 & 2: Gedichte* (Reinbeck bei Hamburg: Rowohlt, 1975), are taken up explicitly by a number of authors.

58. T. S. Eliot, *The Waste Land: A Facsimile Transcript*, ed. Valerie Eliot (London: Faber, 1971).

59. See 'Gesang über der Stadt', in Wüstefeld, *Stadtplan*, 115–19.

60. Thomas Böhme, *Die schamlose Vergeudung des Dunkels* (Berlin and Weimar: Aufbau, 1985), 15, and 'Leipzig mit Löchern', 9.

61. Böhme, *Die schamlose Vergeudung des Dunkels*, 18.

62. Labroisse and Wallace, *DDR-Schriftsteller sprechen in der Zeit*, 215–16. Cf. Kolbe's 'Zitat vom Gott der Stadt', *Bornholm II*, 44, and 'Auf dem Kometen', 53, for further direct references to Heym.

63. Bornholm was an area of allotment gardens which abutted the Wall and had a kind of mirror image in West German allotments just beyond the train lines on the other side. See the poems 'Bornholm I (sentimental)', *Bornholm II*, 67–8, and 'Blattabflug Bornholm I', 69–70, and, for the comments, cf. Labroisse and Wallace, *DDR-Schriftsteller sprechen in der Zeit*, 224–5. For some of the most interesting of the many Berlin poems see: Frank-Wolf Matthies, 'DIE STADT', in *vogel oder käfig sein*, 142–44; Kolbe, 'Berlin' (dedicated to Matthies), in *Vaterlandkanal*, 77; Wenzel, 'Auf dich, mein geliebtes Berlin II', *Lied vom wilden Mohn*, 44; more obliquely, Jansen, *prost neuland*, 8, and, especially, Sascha Anderson's 'Berliner Elegien', in his *brunnen, randvoll* (Berlin/W.: Rotbuch, 1988), 17–27.

64. 'Glimpses & Glances' is the title of the third section of Grünbein's *Grauzone morgens*. The first quotation is from 'Fast ein Gesang', 68–70, the second from 'No. 8', 39–41. See also 'Nullbock', 47, and 'An diesem Morgen gingen. . .', 16–17. A similar mood is found in Mario Persch's 'Stadtbus (Blicktransplantate)', or 'Lichtverkettung', in *Fluchtfreuden Bierdurst. Letzte Gedichte aus der DDR*, Dorothea Oehme (Berlin: Unabhängige Verlagsbuchhandlung, 1990), 60–1 and 71.

65. Heukenkamp, 'Das Ungenügen an der Idylle', 1120. Anthonya Visser argues against this approach in Kolbe's later collections, in 'Überlegungen zur Lyrik Uwe Kolbes', esp. 299–327.

66. Ingrid and Klaus-Dieter Hähnel, 'Junge Lyrik', 131.

67. At an even more basic level, several critics have commented on the prevalence of stone in the poetry. Gerhard Wolf traces the motif in the work of some of the older writers in his ' "Der Stein fällt desto schneller um so tiefer—": Ein Überblick mit einem Exkurs zur "Neuen sächsischen Dichterschule" ', in *Sprachblätter Wortwechsel*, 44–78. Amongst the young generation one could follow a similar 'Steinspur', where stone is used to signal cold, lack of motion, and enclosure.

68. Dennis Tate, 'The Socialist Metropolis? Images of East Berlin in the Literature of the GDR', in Glass, Rösler, and White, *Berlin: Literary Images of a City*, 146–61 (159).

69. *Fahrt mit der S-Bahn: Erzähler der DDR*, ed. Lutz-W. Wolff (Munich: dtv, 1971), 226. Helga Schubert, *Das Verbotene Zimmer: Geschichten* (1982). Quoted in Tate, 'The Socialist Metropolis?', 160.

70. Kolbe, 'Wir leben mit Rissen', *Hineingeboren*, 80–1. See e.g. 'Hoflied', ibid. 20, 'Gedicht eines Fremden', ibid. 47, and 'Möglicher Spaziergang durch eine tote Stadt', ibid. 32.

71. A number of writers negotiate the semantics of the ambivalent 'Sicherheit' of the GDR (including of course that most invasive of securities the *Staatssicherheit*). Cf. also Gabriele Kachold: 'als ich geboren wurde war alles aufgebaut, war alles fertig, perfekt, ein schillerndes förderband mit der richtung nach oben, die ideologie war sicher, der weg war sicher, die häuser, die wohnungen, die rente war sicher', *zügel los*, 79.

72. Richard Pietraß, *Notausgang* (Berlin and Weimar: Aufbau, 1980, 2nd edn. 1988), 9. This theme is very common. Compare Rathenow's 'Aussichten', *Zangenbeburt*, 76, Brinkmann, 'Beschaulich', *Federn und*

Federn lassen (Berlin: Verlag Neues Leben, 1988), 83, or Jansen, 'Alibi', *Poesiealbum*, 10. In Mensching's 'Anfrage beim Amt für Wohnungs- wesen beim Rat des Stadtbezirks Berlin-Prenzlauer Berg', for example, the lyric subject ironically asks whether it is the lack of windows in his workroom which make his poems 'aussichtslos', *Erinnerung an eine Milchglasscheibe*, 50.

73. Kolbe, *Hineingeboren*, 20.
74. Wenzel, *Lied vom wilden Mohn*, 74 and 65.
75. Christa Wolf, *Der geteilte Himmel* (1963), quoted from the West German edition (Munich: dtv, 1973), 187.
76. Köhler, *Deutsches Roulette*, 20. In Mensching's 'World time table', *Erinnerung an eine Milchglasscheibe*, 8–9, it is the 'mit Kurznachrichten geflickten Tuch | Des Himmels, von Bombern zerrissen'. In Kathrin Schmidt's 'Aufzug am Horizont', *Poesiealbum*, 179 (Berlin: Verlag Neues Leben, 1982), 31, 'da | rutscht uns der Himmel doch fast | noch mal weg'. A text by Rathenow begins: ' Der Himmel ist nicht tot. Er stirbt', *Zangengeburt*, 32.
77. Labroisse and Wallace, *DDR-Schriftsteller sprechen in der Zeit*, 221. In Thomas Böhme's *stoff der piloten* the pilots are at once 'pioneers', and representations of illicit (homo)sexual desire. The image is explored throughout the collection and clearly owes something to Brecht and Brinkamnn. Two of the most resonant texts are 'winterflug', 54, and 'piloten der frühe', 46. Cf. also his comments in *DDR-Schriftsteller sprechen in der Zeit*, 303–4.
78. Kolbe, 'ein vogel sein, fliegen so wie er', *Hineingeboren*, 39. 'Komm wir sind Vögel' and 'Spatzenlied' *Abschiede und andere Liebesgedichte*, 27 and 20. See also Wüstefeld, *Stadtplan*, 'Ein Netz von Strassen', 6, and 'Einmal flog durchs Offene', 12; Brinkmann, 'Sturmvogel' (here, after Gorki, as a metaphor for revolution) *Wasserstände und Tauchtiefen*, 8; Drawert, 'Projektion', *Zweite Inventur*, 83; Schmidt, 'Ibykus', *Poesiealbum*, 3. One of the most inventive explorations of this theme is Bert Papenfuß-Gorek's 'Foegel', first published *NdL* 5 (1980), 68–70, and repr. in his *dreizehntanz* (Frankfurt/M: Luchterhand, 1989), 27.
79. *Vogelbühne*, 6. Compare Silvia Schlenstedt's rather doctrinaire: 'Umgang mit einer mythischen Figur: Das Ikarus-Motiv in der neueren DDR-Lyrik', *NdL* 8 (1987), 94–108, and Birgit Lermen, ' "Über die ganze Szene fliegt Ikarus": Das Ikarus-Motiv in ausgewählten Gedichten von Autoren aus der DDR', in *Deutsche Lyrik nach 1945*, ed. Dieter Breuer (Frankfurt/M.: Suhrkamp, 1988), 284–305.
80. Cf. Kunert, 'Ikarus 64', *Verkündigung des Wetters: Gedichte* (Munich: Hanser, 1966), 49–50.
81. Many of the older writers also produced Icarus texts which are much more ambivalent in tone: notably, Berkes, Braun, Biermann, and Kunert. However, the most recent texts are quite distinctive. Cf. Anderson, 'der meissner ikarus', in Anderson and Kerbach, *totenreklame. eine reise*, 12–13; Brinkmann, 'Paar im Flug', *Wasserstände und Tauchtiefen*, 10; Elisabeth Wesuls, 'Für Gerd', Wesuls, *Poesiealbum* (Berlin: Verlag Neues Leben, 1985), 23; Wilhelm Bartsch, 'Kontrapunkt zum Ikarusthema', *Übungen im Joch* (Berlin and Weimar: Aufbau, 1986), 93; Kolbe, 'von der ödnis dieses reden', *Hineingeboren*, 129; Olaf Trunscke, 'Labyrinth', *Auswahl '86: Neue Lyrik. Neue Namen* (Berlin: Verlag Neues Leben,

1986), 116. Recently Wolf Biermann has examined Daedalus and Icarus as symbols for the fall of the GDR and the force of history, in two fascinating essays: 'Der Sturz des Dädalus', in *Klartexte im Getümmel: 13 Jahre im Westen: Von der Ausbürgerung bis zur November Revolution*, ed. Hannes Stein (Cologne: Kiepenheuer & Witsch, 1990), 289–312, and 'à la laterne! à la laterne', in *Der Sturz des Dädalus*, 243–76.

82. Lutz Rathenow, 'Erbe des Ikarus' (1984), VERIRRTE STERNE, oder: WENN ALLES WIEDER MAL GANZ ANDERS KOMMT (Berlin: Merlin, 1994), 63.

83. Gerd Adloff, 'Selbstmord', *Vogelbühne*, 54. The theme of flying and falling, along with figures of Icarus or fallen angels, run obsessively through Lanzendörfer's poetry (for an arresting text see 'trist', in *unmöglich es leben*, 41) and experimental films. He killed himself by jumping from a tower.

84. Wenzel, 'Das Berlin-Lied', from the record 'Reisebilder', and Kolbe, *Bornholm II*, 59.

85. Berendse, 'Zu neuen Ufern: Lyrik der "Sächsischen Dichterschule" im Spiegel der Elbe', in *Studies in GDR Culture and Society 10*, ed. Margy Gerber *et al.* (Lanham, MD: University Press of America, 1991), 197–212. See also Helmut Lethen and Gerrit-Jan Berendse, 'Im Zeichen der Kentauren: Überlegungen zu dem Gedicht "Die Elbe" von Karl Mickel (1973)', in *Jahrbuch zur Literatur in der DDR 6*, ed. Paul Gerhard Klussmann and Heinrich Mohr (Bonn: Bouvier, 1987), 119–42, which analyses Karl Mickel's 'Die Elbe', places it in relation to Hölderlin's mythical landscape of centaurs, and illustrates the links with other GDR writers of the 'Sächsische Dichterschule'.

86. Wenzel, 'Flußbild', *Antrag auf Verlängerung des Monats August*, 59–60; Wüstefeld, 'An den Ufern beginnt der Tag eher', *Heimsuchung* (Berlin and Weimar: Aufbau, 1986), 57–60; Anderson, 'noch treib ich den fluss in die bilder', *totenreklame. eine reise*, 18; Sonja Schüler, 'Die Elbe bei Dresden in März', *Schimmel werden schwarz geboren* (Berlin and Weimar: Aufbau, 1982), 13; Gerd Adloff, 'Mickels Elbe', *Fortgang: Gedichte* (Berlin: Verlag der Nation, 1985), 34–5.

87. *Grauzone morgens*, 71, 35–6, and 39.

88. See esp. the cycle of nine texts 'ELB ALB', *Deutsches Roulette*, 59–68, 'Dresdner Aussichten', 78, 'Niemandsufer. Ein Bericht', 81, and the three-part 'Papierboot', 52–5.

89. This comes from Shakespeare, of course, but is clearly mediated through Ingeborg Bachmann's 1964 poem 'Böhmen liegt am Meer', in Ingeborg Bachmann, *Werke*, ed. Christine Koschel, Inge von Weidenbaum, and Clemens Münster (Munich: Piper, 1978; 3rd edn. 1984), i. 167:

> Liegt Böhmen noch am Meer, so glaub ich den Meeren
> wieder.
> Und glaub ich noch ans Meer, so hoffe ich auf Land.
>
> Bin ich's, so ist ein jeder, der ist soviel wie ich.
> Ich will nichts mehr für mich. Ich will zugrunde gehn.
>
> Zugrund—das heißt zum Meer, dort find ich Böhmen
> wieder.

Köhler's reception of Bachmann is very interesting in its own right; She dedicates a poem to her and takes a motto from Bachmann for her collection.

90. See also Kathrin Schmidt, who in her 'Mittwochs', *Ein Engel fliegt durch die Tapetenfabrik* (Berlin: Verlag Neues Leben, 1987), 16–17, uses a very similar image: 'und wenn ich so lauthals schreibe | und mich bekenne zu papiernen Rettungsbooten, | auf daß ich hoffnungsvoll durch das Jahrhundert treibe | und strande . . .'.

91. In his 'The Divided City: Berlin in Post-War German Literature', in Glass, Rösler, and White, *Berlin: Literary Images of a City*, 162–177 Keith Bullivant understands the 'S-Bahn' as 'a key symbol of the invisible city' (p. 174), although he does not examine any of the texts by the young authors. For him it is centrally as a crossing-point between East and West that it becomes significant.

92. Günter Kunert *Berlin beizeiten* (Munich: Hanser, 1983), 39. See also 'Freudsame U-Bahn-Fahrt', 32 and 'Stadtbahnstenogramme', 40–1.

93. Cf. Gröschner, 'Wir wollten uns nicht verabreden', and 'Muedigkeit zersetzt das Blut', in *vogel oder käfig sein*, 147 and 148, and Kolbe, 'Nachts in der S-Bahn', *Bornholm II*, 45.

94. Grünbein, *Schädelbasislektion*, 27–30 and 31–5.

95. Ibid. 46 and 47. These are both presented in the form of 'Annoncen' on the page.

96. The labyrinth is a central metaphor in recent critical theory, e.g. Deleuze and Foucault. It is frequently used in the poetry and is treated extensively in the essays collected in the volume *ariadnefabrik*. See e.g. Olaf Nicolai 'die fäden der ariadnefabrik—eine annäherung', and Michael Thulin, 'Die zerrissenen Fäden' (which also offers a reading of Foucault's use of myth), both in *abriss der ariadnefabrik*, 324–9 and 332–6 respectively.

97. Elisabeth Wesuls, in *Grenzfallgedichte*, ed. Anna Chiarloni and Helga Pankoke, 33.

98. Wesuls, *Posesiealbum*, 210 (Berlin: Verlag Neues Leben, 1985), 31.

99. *Berührung ist nur eine Randerscheinung*, 15.

100. Ludwig Wittgenstein, 'Tractatus logico-philosophicus', in Wittgenstein, *Schriften 1* (Frankfurt/M.: Suhrkamp, 1969), 140.

101. The phrase comes from the editorial statement of the editors of *Mikado oder Der Kaiser ist nackt*, 10.

102. Papenfuß-Gorek, *vorwärts im zorn &sw.*, 62–3; Anderson, *Jeder Satellit hat einen Killersatelliten*, 25.

103. 'jeder, der spricht, stirbt: pasagen eines gespräches mit sascha anderson', in *Sprache & Antwort*, 55–64 (61–2).

104. See Kolbe, 'Offener Brief an Sascha Anderson', in *Die Zeit*, 22 Nov. 1991, 64, repr. in Böthig and Michael, *MachtSpiele*, 318–20: 'Hast Du es nicht selbst geschrieben: "geh über die grenze auf der anderen seite steht ein mann und sagt: geh über die grenze usw. usf."? Nun war es dieser ganz bestimmte, dieser allbekannte Dunkelmann, der da stand, bereit mit Dir zu reden, wie Du bereit warst, mit ihm zu reden, und Du bist über diese Grenze hin- wie hergegangen, als sei dies bloß kriminelle Halbwelt gewesen.' See also below, Ch. 7.

105. From 'hier k', *Berührung ist nur eine Randerscheinung*, 206.

106. Rainer Schedlinski, 'die unvordenkliche lichtung der worte', in his *die rationen des ja und des nein: Gedichte* (Berlin and Weimar: Aufbau—

Außer der Reihe, 1988), and, in an extended form (Frankfurt/M.: Suhrkamp, 1990). Page references from the Suhrkamp edition, p. 115. Cf. the interview 'vogel oder käfig sein' with Schedlinski, in *Sprache & Antwort*, 157–74.

107. 'überdenken vergangener grundsätze auf die spitze getrieben', *wortBILD: Visuelle Poesie in der DDR*, ed. Guillermo Deisler and Jörg Kowalski (Halle–Leipzig: Mitteldeutscher Verlag, 1990), 57. It is also addressed explicitly, if not very imaginatively, in a number of other concrete texts: e.g. Uwe Warnke's 'abgepackt und eingeschweißt', in *wortBILD*, 26, where the word 'international' is gradually shortened line by line to read 'intern', or the rather more complex and expressive modulations of Papenfuß-Gorek's 'enge', in his *dreizehntanz: Gedichte* (Berlin and Weimar: Aufbau, 1989), here (Frankfurt/M.: Luchterhand, 1989), 99.

108. This, of course, has recently and famously become a metaphor for the GDR as a whole: see Stefan Heym, *Auf Sand gebaut: Sieben Geschichten aus der unmittelbaren Vergangenheit* (Munich: Wilhelm Goldmann Verlag, 1990).

109. A nice comparison can be made with Andreas Koziol's 'pappelvlies liegt auf den kellertreppen', which treats a house of sorts to metaphorical and linguistic play, and ends 'und wo ein wille ist ist auch ein weg versperrt', in *Sprache & Antwort*, 16.

110. Stefan Döring, 'was dich ausmacht—macht', *Heutmorgestern*, 37. Cf., 'mitmachen—mitmacht', 13, 'jede untermauerung ist eine unterwanderung', 33.

111. Ibid. 103.

112. Wolf, *Sprachblätter Wortwechsel*, 161–2 (although there appear to be two odd misprints in his 'version' of the text, 161). It is also discussed in Emmerich, *Kleine Literaturgeschichte*, 434–5 and Alexander von Bormann, 'Rede-Wendungen: Zur Rhetorik des gegenwärtigen Gedichts in der DDR', in *DDR-Lyrik im Kontext*, ed. Cosentino, Ertl, and Labroisse, 89–143 (119–20).

113. Endler, *Den Tiger reiten*, 59–60.

PART II INTRODUCTION

1. Hartmann, 'Der Generationswechsel—ein ästhetischer Wechsel?, 132, and Berendse, 'Outcast in Berlin' 21.

2. Wittstock, 'Literatur als Zuflucht in der Haft': "brunnen randvoll"— Prosa und Lyrik von Sascha Anderson', *FAZ* 9 July 1988, repr. (as 'Literatur als Rettung aus der Haft') in Wittstock, *Von der Stalinallee zum Prenzlauer Berg*, 264–7.

3. *Entgrenzungen*, ed. Kölner Filmhaus, Cologne 1988. See also the review by Hajo Steinert, 'Lyrik mit Nadelstreifen: Entgrenzungen der Literatur im Kölner Filmhaus', *FAZ* 26 May 1988.

4. Erich Arendt, *entgrenzen* (Leipzig: Insel Verlag, 1981). Cf. Böthig, 'Differenz und Revolte', esp. ch. 2.

5. Braun, 'Rimbaud. Ein Psalm der Aktualität', *SuF* 5 (1985), 978–98.

6. Arthur Rimbaud, 'Lettre à Paul Demeny, Charleville, 15 mai 1871', in *Œuvres complètes. Correspondance*, ed. Louis Forestier (Paris: Laffont, 1992), 231–8 (231).

7. Cf. Ursula Heukenkamp, 'Metapher der Befreiung: Volker Braun, "Das innerste Afrika" ', in *DDR-Literatur 1987 im Gespräch*, ed. Siegfried Rönisch (Berlin and Weimar: Aufbau, 1988), 184–96.
8. Rimbaud, 'Vagabonds' (from his *Illuminations*), in *Œuvres complètes*. *Correspondance*, 171–2 (172).
9. This tradition has been widely cultivated in the GDR, particularly in the spirit of Becher, and is a theme explored by Braun with reference to Hölderlin, whom he recalls here also (p. 983).
10. Rimbaud, 'Lettre à Paul Demeny', 235.
11. Of course this is in some ways a more visionary reformulation of his 1970 position, 'Wir schreiben nicht mehr gegen die bestehende Gesellschaft sondern für sie, für ihre immanente Veränderung', in *Es genügt nicht die einfache Wahrheit*. *Notate* (Leipzig: Philipp Reclam jun., 1975), 75.
12. Rimbaud, 'Lettre à Paul Demeny', 233.
13. Braun, 'Das innerste Afrika', in *Langsamer knirschender Morgen*, 61–3.
14. For the poem see Anderson, 'die monologe gehen fremd', *Jeder Satellit hat einen Killersatelliten*, 49. See also Anderson's response, 'Fixierung einer Metapher—Antwort auf Volker Braun', in *schaden*, 1 Aug. 1985, reproduced in *vogel oder käfig sein*, 291–2. Comments by Leonhard Lorek and Elke Erb are also repr. here (p. 293).
15. Cf. the discussion of Braun's 'An Friedrich Hölderlin' in Ch. 4.
16. Gerhard Wolf, *Sprachblätter Wortwechsel*, 24.

CHAPTER 3

1. Bert Papenfuß-Gorek, 'ich', *tiské* (Göttingen: Steidl, 1990), 76. Part of the power of this little poem lies in the Penck drawing of which it is an integral part.
2. Emmerich, 'Gleichzeitigkeit', 206.
3. Peter Geist also makes this point, and interprets it as 'das chimärenhafte Fortgeistern ursprünglicher Idealsetzungen von der Gesellschaft, in der die freie Entwicklung des einzelnen Voraussetzung für die freie Entfaltung aller sei'. Marx's assertion from the *Communist Manifesto* was, of course, famously 'rediscovered' by Stephan Hermlin in his *Abendlicht* (1979). See Geist, *Ein Molotow-Cocktail auf fremder Bettkante*, 382–3.
4. See David Bathrick's 'Kultur und Öffentlichkeit in der DDR', in *Literatur der DDR in den siebziger Jahren*, ed. Peter Uwe Hohendahl and Patricia Herminghouse (Frankfurt/M.: Suhrkamp, 1983), 53–81.
5. ' "Subjektive Authentizität": Gespräch mit Hans Kaufmann', in Christa Wolf, *Die Dimension des Autors: Essays und Ausätze. Reden und Gespräche 1959–1985*, ed. Angela Drescher (Berlin and Weimar: Aufbau, 1986), ii. 317–49 (325).
6. Gerrit-Jan Berendse, *Die 'Sächsische Dichterschule'*.
7. Braun, *Provokation für mich* (Halle/S.: Mitteldeutscher Verlag, 1965). Quotations are taken from the extended collection published in West Germany in the following year: *Vorläufiges* (Frankfurt/M.: Suhrkamp, 1966), 7.
8. Quite apart from début collections by several of the younger authors, there were important controversies over a number of anthologies of

younger writers' work. For a detailed discussion see Anneli Hartmann, *Lyrik-Anthologien als Indikatoren des literarischen und gesellschaftlichen Prozesses in der DDR (1949–1971)*, Deutsche Sprache und Literatur, 643 (Frankfurt/M.: Peter Lang, 1983), 187–272.

9. The quotation comes from a poem by Günther Wünsche entitled 'Die Rehabilitierung des Ich', in *Himmel meiner Stadt. Aus der Werkstsatt der Gruppe 'alex 64'*, ed. Werner Kruse, Richard Christ, and Günther Deicke (Berlin: Verlag der Nation, 1966), 147. The title of the poem was taken up in an important article: Gerhard Kluge, 'Die Rehabilitierung des Ich: Einige Bermerkungen zu Themen und Tendenzen in der Lyrik der DDR', in *Poesie und Politik: Zur Situation der Literatur in Deutschland*, ed. Wolfgang Kuttenkeuler (Stuttgart: W. Kohlhammer, 1973), 206–35. See also Peter Hamm, ' "Glück ist schwer in diesem Land": Zur Situation der jüngsten DDR-Lyrik' in *Merkur*, 19 (1965), 365–99; Fritz J. Raddatz, 'Eine neue Subjektivität formt die neue Realität', in *Traditionen und Tendenzen: Materialien zur Literatur der DDR* (Frankfurt/M.: Suhrkamp, 1972), 167–211.

10. Cf. Klaus Dautel, 'Subjektivität und Unmittelbarkeit. Zur Entwicklung der DDR-Lyrik in den 70er Jahren', in *Text & Kontext*, 1 (1979), 32–66, and Ursula Heukenkamp, 'Poesie und Poetik. Unmittelbarkeit in der Gegenwartslyrik', *WB* 10 (1977), 113–38.

11. This movement which centred (in poetry) on the work of writers like Born, Ralf Dieter Brinkmann, and Jürgen Theobaldy has been widely discussed. One of the best summaries of the developments and critical responses is to be found in Hiltrud Gnüg's *Entstehung und Krise lyrischer Subjektivität: Vom klassischen lyrischen Ich zur modernen Erfahrungswirklichkeit*, Germanistische Abhandlungen, 54 (Stuttgart: Metzler, 1983), esp. 236–87. She discusses the Born poem on p. 249.

12. Emmerich discusses the convergence postulate in his section 'Wieviele deutsche Literaturen?', *Kleine Literaturgeschichte der DDR*, 438–70.

13. Heinrich Mohr, 'Entwicklungslinien der Literatur im geteilten Deutschland', in *Jahrbuch zur Literatur der DDR 1*, ed. Paul Gerhard Klussmann and Heinrich Mohr (Bonn: Bouvier, 1980), 47.

14. For one of the most damning pieces on the failings of 'Neue Subjektivität', see Harald Hartung, 'Eindimensionale Poesie: Zur Lyrik der neuen Subjektivität', in his *Deutsche Lyrik seit 1965*, 48–66.

15. Jay Rosellini, 'Subjektivität contra Politik? Anmerkungen zur Lyrik der DDR', in *Deutsche Gegenwartsliteratur: Ausgangspositionen und aktuelle Entwicklungen*, ed. Manfred Durzak (Stuttgart: Philipp Reclam jun., 1981), 517–51, and Manfred Jäger, 'Subjektivität als politische Kategorie. Zur Emanzipationsgeschichte der Lyrik in der DDR', in *Lyrik von allen Seiten. Gedichte und Aufsätze des ersten Lyrikertreffens in Münster*, ed. Lothar Jordan, Axel Marquardt, and Winfried Woesler (Frankfurt/M.: Fischer, 1981), 304–16.

16. Emmerich, *Kleine Literaturgeschichte der DDR*, esp. 386–8.

17. This widely quoted concept derives from an interview with Maurer conducted by Dieter Schlenstedt in 1968. Schlenstedt asked: 'Könnten Sie [. . .] mit mir einverstanden sein, wenn ich sage: Eine wesentliche allgemeine Funktion der Lyrik ist es, Vorlagen einer denkenden und fühlenden Subjektivität zu geben, Muster einer arbeitenden Subjektivität, die imstande sind, uns rationale und emotionale Beziehungen zwischen

Ich und Welt vorzuspielen?' Maurer's reply is too lengthy to quote here, but takes up Schlenstedt's proposal: 'Die Funktion der Lyrik heute—im allgemeinsten Sinn—ist, am Muster zu einem Weltfrieden zu arbeiten [. . .] Und so stimme ich überein mit Ihnen, daß der Lyriker [. . .] speziell "Vorlagen einer denkenden und fühlenden Subjektivität zu geben", "Muster einer arbeitenden Subjektivität" zu sein hat. [. . .] Nichts wäre mir übrigens lieber, als wenn Ihr Begriff "arbeitende Subjektivität" für den Lyriker zur allgemeinen Selbstverständlichkeit würde'. See 'Lyrik als Empfindungskorrelat der Welt: Gespräch mit Georg Maurer', in *Auskünfte: Werkstattgespräche mit DDR-Autoren*, ed. Anneliese Löffler (Berlin and Weimar: Aufbau, 1974), 15–40 (16–17).

18. Walfried and Christel Hartinger take the Mauerer line in a number of articles. See e.g. 'Von Horizonten und Grenzen: Zum Charakter zeitgenössischer lyrischer Subjektivität', in *DDR-Literatur '83 im Gespräch*, ed. Siegfried Rönisch (Berlin and Weimar, Aufbau, 1984), 268–94. Mathilde Dau also uses the Maurer as a starting-point for understanding the poetry. See Dau, 'Mit meinen Augen', 90–106. The quotation comes from Heinz Plavius, 'Positionsbestimmung', 145.

19. Hartmann, 'Der Generationswechsel,' 109–34.

20. Ingrid and Klaus-Dieter Hähnel, 'Junge Lyrik', 145, Heukenkamp, 'Das Ungenügen an der Idylle', 1121.

21. Cf. Klaus Krippendorf, 'Unruhestiftender Lärm oder Weltentwurf? Die Anfänge zweier Lyrikergenerationen', in *Generationen, Temperamente, Schreibweisen*, ed. Hans Richter, 242–71.

22. Recent critics have discussed this aspect of the writing more fully. Hartmann notes a 'bemerkenswerte solidarische Geschlossenheit' amongst the writers, 'Neue Tendenzen in der DDR-Lyrik', 8, Harald Hartung describes them as a 'geschlossene Phalanx', *Deutsche Lyrik seit 1965*, 100. Berendse's is the most detailed discussion, although he is ultimately arguing for a different collective identity: Berendse, *Die 'Sächsische Dichterschule'*, 131–47.

23. Endler, 'DDR-Lyrik Mitte der Siebziger. Fragment einer Rezension', *ABznG* 7 (1978), 67–95. Kirsch, in a homage to Endler, *Die Zeit*, 15 Apr. 1983, cited in Berendse, *Die 'Sächsische Dichterschule'*, 55.

24. Endler, 'DDR-Lyrik', 73.

25. Braun, *Vorläufiges*, 809.

26. Ibid. 7.

27. Rainer Kirsch, *NdL* 11 (1963), 99. Remarkable in its lexical correspondence is Wolf Biermann's 'An die alten Genossen', Wolf Biermann, *Die Drahtharfe: Balladen Gedichte Lieder* (Berlin/W.: Klaus Wagenbach, 1965; here repr. 1981), 67–8. Raddatz makes the point that Kirsch knew Biermann's text (written in 1962) and published it on the corresponding page of his own *Gespräch mit dem Saurier* (1965), in order to emphasize the link, *Traditionen und Tendenzen*, 196.

28. Hartmann, 'Der Generationswechsel', 117.

29. Volker Braun, *Unvollendete Geschichte*, originally *SuF* 1975, repr. (Frankfurt/M.: Suhrkamp, 1977).

30. Emmerich, *Kleine Literaturgeschichte der DDR*, 390.

31. Heinz Czechowski, *Was mich betrifft: Gedichte* (Leipzig: Mitteldeutscher Verlag, 1981), 17.

32. Cf. Heinz Czechowski, *Kein näheres Zeichen* (Halle–Leipzig: Mitel-

deutscher Verlag, 1987), or Braun, *Langsamer knirschender Morgen* of the same year.

33. Thulin, 'Das Subjekt und sein Spiegel: das dezentrierte subjekt in den texten Rainer Schedlinskis', in *Die andere Sprache*, 160.
34. Emmerich, *Kleine Literaturgeschichte der DDR*, 411, and Hartmann, 'Der Generationswechsel', 120.
35. Cf. Schüler, *Schimmel werden schwarz geboren* (Berlin and Weimar: Aufbau, 1982). Peter Geist takes up this problem in a fairly aggressive review: 'Die Gefühle und die Dinge: Sonja Schüler, 'Schimmel werden schwarz geboren', *NdL* 4 (1983), 153–6.
36. Kurt Drawert, *Privateigentum* (Frankfurt/M.: Suhrkamp, 1989), 47–8.
37. Ibid. 28. This formulation, of course, has very clear echoes of Jürgen Theobaldy's anthology of poetry of 'Neue Subjektivität' in the West: *Und ich bewege mich doch . . .: Gedichte vor und nach 1968* (Munich: Beck, 1977).
38. 'Ein Nein ist keine Lebenshaltung', 19.
39. Kolbe Rönisch, 'Notizen', 7. Cf. Schüler, 'unsere unbestechlichen Augen', *Schimmel werden schwarz geboren*, 39, and Grosz, 'die unbestechliche Zunge', *Blatt vor dem Mund*, 106.
40. *Berührung ist nur eine Randerscheinung*, 39.
41. Anderson, 'lettern schwarz auf weissem grund', *Jeder Satellit hat einen Killersatelliten*, 8.
42. Cosentino uses the difference between 'Zeitungswahrheit und 'Literaturwahrheit' as a starting-point for her investigation. See 'Gedanken zur jüngsten DDR-Lyrik', 83.
43. For Kolbe and Adloff cf. the round-table discussion, 'Ohne den Leser geht es nicht', of 1979, 52; for Mensching's comment see Christel und Walfried Hartinger, ' "Ich sehe das Land nicht als Provinz"': Gespräch mit Steffen Mensching', in *Positionen 2: Wortmeldungen zur DDR-Literatur*, ed. Eberhard Günther and Hinnerk Einhorn (Halle/S.: Mitteldeutscher Verlag, 1986), 65–81 (74); and for Anderson: Labroisse and Wallace, *DDR-Schriftsteller sprechen in der Zeit*, 251.
44. Grosz, *Blatt vor dem Mund*, 26. A large number of texts style themselves as a 'report', 'note', 'plan', or 'snapshot' of reality. See Drawert, 'Tagebuch' and 'Notiz', in *Zweite Inventur*, 42 and 53 respectively, or Jörg Kowalski, 'kurzer bericht', *Vertrauliche Mitteilung* (Halle–Leipzig: Mitteldeutscher Verlag, 1985), 58; Rosenthal, 'Urlaubsfoto', *Berührung ist nur eine Randerscheinung*, 63; Mensching, 'Küchenzettel', *Tuchfühlung*, 71; Wüstefeld, *Stadtplan*. This aspect of the work brings it very close to texts of 'Neue Subjektivität' in the West.
45. Rathenow, *Zangengeburt: Gedichte*.
46. James Knowelton, 'The short prose of Lutz Rathenow', in *Studies in GDR Culture and Society 5*, ed. Margy Gerber et al. (Lanham, MD: University Press of America, 1985), 281–91 (285).
47. 'Interview with Lutz Rathenow', in *Aspect. Art and Literature*, 26/7 (winter 1983), 107–13 (112).
48. Günter Kunert, 'Deutsch-deutsches Exil', in *Aus fremder Heimat. Zur Exilsituation heutiger Literatur*, ed. Kunert (Munich: Hanser, 1988), 100–10 (101 and 107).
49. A number of the poems in *Zangengeburt* end with a paradoxical

statement of immobility. Compare 'Wohnen', 36, 'Die Zunge sieht sich nicht zurück', 92, or 'Das neue Neujahr', 93.

50. Wenzel, *Lied vom wilden Mohn: Gedichte* (Halle–Leipzig: Mitteldeutscher Verlag, 1984).

51. As Wenzel comments: 'Traurig kann nur sein, wer an der wirklichen Welt hängt, barbarisch verliebt ist in seine sinnliche Existenz, in den Genuß und den Ekel', *Antrag auf Verlängerung des Monats August*, 119. Cf. also: 'Geschwindigkeitskontrolle', 6–7, 'Meine Hände', 57–8, or 'Abends, wenn ich noch nicht schlafen kann', 21.

52. Wenzel, *Lied vom wilden Mohn*, p. 38.

53. Mensching, 'Mühsam braut sich das bittere Bier: Hans-Eckardt Wenzels "Ich braue das bittere Bier"', *Lyriker im Zwiegespräch*, ed. Ingrid Hähnel (Berlin and Weimar: Aufbau, 1981), 334–44. Cf. also Wenzel, 'Von meiner Hoffnung laß ich nicht. Vorrat Erich Mühsam', *Temperamente*, 4 (1979), 89–91.

54. Erich Mühsam, 'ich möchte wieder vom Glücke gesunden', in Mühsam, *Gedichte Prosa Stücke* (Berlin: Verlag Volk und Welt, 1978), i. 23.

55. Ibid., i. 302. Wenzel's 'Selbstbildnis, 1981', *Lied vom wilden Mohn*, 10, is dedicated, in a similar way, to Theodor Kramer, and takes up Kramer's 'Selbstbildnis 1946', thus adding a historical dimension to the self-understanding.

56. Mensching, *Erinnerung an eine Milchglasscheibe*, 23.

57. Mensching interviewed by Hartinger, 'Ich sehe das Land nicht als Provinz', 75.

58. Cf. Wenzel, 'Allgemein wiederholte Ausslassungen zu einem hinlänglich bekannten Thema/Diskussionsschrift', in *Positionen 2: Wortmeldungen zur DDR-Literatur*, ed. Eberhard Günther and Hinnerk Einhorn (Halle–Leipzig: Mitteldeutscher Verlag, 1986), 87–106 (89), and Mensching, 'Ich sehe das Land nicht als Provinz', 75.

59. Mensching, 'World time table', *Erinnerung an eine Milchglasscheibe*, 8–9; Wenzel, 'Vorher, wenig später noch und jetzt', *Lied vom wilden Mohn*, 79; Hensel, 'Sonett', *Stilleben mit Zukunft*, 81.

60. Mensching, *Erinnerung an eine Milchglasscheibe*, 66.

61. Dieter Schlenstedt, 'Eine kleine Geste. Zu einem Gedicht von Steffen Mensching', *DDR-Literatur '83 im Gespräch*, ed. Rönisch, 320–5.

62. Bertolt Brecht, *Gesammelte Werke in 20 Bänden*, ed. Suhrkamp Verlag in association with Elisabeth Hauptmann (Frankfurt/M.: Suhrkamp, 1967), ix. 725.

63. Mensching, *Tuchfühlung*, 25.

64. Wenzel, *Lied vom wilden Mohn*, 17.

65. 'Vier Fragen an Hans-Eckardt Wenzel', *NdL* 5 (1984), 71–5 (75).

66. Wenzel takes up Heine in a number of poems and essays, but particularly in his *Reise-Bilder: Satiren, Berichte, Essays* (Halle–Leipzig: Mitteldeutscher Verlag, 1989).

67. 'Vier Fragen an Hans-Eckardt Wenzel', 73–4.

68. Friedrich Hölderlin, 'Das Belebende', *Sämtliche Werke*, Große Stuttgarter Ausgabe, ed. Friedrich Beißner and Adolf Beck, 8 vols. (Stuttgart: W. Kohlhammer Verlag, 1943–1985), v. 289–90.

69. Mensching, *Erinnerung an eine Milchglasscheibe*, 64.

70. Thomas Böhme, 'Auf halbem Weg', in his *Mit der Sanduhr am Gürtel: Gedichte und Gebilde* (Berlin and Weimar: Aufbau, 1983), 5–6; Brigitte

Struzyk, 'Leben auf der Kippe', *Leben auf der Kippe* (Berlin and Weimar: Aufbau, 1984), 5; Kathrin Schmidt, 'Himmels Begängnis' and 'Ins Feld Ins Feld mit Hölderlin', *Ein Engel fliegt durch die Tapetenfabrik*, 7 and 10.

71. Miłosz, *The Captive Mind*, tr. Jane Zielonko (London: Penguin, 1981, repr. 1985). He calls it 'Ketman', see esp. 54–81.

72. Grunenberg, *Aufbruch der inneren Mauer*, esp. 'Jugendliche Subkultur in den Städten', 120–5.

73. This comes from one of the 'Lettres du Voyant', which also form the starting-point of Volker Braun's reception of Rimbaud. See Rimbaud, 'Lettre à Georges Izambard, 13 May 1871', in *Œuvres Complètes Correspondance*, 231. Cf. e.g. Mensching, 'Hotel Smolka', *Bizarre Städte*, Sonderheft 1 (1989), 4, Rainer Schedlinski, 'ich war ein anderer', in his *die männer der frauen* (Berlin: Galrev, 1991), 13.

74. Braun takes up the 'Ich ist ein anderer' quotation, 'Rimbaud. Ein Psalm der Aktualität', 984.

75. Günther cited by Rüdiger Thomas, in Muschter and Thomas, *Jenseits der Staatskultur*, 36. Günther also created *Denn ich ist ein anderer. Ein Versuch und eine Versuchung*, an 89-page cycle of texts and photomontages on the subject of Rimbaud, with photos by Sabine Jahn (Berlin: Günther-Jahn-Bach-Edition, 4 copies, 1989). The Anderson is to be found on a large unfolding sheet of painted graph-paper in *schaden*, 11 (1986), n.p.

76. Hugo Ball, quoted in Arrigo Subiotto, 'Volker Braun, Rimbaud und die DDR', *Die Literatur der DDR 1976–1986*, ed. Chiarloni, Sartori, and Cambi, 241–51 (249). It was also, of course, his life that was exemplary (his experimentation with drugs, his homosexuality, his hatred of the establishment). This was one of the chief sources of the fascination of Rimbaud for the Beat Generation in the United States. In their turn, Kerouac and Ginsberg in particular find their way into much of the poetry of the young GDR writers for similar reasons.

77. A useful examination of the implications of Rimbaud's poetic for an understanding of the lyric subject of Romanticism and Modernism is offered in Marjorie Perloff's *The Poetics of Indeterminacy: Rimbaud to Cage* (Princeton: Princeton University Press, 1984).

78. Cornelia Jentsch, *ariadnefabrik*, 4 (1988), 47–8.

79. Birgit Dahlke takes up this problem in ' "Im Brunnen vor dem Tore" Autorinnen in inoffiziellen Zeitschriften der DDR 1979–90', in *Neue Generation—Neues Erzählen: Deutsche Prosa-Literatur der 80er Jahre*, ed. Walter Delabar, Werner Jung, and Ingrid Pergande (Opladen: Westdeutscher Verlag, 1993), 177–94.

80. Köhler, *Deutsches Roulette*: 'Gedicht', 11, 'American Way of Midlife', 15, 'Aufnahme', 18, 'Brechung', 19, and the series 'Elektra. Spiegelungen', which includes a dedication to Heiner Müller, 23–31.

81. Peter Leistenschneider's, 'Spiegelfrau und Rapunzel: Gedichte von Kerstin Hensel und von Barbara Köhler', *Freitag*, 13 Sept. 1991, is one of the few reviews to engage with this aspect of her work.

82. *Sprache & Antwort*, 56.

83. See e.g. the title poem in Anderson, *Jeder Satellit hat einen Killersatelliten*, 50, 'dresden zum dritten', 15, 'ich bin kein artist', 26, 'ich bin mary westmacott', 32.

84. Cf. Václav Havel's essay, 'The Power of the Powerless', in *Václav Havel or Living in Truth*, ed. Jan Vladislav (London: Faber, 1986).
85. *Sprache & Antwort*, 120.
86. flanzendörfer, *unmöglich es leben*, ed. Peter Böthig and Klaus Michael (Berlin: Janus press, BasisDruck, 1992), 68–72.
87. This is the title of another cycle of poems, *unmöglich es leben*, 161–8. The sense of persecution and impending death is emphasized by the many clear references to Kafka's *Der Bau*. In an editorial essay Peter Böthig suggests that the persecution complex evident in Lanzendörfer's texts might be the result of *Stasi* intimidation (p. 183).
88. Mario Persch, in Oehme, *Fluchtfreuden Bierdurst*, 62–5, and 67–70. Holst in *liane*, 5 (1989), 36. Other texts by Holst are included in the Oehme anthology, 21–5. A posthumous exhibition, 'Es läßt sich keiner umerziehen', of his texts and installations, and documentation about his life (he died in an odd—perhaps deliberate—incident on the eve of the *Währungsunion* in 1990) was held in May 1991 in the Galerie Wohnmaschine in Berlin. Cf. also Thomas Günther, 'Zwischen bunt und bestialisch: Zu "Matthias" BAADER Holst und seinen Texten', *Süddeutsche Zeitung*, 24 Mar. 1991.
89. From the love poem 'für myriam', *liane*, 5 (1989), 37, also repr. in Geist, *Ein Molotow-Cocktail*, 254.
90. Cf. Lubinetski, 'eine haut', in *vogel oder käfig sein*, 74, and 'ich bin das ufer ohne namen', in *Die andere Sprache*, 155.
91. Dorothea Böck, 'Fixierte Realität: Gabriele Kachold, "zügel los" ', *NdL* 11 (1990), 154–6, and Michael Braun, 'Entfesselungsversuche: *Zügel los: Das Prosadebüt von Gabi Kachold aus der Ex-DDR*', *Basler Zeitung*, 2 Nov. 1990.
92. Kachold, 'bauchhöhlenschwangerschaft', *zügel los*, 13–14.
93. Ricarda Schmidt, 'Im Schatten der Titanin: Minor GDR Women Writers—Justly Neglected, Unrecognized or Repressed?', in *Geist und Macht*, ed. Goodbody and Tate, 151–62 (159).
94. See the interview, ' "Kunst ist ein Rhythmus, in dem frau leben kann": In der Werkstatt: Gabriele Kachold', *Temperamente*, 3 (1989), 21–8.
95. Cf. Anderson and Kerbach, *totenreklame. eine reise (1983)*, Anderson, *waldmaschine: übung vierhändig mit Ralf Kerbach, Cornelia Schleime, Michael Wildenhain* (Berlin/W.: Rotbuch, 1984), n.p., and the interviews, 'jeder, der spricht stirbt', in *Sprache & Antwort*, and in Labroisse and Wallace, *DDR-Schriftsteller sprechen in der Zeit*, esp. 248–51.
96. Anderson, *Jeder Satellit hat einen Killersatelliten*, 25.
97. Christine Cosentino discusses a number of Anderson's texts very interestingly in 'ich habe ausser meiner sprache', and creates the useful label 'Kaleidoskop-gedichte' (p. 207), but her own tone takes on too much of the emotional register which she detects in the poems. She describes this text, for example, as 'schmerzhaft schön' and talks of 'Isolation' and 'Ohnmachtsgefühle', expressed in a 'spröde Ton der Trauer' in other texts (p. 211).
98. Michael Thulin, 'die metaphorik des todes: die texte sascha andersons', *ariadnefabrik*, 1 (1988), 6–11.
99. Fredric Jameson, 'The Politics of Theory: Ideological Positions in the Postmodern Debate', in *New German Critique*, 33 (Fall 1984), 53–65 (63).

100. Apart from the texts which I discuss, see also: Grünbein, 'Vorm Fernseher, die Toten', *Schädelbasislektion*, 36–7, and 'Inside out outside in', 39–45; Kolbe, 'TV', *Abschiede*, 46; Mensching, 'Mann am Bahndamm 1928', *Erinnerung an eine Milchglasscheibe*, 17; Wenzel, 'Kleines TV-Epos', *Antrag auf Verlängerung des Monats August*, 17–19; Ralph Grüneberger, 'Abspann. Nicht das', *Frühstück im Stehen*, 9, 'Tele Vision', *Stadt. Name. Land: Gedichte* (Halle–Leipzig: Mitteldeutscher Verlag, 1989), 68–9 and 'Sender Leipzig', 61–2; and Drawert, 'Als wollte sie etwas sagen', *Zweite Inventur*, 20–1.

101. Döring, *Heutmorgestern*, 9.

102. Anderson, *Jeder Satellit hat einen Killersatelliten*, 59. Cf. Visser's illuminating reading of this text in *Blumen im Eis*, 318–20.

103. Böhme, 'dem treuen medium', *stoff der piloten*, 12.

104. See e.g. Böhme, 'Spiegelfechten', *Die schamlose Vergeudung des Dunkels*, 11; Ralph Grüneberger, 'Was tun', *NdL* 3 (1983), 101; Mensching, 'Dein Haar war vollgezogen', *Erinnerung an eine Milchglasscheibe*, 36; Jörg Kowalski, 'Weiterhin ruhiges Spätsommer', *Auswahl '84: Neue Lyrik, Neue Namen* (Berlin: Verlag Neues Leben, 1984), 79.

105. Silvia Schlenstedt, 'Fragen der Nachgeborenen. Aspekte gegenwärtiger Lyrik in der DDR', in *Studies in GDR Culture and Society 9*, ed. Margy Gerber *et al.* (Lanham, MD: University Press of America, 1989), 85–99.

106. Heinz Czechowski, 'Es geht um die Realität des Gedichts', *SuF* 4 (1972), 897–902 (901).

107. In Mensching's 'Drei Radios im Hinterhof', *Erinnerung an eine Milchglasscheibe*, 18–19, for example, news items about atomic war are intercut with dance hits and a documentary piece about the extinction of Neanderthal man. Cf. also Holger Teschke, 'Radiocollage', *Bäume am Hochufer* (Berlin and Weimar: Aufbau, 1985), 80, which Schlenstedt takes to task in another article which adresses similar concerns: 'Das Individuum in der Geschichte: Erkundungen in der Lyrik der DDR', in *Positionen 3: Wortmeldungen zur DDR-Literatur*, ed. Eberhard Günther and Hinnerk Einhorn (Halle–Leipzig: Mitteldeutscher Verlag, 1987), 81–109.

108. Kunert, *Ein englisches Tagebuch* (Berlin and Weimar: Aubau, 1978), 224.

109. Anderson, *Jeder Satellit hat einen Killersatelliten*, 50.

110. Kolbe, 'ich war dabei', in *einst war ich fänger im schnee. Neue Texte und Bilder aus der DDR*, ed. Lutz Rathenow (Berlin/W.: Oberbaum Verlag, 1984), 25.

111. See also Drawert, 'TV I II', *Zweite Inventur*, 111.

112. Wenzel, 'Wir suchten das Verbindungsstück', *Lied vom wilden Mohn*, 88.

113. Cf. Thomas Rosenlöcher, 'Die unentwegte Suche nach dem Verbindungsstück: Zu einem Gedicht von Hans-Eckardt Wenzel', in *Positionen 3: Wortmeldungen zur DDR-Literatur*, ed. Günther and Einhorn, 115–21.

114. Grünbein, 'An diesem Morgen', *Grauzone morgens*, 16.

115. Grünbein, *Schädelbasislektion*, 134–5.

116. Janetzki and Rath, *Tendenz Freisprache*.

117. *Punktzeit: Deutschsprachige Lyrik der achtziger Jahre*, ed. Michael Braun and Hans Thill (Heidelberg: Verlag Das Wunderhorn, 1987).

118. *Sprache & Antwort*, 166.

119. Schedlinski, 'dann leuchten die stätten', *die rationen des ja und des nein*, 98.
120. 'auch ich wollte reden', ibid. 22.
121. Jean Baudrillard, 'The Precession of Simulacra', tr. Paul Foss and Paul Patton, in *Simulations* (New York: Semiotext(e), 1983), 1–79.
122. Schedlinski, '(zungenfilm)', *die rationen des ja und des nein*, 30.
123. Schedlinski, *die männer der frauen*, 14.
124. Bert Papenfuß-Gorek, *SoJa* (Berlin: Galrev, 1990), 51, and *LED SAUDAUS. notdichtung, karrendichtung* (Berlin: Janus press, BasisDruck, 1991), 95.
125. *LED SAUDAUS, 94.*
126. Quoted in David Harvey, *The Condition of Postmodernity: An Enquiry into the Origins of Cultural Change* (Oxford: Blackwell, 1990), 325.
127. *Sprache & Antwort*, 200–1.
128. flanzendörfer, *unmöglich es leben*, 1.
129. Hensel, *Stilleben mit Zukunft*, 46. 'da sagt einer 'WIR', weil er nicht mehr 'ICH' sagen kann': Hensel, 'Lyrik im Stehen: Zu Ralph Grüneberger "Frühstück im Stehen" ', *Temperamente*, 2 (1987), 148–9. See also her comments in interview in 1988, where she relates her statement about the great 'WIR' of the poets to Maurer and his compatriots, and affirms for her own work the importance of the lyric subject: 'ICH ist nicht gleich Bauchnabel mit den eigenen Bauchschmerzen, sondern bewußter Auftritt in der Welt.' See Klaus Hammer, 'Gespräch mit Kerstin Hensel', *WB* 1 (1991), 93–110 (95).

CHAPTER 4

1. Wenzel, 'Drei-Dimensionales Bild einer Dorfkirche bei S.', *Lied vom wilden Mohn*, 60.
2. Joachim Streisand, *Deutsche Geschichte von den Anfängen bis zur Gegenwart. Eine marxistische Einführung* (Cologne: Pahl-Rugenstein, 1976), 10–11.
3. Cf. *Schriftsteller und literarisches Erbe. Zum Traditionsverhältnis sozialistischer Autoren*, ed. Hans Richter (Berlin and Weimar: Aufbau, 1976).
4. Braun, 'Rimbaud. Ein Psalm der Aktualität', 983, 982.
5. Cf. particularly Braun, 'Der Eisenwagen', *Langsamer knirschender Morgen*, 52–7, and further 'Der Frieden', 42–4, 'Das gebremste Leben', 45–6, 'Das innerste Afrika', 61–3.
6. Wallace, for example, fixes the crisis point for Braun in 1974, the shift from 'Detailkritik am System' to 'Systemkritik in Detail'. See Wallace, ' "Das Dennoch und der Triumph der Selbstbehauptung": Identitätssuche und Zivilisationskrise bei Volker Braun', in *Jahrbuch zur Literatur der DDR 3*, ed. Paul Gerhard Klussmann and Heinrich Mohr (Bonn: Bouvier, 1983), 185–208 (186).
7. Brinkmann, 'Narrenschiff. Den Freunden', *Wasserstände und Tauchtiefen*, 86.
8. Bartsch, 'Höllenfahrt. Nach Vergil, Dante, Marx', *Übungen im Joch*, 104–5. This is also a response to Karl Mickel's 'Inferno XXXIV. Für Kirsten', as Peter Geist points out in his 'Gruß, Gerade, Grat', 626–7.
9. Kolbe, *Hineingeboren*, 111–12.
10. Brinkmann, *Wasserstände und Tauchtiefen*, 40.

11. Silvia Schlenstedt, in her article 'Das Individuum in der Geschichte', finds some hope in the fact that 'ein Sinn in der kreisenden Bewegung von Brinkmann nicht ausgeschlossen [sei]', 92. However, the text makes it clear in lines 16–17 that this might only exist 'außerhalb | der Mühle'.

12. Cf. Brinkmann, 'Sisyphos', *Wasserstände und Tauchtiefen*, 42; Kolbe, 'Sisyphos nach Mattheuer', and 'Das ganze Werk oder Sisyphos soundsovielter', *Hineingeboren*, 48–9, and 65–6; Rathenow, 'Sisyphos bleibt zurück', and 'Sisyphos. Wechselnde Einstellungen', *VERRIRTE STERNE*, 50 and 52–4; Brigitte Struzyk, 'Die Tochter des Sisyphos berichtet dem Vater', *Der wild gewordener Tag: Gedichte* (Berlin and Weimar: Aufbau, 1989), 88.

13. See Heiner Müller, *Traktor*, in *Geschichten aus der Produktion 2* (Berlin/ W.: Rotbuch, 1974; repr. 1991), 9–24 (21). Müller's image, of course, is also very ambivalent in its implications.

14. Cf. Silvia Schlenstedt, 'Das Individaum', 90; and Kolbe, *Hineingeboren*, 48–9.

15. *Berührung ist nur eine Randerscheinung*, 42.

16. Hartmann, 'Der Generationswechsel', 119.

17. See also Hartmann, 'Neue Tendenzen in der DDR-Lyrik', 5–29, and 'Schreiben in der Tradition der Avantgarde. Neue Lyrik in der DDR', 1–37. See Bibliography.

18. Heukenkamp, 'Gedanken zur jungen Lyrik', *NdL* 2 (1978), 110–18 (111), and 'Wandel einer Mitteilung', *SuF* 5 (1978), 1079–91 (1088).

19. Rönisch, 'Notizen', 5. Ingrid Pergande points out that the problem of young writers having to coming to terms with an 'anglernte[s] Sozialismusbild', frequently at odds with the everyday realities of socialism, was even officially raised at the Ninth Writers' Congress. Cf. Pergande, 'Volker Braun?', 235.

20. Drawert, 'Wunsch', *Zweiter Inventur*, 74 and Grünbein, 'Zerebralis', *Schädelbasislektion*, 134–5. In this context, Anderson's comments about the impossibility of gaining access to works of art in Dresden also has a resonance far beyond the particular instance: '*Ich* hatte keine Originale gesehen, ich habe von Reproduktionen gelebt'. Labroisse and Wallace, *DDR-Schriftsteller sprechen in der Zeit*, 246.

21. Elisabeth Wesuls, 'Sich einlassen auf das Langwierige', *NdL* 1 (1981), 75–8 (78), and Bernd Rump, a speech at the Ninth Writers' Congress from 'Diskussion', *NdL* 9 (1983), 100–81 (162). Cf. also Thomas Böhme, 'Unarten eines Sachsen aus Leipzig', *NdL* 3 (1983), 87–91 (90–1) and Hans-Eckardt Wenzel, 'Allgemein wiederholte Auslassungen zu einem hinlänglich bekannten Thema/Diskussionsschrift', in *Positionen 2: Wortmeldungen zur DDR-Literatur*, ed. Eberhard Günther and Hinnerk Einhorn (Halle–Leipzig: Mitteldeutscher Verlag, 1986), 86–106.

22. See Kolbe, *Hineingeboren*, 135 and *Vaterlandkanal*, 43 for quotations; see also 'Gedichte, dacht ich werden nachts geschrieben', *Vaterlandkanal*, 44. These find a response in his much-quoted 'Gespräch ohne Ende', *Bornholm II*, 24–5: 'Glauben ersetze ich nicht | durch weiterer Glauben'.

23. Holger Teschke, 'Weihnachten in Saßnitz', *Bäume am Hochufer*, 46.

24. Drawert, 'Gedicht im Juni, Juli, August', *Zweite Inventur*, 9–15 (14).

25. Mensching, 'Lied für meine Freunde', *Poesiealbum*, 146 (Berlin: Verlag Neues Leben, 1979), 5.

26. Dau, 'Mit meinen Augen', 100.

27. Mensching began his poetic career in the 'Poetenseminar' of the FDJ. For texts which takes up a very similar theme, see Brinkmann, 'Kino', which starts 'Wir kennen den Krieg | vom Pflichtfilmsehen', *Poetenseminar 1979*, Poesiealbum: Sonderheft (Berlin: Verlag Neues Leben, 1980), 6, or Jansen, 'Vorbereitung auf einen Kriegsfilm', *Poesiealbum*, 20.
28. T. S. Eliot, 'Tradition and the Individual Talent', in *Selected Essays* (London: Faber, 1957), 14. Wenzel, quoted by Christel and Walfried Hartinger, 'Zu Hans-Eckardt Wenzel: "Lied vom wilden Mohn" ', in *Im Blick: Junge Autoren. Lesarten zu neuen Büchern*, ed. Walfried Hartinger and Klaus Schuhmann (Halle–Leipzig; Mitteldeutscher Verlag, 1987), 115–20 (117).
29. Wenzel, 'Vor allem suchen wir', *Sonntag*, 3 (1981), 5, quoted in Hagemann, 'Die Analyse der Wertvorstellungen', 64. Among the young writers Wenzel is probably the one who has written most about the problem of the acquisition of historical understanding. See also: 'Arbeit mit Geschichte', *NdL* 1 (1981), 108–11, and 'Halteverbot in der Dunkelheit: Variationen zum Begriff der Geschichte', *NdL* 8 (1991), 53–65.
30. Christel and Walfried Hartinger, 'Gespräch mit Heinz Czechowski', repr. in Czechowski, *Ich beispielsweise* (Leipzig: Philipp Reclam jun., 1982), 117 and 133.
31. Kowalski, *Vertrauliche Mitteilung*, 66–8.
32. Cf. Adloff, 'Ortsbestimmung', *Fortgang*, 19–21; Uta Mauersberger, 'Ausflüge ja sonntags alle zusammen', *Balladen Lieder Gedichte* (Berlin: Verlag Neues Leben, 1983; 2nd edn., 1985), 64; Teschke, 'Weihnachten in Saßnitz', *Bäume am Hochufer*, 46.
33. Steffen Mensching, 'Grenzwertberechnung', *NdL* 5 (1984), 45–8 (47).
34. Mensching, *Tuchfühlung*, 35–61 (44 and 61).
35. Wenzel, 'Amtliches Schuldbekenntnis', *Lied vom wilden Mohn*, 35. Geist points out the Marx reference from 'Lucretius Über die Natur der Dinge', in his 'Gedicht-Schreiben', 99.
36. Cf. Marx, 'Der achtzehnte Brumaire des Louis Bonaparte', in *Karl Marx, Friedrich Engels, Studienausgabe in 4 Bänden*, ed. Iring Fetscher (Frankfurt/M.: Fischer, 1966; 9th edn. 1980), iv. 34–121 (34).
37. Wilhelm Girnus, 'Die Glätte des Stroms und seine Tiefe', in *Wozu Literatur: Essays Reden Gespräche* (Leipzig: Philipp Reclam jun., 1976), 167.
38. Two examples will have to suffice for this very wide-ranging strand of reception. See, e.g. Kolbe in interview in 1982: 'Alles hat für mich mit der "Menschheitsdämmerung" angefangen. Ich komme immer wieder auf die Expressionisten zurück', in ' "Ein Nein ist keine Lebenshaltung" ', 17–35 (21); and Mensching, 'Weltanfang' (with a dedication for von Hoddis), *Erinnerung an eine Milchglasscheibe*, 16.
39. Hans Magnus Enzensberger, *Die Furie des Verschwindens* (Frankfurt/M.: Suhrkamp, 1980).
40. Günter Kunert 'Unterwegs nach Utopia I', *Unterwegs nach Utopia: Gedichte* (Munich: Hanser, 1977), 75.
41. Wolf Biermann, 'Das macht mich populär', in *Für meine Genossen: Hetzlieder, Balladen, Gedichte*, (Berlin, Verlag Klaus Wagenbach, 1972), 49.
42. Braun, *Gegen die symmetrische Welt*, 32.

43. Anderson and Kerbach, *totenreklame. eine reise.* Anderson talks about the extraordinary journey (the very length of which emphasizes in some ways the sense of enclosure) in Labroisse and Wallace, *DDR-Schriftsteller sprechen in der Zeit,* esp. 241–2 and 254–5. Here he claims: 'ich suche überhaupt nicht nach der Vergangenheit. Ich bin nur ununterbrochen auf sie gestoßen' (p. 255), although the texture of the composition would seem to work against this. There is no space here to discuss Bartsch in detail either; however, special mention might be made of the poems in the section 'Wüste Mark Maltritz', in *Übungen im Joch,* 9–61, esp. those on pp. 13–17, and 'Die Doppelkapelle in Landesberg', 43–5.

44. Cf. Mauersberger, 'Die Erde tragen helfen', quoted in Hagemann, 'Die Analyse der Wertvorstellungen', 123–4. Mauersberger explains the origin of a number of her poems in her historical investigations about the ancestors of those in the villages of the area.

45. Mauersberger, *Balladen Lieder Gedichte,* 7–9, 10–12, 13–14 respectively.

46. Domašcyna, *Zaungucker: gedichte, texte* (Berlin: Janus press, Basis-Druck, 1992).

47. From an interview with Gregor Laschen in 1976, reprinted in Labroisse and Wallace, *DDR-Schriftsteller sprechen in der Zeit,* 3–11 (7).

48. In *Poetenseminar 1979,* 6.

49. Müller, 'Das Böse ist die Zukunft', in Heiner Müller, *'Jenseits der Nation'* (Berlin: Rotbuch, 1991), 74. Müller takes up Nietzsche's 'Vom Nutzen und Nachteil der Historie für das Leben', and pushes it to an extreme, by calling for an orgiastic, necrophiliac exchange with the past.

50. Cf. Wenzel, *Lied vom wilden Mohn,* 60, 9, 22, 39, 48, 54, 59, 73–7, 80, 82, and 85.

51. Hensel, *Stilleben mit Zukunft,* 107. See also the series of poems, 119–25. Hensel's prize-winning *Hallimasch: Erzählungen* (Frankfurt/M.: Luchterhand, 1989) is also an exploration of the realities of Fascism in the past of the GDR. Cf. also Anderson, 'der krieg VATER', and 'die deutsche Frau klagt an', *Jeder Satellit hat einen Killersatelliten,* 18 and 19.

52. Mensching, *Erinnerung an eine Milchglasscheibe,* 84–6. See also, in the same collection, 'Späte Elegie', dedicated to the Spanish Civil War fighter Eberhard Schmidt, 42; Holger Teschke, 'Regen gräbt sich ins Mauerwerk', *Bäume am Hochufer,* 51; and Kathrin Schmidt, 'Beispiele Jahre', which takes up the 1936 Olympic Games in Berlin, *Ein Engel fleigt durch die Tapetenfabrik,* 6. Sascha Anderson's *Jewish Jetset* (Berlin: Galrev, 1991) also deals explicitly with Fascism (and the persecution of the Jews in history more generally) in two cycles of texts (15–24 and 27–32), but brings the threat firmly up into the present with his warning: 'das böse trägt von jetzt an keine stiefel' (22).

53. Walter Benjamin, 'Über den Begriff der Geschichte', in Benjamin, *Gesammelte Schriften,* ed. Roy Tiedemann and Hermann Schweppenhäuser (Frankfurt/M.: Suhrkamp, 1974), i. 690–706 (693–4).

54. See Hähnel, *Lyriker im Zwiegespräch. Traditionsbeziehungen im Gedicht,* and cf. the comments by Ingrid Hähnel herself (p. 15), and Stefan Stein (p. 300). See also esp. Ursula Heukenkamp, 'Dichterporträts', *Lyriker im Zwiegespräch,* 217–64, and Achim Trebeß, ' "wir würschten" in den Kämpfen unserer Zeit: Porträtgedichte junger Autoren', 312–31.

55. Silvia Schlenstedt in 'Das Individuum in der Geschichte', 100–3.
56. Cf. Heukenkamp, 'Dichterporträts', 218. Schlenstedt develops a similar category and uses Wenzel's 'Max Hoelz', *Lied vom wilden Mohn*, 34, and Bernd Rump's 'Schlußlied fur Max Hoelz', *Sing-Gedichte* (Leipzig: Philipp Reklam jun., 1983), 107, as examples for a successful and less successful exploitation of this method.
57. Geist, 'Zu Steffen Mensching: "Erinnerung an eine Milchglasscheibe" ' in Hartinger and Schuhmann, *Im Blick: Junge Autoren. Lesarten zu neuen Büchern*, 67–73 (69). Cf. Wilhelm Bartsch, 'Marxens Führung', *Übungen im Joch*, 103, and Mensching, 'Blanqui in der Boutique', and 'Hegel bei den Statuen', *Erinnerung an eine Milchglasscheibe*, 25–7 and 30–1.
58. Kathrin Schmidt, 'Die Deutsche Reichsbahn lädt zum revolutionären Ausflug', *Poesiealbum*, 179 (Berlin: Verlag Neues Leben, 1982), 23–4, and ' "Es liegt an uns, Überkommenes aufzubrechen": *Temperamente* im Gespräch mit Kathrin Schmidt', *Temperamente*, 3 (1982), 39–44.
59. Cf. Hans Richter, 'Dialoge mit Kathrin Schmidts Gedichten', and Katrin Schmidt, 'Ebenfalls zu Kathrin Schmidts Gedichten', in *WB* 6 (1989), 990–5 and 995–9.
60. Mensching, *Erinnerung an eine Milchglasscheibe*, 14–15. In the July edition of 1985, the journal *Weimarer Beiträge* published one of its collections of reviews 'Für und Wider' on Mensching's first collection, including contributions from Geist, Haase, Dau, Hähnel, Hartinger, Gelbrich, Franz, and others (see Bibliography). See also in particular the articles on this poem: Hans-Eckardt Wenzel, 'Traumhafter Ausflug des Dichters Steffen M. mit Rosa L.: Steffen Menschings "Traumhafter Ausflug mit Rosa L." ', in *Lyriker im Zwiegespräch*, ed. Ingrid Hähnel, 345–67, and Mathilde and Rudolf Dau, 'Steffen Mensching: "Traumhafter Ausflug mit Rosa L." ', in *Werkinterpretationen zur deutschen Literatur*, ed. Horst Hartmann *et al.* (Berlin: Verlag Volk und Wissen, 1986), 257–63.
61. Becher, 'Hymne auf Rosa Luxemburg', from 'Der Glückssucher und die sieben Lasten', in Johannes R. Becher, *Gedichte 1936–1941*, (Berlin and Weimar: Aufbau, 1966), 354, and Bobrowski, 'Rosa Luxemburg' (1960), in Johannes Bobrowski, *Gesammelte Werke in 6 Bänden* (Berlin: Union Verlag, 1987), ii. *Gedichte aus dem Nachlaß*, 336.
62. The references to the prison letters are primarily to the letters of 2 May 1917, 3 June 1917, 14 Jan. 1918, and 24 Mar. 1918. The May letter is particularly significant: 'ich habe manchmal das Gefühl, ich bin kein richtiger Mensch, sondern irgendein Vogel oder ein anderes Tier in Menschengestalt; innerlich fühle ich mich in so einem Stückchen Garten wie hier oder im freien Feld unter Hummeln und Gras viel mehr in meiner Heimat als—auf einem Parteitag. Ihnen kann ich ja wohl alles sagen: Sie werden nicht gleich Verrat am Sozialismus wittern. Sie wissen, ich werde trotzdem hoffentlich auf dem Posten sterben: in einer Straßenschlacht oder im Zuchthaus. Aber mein innerstes Ich gehört mehr meinen Kohlmeisen als den "Genossen". Und nicht etwa, weil ich in der Natur, wie so viele innerlich bankrotte Politiker, ein Refugium, ein Ausruhen finde. Im Gegenteil, ich finde auch in der Natur auf Schritt und Tritt soviel Grausames, daß ich sehr leide.' Rosa Luxemburg, *Briefe aus dem Gefängnis* (Berlin: Verlag Volk und Wissen, 1977), 36.
63. Wenzel, 'Traumhafter Ausflug des Dichters Steffen M.', 361. Wenzel's

analysis focuses centrally on the temporal aspect of the poem. This is perhaps because the generation of an ahistorical moment which can feed back into history as a productive revolutionary force is also central to his own poetic understanding. Cf. the title poem of *Antrag auf Verlängerung des Monats August* (73–5), in which the lyric subject requests a 32 August, as the intimation of an ideal world governed by peace and equality: 'An diesem Tag werde ich BRÜDER sagen'.

64. Adolf Endler's comment that this 'mediocre' poem can only be seen as bold or innovative by those 'Alt-Stalinisten' who produce it as their trump card at every given occasion, is really very wide of the mark. Cf. Endler, *Den Tiger reiten*, 46.

65. Heukenkamp, 'Funktion und Ausdruck', 295–302.

66. The most comprehensive and up-to-date account is Sture Packalén's *Zum Hölderlinbild in der Bundesrepublik und der DDR. Anhand ausgewählter Beispiele der produktiven Hölderlinrezeption*, Studia Germanistica Upsalensia, 28 (Stockholm: Almquist and Wiksell, 1986). See also: Helen Fehervary, *Hölderlin and the Left: The Search for a Dialectic of Art and Life* (Heidelberg: Carl Winter Universitätsverlag, 1977); and Bernhard Greiner, 'Zersprungene Identität: Bildnisse des Schriftstellers in zeitgenössischen Dichtungen über Hölderlin', in *Die deutsche Teilung im Spiegel der Literatur: Beiträge zur Literatur und Germanistik der DDR*, ed. Karl Lamers (Bonn: Verlag Bonn Aktuell, 2nd edn. 1978), 85–120.

67. Cf. my 'Towards a Profane Hölderlin: Representations and Revisions of Hölderlin in some GDR poetry', in *Neue Ansichten: The Reception of Romanticism in the Literature of the GDR*, ed. Howard Gaskill, Karin McPherson, and Andrew Barker, GDR Monitor Special Series, 6 (Amsterdam: Rodopi, 1990), 212–31; and Oscar van Weerdenburg, 'Hölderlin am Prenzlauer Berg. Zur Hölderlin Rezeption Hans-Eckardt Wenzels', in *Literarische Tradition Heute: Deutschsprachige Gegenwartsliteratur in ihrem Verhältnis zur Tradition*, ed. Gerd Labroisse and Gerhard P. Knapp, ABznG 24 (Amsterdam: Rodopi, 1988), 61–77.

68. 'Die Goethepächter', in Braun, *Es genügt nicht die einfache Wahrheit*, 48.

69. In 1970 the bicentenary of Hölderlin's birth occasioned an unprecedented celebration of the poet as a legitimate herald of the socialist state. The new understanding of Hölderlin was ushered in by a range of cultural and political developments, especially Bertaux's critical reappraisal of the Romantic period, not as a time of flight from reality, but as a time of concrete social concern. Pierre Bertaux, 'Hölderlin und die Französische Revolution', in *Hölderlin-Jahrbuch*, 15, (1967–8), 1–27. Günther Deicke's essay 'Wiederbegegnung mit Hölderlin', *NdL* 5 (1970), 107–16, and his poem 'Tübingen, Oktober', 116–18, can be regarded as examples of this strand. They take up Hölderlin as poet of revolution and productive 'homo faber' and are also a direct response to the 'decadent' reception of Hölderlin in the West, especially by Celan.

70. 'An die klugen Rathgeber' is the title of one of Hölderlin's poems. See Hölderlin, *Sämtliche Werke*, ed. Beißner and Beck, i. 223. References given in the text are to volume and page numbers in this edition. For a general study about the shaking of the Classical foundations of the GDR literary tradition see Bernd Leistner, *Unruhe um einen Klassiker. Zum*

Goethe-Bezug in der neueren DDR-Literatur (Halle–Leipzig: Mittel-deutscher Verlag, 1978).
71. Trebeß, ' "wir würschten" in den Kämpfen unserer Zeit', 315.
72. Christa Wolf speaks specifically about the effect of the *Ausbürgerung* of Wolf Biermann on the reception of Romanticism in the GDR in Christa and Gerhard Wolf, *Ins Ungebundene gehet eine Sehnsucht: Gesprächs-raum Romantik* (Belin and Weimar: Aufbau, 1985), 376.
73. First published in *Die Zeit*, 13 Aug. 1982, and recently taken up into Czechowski, *Nachtspur: Gedichte und Prosa 1987–1992* (Zurich: Ammann Verlag, 1993). I discuss this poem in more detail in 'Towards a profane Hölderlin', 219–20.
74. Braun, 'An Friedrich Hölderlin', *Gegen die symmetrische Welt*, 18.
75. A later poem develops the same themes. Quotations from Hölderlin and Guevara are set side by side and Braun identifies himself in a line with the revolutionary social concern of both these models. Braun, 'Material IV: Guevara', in Volker Braun, *Training des aufrechten Gangs* (Halle/S.: Mitteldeutscher Verlag, 1979), 55–8.
76. Biermann, *Für meine Genossen*, 19.
77. This affinity is underlined in two later poems about Hölderlin: 'Hölderlin in Bordeaux', in which the two poets conspire to elude repressive political measures (and which also quotes the 'Fremdlinge' speech), and 'Hölderlin im Turm' of 1986, where Hölderlin is hailed as 'Ikarus' (l. 12)—an epithet which Biermann also applied to himself at the time of his exile. Wolf Biermann, *Verdrehte Welt—das seh' ich gerne: Gedichte* (Munich: dtv, 1985), 136–8 (first published by Kiepenheuer & Witsch, 1982), and *Affenfels und Barrikade* (Cologne: Kiepenheuer & Witsch, 1986), 107–8.
78. Fehervary, *Hölderin and the Left*, 140, and 141–2.
79. Biermann, 'Gesang für meine Genossen', *Für meine Genossen*, 7–9.
80. Cf. Roland Erb, 'An Hölderlin', *Die Stille des Taifuns* (Berlin and Weimar: Aufbau, 1981), 102; and Jan Flieger, 'Hölderlin', in Flieger and Peter Tiller, *Floßfahrt* (Halle/S.: Mitteldeutscher Verlag, 1977), 12.
81. Kowalski, 'Hölderlin kehrt aus Bordeaux zurück', *Vertrauliche Mitteilung*, 37.
82. Cf. Ch. 6 for a discussion of Hölderlin's poem in the context of Christa Wolf's *Was bleibt*.
83. Rüdiger Bernhardt, ' "Vertrauliche Mitteilung" über Geschichte', *Wort Wechsel: Studien zur DDR-Literatur*, Wissenschaftliche Zeitschrift der Friedrich Schiller Universität Jena, 3 (1990), 151–5 (154). Contrast Packalén's reading, *Zum Hölderlinbild*, 221–3.
84. The other poems in the historical section of the collection contain any number of phrases like 'leerer raum', 'blind und in ketten', 'stumm', or 'henker'. The only historically hopeful text is 'beton(fabrik an einer eisenbahnstrecke)' (p. 41), in which 'der arbeitsfrieden' of the bosses is disrupted by a twist of Brechtian smoke: 'einzig | der rauch überm schornstein | mahnt: im kesselhaus arbeiten unruhestifter', 41.
85. Roland Erb, 'An Friedrich Hölderlin', *Die Stille des Taifuns*, 102.
86. Steffen Mensching, 'Hölderlin', first published in NdL 3 (1981), 120–1. When it was taken up into *Erinnerung an eine Milchglasscheibe*, 76, it included a dedication to Wenzel.
87. Packalén, *Zum Hölderlinbild*, 228.

88. The 'ins offene' could also, of course, be read as referring to the blade of the knife.
89. Schmidt, *Ein Engel fliegt durch die Tapetenfabrik*, 10.
90. 'Vier Fragen an Hans-Eckardt Wenzel', 75. See also the discussion of Hölderlin's 'Chiron' in Ch. 3. Wenzel's is the most wide-ranging response to Hölderlin among the young writers. His *Lied vom wilden Mohn*, for example, includes a cycle of six poems dedicated to Hölderlin and entitled 'Grenzen'. I discuss one of the other Hölderlin poems in 'Towards a Profane Hölderlin', 222–4. The treatment of Chiron is taken up in detail in Oscar van Weerdenburg's 'Holderlin am Prenzlauer Berg'.
91. Köhler, 'Endstelle', *Deutsches Roulette*, 39. An interesting comparison is with the much more closed opposition in Barbara Struzyk's 'Verschlossen', from 1975, *Leben auf der Kippe*, 30. It is a poetic 'dialogue' with the text of Hölderlin's 'Der Gang aufs Land', but one in which contemporary failings serve to shut down the historical perspectives line by line, until the whole becomes a static list of oppositions, for example, the first lines: '*Komm! ins Offene, Freund!*— | aber mach fest die Tür zu'.
92. Parts of this dialogue are reprinted in *vogel oder käfig sein*, 46–54.
93. Parts of the collection are clearly a diaglogue with Müller; cf. pp 23 and 31 and also above, Ch. 3. See also *Die Hamletmaschine: Heiner Müllers Endspiel*, ed. Theo Girshausen (Cologne: Prometh Verlag, 1978).
94. See Köhler, *Deutsches Roulette*, 12. See also 'Letztes Erinnern' (p. 44), which clearly thematizes a similar division. The poem carries a quotation from a poem by Melle as an epigraph, and takes up Hölderlin's Bellarmin, and the famous quotation from the 'Scheltrede', 'So kam ich unter die Deutschen'.
95. In this opposition, and in the link between language, love and death, Köhler reveals also a much darker engagement, namely with Ingeborg Bachmann, and in particular with her essays, with *Malina* (from which the epigraph for the collection is taken), and with the 'Todesarten' cycle.
96. David Constantine, *Hölderlin* (Oxford: Clarendon Press, 1988), 27.
97. All of these older writers (especially perhaps Czechowski) have had a long and shifting poetic dialogue with Hölderlin in their work, and cannot, of course, be firmly tied to any one particular category of response.
98. Papenfuß-Gorek, *tiské* (Göttingen: Steidl, 1990), 8. See Erik Grimm, 'Der Tod der Ostmoderne oder Die BRDigung des DDR-Untergrunds: Zur Lyrik Bert Papenfuß-Goreks', *ZfG*, 1 (1991), 9–20.
99. Cf. Walfried Hartinger, Klaus Werner, 'DDR Lyrik der siebziger und achtziger Jahre: Thesen', *WB* 12 (1990), 1987–92 (1190).
100. Cf. Hartmann, 'Generationswechsel', 130.
101. Braun, *Langsamer knirschender Morgen*, 35–9.
102. Grünbein, *Grauzone morgens*, 53.
103. Papenfuß-Gorek's fondness for such linguistic reversals can be seen in a number of texts; 'Tyske' is also Danish for 'German'. Given the large number of poems in the collection on the subject of the W*ende* and on the end of post-war understandings of German national and historical identity, this seems to be a characteristically wry comment.

CHAPTER 5

1. Volker Braun, 'Das Unersetzliche wird unser Thema bleiben', *NdL* 6 (1990), 6–9 (7).
2. The liberalizations of the 1980s meant that some of the most interesting GDR theorists, critics, and philosophers could engage with previously taboo areas (the historical avant-garde, French surrealism, structuralism, and even post-structuralism). Nevertheless, the attitudes of those cultural politicians in charge of publishing and censorship lagged a long way behind. For a useful account of the shifts in attitude, see Günter Erbe, *Die verfemte Moderne: Die Auseinandersetzung mit dem 'Modernismus' in Kulturpolitik, Literaturwissenschaft und Literatur der DDR* (Opladen: Westdeutscher Verlag, 1993).
3. Quoted in Endler, *Den Tiger reiten*, 17.
4. Papenfuß-Gorek, 'krampf–kampf–tanz–saga', *dreihzehntanz*, 181–204 (183). Döring, 'Introview. Egmont Hesse—Stefan Döring. das interview vom gespräch', in *Sprache & Antwort*, 100. See also Döring's 'was dich ausmacht—macht', *Heutmorgestern*, 37.
5. See Kolbe in discussion with Elke Erb in *Berührung ist nur eine Randerscheinung*, 40–1.
6. Anderson, *Jeder Satellit hat einen Killersatelliten*, 72.
7. Kolbe, 'Beschreibung der Möglichkeiten', *Abschiede und andere Liebesgedichte*, 12–13. Several of these formulations, and indeed the writers' whole understanding of this issue, are coloured by the writings of Foucault, the rhetoric of whose analysis was taken up widely (probably rather more widely than he was actually read).
8. Marieluise de Waijer-Wilke: '*ünf Fragen an Kito Lorenc*', in Lorenc, *Wortland: Gedichte* (Leipzig: Verlag Philipp Reclam jun., 1984), 165–6.
9. Ibid. 166. For a taste, compare his 'Rede-Wendungen', *Wortland*, 102.
10. Döring, 'willelei', in *Sprache & Antwort*, 91.
11. *Berührung ist nur eine Randerscheinung*, 41.
12. Anderson, 'Das Prinzip Subversion und seine Folgen', *Neue Rundschau*, 1 (1990), 94–8 (97).
13. Cf. Hartmann, 'Der Generationswechsel'. She notes 'eine tiefgreifende Sprachskepsis, sowie ein fundamentaler Erkenntnisrelativismus' (p. 122).
14. Ibid. 125, and Hartmann, 'Schreiben in der Tradition der Avantgarde', 32.
15. See Hartmann, 'Schreiben in der Tradition der Avantgarde', 9; and Cosentino, 'ich habe ausser meiner sprache', 201.
16. Kolbe, in *Berührung ist nur eine Randerscheinung*, 39.
17. Ibid. 15.
18. Papenfuß-Gorek, quoted in Gerhard Wolf, *Sprachblätter Wortwechsel*, 10.
19. Endler, *Den Tiger reiten*, 29. Endler also makes the nice point that when some (less interesting) examples of experimental work were included in the anthology *Auswahl '84* the editors glossed the experiments instead with the anodyne formula 'Liebe zu den Wörtern' (p. 30).
20. Alexander von Bormann has compiled a more detailed scheme of

disctinctions for poetry of the 1980s as a whole: 'Begrenzte Andersheit: Zur DDR-Lyrik der achtziger Jahre', *Der Deutschunterricht*, 4 (1990), 77–99.

21. Heiner Müller: 'Der Autor ist klüger als die Allegorie, die Metapher klüger als der Autor', from 'Fatzer ± Keuner', in Müller, *Rotwelsch*, 140–9 (141).

22. Cf. a review of Kathrin Schmidt's collection, which takes up the controversial nature of her metaphors. Rainer Zekert, 'Das Wagnis Metapher. Kathrin Schmidt: "Ein Engel fliegt durch die Tapetenfabrik" ', *NdL* 6 (1989), 157–61.

23. I am indebted to this illuminating piece: Geist, 'Die Metapher in der poetologischen Reflexion und Dichtungspraxis von DDR-Lyrikern in den siebziger und achtziger Jahren—Eine Problemskizze', *DDR-Lyrik im Kontext*, 61–87.

24. From 'Was vermag Lyrik?', quoted ibid. 63.

25. Rainer Kirsch, 'Georg Maurer zum 60 Geburtstag', quoted ibid. 63.

26. Elke Erb, *Der Faden der Geduld* (Berlin and Weimar: Aufbau, 1978), 120.

27. This he traces to the 'Metapherndiskussion' of 1973, which was initiated at the conference 'Welt im sozialistischen Gedicht' in April of that year (p. 62).

28. Richard Pietraß, 'Raum des Lebbaren: Interview mit Christian Löser', *NdL* 9 (1976), 119–21 (120).

29. Cf. Rimbaud, 'Lettre à Paul Demeny, Charleville, 15 mai 1871', in *Œuvres Complètes. Correspondance*, 233.

30. Rönisch, 'Notizen', 9. Walfried Hartinger makes the same point in ' "Vom Machen einleuchtender Bilder": Versuche zur geschichtlichen Positionsbestimmung in der Lyrik in der DDR', in *Selbsterfahrung als Welterfahrung*, ed. Nalewski and Schuhmann, 5–20 (15).

31. Rainer Schedlinski, 'Zwischen Nostalgie und Utopie. Ein Postskriptum', in *'Die Geschichte ist offen': DDR 1990: Hoffnung auf eine neue Republik. Schriftsteller aus der DDR über die Zukunftschancen ihres Landes*, ed. Michael Naumann (Reinbek bei Hamburg: Rowohlt, 1990), 183. Schmidt is the writer most associated with innovative use of metaphor. See her own comments in the interview, 'Es liegt an uns, Überkommenes aufzubrechen', 44.

32. Mensching, *Erinnerung an eine Milchglasscheibe*, 83.

33. This poem, which in many ways embodies the moral injunction of Mensching's poetry as a whole, gave rise to a critical controversy. Cf. particularly: Bernd Leistner, '. . . Dich zu treiben bis aufs Blut', *SuF* 5 (1985), 1094–1102; and Mathilde and Rudolf Dau, 'Vivisektion mit stumpfem Skalpell', *SuF* 2 (1986), 442–7.

34. Alexander von Bormann, 'Rede-Wendungen: Zur Rhetorik des gegenwärtigen Gedichts in der DDR', in Cosentino, Ertl, and Labroisse, *DDR-Lyrik im Kontext*, 89–143 (114).

35. This gesture is recognizable from a number of Mensching's poems, some of which have already been discussed. See, e.g. 'Auf einem Bein, nachts, nackt', *Erinnerung an eine Milchglasscheibe*, 88, or 'World time table', ibid. 8–9.

36. Hensel, *Stilleben mit Zukunft*, 90.

37. Kolbe, *Bornholm II*, 28.
38. Bormann ('Rede-Wendnugen', 115) makes the point that 'glasnost', one of the central pillars of Gorbachev's *perestroika*, was ironically referred to as 'Milchglasnost' in the GDR, because of the attempts of the authorities to water down the reforms. It seems to me that the dates of both of these texts—1980 in the case of Kolbe, and 1982–3 for the Mensching—are a little early for this to play a role in the conception. However, it adds a further political dimension to the reception of the texts.
39. Kolbe, 'Das wirkliche Grün', *Bornholm II*, 106.
40. See Bormann, 'Rede-Wendungen' 119–43.
41. Müller, *Gedichte* (Berlin: Alexander Verlag, 1992), 13.
42. Cf. Michael Thulin [i.e. Klaus Michael], 'Sprache und Sprachkritik: Die Literatur des Prenzlauer Bergs in Berlin/DDR', in *Die andere Sprache*, 234–42 (239).
43. Ibid.
44. Andreas Koziol, 'ein letterleuchten', *mehr über rauten und türme: gedichte* (Berlin and Weimar: Aufbau—Außer der Reihe, 1991), 83.
45. Koziol, 'rumor', *mehr über rauten und türme*, 81. Cf. also 'verfallener wortwechsel', 80.
46. Döring, ' "mit den worten sterben die bilder" ', *Heutmorgestern*, 94. Döring explicitly addresses the ambivalence towards metaphor in his work: 'Ich lasse die Metapher keine Zeit. Wo und wie sie sich entwickelt, nehme ich sie wieder zurück'. See 'Introview', in *Sprache & Antwort*, 96–7.
47. McCaffery is often associated with the Language Poets of the United States, who in many ways can be compared with the experimental poets of Prenzlauer Berg. See e.g. George Hartley, *Textual Politics and the Language Poets* (Bloomington and Indianapolis: Indiana University Press, 1989).
48. McCaffery, 'The Death of the Subject', [n.p.]. The phrase 'the referential fallacy of language' provoked so many attacks against the 'language' poetry, that in a heavily revised version of the essay McCaffery deleted it altogether.
49. I have already mentioned Mensching and Wenzel's cabaret performances, the texts for some of which are collected in *Allerletztes aus der Da Da eR, Hundekomödie: Textbücher*, ed. Andrea Doberenz (Halle–Leipzig: Mitteldeutscher Verlag, 1991). *Die andere Sprache* also carries an extract from a piece by the free theatre and cabaret group 'zinnober', with a note by Rainer Schedlinski, 78–87.
50. Kolbe, 'Ein Gruß', *Bornholm II*, 77.
51. An exception is, of course, his notorious text 'Kern meines Romans'. This string of unconnected nouns and noun forms functioned as a kind of vast acrostic. When read for its hidden meaning, it revealed the inner biography of a generation and scathing attack on the GDR. The scandal was discovered, and passed by word of mouth, while the anthology was removed from libraries. Cf. *Bestandsaufnahme 2: Debütanten 1976–1980*, ed. Brigitte Böttcher (Halle–Leipzig: Mitteldeutscher Verlag, 1981), 82–3.
52. Endler, *Den Tiger reiten*, 25.
53. The first four of the 'Manifeste der Trivialpoesie' are reprinted in Faktor's

Georgs Versuche an einem Gedicht, 87–102. In his second collection *Henry's Jupitergestik in der Blutlache Nr.* *3 und andere positive Texte aus Georgs Besudelungs- und Selbstbesudelungskabinett: Texte, Manifeste, Stücke und ein Bericht* (Berlin: Janus press, BasisDruck, 1991), there is an 'Antwort auf die Manifeste der Trivialpoesie', which explores the equally ironic notion of a 'Paralyrik' (79–87).

54. For very different examples see Faktor, 'sterbender Papa steht auf', *Georgs Versuche an einem Gedicht*, 79, 'wie praktisch ist unsere Haut', ibid. 28–33, or 'Das Selbstbesudelungsmanifest fünf tapferer Literaturrevoluzzer, wie es die Zeit verlangt', *Henry's Jupitergestik in der Blutlache Nr. 3*, 39–77.

55. Cf. Endler, *Den Tiger reiten*, 27.

56. There are six numbered 'eNDe' texts in Anderson, *Jeder Satellit hat einen Killersatelliten*, and three further texts in *totenreklame. eine reise.*

57. Cf. 'eNDe' I, II, and IV, in Anderson, *Jeder Satellit hat einen Killersatelliten*, 20, 21, and 59.

58. Cf. 'eNDe' V, ibid. 64, or, for a more pointed unmasking of ideology, 'eNDe' VI, ibid. 65.

59. Anderson, *totenreklame. eine reise*, 76.

60. Cosentino, in 'ich habe ausser meiner sprache', calls this series of poems Anderson's distinctive contribution to the 'Politgedicht' of the 1980s. Visser offers a detailed political interpretation of them, *Blumen im Eis*, 317–28.

61. Papenfuß-Gorek, 'wustsein im unterwolz', *dreizehntanz*, 9.

62. Thulin, 'Sprache und Sprachkritik', 238.

63. Cf. Faktor, 'Georgs Sorgen um die Zukunft', *Georgs Versuche an einem Gedicht*, 37–70, 'Hans kam außer Atem an nur so', which runs through the formation of questions and prepositions in German to comic effect, 80–1, and 'Parallelepiped', 103–10. In *Henrys Jupitergestik in der Blutlache Nr. 3* this is taken even further, as in 'Rangreihe der 323 häufigsten Wortformen der deutschen Sprache', 20–1, or 'Ein Versuch, den Konsonanten "f" stimmhaft auszusprechen', 23–6.

64. Cf. also texts by Thom di Roes (i.e. Thomas Roesler), which work on a similar principle: 'ICH's APOKALYPTUS eine autobiographische Weltgeschichte', in *Berührung ist nur eine Randerscheinung*, 209–19.

65. Wolfgang Müller, 'Die Kunst der (simulierten?) Rebellion: Zur Lyrik aus Prenzlauer Berg', *GDR Bulletin*, 2 (Fall 1992), 21–6, (23).

66. Frank-Wolf Matthies, 'Auf der Suche nach Herrn Naumann (ein Manifest)', in *Für Patricia im Winter: Gedichte* (Reinbek bei Hamburg: Rowohlt, 1981), 17.

67. Anderson, *totenreklame. eine reise*, 83–4.

68. Kachold, *zügel los*, 44.

69. Jansen, *prost neuland*, 78.

70. The term 'fragmentbaukasten' comes from Johannes Jansen, *Schlackstoff: Materialversionen*, Text und Porträt 3 (Berlin: Literarisches Colloquium and DAAD, 1991), 60. The poem, 'gangart 1', is from *prost neuland*, 10.

71. Both quotations from Jansen, *Schlackstoff*, 10.

72. Jansen, *prost neuland*, 140. A useful example is the impressive final poem 'sollte ich fallen find ich was beßres im tod allemal', 140–1, which is a macabre echo of the story of the 'Bremer Stadtmusikanten', and also a

concrete political comment. Jansen worked very closely with Frank Lanzendörfer (some of their texts and drawings were done jointly), and his work resembles Lanzendörfer's own in its preoccupation with silence and death.

73. Kolbe, *Abschiede und andere Liebesgedichte*, 43.
74. Christine Cosentino has documented Kolbe's poetic struggle against silence, in ' "Aber die Sprache. | Warum spreche ich?": Zur "Metasprache" und Sprachhinterfragung in der Lyrik Uwe Kolbes', *GDR Monitor*, 18 (1987/8), 71–85.
75. Grünbein, 'Errata', in Druckhaus Galrev (ed.), *Proë*, Druckhaus Galrev Sonderband (Berlin: Galrev, 1992), [n.p.].
76. Grünbein, 'Die Leeren Zeichen 1', *Schädelbasislektion*, 69.
77. A sensitive approach to the problems of reading his more hermetic early work is offered in Cosentino's 'ich habe ausser meiner sprache'. See my comments in Ch. 7 about reading Anderson after 1991.
78. Jan Faktor, 'Was ist neu an der jungen Lyrik der achtziger Jahre?', in *vogel oder käfig sein*, 367–89 (374).
79. Manfred Jäger ' "Wem schreibe ich": Adressen und Botschaften in Gedichten jüngerer Autoren aus der DDR seit dem Beginn der achtziger Jahre', in *Die andere Sprache*, 61–71.
80. This dilemma is most interestingly documented by Gerd Neumann, a GDR prose writer a little older than many of the Prenzlauer Berg writers, who nevertheless shares many of the same preoccupations. See e.g. his *Die Schuld der Worte* (Rostock: Hinstorff Verlag, 1979), and 'Die Wörter des reinen Denkens', in *abriss der ariadnefabrik*, 249–54.
81. Papenfuß-Gorek, *dreizehntanz*, 123–4.
82. Jean-François Lyotard, *The Postmodern Condition*, p. xxv.
83. See particularly Achim Trebeß, ' "im rechten augenblick das linke tun": Spracherneuerung in Texten von Bert Papenfuß-Gorek', *WB* 4 (1990), 617–36; Michael Thulin, 'Die Imagination der poetischen Sprache. dichtung und arkdichtung von Bert Papenfuß-Gorek', in *Die andere Sprache*, 114–19; and Erik Grimm, 'Der Tod der Ostmoderne oder Die BRDigung der DDR-Untergrunds'.
84. Martin Kane, 'From Oobliadooh to Prenzlauer Berg: Literature, Alternative Lifestyle and Identity in the GDR', in Goodbody and Tate, *Geist und Macht*, 90–103 (101). He offers a very persuasive and personal reading of Papenfuß-Gorek's work.
85. Wolf Biermann, 'Ein öffentliches Geschwür: Offener Brief an Lew Kopelew', *Der Sturz des Dädalus*, 108.
86. Papenfuß-Gorek, *SoJa*, 70.
87. Cf. Trebeß, 'im rechten augenblick', 625. All the examples are from Papenfuß-Gorek, *dreizehntanz*.
88. See Karl Mickel, 'Lesarten: Das Einfache, das selten gelingt', *NdL* 8 (1980), 67–71. and 'Aussagen über Papenfuss', *SuF* 6 (1986), 1230–31 and Gerhard Wolf, *Sprachblätter Wortwechsel*, 36.
89. Endler, *Den Tiger reiten*, 49–50.
90. Papenfuß-Gorek, *dreihzehntanz*, 183.
91. Cf. Papenfuß-Gorek, LED SAUDAUS, 66 and 32. His subsequent collection is even more provocative in this respect. Cf. NUNFT: FKK/IM *endart*. *novemberklub: Gedichte, mit Grafiken der Gruppe Endart und einer CD des Novemberklub* (Göttingen: Steidl, 1992).

92. See LED SAUDAUS, 41–109. Papenfuß-Gorek explained in conversation that the 'Karren' of the title refers to the cart in the French romance. The two paces which Lancelot hesitates before he gets in mark the beginning of his trials of love and are a symbol of his betrayal.

93. Papenfuß-Gorek *SoJa*, 76.

94. *Sprache & Antwort*, 216–35 (228). A useful example of the fascination with individual words can also be seen here. A discussion of the word 'landläufig' led, for example, to a whole cycle of poems, in which all sorts of historical and artistic associations of the word are explored. See *Sprache & Antwort*, 236–40.

95. Michael Gratz offers a very convincing reading of Papenfuß-Gorek's political and linguistic strategies, 'Sprachspiel gegen Bewußtseinsbesetzung. Eine andere politische Dichtung aus der DDR', *Diskussion Deutsch*, 12 (1991), 606–18. See also Trebeß, 'im rechten augenblick', 632–5.

96. From Papenfuß-Gorek, 'SOndern', *dreihzehntanz*, 125–33 (133) and 'bewegung, d. h. bewegung', *vorwärts im zorn &sw.: gedichte* (Berlin and Weimar: Aufbau, 1990), 104.

97. Papenfuß-Gorek, *dreizehntanz*, 133.

98. Papenfuß-Gorek, *SoJa*, 8–9.

99. Hartmann, 'Neue Tendenzen in der DDR-Lyrik', 25.

100. Koziol, *mehr über rauten und türme*, 86.

101. Köhler, *Deutsches Roulette*, 63.

102. Cf. J. R. Becher, 'Philosophie des Sonetts—oder Kleine Sonettlehre: Ein Versuch', in Becher, *Über Literatur und Kunst* (Berlin: Aufbau, 1962), 664–75. Jürgen Engler latched on to this revival of interest in form in an interesting article: 'Gedrängte Kränze? Bemerkungen zum Sonett in der jüngsten Lyrik', in *Positionen 4: Wortmeldungen zur DDR-Literatur*, ed. Eberhard Günther and Hinnerk Einhorn (Halle–Leipzig: Mitteldeutscher Verlag, 1988), 149–68.

103. Drawert, 'Das Sonett', *Zweite Inventur*, 67.

104. Cf. Schmidt, 'Pupillenfliegen', *Ein Engel fliegt durch die Tapetenfabrik*, 75–92; and Kerstin Hensel, 'Märchen-Land', *Temperamente*, 2 (1984), 32–8. The 'Meistersonett' of Hensel's sequence, formed out of the first lines of the fourteen preceding sonnets, is reprinted in Hensel, *Stilleben mit Zukunft*, 104.

105. Dahlke, 'Im Brunnen vor dem Tore', 177–94.

106. *ich fühle mich in grenzen wohl: Fünfzehn deutsche Sonette*, ed. Sascha Anderson (Berlin/W.: Mariannenpresse, 1985).

107. Emmerich, *Kleine Literaturgeschichte*, 415, Böthig, 'Differenz und Revolte', 4, Peter Geist, 'Die Schatten werfen ihre Ereignisse voraus: Nachsichtendes zur Lyrik aus der DDR', in *Re-assessing the GDR*, ed. J. H. Reid, German Monitor, 33 (Amsterdam: Rodopi, 1994), 129–52, (142).

108. Hans Magnus Enzensberger, 'Meldungen vom lyrischen Betrieb', *FAZ* 14 Mar. 1989.

109. Braun, 'Rimbaud Ein Psalm der Aktualität', 990.

110. The more liberal literary critics in the GDR were moving in that direction. Cf. *Künstlerische Avantgarde: Annäherungen an ein unabgeschlossenes Kapitel*, ed. Karlheinz Barck, Dieter Schlenstedt, and Wolfgang Thierse (Berlin: Akademie-Verlag, 1979).

111. Hans Magnus Enzensberger 'Die Aporien der Avantgarde', in Enzenberger *Einzelheiten* (Frankfurt/M.: Suhrkamp, 1962), 290–315 (314–15).
112. Jäger speaks of 'das verspätete Nachholen der Moderne in der realismusgeschädigten DDR' in 'Wem schreibe ich?', 70 and Fritz Raddatz criticizes elements of an 'Avantgarde aus einer Konserve' in his ' "bebe go ehed". Lyrik von Flanzendörfer, Jan Faktor, Bert Papenfuß-Gorek und anderen: Rückblick auf die alternative Literatur der DDR', *Die Zeit*, 8 May 1992.
113. Anderson, *Jeder Satellit hat einen Killersatelliten*, 72.
114. Cf. Peter Bürger, *Theorie der Avantgarde* (Frankfurt/M.: Suhrkamp, 1974).
115. Papenfuß-Gorek, 'arianrhod von der überdosis', in Döring and Steinert, *Schöne Aussichten: Neue Prosa aus der DDR*, 113. Cf. Penck, 'Das Ende des Untergrundes', *ariadnefabrik*, 3 (1987), repr. in *abriss der ariadnefabrik*, 57–78.
116. Böthig, 'Differenz und Revolte', 143.
117. Cf. Steffen Mensching and Hans-Eckardt Wenzel, 'Entwürfe einer anderen Welt: Ein Gespräch mit Frauke Meyer-Gosau', in *Macht-ApparatLiteratur: Literatur und 'Stalinismus'*, ed. Frauke Meyer-Gosau, *Text und Kritik*, 108 (1990), 86–94.
118. Sascha Anderson, 'ich rede von Deutschland. Die junge Opposition in der DDR spricht mit der Macht von gleich zu gleich', *FAZ* 12 Feb. 1988, 29.
119. T. W. Adorno, 'Engagement', in *Notizen zur Literatur II* (Frankfurt/M.: Suhrkamp, 1965), 109–35, (130).
120. Anderson, *Jeder Satellit hat einen Killersatelliten*, 7.

PART III INTRODUCTION

1. Christa Wolf, *Was bleibt: Erzählung* (Frankfurt/M.: Luchterhand, 1990). Page references will be given to this edition in the text.
2. This has been widely discussed. See e.g. Wolf Lepenies, 'Das Ende der Utopie und die Rückkehr der Melancholie: Blick auf die Intellektuellen eines alten Kontinents', in *Intellektuellendämmerung? Beiträge zur neuesten Zeit des Geistes*, ed. Martin Meyer, 15–26, or 'Von linker Melancholie', in Rolf Schneider, *Volk ohne Trauer: Notizen nach dem Untergang der DDR* (Göttingen: Steidl, 1992), 183–94. I am particularly indebted to Wolfgang Emmerich's article, 'Status melancholicus. Zur Transformation der Utopie in der DDR-Literatur', in Arnold and Meyer-Gosau, *Literatur in der DDR: Rückblicke*, 232–45, which seems to me the most compelling and differentiated analysis to date.
3. Many of the important contributions to the 'Literaturstreit' of 1990–1 have been collected in two critical anthologies: *'Es geht nicht um Christa Wolf': Der Literaturstreit im vereinten Deutschland*, ed. Thomas Anz (Munich: edition spangenberg, 1991; cited hereafter as Anz); and *Der deutsch–deutsche Literaturstreit oder 'Freunde es spricht sich schlecht mit gebundener Zunge': Analysen und Materialien*, ed. Karl Deiritz and Hannes Krauss (Hamburg: Luchterhand, 1991; cited hereafter as Deiritz and Krauss).

4. See Horst Domdey, 'Die DDR-Literatur als Literatur der Epochenillusion. Zur Literaturgeschichtsschreibung der DDR-Literatur', in *Die DDR im vierzigsten Jahr. Geschichte, Situation, Perspektiven*, ed. Ilse Spittmann and Gisela Hellwig, xxii. Tagung zum Stand der DDR-Forschung in der BRD 16–19 Mai 1989 (Cologne: Edition Deutschland Archiv, 1989), 141–9.

5. Andreas Huyssen, 'After the Wall: The Failure of German Intellectuals', *New German Critique*, Special Issue on German Unification', 52 (winter 1991), 109–33. This important attempt by Huyssen to address a difficult issue stands in marked contrast to Frank Schirrmacher's demand that intellectuals should do a kind of public penance for their 'Blindheit gegenüber einem verbrecherischen Gesellschaftsmodell'. See the section 'Der Streit geht weiter: Neue Stellungnahmen zur Debatte', in Anz, 241–60 (257).

6. The essay 'Volk ohne Trauer' was first published in *Der Spiegel*, 29 Oct. 1990, 264–70. Page references are given to the collection of essays bearing the same title: Schneider, *Volk ohne Trauer*, here, 206.

CHAPTER 6

1. Cf. Alexander Stephan, 'Ein deutscher Forschungsbericht 1990/91: Zur Debatte um das Ende der DDR-Literatur und den Anfang einer gesamtdeutschen Kultur', *Germanic Review*, Theme Issue: 'The End of GDR Literature', 3 (summer 1992), 126–34 (126) and Irene Heidelberger-Leonard, 'Der Literaturstreit—ein Historikerstreit im gesamtdeutschen Kostüm?', in Deiritz and Krauss, 69–79 (71).

2. See e.g. the essays and interviews collected in Christa and Gerhard Wolf, *Ins Ungebundene gehet eine Sehnsucht: Gesprächsraum Romantik*.

3. References to Friedrich Hölderlin, *Sämtliche Werke*, ii. 188–9. See David Constantine's discussion of Hölderlin's ambivalent preoccupation with memory in 'Andenken' and 'Mnemosyne', in his *Hölderlin*, 275–8.

4. Heiner Müller, *Verkommenes Ufer Medeamaterial Landschaft mit Argonauten*, in *Herzstück* (Berlin: Rotbuch, 1983), 91–101 (99).

5. Compare Volker Hage, ' "Wir müssen uns dem Schicksal stellen": Über den Fall von Christa Wolf', *Der Spiegel*, 8 Feb. 1993, 197–9.

6. With hindsight it becomes clear that the theme of the 'Faustian bargain' is central in Wolf's work. It would be crude to interpret this motif solely as a reflection of Wolf's early involvement with the *Staatssicherheit*, however.

7. Apart from the anthologies edited by Anz and by Deiritz and Krauss, I have drawn particularly on the essays in the *New German Critique*, 'Special Issue on German Unification', 52 (winter 1991), the analysis of Alexander Stephan, 'Ein deutscher Forschungsbericht 1990/91', and articles in *Zum gegenwärtigen Zustand der deutschen Literatur*.

8. See 'Was bleibt. Bleibt was? Pro und Contra: eine *Zeit*-Kontroverse über Christa Wolf und ihre neue Erzählung', in *Die Zeit*, 1 June 1990. This consists of articles by Ulrich Greiner, 'Mangel an Feingefühl', repr. in Anz, 66–70, and Volker Hage, 'Kunstvolle Prosa', repr. in Anz, 71–6. See

also: Frank Schirrmacher, ' "Dem Druck des härteren strengeren Lebens standhalten": Auch eine Studie über den autoritären Charakter: Christa Wolfs Aufsätze, Reden und ihre jüngste Erzählung "Was bleibt" ', *FAZ* 2 June 1990, repr. in Anz, 77–89. Henceforward page references, unless otherwise stated, will be to texts as printed in Anz.

9. Jürgen Serke, 'Was bleibt, das ist die Scham', *Die Welt*, 23 June 1990, quoted in Stephan, 'Ein deutscher Forschungsbericht 1990/1', 127.

10. Biermann's full comment runs: 'Es geht um Christa Wolf, genauer: Es geht nicht um Christa Wolf', in Wolf Biermann, 'Nur wer sich ändert bleibt sich treu: Der Streit um Christa Wolf, das Ende der DDR, das Elend der Intellektuellen: Das alles ist auch komisch', *Die Zeit*, 24 Aug. 1990, repr. in Anz, 139–56 (139).

11. Emmerich argues the case for the differing attitudes of the generations very well in his 'Im Zeichen der Wiedervereinigung: die zweite Spaltung der deutschen Literatur', in *Kultur und Macht*, 26–40.

12. Quoted in Lew Kopelew, 'Für Christa Wolf', *die tageszeitung*, 14 June 1990, repr. in Anz, 117–21 (120).

13. Uwe Wittstock, 'Die Dichter und ihre Richter: Literaturstreit im Namen der Moral: Warum die Schriftsteller aus der DDR als Sündenböcke herhalten müssen', *Süddeutsche Zeitung*, 13/14 Oct. 1990, repr. in Anz, 198–207 (207).

14. Emmerich makes the point that it was also a reckoning between those who had left or been forced out of the GDR and those who had stayed behind, 'Im Zeichen der Wiedervereinigung', 29–30, as does Ian Wallace, 'Deutscher Literaturstreit aus britischer Sicht', *NdL*, 3 (1991), 150–5.

15. Reich-Ranicki reject the much used term 'Mitläufer' but only to substitute the term 'Mitverantwortliche', which is equally historically loaded, *Süddeutsche Zeitung*, 26 June 1990, quoted in Andrea Jäger, 'Schriftsteller-Identität und Zensur: Über die Bedingungen des Schreibens im "realen Sozialismus" ', in *Literatur in der DDR. Rückblicke*, ed. Arnold, 137–48 (139).

16. See Karl Heinz Bohrer, 'Kulturschutzgebiet DDR?', *Merkur*, 10/11 (Oct./Nov. 1990), 1015–18, (1017). The contention that GDR literature functioned as 'intellectual balm [. . .] that sustained rather than exposed the hard-edged, brutal reality of a dictatorship', is a common charge, especially from outside Germany. See Katie Hafner, 'A Nation of Readers Dumps its Writers', *New York Times*, 10 Jan. 1993, 23–6 and 45–8 (24). Emmerich rejects the idea absolutely, 'Status melancholicus', 241. Wallace defends the caution as pragmatic: as 'eine Kunst des Möglichen'. See 'Deutscher Literaturstreit aus britischer Sicht', 153.

17. Cf. the 'Aufruf': 'Für unser Land' of 28 Nov. 1989, pub. in *Neues Deutschland*, 28 Nov. 1989, and *Frankfurter Rundschau*, 30 Nov. 1989, and repr. in Christa Wolf, *Im Dialog. Aktuelle Texte* (Frankfurt/M.: Luchterhand, 1990), 170–1.

18. Cf. Heiner Müller's reflections on this animosity ' "Ohne Hoffnung, ohne Verzweiflung": Spiegel-Interview mit dem DDR-Dramatiker Heiner Müller in Ost Berlin', *Der Spiegel*, 4 Dec. 1989, 264–5 (264).

19. Cf. Stefan Heym, 'Aschermittwoch in der DDR', in *'Die Geschichte ist offen'* 71–8, and the sheer incomprehension of Christa Wolf, ' "Aufforderung zum Dialog": Gespräch mit Gerhard Rhein', 8 Oct. 1989, in Christa Wolf, *Im Dialog*, 77–89.

20. Many of the essays gathered in Kunert's *Der Sturz vom Sockel* deal with the end of this very special function of literature.
21. Cf. Grass, 'Ein Schnäppchen namens DDR', *Die Zeit*, 5 Oct. 1990, repr. in Günter Grass, *Ein Schnäppchen namens DDR: Letzte Reden vorm Glockengeläut* (Frankfurt/M.: Luchterhand, 1990), 39–60 (58).
22. Braun's comment is quoted in Huyssen, 'The Failure of German Intellectuals', 127, and Müller's contribution to a panel discussion in Berlin is reported in Ulrich Greiner, 'Die deutsche Gesinnungsästhetik. Noch einmal: Christa Wolf und der deutsche Literaturstreit. Eine Zwischenbilanz', *Die Zeit*, 2 Nov. 1990, repr. in Anz, 208–16 (215). For an examination of the broader context compare Ulrich Greiner, 'Keiner ist frei von Schuld. Deutscher Literaturstreit: Der Fall Christa Wolf und die Intellektuellen', *Die Zeit*, 25 July 1990, repr. in Anz, 179–83, and the telling article by Ivan Nagel, 'Die Volksfeinde: Literaturstreit und Intellektuellenjagd', *Süddeutsche Zeitung*, 22/23 Dec. 1990, repr. in Anz, 184–8.
23. Günter Grass, Hellmuth Karasek, and Rolf Becker, ' "Nötige Kritik oder Hinrichtung": Spiegel-Gespräch mit Günter Grass über die Debatte um Christa Wolf und die DDR-Literatur', *Der Spiegel*, 16 July 1990, repr. in Anz, 122–34.
24. The word 'Hexenjagd' was used by Wolf herself in one of her very few comments on the debate, quoted in Greiner, 'Die deutsche Gesinnungsästhetik'; Anz, 216. It is almost certainly not a coincidence that it is a woman writer who was attacked; see Anna Kuhn's persuasive analysis: 'Rewriting GDR history: The Christa Wolf Controversy', *GDR Bulletin*, 1 (1991), 7–11 (10).
25. Greiner: 'Ein trauriger Fall. Ein kleines Kapitel aus der langen Geschichte "Deutsche Dichter und die Macht" '; Anz, 70. Schirrmacher: 'Die vierzig Jahre DDR [schreiben] das längst abgeschlossen geglaubte Unglücksverhältnis des deutschen Intellektuellen mit der Macht bis in die Gegenwart fort', Anz, 83.
26. Theodor W. Adorno *et al.*, 'Studies in Authoritarian Personality', *Soziologische Schriften* 11, ed. Susan Buck-Morrs and Rolf Tiedemann (Frankfurt/M.: Suhrkamp, 1975), 237–509; see Anz, 89.
27. See Hellmuth Karasek, 'Selbstgemachte Konfitüre: Über die Diskussion um Christa Wolfs Erzählung "Was bleibt" ', *Der Spiegel*, 25 June 1990, 162–8. He claims that Wolf is 'weniger eine Opportunistin, kaum eine engagierte Schriftstellerin, mehr eine ins Innerliche emigrierte Autorin' (168).
28. Walter Jens, 'Pläydoyer gegen die Preisgabe der DDR-Kultur: Fünf Forderungen an die Intellektuellen im geeinten Deutschland', *Süddeutsche Zeitung*, 16/17 June 1990, repr. in Anz, 167–78 (175).
29. Quoted in Karasek, 'Selbstgemachte Konfitüre', 162.
30. Anz, 96–7.
31. Frank Schirrmacher, 'Abschied von der Literatur der Bundesrepublik. Neue Pässe, neue Identitäten, neue Lebensläufe: über die Kündigung einiger Mythen des westdeutschen Bewußtseins', *FAZ* 2 Oct. 1990.
32. As also highlighted by the impassioned response to the claims of Schirrmacher (b. 1959) by Wolfram Schütte (b. 1939). See Schütte, 'Auf dem Schrotthaufen der Geschichte. Zu einer denkwürdig-voreiligen

Verabschiedung der "bundesdeutschen Literatur" ', *Frankfurter Rundschau*, 20 Oct. 1990.

33. The term comes from Veit-Ulrich Müller, 'Stillhalteliteratur in Ost und West', *FAZ* 13 Oct. 1990, quoted in Stephan, 'Ein deutscher Forschungsbericht 1990/1', 130.

34. Ulrich Schmidt takes issue with Schirrmacher's claims for Celan and Bernhard: 'Engagierter Ästhetizismus. Über neudeutsche Literaturkritik', in *Zum gegenwärtigen Zustand der deutschen Literatur*, ed. Arnold, 86–96.

35. Greiner, 'Die deutsche Gesinnungsästhetik', in Anz, 208–16.

36. Huyssen sees him as the *éminence grise* ('After the Wall', 138), Baumgart as the 'heimlicher Pater' of the debate, who has in effect choreographed the discussion. Reinhard Baumgart, in *Zum gegenwärtigen Zustand der deutschen Literatur*, ed. Arnold, 77. While one should be cautious in overemphasizing the similarities between the critics' positions, Schirrmacher's call for 'ästhetische Weltliteratur' instead of 'engagierte Provinzliteratur', clearly owes something to Bohrer's own rhetoric, see especially: Karl Heinz Bohrer, 'Provinzialismus', *Merkur*, 12 (1990), 1096–1102.

37. Karl Heinz Bohrer, 'Die Ästhetik am Ausgang ihrer Unmündigkeit', *Merkur*, 10/11 (1990) 851–65. This issue also includes the now notorious article, 'Kulturschutzgebiet DDR?' (pp. 1015–18), in which he attacks the resacralization of art in the form of 'the writer as priest' (p. 1016), and takes to task those intellectuals who are still mourning the loss of the socialist utopia in the GDR.

38. Huyssen offers the brief hypothesis that the 'Literaturstreit' is 'a second historians' debate' ('After the Wall', 125). Irene Heidelberger-Leonard also makes the point in her 'Der Literaturstreit—ein Historikerstreit im gesamtdeutschen Kostüm?', but does not quite have the courage of her title. It is left to Keith Bullivant to draw more detailed and disturbing parallels in his *The Future of German Literature* (Oxford: Berg, 1994).

39. For a detailed analysis of Bohrer's stance compare Huyssen 'After the Wall', 138–42, and Schmidt, 'Engagierte Ästhetizismus', 93–5.

40. Greiner's much-quoted 'Wer bestimmt, was gewesen ist, der bestimmt auch, was sein wird. Der Streit um die Vergangenheit ist ein Streit um die Zukunft' (Anz, 208), was understood as a threat by some and a simple statement of fact by others.

41. Hajo Steinert, 'Die neuen Nix-Künstler: Die DDR-Literatur ist tot, es lebe die DDR-Literatur', *Die Zeit*, 7 Dec. 1990. The paradox of Steinert's subtitle makes the point very neatly. He goes on to argue that, with the flood of previously inaccessible work from Prenzlauer Berg, perhaps the literature of the GDR 'has only just begun'. Lutz Rathenow warns against a quite different scenario, and fears 'daß jetzt eine ganze Künstlergeneration, auch von Malern und Musikern, abgewertet wird, ohne daß sie überhaupt zur Kenntnis genommen wurde'. See ' "... an Vernachlässigtes erinnern": *tacheles* im Gespräch mit Lutz Rathenow', *tacheles*, 10 (1990), 5–7 (7).

42. The two quotations come from Ulf Christian Hasenfelder, 'Die Generation, die nicht zu sich kommen durfte: Junge Avantgarde der ehemaligen DDR', *Der Literat*, 4 Apr. 1991, 18–20, and 'Fortsetzung', *Der Literat*, 5 May 1991, 16–19, and Thomas Günther, 'Die subkulturellen Zeitschriften in der DDR und ihre kulturgeschichtliche

Bedeutung', 'Aus Politik und Zeitgeschichte', *Das Parlament*, 8 May 1992, 27–36 (36).
43. Emmerich, 'Status melancholicus', 243. Cf. also Klaus Jarmatz, ' "Was bleibt, stiften die Dichter": Nachdenkliches zu einer Diskussion um die DDR-Literatur', *tacheles*, 10 (1990), 34–7. He again singles out the texts of the young writers (35).
44. See Emmerich's detailed analysis in 'Im Zeichen der Wiedervereinigung', 31–6.
45. Biermann, 'Nur wer sich ändert', in Anz, 149.
46. Kolbe, 'Die Heimat der Dissidenten: Nachbemerkungen zum Phantom der DDR Opposition', in Deiritz and Krauss, 33–9 (38). It is for this reason that the older generations of the GDR did not produce an 'opposition' figure amongst the intelligentsia of the type of Václav Havel in Czechoslovakia or Gyorgy Konrad in Hungary, but rather simply 'Dissidenten', see also Kolbe, esp. 37–8.
47. Kurt Drawert, 'Niemand braucht sie, sie brauchen niemand: Über das Volk und die Intellektuellen in Deutschland', *Monatshefte*, 4 (winter 1990), 399–402.
48. Cf. the titles of publications since 1989: *Die andere Sprache. Neue DDR-Literatur der 8oer Jahre*, ed. Arnold and Wolf, or *Sprache & Antwort. Stimmen und Texte einer anderen Literatur aus der DDR*, ed. Hesse. Adolf Endler discusses the problematic implications of references to this 'other' literature in a review of *Sprache & Antwort* of 1988: 'Alles ist im untergrund obenauf; einmannfrei . . .', in Endler, *Den Tiger reiten*, 40–64 (42–4).
49. Quoted in Matthias Ehlert, 'Zerfallen die Dichter?', *Junge Welt*, 23 Dec. 1991.
50. Greiner points out the importance of generational clashes in the debate (both between writers and between critics), 'Die deutsche Gesinnungs-ästhetik', Anz, 210. Cf. of the comments by Kolbe and the more cautious observations by Habermas on this aspect of the debate quoted in Anz, 14–16.
51. Endler, *Den Tiger reiten*, 43.
52. Cf. also Emmerich, 'Status melancholicus', 242.
53. See e.g. *Postmoderne: Zeichen eines kulturellen Wandels*, ed. Andreas Huyssen and Klaus R. Scherpe (Reinbek bei Hamburg: Rowohlt, 1986); *Wege aus der Moderne. Schlüsseltexte der Postmoderne-Diskussion*, ed. Wolfgang Welsch (Weinheim: VCH Verlagsgesellschaft, 1988); *Spätmoderne und Postmoderne: Beiträge zur deutschsprachigen Gegenwartskultur*, ed. Paul Michael Lützeler (Frankfurt/M.: Fischer, 1991); *Pluralismus und Postmodernismus: Zur Literatur- und Kulturgeschichte der achtziger Jahre*, ed. Helmut Kreuzer, Forschungen zur Literatur- und Kulturgeschichte, 25 2nd rev. and extended edn. (Frankfurt/M.: Peter Lang, 1991).
54. Cf. e.g. the extraordinary pathos in Günther Rüther's celebration of the 'Furchtlosigkeit und Freiheitswille' of the young writers, in his *'Greif zur Feder Kumpel': Schriftsteller, Literatur und Politik in der DDR 1949–1990* (Düsseldorf: Droste Verlag, 1991), 170.
55. Jurek Becker, 'Die Wiedervereinigung der deutschen Literatur', *German Quarterly*, 3/4 (1990), 361.
56. Erik Grimm criticizes what he sees as an inappropriate reinstitution of a

moral and political index in a reading of Papenfuß-Gorek's work, in his 'Der Tod der Ostmoderne oder Die BRDigung des DDR-Untergrunds', 9–20.
57. The rhetoric of heroism is important. I come back to it in the Conclusion. See e.g. the titles of a selection of recent articles: Michael Braun, 'Ende einer Mythos?', *Freitag*, 22 Nov. 1991; Karl Corino, 'Zerstörte Legende: Über den Fall Sascha Anderson', *Stuttgarter Zeitung*, 30 Nov. 1991; Stefan Eggert, 'Der schwankende Mythos vom tapferen Partisanen: Das Druckhaus "Galrev" und die Affäre Sascha Anderson', *Frankfurter Rundschau*, 18 Nov. 1991; Bascha Mika und Ute Scheub, 'Untergrundhelden und Stasi-Spitzel am Prenzelberg', *die tageszeitung*, 11 Jan. 1992.

CHAPTER 7

1. Schedlinski, 'es beginnt fast immer mit einem gedicht', *die männer der frauen*, 7.
2. 'Es gibt Worte, die sollten bleiben, wo sie entstanden sind, in der Kälte.' Ein Wort wie Staatssicherheit erwärmt sich enorm in seiner lieblichen Kurzform; als *Stasi* ist es klebrigster Euphemismus, fast Brüderlichkeit. Bleiben wir also kühl.' Durs Grünbein, 'Im Namen der Füchse: Gibt es eine neue literarische Zensur', *FAZ* 26 Nov. 1991.
3. Many of the important contributions to the debates to date have been collected in *MachtSpiele: Literatur und Staatssicherheit im Fokus Prenzlauer Berg*, ed. Peter Böthig and Klaus Michael (Leipzig: Reclam, 1993). Where individual articles have been reprinted here, references will be given as *MachtSpiele*.
4. For example, between 1989 and 1993 Bert Papenfuß[-Gorek] published no fewer than five full-length poetry collections, in which some work dates back to the 1970s.
5. Thomas Günther, 'Wo auf Trümmern die Buchstaben tanzen', *Rheinische Merkur*, 24 Jan. 1992.
6. Anon., 'Pegasus an der *Stasi*-Leine', *Der Spiegel*, 18 Nov. 1991, 276–80 (277–8).
7. Rathenow, 'Die Vergangenheit beginnt erst jetzt', *Hamburger Morgenpost*, 9 Dec. 1991, repr. in *MachtSpiele*, 334–5 (334). Cf. Konrad Franke, 'Fuchteln gilt nicht, Anmerkung zur absurden These, die DDR-Literaturgeschichte müsse umgeschrieben werden', *Süddeutsche Zeitung*, 2 Dec. 1991.
8. The revelation in early 1993 that both Heiner Müller and Christa Wolf herself had acted as 'inoffizielle Mitarbeiter' for the 'Staatssicherheit' added a new urgency—and a new desperation—to the massive task of revision. Although I shall not deal with Müller and Wolf directly here, the similarities—and differences—between the response to these writers and to Anderson and Schedlinski is instructive in itself. Cf. the emotional article by Fritz Raddatz, 'Von der Beschädigung der Literatur durch ihre Urheber: Bemerkungen zu Heiner Müller und Christa Wolf', *Die Zeit*, 29 Jan. 1993.
9. Kurt Drawert, 'Es gibt keine Entschuldigung. Offener Brief an Rainer Schedlinski', *Süddeutsche Zeitung*, 11/12 Jan. 1992. Cornelia Geißler takes a similar line: 'Gerüchte, Mutmaßungen, Verdächtigungen. . . Der

"Fall" Sascha Anderson: Mit der Frage seiner *Stasi*-Mitarbeit wird eine ganze literarische Generation in Mißkredit gebracht', *Badische Zeitung*, 30 Oct. 1991.

10. The bibliography of *MachtSpiele*, for example, lists thirty-seven books directly about the *Staatssicherheit*, published since 1989.

11. Péter Nádas, 'Armer Sascha Anderson', trans. from the Hungarian by Zsuzsanna Gahse, first published in *Kursbuch*, 108 (July 1992), 163–88 (165). This is a much longer and more wide-ranging version than the one printed in *Machtspiele*, 378–91. Quotations will be from the *Kursbuch* essay. Nádas's examination of the battle between 'Moral' and 'Vernunft' and his resistance to the secret police of his own country is one of the most acute and unflinching accounts of the whole complex of issues to date.

12. *MachtSpiele*, 49.

13. Few critics have had the courage to put it as bluntly as Sieglinde Geisel. See 'Die Moral des Grenzhundes: Müssen Dichter gute Menschen sein?', *Freitag*, 14 Feb. 1992.

14. Frank Schirrmacher, 'Aufgeklärt. Der Fall Anderson', *FAZ* 8 Jan. 1992.

15. Kurt Drawert, 'Sie schweigen oder sie lügen: Von der Beschaffenheit einer gescheiterten Elite', in *MachtSpiele*, 74–82 (80).

16. Markus Clauer, ' "Das endet dann in Mord und Totschlag": Der neudeutsche Literaturstreit zwischen Wolf Biermann und Sascha Anderson—Ein altes Trauma', *Die Rheinpfalz*, 15 Nov. 1992.

17. See the Stuttgart historian Eberhard Jäckel, 'Die doppelte Vergangenheit', *Der Spiegel*, 23 Dec. 1991, 39–43.

18. As a single, disturbing, example of this: 'Kein Verbrechen ohne Schuld', *Der Spiegel*, 23 Dec. 1991, 30–8. Péter Nádas offers a persuasive refutation of such a comparison, in his 'Armer Sascha Anderson'.

19. Quoted from Frank Schirrmacher, 'Verdacht und Verrat', in *MachtSpiele*, 306. Karl Corino, in 'Absolution vor der Beichte?', *Die Welt*, 2 Jan. 1992, repr. in *MachtSpiele*, 341–7, compares the denials of those accused of working with the *Staatssicherheit* with the excuses of those accused of working with the *Gestapo*. Wolf Biermann takes up the attacks on Fuchs's phrase and defends the rhetoric of such comparisons in: 'Ein öffentliches Geschwür: Offener Brief an Lew Kopelew', *Der Sturz des Dädalus*, 107–8.

20. See Detlef Opitz, 'Verrat und Verräter: Ein Versuch über die Psychopathologie von Spitzeln und über eine Gesellschaft, die nach Spitzeln giert', *Freitag*, 13 Aug. 1993.

21. This is illustrated neatly by the fact that when writers and critics were outraged by Biermann's (at that time) unproven accusations against Sascha Anderson they simply turned the issue on its head and accused Biermann himself of being a 'rechthaberischer Denunziant'; see Hans Krieger 'Die neue Unfähigkeit zu trauern. Nachbemerkung zu Wolf Biermann und seinen "lieben Ossis" ', *NdL*, 1 (1992), 165–8. Biermann takes up the attacks on him as 'Großinquisitor' (Grass) and 'Blutrichter und Scharfrichter' (Kopelew), in his 'Ein öffentliches Geschwür', 98 and 110.

22. Compare Iris Radisch, 'Die Krankheit Lüge: Die Stasi als sicherer Ort: Sascha Anderson und die Staatssicherheit', *Die Zeit*, 24 Jan. 1992, 51–2. A shortened version is reprinted in *MachtSpiele*, 357–67 (364).

23. Cf. Axel Vornbäumen, 'Mit Phänomenen wie Chaos und Liebe kam die Stasi nicht klar', *Frankfurter Rundschau*, 9 Jan. 1992.
24. For an exact explanation see the articles accompanying the publication of documentation linking Anderson with the IM and IMB ('Inoffizieller Mitarbeiter mit Feindberührung') code names 'David Menzer', 'Fritz Müller' and 'Peters', in Jürgen Fuchs, 'Landschaften der Lüge: Schriftsteller im Stasi Netz (II) 'Pegasus, Spinne, Qualle, Apostel', *Der Spiegel*, 25 Nov. 1991, 72–92; 'Der Verräter seiner Freunde', *Der Spiegel*, 2 Dec. 1991, 22–4, 'Maßnahme Totenhaus', *Der Spiegel*, 23 Dec. 1991, 28–9.
25. For the procedure see Joachim Gauck, *Die Stasi-Akten: Das unheimliche Erbe der DDR*, ed. Margarethe Steinhausen und Hubertus Knabe (Reinbek bei Hamburg: Rowohlt, 1991).
26. The ZDF programme 'Kennzeichen D', on 23 Oct. 1991, went public with accusations against Anderson. It was the ZDF 'Kontraste' programme of 6 Jan. 1992 which delivered further proof about Anderson and also exposed Schedlinski, and it was also the television which denounced Gabriele Eckart as IM Hölderlin. 'Keine Gerechtigkeit für IM "Hölderlin"?', *Das Parlament*, 29 Jan. 1993, 13.
27. See in particular Josef Singldinger, 'Sich einlassen auf ein Stück möglicher Selbsterkenntnis: Anmerkungen zum Umgang der Medien mit der Staatssicherheit der DDR', *Publizistik & Kunst. Zeitschrift der IG Medien*, 3 (1992), 10–14, and Ulrich Greiner, 'Plädoyer für den Schluß der Stasi-Debatte', *Die Zeit*, 5 Feb. 1993.
28. Cf. Ulrich Schröter, 'Wie wurde man ein IM?: Viele Gesprächspartner der Stasi waren Spitzel—aber nicht alle', *Die Zeit*, 6 Mar. 1993, repr. in *MachtSpiele*, 372–8. Cf. also the comments of Herr K., one of the *Stasi* officials assigned to Prenzlauer Berg, about IM 'Bendel', another writer from the underground scene. Peter Böthig, 'Gedächtnisprotokoll mit Herrn K.', in *MachtSpiele*, 288–95.
29. Compare *MachtSpiele*, 47, 304, and 369, for various attempts to define the activities and scope of the *Stasi*, and see Schedlinski's important essay 'Die Unzuständigkeit der Macht', *NdL* 6 (1992), 75–105 (96).
30. Several critics report this fact and point to the lists published in *die tageszeitung*, which documented a record number of 'konspirative Wohnungen' (secret addresses to be used for meetings with IMs) in Prenzlauer Berg. Compare Mika and Scheub, 'Untergrundhelden und Stasi-Spitzel am Prenzelberg'. For Rathenow's comment see Vornbäumen, 'Mit Phänomenen wie Chaos und Liebe'. Jan Faktor, among others, contests that it was especially infiltrated, 'Sechzehn Punkte zur Prenzlauer-Berg-Szene', *MachtSpiele*, 91–111 (94).
31. ' "Das ist nicht so einfach": Ein *Zeit*-Gespräch mit Sascha Anderson', *Die Zeit*, 1 Nov. 1991, and ' "Das ist mir ein völliges Rätsel": Detlev Kuhlbrodt, Gespräch mit Sascha Anderson', *Freitag*, 10 Jan. 1992.
32. Gabriele Dietze, 'Die hilflose Wiedervereinigung', *MachtSpiele*, 35.
33. Rainer Schedlinski, 'Dem Druck, immer mehr sagen zu sollen, hielt ich nicht stand', *FAZ*, 14 Jan. 1992, ' "Was ein IM ist, weiss ich erst heute": Gespräch mit Rainer Schedlinski', *Neue Zürcher Zeitung*, 14 Jan. 1992, and ' "Nach vier Wochen hatten sie mich klein." Ein Gespräch mit dem Berliner Autor Rainer Schedlinski', *Berliner Zeitung*, 18/19 Jan. 1992.
34. See Peter Böthig, 'Wie man mit Wahrheiten lügt. Eine Entgegnung auf

Rainer Schedlinski, "Die Unzuständigkeit der Macht" ', *NdL* 10 (1992), 157–63; Andreas Koziol, 'Korrektur einer Vergangenheit: Entgegnung auf Rainer Schedlinski, "Die Unzuständigkeit der Macht" ', *NdL* 10 (1992), 164–8; and Kurt Drawert, 'Sie schweigen oder sie lügen: Von der Beschaffenheit der geistigen Elite', *MachtSpiele*, 74–82.

35. Uwe Kolbe, 'Offener Brief an Sascha Anderson', *Die Zeit*, 22 Nov. 1991, repr. in *MachtSpiele*, 318–20.

36. Klaus Michael, quoted in Singldinger, 'Literatur, Politik, die Dichter und ein Verlag. Der Prenzlauer Berg und seine mehrdimensionalen Geschichten', *Publizistik & Kunst. Zeitschrift der IG Medien*, 5 (1992), 27–9 (29). Detlef Opitz, 'Literatur in diesen Zeiten: Staatssicherheit und Prenzlauer Berg', [an extract from: Opitz, ' "Literatur zu sagen in diesen Zeiten—ein Sakrileg", Rede anläßlich der Verleihung des Klaus-Piper-Stipendiums', Berlin, Jan. 1992], *Freitag*, 7 Feb. 1992.

37. Schedlinski, 'Die Unzuständigkeit der Macht', 89–91.

38. Johannes Jansen, 'Enttarnt mich auch!', *MachtSpiele*, 138–43 and Fritz Hendrik Melle, 'I.M.', *MachtSpiele*, 144–62.

39. Wolf Biermann 'Tiefer als unter die Haut: Über Schweinehunde, halbe Helden, Intimitäten und andere Funde aus meinen Stasi-Akten', *Der Spiegel*, 27 Jan. 1992, repr. in Biermann, *Der Sturz des Dädalus*, 112–27.

40. This is also Heiner Müller's claim. See ' "Es gibt ein Menschenrecht auf Feigheit": Ein Gespräch mit dem Dramatiker Heiner Müller über seine Kontakte mit der Staatssicherheit', *Frankfurter Rundschau*, 22 May 1993.

41. *MachtSpiele*, 250–73.

42. Schedlinski in ' "Wolltest Du nie bei der Stasi aussteigen?": Die Schriftsteller Rainer Schedlinski und Detlef Opitz im Gespräch', *Süddeutsche Zeitung* MAGAZIN, 16 Apr. 1992, 12–20. This dialogue is the result of twenty-five hours of discussion between the friends. A year later Opitz distanced himself from Schedlinski's continued denials: Detlef Opitz, 'Verrat und Verräter'.

43. See Opitz's incredulity, 'Wolltest Du nie bei der Stasi aussteigen', 20.

44. 'Bearbeitung' and 'Zersetzung' were the official terms used when an individual was to come under active pressure. Compare the account of Gerd Poppe in *MachtSpiele*, 228–41. This becomes particulary significant when one remembers that two of the writers associated with Prenzlauer Berg apparently committed suicide in the late 1980s (Frank Lanzendörfer and "Matthias" BAADER Holst), and there is a suspicion in both cases that pressure from the *Stasi* was involved. Compare Karl Corino 'Vom Leichengift der Stasi: Die DDR-Literatur hat an Glaubwürdigkeit verloren. Eine Entgegnung', *Süddeutsche Zeitung*, 6 Dec. 1991.

45. Lutz Rathenow, 'Die blockierte Erinnerung', *Kommune*, 6 (1992), 37–9.

46. Wolf Biermann, 'Der Lichtblick im gräßlichen Fatalismus der Geschichte: Büchner-Preis-Rede', *Die Zeit*, 25 Oct. 1991, repr. in *Der Sturz des Dädalus*, 48–63 (56). Biermann later took back the word 'Arschloch', not because it had caused so much offence, but rather because he thought that it trivialized Anderson's real nature. See 'Eine kleine Rede über Utz Rachowski, in *Der Sturz des Dädalus*, 80–6 (84). It is worth noting how far Biermann's attitudes have hardened since an earlier more differentiated examination of the fluidity between resistance and collaboration. Wolf Biermann, 'Auch ich war bei der Stasi', *Die Zeit*, 11 May 1990.

47. Wolf Biermann, ' "Laß, o Welt, o laß mich sein!": Rede zum Eduard-Mörike-Preis', *Die Zeit*, 15 Nov. 1991, repr. in *Der Sturz des Dädalus*, 64–79.
48. Frank Schirrmacher, 'Ein grausames Spiel: Der Fall Sascha Anderson und die Stasi-Akten', *FAZ* 25 Oct. 1991.
49. Schedlinski, 'Wolltest Du nie bei der Stasi aussteigen?', 17. Stefan Eggert, 'Der schwankende Mythos vom tapferen Partisanen: Das Druckhaus "Galrev" und die Affäre Sascha Anderson', *Frankfurter Rundschau*, 18 Nov. 1991.
50. Faktor, 'Sechzehn Punkte zur Prenzlauer-Berg-Szene', 106.
51. Papenfuß-Gorek, for example, notes that much harsher measures were instituted by the *Stasi* against the punks and against some of the other groups in Prenzlauer Berg, see 'Sascha Andersons letzter Freund': Bert Papenfuß-Gorek zu Sascha Anderson, Rainer Schedlinski und der "Ortsbestimmung" von Literatur zwischen Häresie und Staatssicherheit, von Ute Scheub und Bascha Mika', *die tageszeitung*, 29 Jan. 1992. A shortened version of this (under a different title) is included in *MachtSpiele*, 182–7. Faktor also remarks bitterly on the worth of a freedom which needs a *Stasi* 'Führungsoffizier als Schutzengel'. 'Sechzehn Punkte zur Prenzlauer-Berg-Szene', 107.
52. Lorek, 'Ciao! Von der Anspruchslosigkeit der Kapitulationen', 119. Faktor, 'Sechzehn Punkte zur Prenzlauer-Berg-Szene', 106. Biermann, 'Ein öffentliches Geschwür', 102.
53. ' "Die ganze Szene von der Stasi gesteuert?—Quatsch!": Ein Gespräch mit Lutz Rathenow über den Fall Anderson und die DDR', *Süddeutsche Zeitung*, 3 Dec. 1991, and Frank-Wolf Matthies, 'Einer, der tatsächlich etwas getan hat: Zorniger Widerspruch zur Sascha Anderson-Kampagne', *Frankfurter Rundschau*, 3 Jan. 1992. But see also the tart response, again from Rathenow: 'Tatsächlich: er hat etwas getan: Eine Replik zu Frank-Wolf Matthies über Sascha Anderson', *Frankfurter Rundschau*, 15 Jan. 1992. For what it is worth, Anderson himself also denies that Prenzlauer Berg was 'steered' by the *Stasi*, in his essay 'Ein hoffentlich schöner und lang anhaltender Amoklauf: Zum Thema AIM 7423/91: Ein Bericht', *FAZ* 30 Oct. 1991.
54. Wolfgang Emmerich makes it too easy for himself when, of Prenzlauer Berg, he says: 'Die Verweigerungshaltung dieser Szene-Künstler wird übrigens nicht dadurch entwertet, daß einer (oder einige) von ihnen der Staatssicherheit Spitzeldienste leisteten.' See his 'Wahrenehmung', 16.
55. Böthig, 'Spiele der Revolte', in *MachtSpiele*, 59–64 (63).
56. Thomas Assheuer, 'Den Versen der Verrat verraten', *Frankfurter Rundschau*, 23 Jan. 1992.
57. Faktor, 'Sechzehn Punkte zur Prenzlauer-Berg-Szene', 108.
58. Drawert, 'Es gibt keine Entschuldigung. Offener Brief an Rainer Schedlinski', 14.
59. The image from 'Riña a Garotazos' has been used extensively by Heiner Müller as representative of a historical fight to the death.
60. One of the reasons Anderson claims he was imprisoned (and tortured) was for illegally printing and performing Biermann's songs after Biermann had been exiled. Cf. the unprepared confrontation of Anderson and Biermann, arranged by the television crew, and the harrowing

dialogue that results in 'Biermann äußert eine Meinung . . . und Sascha Anderson versucht, sich zu wehren' [transcript of a dialogue between Anderson and Biermann on the ZDF programme 'Kennzeichen D'], *Süddeutsche Zeitung*, 25 Oct. 1991, 15.

61. Schirrmacher, 'Verdacht und Verrat', in *MachtSpiele*, 305, sees it as a moral reckoning between those who left and those who stayed; Jane Kramer, in an otherwise snide attack on Prenzlauer Berg (which has nevertheless been taken seriously) formulates the generation aspect quite usefully: Jane Kramer, 'Letter from Europe', *New Yorker*, 25 May 1992, 40–64; Gabriele Stötzer-Kachold, in a rabid piece about the sexism of the Prenzlauer Berg, identifies the struggle as a sexual 'Potenzkampf': ' "Denn wir haben uns nur bekämpft und verletzt": Gespräch mit Gabriele Stötzer-Kachold', *Freitag*, 23 Jan. 1992.

62. Biermann, 'Ein öffentliches Geschwür', 108. This takes up the scathing references to Dada in Biermann's Mörike Prize speech, see 'Laß, o Welt, o laß mich sein!', 71.

63. Volker Braun makes the point more cautiously: 'Ihr Desinteresse am politischen Konflikt machte die Szene am Prenzlauer Berg aber unwillentlich für die Stasi interessant, sozusagen kompatibel.' Braun, 'Monströse Banalität', *Die Zeit*, 22 Nov. 1991, repr. in *MachtSpiele*, 321–4.

64. Opitz, 'Literatur in diesen Zeiten: Staatssicherheit und Prenzlauer Berg', 12.

65. Durs Grünbein, 'Im Namen der Füchse', in *MachtSpiele*, 325–9.

66. Papenfuß-Gorek also points out that the discussion about the *Staatssicherheit* has been fuelled by long-standing aesthetic disagreements within the underground itself—between expressly political writers like Rathenow and those like Schedlinski, who were more concerned with theory. These disagreements were previously suppressed because of the need for solidarity. See Papenfuß-Gorek, 'Sascha Andersons letzter Freund'.

67. Biermann, 'Laß, o Welt, o laß mich sein!', 76.

68. Wolf Biermann, 'Das Kaninchen frißt die Schlange: Die Stasi-Debatte und das Drehbuch meiner Ausbürgerung', *Der Spiegel*, 2 Mar. 1992, repr. in *Der Sturz des Dädalus*, 139–60 (140). Cf. Karl Corino, 'Zerstörte Legende: Über den Fall Sascha Anderson', *Stuttgarter Zeitung*, 30 Nov. 1991.

69. ' "Das ist nicht so einfach": Ein *Zeit*-Gespräch mit Sascha Anderson'. Schedlinski takes up the notion of the *Stasi* as a system of information in 'Die Unzuständigkeit der Macht'. As if by chance there is a review of Biermann's poetry by Sascha Anderson printed directly below the *Zeit* interview, in which Anderson also distances himself from the 'Scheindialektik' and 'von Dogmatik durchschimmerte Gebärde' of Biermann's work: 'Ich hab euch lieb: Wolf Biermanns gesammelte Lieder', *Die Zeit*, 1 Nov. 1991.

70. Compare Biermann, 'Laß, o Welt, o laß mich sein!', 76, with the article 'Jean meets Sascha', *Frankfurter Rundschau*, 5 Nov. 1991. This piece is the most acerbic attack on post-structuralist theory in Prenzlauer Berg, esp. regarding the theories of (Jean) Baudrillard. Only the motto 'ass' is given. The tone and the opinions expressed suggest that this signifies Thomas Assheuer.

71. Frank Schirrmacher, 'Der große Verdacht: Am Beispiel der Akten. Literatur und Stasi', *FAZ* 23 Nov. 1991.
72. *MachtSpiele*, 244.
73. Quoted in Horst Domdey, 'Duftmarken: Eine Anthologie über Kunst und Literatur aus unabhängigen Zeitschriften in der DDR 1979–1989', *Freitag*, 8 May 1992.
74. See Grünbein, 'Im Namen der Füchse', 326. Peter Böthig even goes so far as to claim that some of poetry can only truly be read now, *MachtSpiele*, 63.
75. There are dissenting voices. The former GDR writer Ulrich Schacht, for example, has claimed that the authors involved with the *Stasi* and their texts have forfeited any moral or aesthetic legitimacy, *MachtSpiele*, 68.
76. Hajo Steinert, 'Die Szene und die Stasi: Muß man die literarischen Texte von Prenzlauer Berg jetzt anders lesen?', *Die Zeit*, 29 Nov. 1991. A shortened version appears in *MachtSpiele*, 329–33. This is in many ways reminiscent of the 'Wunderbrille', in Günter Grass's *Hundejahre*, which allowed the children to see through to their parent's true past.
77. Jan Faktor, 'hinter unten oben auf: Eine Szene demontiert sich', *Freitag*, 22 Nov. 1991.
78. Dorothea von Törne, 'Jeder Killer hat seinen Killersatelliten: Der Fall Sascha Anderson oder Wie Gespaltenheit zur Überlebensstrategie wird', *Neue Zeit*, 4 Jan. 1992.
79. For example, Andreas Koziol describes his fellow writers as 'notorisch betörte neunmalkluge tabuversetzer | aura-toren staatliche ohren und überschaetzer', and Papenfuß-Gorek hints about shadows and illicit recordings in a text entitled 'unter uns gesagt aber behalt es für dich'. Both taken up by Steinert, in the longer version of his essay from *Die Zeit*.
80. Steinert, 'Die Szene und die Stasi', in *MachtSpiele*, 330.
81. Schedlinski, 'Die Unzuständigkeit der Macht', 99 and 101.
82. From Schedlinski, *die rationen des ja und des nein*, 150.
83. See Charitas Jenny-Ebeling, ' "mit doppeltem boden" Zum Beispiel: Rainer Schedlinski', *Neue Zürcher Zeitung*, 24 Mar. 1992. This reading is linguistically very inventive, but does not address the very specific moral ambiguities of the text.
84. See also the detailed reading of Schedlinski's 'als redeten wir nur mit der sprache', another poem from the same cycle as the one above, in Stefan Rosinski, 'Der Fall Schedlinski oder Konjekturen des Unglücks', in *MachtSpiele*, esp. 68–74.
85. Sascha Anderson, *Jewish Jetset*, 6.
86. Michael Braun, 'Ende eines Mythos', *Freitag*, 22 Nov. 1991.
87. Assheuer, 'Den Versen den Verrat verraten'.
88. Cf. 'einmal bekam ich ein glas eingewecktes ohne absender', in Anderson, *brunnen, randvoll*, 67–73. This tells of Löwenthal's death.
89. See ' "Das ist nicht so einfach": Ein *Zeit*-Gespräch mit Sascha Anderson'.
90. Anderson, *Jewish Jetset*, 8.
91. Anderson, 'wenn ich über grün spreche | stirbt grün', *Jeder Satellit hat einen Killersatelliten*, 66.
92. It is perhaps worth recalling here the passage from the collection *totenreklame*, also quoted in Ch. 3: 'dann werden die dinge zeichen, und sie als das zu sehen, was sie sind ist unmöglich. die errichteten denkmäle werden spiegel, der weitere weg, schritte im labyrinth. die scherben

spalten deine erscheinung und werfen deine abbilder in den sammelnden raum.' Anderson and Kerbach, *totenreklame. eine reise*, 53.

93. In a schematic essay Assheuer rejects the 'Pietismus der "deconstruction" ', and insists that this text is not an allegory of reading, but rather an allegory of a split identity which is the result of the 'Katastrophe', which Anderson's time in prison represented to his identity. See 'Den Versen den Verrat verraten'.

94. Harald Hartung greets this text with obvious relief as intelligible because based on personal experience of interrogation but scorns what he otherwise considers a collection of 'Sprachverdunklung' and 'Hermetik', 'Placebos, Kwerdeutsch, Vaterlandkanal', *Merkur*, 12 (Dec. 1991), 1143–52 (1148).

95. Cf. Rosinski, 'Der Fall Schedlinski', esp. 72–3. Christa Wolf's use of metaphor came under attack in very much the same way during the *Was bleibt* debate. Huyssen takes this up in his 'After the Wall', 123.

96. Assheuer considers Anderson's texts as a form of deliberately concealed 'Beichte'. See 'Den Versen den Verrat verraten'; and Rosinski, 'Der Fall Schedlinski', 73, consideres Schedlinski's texts as 'doubly camouflaged', and doubly treacherous.

97. Schedlinski, 'Die Unzuständigkeit der Macht', 99.

98. Schirrmacher 'Verdacht und Verrat', 305.

99. Biermann, 'Laß, o Welt, o laß mich sein!', 76. A number of writers have commented that, unlike many reports by other IMs, Anderson's reports were extraordinarily detailed, direct and damaging. The extracts of reports reproduced in *MachtSpiele* appear to bear this out.

100. Biermann's controversial comparison with Viktor Klemperer's analysis of the language of the Third Reich ('Lingua Tertii Imperii') is made in his essay 'Ein öffentliches Geschwür', 109. Jürgen Fuchs also analyses the language of the *Staatssicherheit*, in 'Landschaften der Lüge (IV): "Aktion Gegenschlag" im Namen Fuchs', *Der Spiegel*, 9 Dec. 1991, 103–21.

101. Hilbig, *'Ich': Roman* (Frankfurt/M.: Fischer, 1993), 197. This extraordinary novel is one of the first fictional works to explore the unstable identity of the writer in the GDR.

102. Quoted in Bascha Mika und Ute Scheub, 'Untergrundhelden und Stasi-Spitzel am Prenzelberg'.

103. See ' "Anderson ist reif für die Therapie": Gespräch mit Karl Corino', *Hamburger Morgenpost*, 16 Jan. 1992, and Christine Cosentino, 'Noch einmal Sascha Anderson', in *Literatur und Politische Aktualität*, ed. Elrud Ibsch and Ferdinand van Ingen, ABznG 36 (Amsterdam: Rodopi, 1993), 3–20 (14).

CONCLUSION

1. Ulrich Zieger, *Grosse beruhigte Körper* (Berlin: Galrev, 1992), poem xxiii [n.p.].

2. Volker Braun, 'Verbannt nach Atlantis', *Die Zickzackbrücke: Ein Abrißkalender*, 57.

3. Franz Fühmann, 'Anläßlich der Gedichte Uwe Kolbes', in Kolbe, *Hineingeboren*, 131–7. Heinz Czechowski makes similar observations

306 Notes to Conclusion

in his short essay 'Lektüre' in Kurt Drawert's volume *Zweite Inventur*, 130–8.

4. Hartmann, 'Der Generationswechsel', 111.

5. See, e.g. my ' "Poesie ist eine Gegensprache": Young GDR Poets in Search of a Political Identity', in *German Literature at a Time of Change 1989–1990: German Unity and German Identity in Literary Perspective*, ed. Arthur Williams, Stuart Parkes and Roland Smith (Frankfurt/M.: Peter Lang, 1991), 413–28.

6. Stötzer-Kachold, *grenzen los fremd gehen*, 3, Kolbe, from 'Der eherne Kreis', in his *Vaterlandkanal*, 7, Drawert from his *Spiegelland*, 12.

7. Gröschner, *Herzdame Knochensammler*, [n.p.].

8. Kerstin Hensel, 'Gänze des Lebens', in Hensel, *Angestaut. Aus meinen Sudelbuch* (Halle: Mitteldeutscher Verlag, 1993), 42–3; Rathenow, 'Biographie', VERIRRTE STERNE, 7, and a number of echoes in Kolbe, *Vaterlandkanal*.

9. Köhler, 'A la Recherche de la révolution perdue: Ein innerdeutscher Monolog', in Boa and Wharton, *Women and the* Wende: *Social Effects and Cultural Reflections of the German Unification Process*, 2.

10. 'Niemands Land Stimmen' is the title of a section of poems in Grünbein's *Schädelbasislektion* from which the quotation also comes, 31. See also Grünbein, *Falten und Fallen: Gedichte* (Frankfurt/M.: Suhrkamp, 1994), and the extraordinary reception Grünbein has enjoyed in articles by Drawert, Geisel, Hartung, Peukert, Schirrmacher, and Wichner (see Bibliography).

11. See the poem 'La vie ou la vite' from the selection printed under the title 'Simulis, simulis', *NdL* 4 (1992), 31–6 (35–6).

12. Hensel, 'IM STAU', *Angestaut*, 64.

13. Papenfuß-Gorek, '... gleich mal aufschreiben:' and 'soziale markt-monarchie', *tiské*, 59 and 61.

14. Papenfuß-Gorek, 'erweiterte versatzstücke einer gewissenhaften tätlichkeit', LED SAUDAUS, 16. Many texts from this collection would provide useful examples.

15. Gert Neumann, 'Geheimsprache "Klandestinität" ', based on a reading of Gilles Deleuze, *Sprache & Antwort*, 129–44.

16. Adorno, 'Rede über Lyrik und Gesellschaft,' in *Gesammelte Schriften*, ed. Ralf Tiedemann (Frankfurt/M.: Suhrkamp, 1974), xi. 49–68 (51).

17. Václav Havel examines the problematic readings of the word 'opposition' in his essay 'The Power of the Powerless', in *Václav Havel or Living in Truth*, ed. Jan Vladislav (London: Faber, 1986), 72–80.

18. Braun, 'Rimbaud. Ein Psalm der Aktualität', 982.

19. Rainer Schedlinski, 'Zwischen Nostalgie und Utopie. Ein Postscriptum', 185.

20. Hans Magnus Enzensberger, *Museum der modernen Poesie* (originally Frankfurt/M.: Suhrkamp, 1960; here Munich: dtv, 1964), 21.

21. See Papenfuß-Gorek, *tiské*, 57 and 73.

22. Faktor, 'Sechzehn Punkte zur Prenzlauer-Berg-Szene', in *MachtSpiele*, 91–111 (111).

23. A number of anthologies had pointed up the connections even before the end of the GDR: see Hans Bender's *Was sind das für Zeiten: Deutschsprachige Gedichte der achtziger Jahre* (Munich: Hanser, 1988); or *Punktzeit: Deutschsprachige Lyrik der achtziger Jahre*. Cf. e.g. the

journals: *Zwischen den Zeilen*, 1 (1993); *bateria*, 13/14 (1993); and *Schreibheft*, 41 (1993).

24. Peter Geist suggests that the shift away from Berlin as a central focus of critical attention will be one of the important developments in the future. 'Lyrik aus der Lychener Straße, Karl-Chemnitz-Stadt und NiemandsLand. Weniger ein Rückblick', in *Verrat an der Kunst? Rückblicke auf die DDR-Literatur*, ed. Karl Deiritz and Hannes Krauss (Berlin: Aufbau Taschenbuch Verlag, 1993), 233–54.

25. Köhler, 'A la Recherche de la révolution perdue: Ein innerdeutscher Monolog', 2.

26. Papenfuß-Gorek, 'Mein Lieblingspreis wäre der Franz-Jung-Preis: Gespräch mit dem Dichterwerker Bert Papenfuß-Gorek', *Freitag*, 7 June 1991.

27. Papenfuß-Gorek, 'strohtod in stiefeln', *LED SAUDAUS*, 106.

28. Cf. Papenfuß-Gorek, 'Sascha Andersons letzter Freund'.

29. Karen Leeder, ' "eine abstellhalle des authentischen": Postmodernism and Poetry in the New Germany', in *The Individual, Identity and Innovation: Signals from Contemporary Literature and the New Germany*, ed. Arthur Williams and Stuart Parkes (Frankfurt M.: Peter Lang, 1994), 201–20.

30. See Frank Schirrmacher, 'War da irgendein Mythos?: Porträt des Künstlers als junger Grenzhund', *FAZ* 28 Mar. 1992, and Karl Deiritz, ' "Ich halt's halt mit der Kunst": Ein Gespräch mit Gerhard Wolf', in *Verrat an der Kunst?*, 255–72 (270).

31. Kolbe, 'Die Heimat der Dissidenten: Nachbemerkung zum Phantom der DDR-Opposition', in Deiritz and Krauss, *Der deutsch–deutsche Literaturstreit*, 33–9 (37). For one of the most influential of critics who take this line, see Wolfgang Emmerich, 'Status melancholicus', in *Literatur in der DDR: Rückblicke*, ed. Arnold and Meyer-Gosau, 232–45.

32. Geist, 'Lyrik aus der Lychener Straße', 249.

33. Mensching, *NdL* 36. Compare Köhler, *Deutsches Roulette*.

34. The negative vision of 'Praxis als Esserin der Utopien', is Heiner Müller's and is taken up by Frank Hörnigk, in 'Die Literatur bleibt zuständig: Ein Versuch über das Verhältnis von Literatur, Utopie und Politik in der DDR—am Ende der DDR', *Germanic Review*, Theme Issue: 'The End of GDR Literature', 3 (summer 1992), 99–105.

35. Cohen-Pfister, 'Defining the End of GDR Literature', 151–8.

36. Bullivant, *The Future of German Literature*, 165.

37. Hans-Eckardt Wenzel, 'UNLUST UND SCHWERMUT', 'Die herrenlosen Hunde des Mittags', *NdL* 2 (1991), 41–7 (41); Wenzel, 'Halteverbot in der Dunkelheit', 53–4.

38. Wenzel's preoccupation with Benjamin, for example, and an increasingly dark vision of historical progress also date back much earlier. Cf. Wenzel, *Antrag auf Verlängerung des Monats August*.

39. Müller, *Die Hamletmaschine* in *Mauser* (Berlin/W.: Rotbuch 1978), 89–97.

40. Mohr, *Zaungäste*, 11.

41. Cf. Stefan Pannen, *Wir Mauerkinder* (Weinhein: Quadriga, 1994) and Walter Wüllenweber, *Wir Fernsehkinder: Eine Generation ohne Programm* (Reinbek bei Hamburg: Rowohlt, 1994).

42. Greiner, 'Plädoyer für den Schluß der Stasi-Debatte'.
43. Günter Kunert attacks this attitude most roundly in the essays collected in Kunert, *Der Sturz vom Sockel*.
44. Deiritz, 'Zur Klärung eines Sachverhalts—Literatur und Staatssicherheit', in Deiritz and Krauss (eds.), *Verrat an der Kunst?*, 11–17 (15). Raddatz, 'Von der Beschädigung der Literatur durch ihre Urheber: Bemerkungen zu Heiner Müller und Christa Wolf'.
45. Drawert, 'Verpatzte Gelegenheiten: Die Stasi. Eine dauernde Realität', *Freitag*, 3 Sept. 1993.
46. Müller in interview in 1990 in Heiner Müller, *Zur Lage der Nation* (Berlin: Rotbuch, 1990), 21 and 23.
47. Emmerich, 'Wahrnehmung', 7–22.
48. Thomas Rietzschel, 'Kalauer und geliehene Fragmente: Gedichte aus der DDR verlieren ihren Reiz', *FAZ* 12 Feb. 1990.
49. Gerd Labroisse, 'The Literature of the GDR and the Revolution of 1989/90', *German Monitor*, 26 (1992), 37–49 (45–6).
50. See the chapter 'What will Remain' in Bullivant, *The Future of German Literature*, 161–84 (169 and 170).
51. Deiritz and Krauss, *Verrat an der Kunst?*.
52. Ibid. Geist, 'Lyrik aus der Lychener Straße', 233.
53. Cf. particularly the article by Wolfgang Emmerich, 'solidare—solitare. Volker Braun: Drei Gedichte', 195–205, Michael Gratz, 'Was sollte sich daran ändern? Anmerkungen zur Debatte um DDR-Literatur und "Underground"-Kultur', 41–63, in Deiritz and Krauss, *Verrat an der Kunst?*.
54. Cf. Kerstin Hensel on Stephan Hermlin's *Abendlicht*, 109–19, Ursula Heukenkamp on Franz Fühmann, 'Konjunktur—und was danach', 29–40, in Deiritz and Krauss, *Verrat an der Kunst?*.
55. Compare Linda Hutcheon, *The Politics of Postmodernism* (London: Routledge, 1989), and various of the essays in *New German Critique*, Modernity and Postmodernity, 33 (Fall 1984).
56. Müller, 'Es gibt ein Menschenrecht auf Feigheit'.
57. Kunert, 'Fortgesetzt was geht', *NdL* 6 (1993), 5–11 (5).
58. Cf. Katie Hafner, 'A Nation of Readers Dumps its Writers', *New York Times*, 10 Jan. 1993, 23–6 and 45–8.
59. Brecht, *Gesammelte Werke*, iii. 1329.
60. Faktor, 'hinter unten oben auf: Eine Szene demontiert sich'.
61. Geist, 'Lyrik aus der Lychener Straße'. See also Emmerich, 'solidare—solitare', 204.
62. Quoted in Deiritz, 'Zur Klärung eines Sachverhalts', 17.
63. Papenfuß-Gorek, 'ihr seid ein volk von sachsen', *tiské*, 69.
64. Durs Grünbein, 'Völlig daneben', originally in *ariadnefabrik*, 4 (1989), repr. in *abriss der ariadnefabrik*, 259–61 (261).
65. Köhler, *Deutsches Roulette*, 83.
66. Grünbein, 'Vollig daneben', 261.

Select Bibliography

I. THE YOUNG AUTHORS

1. *Major Published Collections.*

This is not intended to be an exhaustive list, but represents the body of material on which this study is based. It does not include 'Künstlerbücher', or individual collections published in the unofficial magazines in the GDR. Dates of birth are given for the young authors. Dates marked * indicate the dates when writers left the GDR. Only in the case of authors not elsewhere collected is specific reference made to anthologies.

ADLOFF, GERD (b. 1952), *Fortgang: Gedichte* (Berlin: Verlag der Nation, 1985).

ANDERSON, SASCHA (b. 1953) *1986, *Jeder Satellit hat einen Killersatelliten* (Berlin/W.: Rotbuch, 1982).

—— *waldmaschine: übung vierhändig mit Ralf Kerbach, Cornelia Schleime, Michael Wildenhain*, Rotbuch, 298 (Berlin/W.: Rotbuch, 1984).

—— *brunnen randvoll* (Berlin/W.: Rotbuch, 1988).

—— *Jewish Jetset* (Berlin: Galrev, 1991).

—— and KERBACH, RALF, *totenreklame. eine reise: texte und zeichnungen*, Rotbuch, 273 (Berlin/W: Rotbuch, 1983).

BARTSCH, WILHELM (b. 1950), *Poesiealbum*, 208 (Berlin: Verlag Neues Leben, 1985).

—— *Übungen im Joch* (Berlin and Weimar: Aufbau, 1986).

BÖHME, THOMAS (b. 1955), *Mit der Sanduhr am Gürtel: Gedichte und Gebilde* (Berlin and Weimar: Aufbau, 1983).

—— *Die schamlose Vergeudung des Dunkels* (Berlin and Weimar: Aufbau, 1985).

—— *stoff der piloten: gedichte* (Berlin and Weimar: Aufbau, 1988)

—— *ich trinke dein · plasma november: 2 dreizehnzeilige und 100 zwölfzeilige gedichte (1987–1990)* (Berlin and Weimar: Aufbau, 1991).

BRINKMANN, HANS (b. 1956), *Poesiealbum*, 170 (Berlin: Verlag Neues Leben, 1981).

—— *Wasserstände und Tauchtiefen: Gedichte* (Berlin: Verlag Neues Leben, 1985).

—— *Federn und Federn lassen: Gedichte* (Berlin: Verlag Neues Leben, 1988).

310 *Select Bibliography*

DÖRING, STEFAN (b. 1953), *Heutmorgestern* (Berlin and Weimar: Aufbau—Außer der Reihe, 1989).
—— *ZEHN* (Berlin: Galrev, 1990).
DOMAŠCYNA, RÓŽA (b. 1951), *Zaungucker: gedichte, texte* (Berlin: Janus press, BasisDruck, 1992).
DRAWERT, KURT (b. 1956), *Zweite Inventur: Gedichte* (Berlin and Weimar: Aufbau, 1987).
—— *Privateigentum: Gedichte*, es 1584 (Frankfurt/M.: Suhrkamp, 1989).
—— *Fraktur: Lyrik, Prosa, Essay*, Reclam-Bibliothek, 1492 (Leipzig: Reclam, 1994).
ECKART, GABRIELE (b. 1954) *1986, *Poesiealbum*, 80 (Berlin: Verlag Neues Leben, 1974).
—— *Sturzacker* (Berlin: Buchverlag der Morgen, 1985).
FAKTOR, JAN (b. 1951), *Georgs Versuche an einem Gedicht und andere positive Texte aus dem Dichtergarten des Grauens* (Berlin and Weimar: Aufbau—Außer der Reihe, 1989).
—— *Henry's Jupitergestik in der Blutlache Nr. 3 und andere positive Texte aus Georgs Besudelungs- und Selbstbesudelungskabinett: Texte, Manifeste, Stücke und ein Bericht* (Berlin: Janus press, BasisDruck, 1991).
FLANZENDÖRFER [Frank Lanzendörfer] (1962–88), *unmöglich es leben: texte bilder fotos*, ed. Peter Böthig and Klaus Michael (Berlin: Janus press, BasisDruck, 1992).
GRÖSCHNER, ANNETT (b. 1964), *Herzdame Knochensammler: Gedichte* (Berlin: KONTEXTverlag, 1993).
GRÜNBEIN, DURS (b. 1961), *Grauzone morgens: Gedichte*, es 1507 (Frankfurt/M.: Suhrkamp, 1988).
—— *Schädelbasislektion: Gedichte* (Frankfurt/M.: Suhrkamp, 1991).
—— *Falten und Fallen: Gedichte* (Frankfurt/M.: Suhrkamp, 1994).
GRÜNEBERGER, RALPH (b. 1951), *Frühstuck im Stehen: Gedichte* (Halle–Leipzig: Mitteldeutscher Verlag, 1986).
—— *Stadt. Name. Land: Gedichte* (Halle–Leipzig: Mitteldeutscher Verlag, 1989).
GÜNTHER, THOMAS (b. 1952), poems in *Berührung ist nur eine Randerscheinung* and *vogel oder käfig sein* (see under Anthologies).
HENSEL, KERSTIN (b. 1961), *Poesiealbum*, 222 (Berlin: Verlag Neues Leben, 1986).
—— *Stilleben mit Zukunft: Gedichte* (Halle–Leipzig: Mitteldeutscher Verlag, 1988).
—— *Schlaraffenzucht* (Frankfurt/M.: Luchterhand, 1990).
—— *Gewitterfront: Lyrik* (Halle–Leipzig: Mitteldeutscher Verlag, 1991).
—— *Angestaut. Aus meinem Sudelbuch* (Halle: Mitteldeutscher Verlag, 1993).
HESSE, EGMONT (b. 1958), *aus der welt kann man nur fallen* (Berlin–Dresden: Galrev and LEITWOLFVERLAG, 1993).

HOLST, "MATTHIAS" BAADER [Matthias Holst] (1962–1990), *traurig wie hans moser im sperma weinholds. texte* (Berlin: Produzenten Verlag, 1990).

IGEL JAYNE-ANN (b. 1954), [before 1989 Bernd Igel], *Poesiealbum 259* (Berlin: Verlag Neues Leben, 1989).

—— *Das Geschlecht der Häuser gebar mir fremde Orte: Gedichte,* Collection S. Fischer, 2363 (Frankfurt/M.: Fischer, 1989).

JANSEN, JOHANNES (b. 1966), *Poesiealbum,* 248 (Berlin: Verlag Neues Leben, 1988).

—— *prost neuland: spottklagen und wegzeug* (Berlin and Weimar: Aufbau, 1990).

KACHOLD, GABRIELE (b. 1953), *zügel los: prosatexte* (Berlin and Weimar: Aufbau—Außer der Reihe, 1989). [From 1992 see Gabriele Stötzer-Kachold.]

KERSCHEK, DIETER (b. 1953), *Poesiealbum,* 188 (Berlin: Verlag Neues Leben, 1983).

KIRCHNER, ANNEROSE (b. 1951), *Mittagsein: Gedichte* (Berlin and Weimar: Aufbau, 1979).

—— *Im Maskensaal: Gedichte* (Berlin and Weimar: Aufbau, 1989).

KÖHLER, BARBARA (b. 1959), *Deutsches Roulette: Gedichte,* es 1642 (Frankfurt/M.: Suhrkamp, 1991).

KOLBE, UWE (b. 1957) *1987, Hineingeboren: Gedichte 1975–1979* (Berlin and Weimar: Aufbau, 1980); also es 1110 (Frankfurt/M.: Suhrkamp, 1982).

—— *Abschiede und andere Liebesgedichte* (Berlin and Weimar: Aufbau, 1981); also es 1178 (Frankfurt/M.: Suhrkamp, 1983).

—— *Bornholm II: Gedichte* (Berlin and Weimar: Aufbau, 1986); also es 1402 (Frankfurt/M.: Suhrkamp, 1987).

—— *Vaterlandkanal: Ein Fahrtenbuch* (Frankfurt/M.: Suhrkamp, 1990).

KOWALSKI, JÖRG (b. 1952), *Vertrauliche Mitteilung* (Halle–Leipzig: Mitteldeutscher Verlag, 1985).

KOZIOL, ANDREAS (b. 1957), BESTIARIUM LITERARICUM (Berlin: Galrev, 1990).

—— *mehr über rauten und türme: gedichte* (Berlin and Weimar: Aufbau—Außer der Reihe, 1991).

KUNST, THOMAS (b. 1965) *besorg noch für das segel die chaussee: gedichte und eine erzählung* (Leipzig: Reclam, 1991).

—— *die verteilung des lächelns bei gegenwehr: gedichte, texte 1986–1988* (Leipzig: Connewitzer Verlagsbuchhandlung, 1992).

—— *medelotti* (Berlin: Galrev, 1994).

LOREK, LEONHARD (b. 1958), *1988, poems in *Berührung ist nur eine Randerscheinung, Sprache & Antwort,* and *vogel oder käfig sein* (see under Anthologies).

LUBINETSKI, RAJA (b. 1962) *1987, poems in *abriss der ariadnefabrik, Die andere Sprache, Mikado,* and *vogel oder käfig sein* (see under Anthologies).

MATTHIES, FRANK-WOLF (b. 1951) *1981, *Für Patricia in Winter: Gedichte* (Reinbeck bei Hamburg: Rowohlt, 1981).

MAUERSBERGER, UTA (b. 1952), *Poesiealbum,* 153 (Berlin: Verlag Neues Leben, 1980).

—— *Balladen Lieder Gedichte* (Berlin: Verlag Neues Leben, 1983; 2nd edn. 1985).

MELLE, FRITZ HENDRICK (b. 1960) *1985, poems in *Berührung ist nur eine Randerscheinung, vogel oder käfig sein* (see under Anthologies).

MENSCHING, STEFFEN (b. 1958), *Poesiealbum,* 146 (Berlin: Verlag Neues Leben, 1979).

—— 'Military Look, deine schönste Bluse', *Sonntag,* 38 (1979), 6.

—— *Erinnerung an eine Milchglasscheibe: Gedichte* (Halle–Leipzig: Mitteldeutscher Verlag, 1984).

—— *Tuchfühlung: Gedichte* (Halle–Leipzig: Mitteldeutscher Verlag, 1986).

OPITZ, DETLEF (b. 1956), poems in *Die andere Sprache; abriss der ariadnefabrik, 'Alles ist im untergrund obenauf; einmannfrei ...', Berührung ist nur eine Randerscheinung, Mikado,* and *vogel oder käfig sein* (see under Anthologies).

PAPENFUß-GOREK, BERT [From 1992 publishing under his original name Bert Papenfuß] (b. 1956), *harm. arkdichtung 77* (Berlin/W.: KULTuhr, 1985).

—— *dreizehntanz: Gedichte* (Berlin and Weimar: Aufbau—Außer der Reihe, 1989); also (Frankfurt/M.: Luchterhand, 1989).

—— *tiské* (Göttingen: Steidl, 1990).

—— *vorwärts im zorn &sw.: gedichte* (Berlin and Weimar: Aufbau, 1990).

—— *SoJa* (Berlin: Galrev, 1990).

—— LED SAUDAUS. *notdichtung, karrendichtung* (Berlin: Janus press, BasisDruck, 1991).

—— NUNFT: *FKK/IM endart. novemberklub: Gedichte, mit Grafiken der Gruppe Endart und einer CD des Novemberklub* (Göttingen: Steidl, 1992).

—— *naif: gedichte 1973 bis 1976,* Gesammelte Texte, 1 (Berlin: Gerhard Wolf Janus press, 1993).

—— *till: gedichte 1973–1976,* Gesammelte Texte, 2, (Berlin: Gerhard Wolf Janus press, 1993).

—— *harm: arkdichtung 1977,* Gesammelte Texte, 3 (Berlin: Gerhard Wolf Janus press, 1993).

PERSCH, MARIO (b. 1963), poems in *Fluchtfreuden Bierdurst* (see under Anthologies).

RATHENOW, LUTZ (b. 1952), *Zangengeburt: Gedichte*, SP 654 (Munich: Piper, 1982).

—— VERIRRTE STERNE, *oder:* WENN ALLES WIEDER MAL GANZ ANDERS KOMMT (Berlin: Merlin, 1994).

ROES, THOM DI [see Thomas Roesler].

ROESLER, THOMAS (b. 1960) *1985, poems in *Berührung ist nur eine Randerscheinung* and *vogel oder käfig sein* (see under Anthologies).

ROSENTHAL, RÜDIGER (b. 1951) *1987, poems in *Berührung ist nur eine Randerscheinung*, Kroh (ed.), 'Freiheit ist immer Freiheit . . .', *vogel oder käfig sein* and *Vogelbühne* (see under Anthologies).

SCHEDLINSKI, RAINER (b. 1956), *die rationen des ja und des nein: Gedichte* (Berlin and Weimar: Aufbau—Außer der Reihe, 1988); also es 1606 (Frankfurt/M.: Suhrkamp, 1990).

—— *die männer der frauen* (Berlin: Druckhaus Galrev, 1991).

SCHLEIME, CORNELIA (b. 1953) *1984, poems in *Berührung ist nur eine Randerscheinung* and *vogel oder käfig sein* (see under Anthologies).

SCHMIDT, KATHRIN (b. 1958), *Poesiealbum*, 179 (Berlin: Verlag Neues Leben, 1982).

—— *Ein Engel fliegt durch die Tapetenfabrik* (Berlin: Verlag Neues Leben, 1987).

SCHÜLER, SONJA (b. 1950), *Schimmel werden schwarz geboren* (Berlin and Weimar: Aufbau, 1982).

SCHWARZ, KLAUS-PETER (b. 1955) *Poesiealbum*, 174 (Berlin: Verlag Neues Leben, 1982).

STÖTZER-KACHOLD, GABRIELE [see also Gabriele Kachold], *grenzen los fremd gehen* (Berlin: Janus press, Basisdruck, 1992).

TESCHKE, HOLGER (b. 1958), *Bäume am Hochufer* (Berlin and Weimar: Aufbau, 1985).

WALSDORF, LOTHAR (b. 1951), *Der Wind ist auch ein Haus: Gedichte* (Berlin and Weimar: Aufbau, 1981).

—— *Im gläsernen Licht der Frühe: Gedichte* (Berlin and Weimar: Aufbau, 1983).

—— *Über die Berge kam ich: Gedichte* (Berlin and Weimar: Aufbau, 1987).

WENZEL, HANS-ECKARDT (b. 1955), *Poesiealbum*, 193 (Berlin: Verlag Neues Leben, 1983).

—— *Lied vom wilden Mohn: Gedichte* (Halle–Leipzig: Mitteldeutscher Verlag, 1984).

—— *Antrag auf Verlängerung des Monats August: Gedichte* (Halle–Leipzig: Mitteldeutscher Verlag, 1986).

WESULS, ELISABETH (b. 1954), *Poesiealbum*, 216 (Berlin: Verlag Neues Leben, 1985).

WILLINGHAM, HEIKE (b. 1962) [Former Heike Drews], *1988, *vom fegen

weiß ich wird man besen: Gedichte (Berlin: Janus press, BasisDruck, 1992).
WÜSTEFELD, MICHAEL (b. 1951) *1988, *Heimsuchung* (Berlin and Weimar: Aufbau, 1987).
—— *Stadtplan: Gedichte* (Berlin and Weimar: Aufbau, 1990).
ZIEGER, ULRICH (b. 1961) *1988, *neunzehnhundertfünfundsechzig* (Berlin: Edition qwert zui opü, 1990).
—— *Groß beruhigte Körper* (Berlin: Galrev, 1992).

In addition I have consulted a wide range of unofficial magazines publishing work by the young authors. Particularly useful were: *ariadnefabrik*, Berlin, 1986–89; *Bizzare Städte*, Berlin, 1987–89; LIANE, Berlin, 1988–89; *schaden*, Berlin, 1984–7.

2. Interviews, Anthologies, Further Texts

This is a select bibliography of those interviews, further texts by the young authors, and anthologies presenting their work which have been particularly useful to me. It is not intended to be a comprehensive account of the young writers' work, and I have not listed individual essays, poems, and interviews from the 'unofficial' magazines nor from published anthologies devoted to the the the young writers' work unless they are discussed specifically in the text.

abriss der ariadnefabrik [see under Koziol and Schedlinski below].
'*Alles is im untergrund obenauf, einmannfrei . . .*' [see under Metelka below].
ANDERSON, SASCHA (ed.), *ich fühle mich in grenzen wohl: Fünfzehn deutsche Sonette* (Berlin/W.: Mariannenpresse, 1985).
—— 'Die Generation nach uns ist freier. Gespräch mit Sascha Anderson', *Der Spiegel*, 1 Sept. 1986, 74–8.
—— 'Das Fleisch vom Knochen lösen: Gespräch mit dem Lyriker und Sänger Sascha Anderson', *Süddeutsche Zeitung*, 12 Sept. 1986.
—— 'Gespräch mit Sascha Anderson', *DB* 1 (1987), 1–21.
—— 'ich rede von Deutschland. Die junge Opposition in der DDR spricht mit der Macht von gleich zu gleich', *FAZ* 12 Feb. 1988.
—— 'Das Prinzip Subversion und seine Folgen', *Neue Rundschau*, 1 (1990), 94–8.
—— 'Biermann äußert eine Meinung . . . und Sascha Anderson versucht, sich zu wehren' [transcript of a dialogue between Anderson and Biermann on the ZDF programme 'Kennzeichen D'], *Süddeutsche Zeitung*, 25 Oct. 1991.
—— 'Ein hoffentlich schöner und lang anhaltender Amoklauf: Zum Thema AIM 7423/91: Ein Bericht', *FAZ* 30 Oct. 1991.

—— ' "Das ist nicht so einfach": Ein *Zeit*-Gespräch mit Sascha Anderson', *Die Zeit*, 1 Nov. 1991.

—— ' "Ich hab euch lieb": Wolf Biermanns gesammelte Lieder', *Die Zeit*, 1 Nov. 1991.

—— ' "Das ist mir ein völliges Rätsel": Detlev Kuhlbrodt, Gespräch mit Sascha Anderson,', *Freitag*, 10 Jan. 1992.

—— 'Fixierung einer Metapher—Antwort auf Volker Braun', repr. in *vogel oder käfig sein*, 291–92.

—— and ERB, ELKE (eds.), *Berührung ist nur eine Randerscheinung. Neue Literatur aus der DDR* (Cologne: Kiepenheuer & Witsch, 1985).

ARNOLD, HEINZ LUDWIG, and WOLF GERHARD, (eds.), *Die andere Sprache: Neue DDR-Literatur der 80er Jahre*, Text + Kritik Sonderband (Munich: edition text + kritik, 1990).

BARTSCH, WILHELM, 'Ich bin kein Vielschreiber', *Temperamente*, 4 (1987), 61–7.

Berührung is nur eine Randerscheinung [see under Anderson and Erb above].

BÖHME, THOMAS, 'Unarten eines Sachsen aus Leipzig', *NdL* 3 (1983), 87–91.

—— 'Werkstattgespräch mit Thomas Böhme', *Temperamente* 3 (1987), 119–22.

—— Interview, *DB* 2 (1989), 89–102.

BÖTTCHER, BRIGITTE (ed.), *Bestandsaufnahme 2. Debütanten 1967–1980* (Halle–Leipzig: Mitteldeutscher Verlag, 1981).

BRINKMANN, HANS, 'Temperamente im Gespräch mit Hans Brinkmann', *Temperamente*, 7 (1982), 66–74.

DEISLER, GUILLERMO and KOWALSKI, JÖRG (eds), *wort*BILD: *Visuelle Poesie in der DDR* (Halle–Leipzig: Mitteldeutscher Verlag, 1990).

Die andere Sprache [see Arnold and Wolf above].

Döring, Christian and STEINERT, HAJO (eds.), *Schöne Aussichten: Neue Prosa aus der DDR*, es 1593 (Frankfurt/M.: Suhrkamp, 1990).

DRAWERT, KURT (ed.), *Die Wärme die Kälte des Körpers. Liebesgedichte* (Berlin and Weimar: Aufbau, 1988).

—— ' ". . . Die Tür ist zu, das ist alles": Robert Stauffer im Gespräch mit Kurt Drawert 19. 12. 1988', in Drawert, *Fraktur*, 230–41.

—— 'Niemand braucht sie, sie brauchen niemand: Über das Volk und die Intellektuellen in Deutschland', *Monatshefte*, 4 (winter 1990), 399–402.

—— 'Die Unaufgeklärtheit der Revolution. Aufsätze und Gedichte von Rainer Schedlinski', *Süddeutsche Zeitung*, 6 Nov. 1991.

—— 'Es gibt keine Entschuldigung. Offener Brief an Rainer Schedlinski', *Süddeutsche Zeitung*, 11/12 Jan. 1992.

—— 'Dieses Jahr, dachte ich, müßte das Schweigen der Text sein: Über den Verfall der DDR und den Doppelcharakter der Macht', *Freitag*, 15 May 1992.

—— 'Die leeren Zeichen: Durs Grünbein: "Schädelbasislektion" ', *NdL* 6 (1992), 132–7.

—— *Spiegelland: Ein deutscher Monolog,* es 1715 (Frankfurt/M.:, Suhrkamp, 1992)

—— 'Der Text und die Freiheit des Textes: Einige Bemerkungen zum Thema Zensur und Selbstzensur in der DDR-Literatur', *Freitag,* 18 June 1993.

—— 'Verpatzte Gelegenheiten: Die Stasi. Eine dauernde Realität', *Freitag,* 3 Sept. 1993.

—— 'Haus ohne Menschen', *Der Spiegel,* 5 July 1993, 149–51.

—— 'Die Gespräche finden nicht statt. Die DDR und ihr Mythos', in Rietzschel (ed.), *Über Deutschland,* 51–72.

—— 'Sie schweigen oder sie lügen: Von der Beschaffenheit einer gescheiterten Elite', in Böthig and Michael (eds.), *MachtSpiele,* 74–82.

Druckhaus Galrev, *Proë,* Sonderband (Berlin: Galrev, 1992).

ECKART, GABRIELE, ' "ich verstehe Deinen Zorn": Dokument einer Stasi-Verstrickung: Gabriele Eckarts offener Brief an Sarah Kirsch', *Stuttgarte Zeitung,* 5 Sept. 1992.

FAKTOR, JAN, 'Diese 8oer gingen zwei Jahre früher zu Ende: Über die inoffizielle Literatur der DDR in den achtziger Jahren', *wespennest: zeitschrift für brauchbare texte und bilder,* 78 (1990), 21–6.

—— 'Was ist neu an der Literatur der 8oer Jahre?', in *vogel oder käfig sein,* 367–89.

—— 'hinter unten oben auf: Eine Szene demontiert sich', *Freitag,* 22 Nov. 1991.

—— 'Das wozu die Berliner Szene geworden ist', *vogel oder käfig sein,* 399–400.

—— 'Sechzehn Punkte zur Prenzlauer-Berg-Szene', in Böthig and Michael (eds.), *MachtSpiele,* 91–111.

—— 'Realität von nebenan: Der besondere Stand der jungen, linken DDR-Intellektuellen im ehemaligen Ostblock', in Rietzschel (ed.), *Über Deutschland,* 73–88.

—— ' "Das Polster um uns war künstlich": Was inoffizielle Mitarbeiter zur Entstehung des Freiraums im Prenzlauer Berg beigetragen haben und was dabei zerstört wurde', *FAZ* 5 Jan. 1993.

Fluchtfreuden Bierdurst [see under Oehme below].

GEIST, PETER (ed.), *Ein Molotow-Cocktail auf fremder Bettkante: Lyrik der siebziger/achtziger Jahre von Dichtern aus der DDR—Ein Lesebuch,* Reclam-Bibliothek, 1399 (Leipzig: Reclam, 1991).

GRÜNBEIN, DURS, 'Völlig daneben', in *abriss der ariadnefabrik,* 259–61.

—— 'Im Namen der Füchse. Gibt es eine neue literarische Zensur?' *FAZ* 26 Nov. 1991.

—— 'Bewußtsein als Verhängnis', *Konzepte,* 11 (1992), 125–38.

—— 'Drei Briefe', *SitZ*, 122 (1992), 172–80.

—— ' "Poetry from the bad side": Gespräch mit Thomas Naumann', *SitZ*, 122 (1992).

—— 'Transit Berlin', *Zwischen den Zeilen*, 2 (1992) 12–19.

—— 'Reflex und Exegese: Rede anläßlich der Verleihung des Bremer Literatur-Förderpreis 1992 der Rudolf-Alexander-Schröder-Stiftung', *Akzente*, 6 *(1993)*, 43–6.

Grüneberger, Ralph, 'Was tun', *NdL* 3 (1983), 95–7.

—— ' "So offensichtlich aus gutem Stoff": Zu Steffen Mensching, "Erinnerung an eine Milchglasscheibe" ', *Temperamente*, 2 (1985), 149–51.

GÜNTHER, THOMAS, *Denn ich ist ein anderer. Ein Versuch und eine Versuchung*, with photos by Sabine Jahn (Berlin: Günther-Jahn-Bach-Edition, 4 copies, 1989).

—— 'Zwischen bunt und bestialisch: Zu "Matthias" BAADER Holst und seinen Texten', *Süddeutsche Zeitung*, 24 Mar. 1991.

—— 'Die subkulturellen Zeitschriften in der DDR und ihre kultur-geschichtliche Bedeutung', in 'Aus Politik und Zeitgeschichte', *Das Parlament*, 8 May 1992, 27–36.

—— 'Wo auf Trümmern die Buchstaben tanzen', *Rheinische Merkur*, 24 Jan. 1992.

HENSEL, KERSTIN, 'Märchen-Land', *Temperamente*, 2 (1984), 32–8.

—— 'Lyrik im Stehen: Zu Ralph Grüneberger "Frühstück im Stehen" ', *Temperamente*, 2 (1987), 148–49.

—— 'Ein Stück Land im Lande: Lesart zu Gedichten von Kathrin Schmidt', *Temperamente*, 1 (1988), 147–9.

—— 'Kerstin Hensel: "Grundstrukturen von Leben gestalten" ', *Börsenblatt für den deutschen Buchhandel*, 14 (15 Apr. 1988), 252–3.

—— ' "Letztlich will ich nichts, als Aufklärer sein. . .": Ein Gespräch mit Kerstin Hensel', *Temperamente*, 3 (1989), 3–7.

—— *Hallimasch: Erzählungen* (Frankfurt/M.: Luchterhand, 1989).

—— 'Welsch', *Sondeur*, 2 (1990), 56–61.

—— 'Wende', *Temperamente*, 1 (1991), 138.

—— Klaus Hammer, 'Gespräch mit Kerstin Hensel', *WB* 1 (1991), 93–110.

—— *Im Schlauch. Erzählung*, es 1815 (Frankfurt/M.: Suhrkamp, 1993).

—— ' "Mein Thema ist die Dummheit—die gibt es auch heute nicht zu knapp": Karl-Heinz Jakobs im Gespräch mit Kerstin Hensel', *Neues Deutschland*, 22 Jan. 1993.

HESSE, EGMONT (ed.), *Sprache & Antwort. Stimmen und Texte einer anderen Literatur aus der DDR* (Frankfurt/M.: Fischer, 1988).

—— and TANNERT, CHRISTOPH (eds.), *Zellinnendruck* (Leipzig: Katalog der Galerie EIGEN+ART, 1990).

IGEL, JAYNE-ANN, 'Fahrwasser', *SuF* 2 (1991), 300–5.

—— [Bernd], ' "ich weiß, daß ihr da seid"; Zu Steffen Mensching, "Tuchfühlung" ', *Temperamente*, 4 (1987), 149–51.

—— 'Gedichte', *SitZ*, 122 (June 1992), 140–2.

JANSEN, JOHANNES, 'eine beunruhigung das behagen der landschaft betreffend (wegen uta ackermann, gudula ziemer, bernd igel): Lesart zu ihren Poesiealben', *Temperamente*, 5 (1989), 156–8.

—— 'BLEIBT AUF DER STRASSE!', *Temperamente*, 1 (1991), 130.

—— *Schlackstoff: Materialversionen*, Text und Porträt, 3 (Berlin: Literarisches Colloquium and DAAD, 1991).

—— *Reisswolf: Aufzeichnungen*, es 1693 (Frankfurt/M.: Suhrkamp, 1992).

—— 'Enttarnt mich auch!', in Böthig and Michael (eds.), *MachtSpiele*, 138–43.

—— *Splittergraben: Aufzeichnungen II*, es 1873 (Frankfurt/M.: Suhrkamp, 1993).

KACHOLD, GABRIELE [see also Stötzer-Kachold], ' "Kunst ist ein Rhythmus, in dem frau leben kann": In der Werkstatt: Gabriele Kachold', *Temperamente*, 3 (1989), 21–8.

KOLBE, UWE, ' "Ein Nein ist keine Lebenshaltung": Vier Gespräche mit Uwe Kolbe' (geführt von Ellen Barthels), in Siegfried Radlach (ed.), *Absage—Ansage*, Schriftenreihe DDR-Kultur, 2 (Berlin/W.: Paul Löbe-Institut, 1982), 17–35.

—— 'Die neunte Stunde: 9 Gedichte von Uwe Kolbe und 9 Radierungen von Hans J. Scheib', in Siegfried Radlach (ed.), *Absage—Ansage*, Schriftenreihe DDR-Kultur 2 (Berlin/W.: Paul Löbe-Institut, 1982), 36–63.

—— Interview, *DB* 3 (1986), 85–98.

—— 'Neue Gedichte', *NdL* 12 (1993), 5–8.

—— 'Offener Brief an Sascha Anderson', *Die Zeit*, 22 Nov. 1991.

—— 'Rundfunk Essay', in *vogel oder käfig sein*, 391–2.

—— 'Frau Wolf, warum lächeln Sie nicht?', in Muschter and Thomas (eds.), *Jenseits der Staatskultur*, 250–8.

—— 'Die Heimat der Dissidenten: Nachbemerkung zum Phantom der DDR-Opposition', in Deiritz and Krauss (eds.), *Der deutsch-deutsche Literaturstreit*, 33–9.

—— TROLLE, LOTHAR, and WAGNER, BERND (eds.), *Mikado oder Der Kaiser ist nackt: Selbstverlegte Literatur in der DDR*, SL 809 (Darmstadt: Luchterhand, 1988).

KÖHLER, BARBARA, 'Eröffnung des Labyrinths', *NdL* 10 (1987), 75–7.

—— 'A la Recherche de la révolution perdue: Ein innerdeutscher Monolog', in Elizabeth Boa and Janet Wharton (eds.), *Women and the Wende: Social Effects and Cultural Reflections of the German Unification Process*, German Monitor, 31 (Amsterdam: Rodopi, 1994), 1–5.

KOZIOL, ANDREAS and SCHEDLINSKI, RAINER (eds.), *abriss der ariadnefabrik* (Berlin: Druckhaus Galrev, 1990).

—— 'Korrektur einer Vergangenheit?: Entgegnung auf Rainer Schedlinskis "Die Unzuständigkeit der Macht" ', *NdL* 10 (1992), 164–8.

KROH, FERDINAND (ed.), *'Freiheit ist immer Freiheit . . .': Die Andersdenkenden in der DDR* (Berlin: Ullstein, 1988).

LOREK, LEONHARD, 'Ciao! Von der Anspruchslosigkeit der Kapitulationen', in Böthig and Michael (eds.), *MachtSpiele*, 122–5.

MATTHIES, FRANK-WOLF, 'Offener Brief', *Frankfurter Rundschau*, 11 May 1982.

—— 'DIE STADT', *vogel oder käfig sein*, 142–4.

—— 'Einer, der tatsächlich etwas getan hat: Zorniger Widerspruch zur Sascha Anderson-Kampagne', *Frankfurter Rundschau*, 3 Jan. 1992.

MELLE, FRITZ HENDRICK, ' "Demokratiespiel für alle": Im Gespräch mit F. Hendrick Melle', *Berliner Zeitung*, 27 Mar. 1991.

—— 'I.M.', in Böthig and Michael (eds.), *MachtSpiele*, 144–62.

MENSCHING, STEFFEN, 'Grenzwertberechnung', *NdL* 5 (1984), 45–8.

—— ' "Präzision ohne Pingelichkeit": Karin Hirdina im Gespräch mit Steffen Mensching und Hans-Eckardt Wenzel', *Temperamente*, 4 (1984), 35–43.

—— Christel and Walfried Hartinger: 'Ich sehe das Land nicht als Provinz. Gespräch mit Steffen Mensching', in Eberhard Günther and Hinnerk Einhorn (eds.), *Positionen 2: Wortmeldungen zur DDR-Literatur*, 65–81.

—— 'Filmfetzen von Wirklichkeit in den Blick bekommen', *Börsenblatt für den deutschen Buchhandel*, 7 (1987), 774–6.

—— 'Mühsam braut sich das bittere Bier: Hans-Eckardt Wenzels "Ich braue das bittere Bier" ', in Hähnel (ed.), *Lyriker im Zwiegespräch*, 334–44.

—— 'Berliner Elegien', *SuF* 5 (1989), 1054–60.

—— 'Its money that matters', *NdL* 4 (1990), 108.

—— 'Notate im November 1989', *Sondeur*, 1 (1990), 43–5.

—— Steffen Mensching and Hans-Eckardt Wenzel, 'Entwürfe einer anderen Welt: Ein Gespräch mit Frauke Meyer-Gosau', in Frauke Meyer-Gosau (ed.), *MachtApparatLiteratur: Literatur und 'Stalinismus'*, *Text + Kritik*, 108 (1990), 86–94.

—— *Pygmalion: ein verloren geglaubter dubioser Kolportage-Roman aus den späten 80er Jahren entschlüsselt und herausgegeben von Steffen Mensching* (Leipzig: Mitteldeutscher Verlag, 1991).

—— 'Von mir aus' and 'Perleberger Zettelkasten', *Lifass*, 33 (1992), 41–50.

—— 'Simulis, simulis', *NdL* 4 (1992), 31–3.

—— and WENZEL, HANS-ECKARDT 'Kunst = Arbeit: Einwürfe und

Auszüge zu "Einblicke und Ausblicke" der 4. Werkstatt "Lieder und Theater"—Dresden 1983', *Temperamente*, 2 (1984), 140–3.

—— *Letztes aus der Da Da eR*, film, directed by Jörg Foth, DEFA 1990.

—— *Allerletztes aus der Da Da eR, Hundekomödie: Textbücher*, ed. Andrea Doberenz (Halle–Leipzig: Mitteldeutscher Verlag, 1991).

METELKA, TORSTEN (ed.), *'Alles ist im untergrund obenauf; einmannfrei. . .': ausgewählte beiträge aus der zeitschrift* KONTEXT 1–7 (Berlin: KONTEXTverlag, 1990).

MICHAEL, KLAUS, and WOHLFAHRT, THOMAS (eds.), *vogel oder käfig sein: Kunst und Literatur aus unabhängigen Zeitschriften in der DDR 1979– 1989* (Berlin: Galrev, 1992).

Mikado [see under Kolbe, Trolle, and Wagner above].

OEHME, DOROTHEA (ed.), *Fluchtfreuden Bierdurst. Letzte Gedichte aus der DDR* (Berlin: Unabhängige Verlagsbuchhandlung, 1990).

OPITZ, DETLEF, 'Die Literaturpolizei der DDR greift zu', *Die Zeit*, 16 Nov. 1984.

—— *Idyll: Erzählungen und andere Texte* (Halle: Mitteldeutscher Verlag, 1990).

—— 'Die Fremde des Beobachters: Eine Erwiderung auf Uwe Kolbes Kritik an der DDR-Opposition', *Freitag*, 4 Oct. 1991.

—— 'Literatur in diesen Zeiten: Staatssicherheit und Prenzlauer Berg', *Freitag*, 7 Feb. 1992 (an extract from: Opitz, ' "Literatur zu sagen in diesen Zeiten—ein Sakrileg", Rede anläßlich der Verleihung des Klaus-Piper-Stipendiums', Berlin, Jan. 1992).

—— ' "Ich weiß, wie zehn Stunden Verhör bei der Stasi sind"—Ein Gespräch mit dem Ostberliner Schriftsteller Detlef Opitz', *Süddeutsche Zeitung*, 25 Jan. 1992.

—— 'Verrat und Verräter: Ein Versuch über die Psychopathologie von Spitzeln und über eine Gesellschaft, die nach Spitzeln giert', *Freitag*, 13 Aug. 1993.

PANKOKE, HELGA, and TRAMPE, WOLFGANG (eds.), *Selbstbildnis zwei Uhr nachts. Gedichte. Eine Anthologie* (Berlin and Weimar: Aufbau, 1989).

PAPENFUß-GOREK, BERT, 'Gedichte', *SuF* 6 (1986), 1232–6.

—— 'Der Blutspur', *SuF* 5 (1989), 1057–63.

—— 'Zwiespaltiges Mutual-Innerview (Auszüge) der Begegner Michoacan & Mandragorek (in halbseidigten Flaggen & übergreifenden Entworten) verfasslt, abgejandlt, drunter- und drübergearbeitet von Mitch Cohen und Bert Papenfuß-Gorek', in Per Ketman (ed.), *'Geh doch rüber!': Begegnungen von Menschen aus Ost und West*, SL 631 (Darmstadt and Neuwied: Luchterhand, 1986), 84–90.

—— 'Mein Lieblingspreis wäre der Franz-Jung-Preis: Gespräch mit dem Dichterwerker Bert Papenfuß-Gorek', *Freitag*, 7 June 1991.

—— 'Sascha Andersons letzter Freund: Bert Papenfuß-Gorek zu Sascha Anderson, Rainer Schedlinski und der "Ortsbestimmung" von Literatur zwischen Häresie und Staatssicherheit, von Ute Scheub und Bascha Mika', *die tageszeitung*, 29 Jan. 1992.

—— ' "Verlust ist eine Herausforderung": Über Verrat, Stasi und literarische Produktion nach 1989. Gespräch mit Bert Papenfuß', *Freitag*, 24 Dec. 1993.

PIETRAß, RICHARD, SCHUBERT, HOLGER J., and TRAMPE, WOLFGANG (eds.), *Auswahl 78. Neue Lyrik—Neue Namen* (Berlin: Verlag Neues Leben, 1978).

RATHENOW, LUTZ, 'Interview with Lutz Rathenow', *Aspect. Art and Literature*, 26/27 (winter 1983), 107–13.

—— *Mit dem Schlimmsten wurde schon gerechnet: Erzählungen*, SP 935 (Munich: Piper, 1989); first appeared (Berlin: Ullstein, 1984).

—— *Boden 411: Stücke zum Lesen und Texte zum Spielen* (Munich: Piper, 1984).

—— (ed.), *einst war ich fänger im schnee. Neue Texte und Bilder aus der DDR* (Berlin/W.: Oberbaum Verlag, 1984).

—— ' "... an Vernachlässigtes erinnern": *tacheles* im Gespräch mit Lutz Rathenow', *tacheles*, 10 (1990), 5–7.

—— ' "Die ganze Szene von der Stasi gesteuert?—Quatsch!": Ein Gespräch mit Lutz Rathenow über den Fall Anderson und die DDR', *Süddeutsche Zeitung*, 3 Dec. 1991.

—— ' "ich untersage Ihnen, doppeldeutige Gedichte zu schreiben": Zwischen Überlegenheit und Hilfslosigkeit—der Schriftsteller Lutz Rathenow hat Stasi-Akten eingesehen', *Berliner Zeitung*, 28/9 Dec. 1991.

—— 'Tatsächlich: er hat etwas getan: Eine Replik zu Frank-Wolf Matthies über Sascha Anderson', *Frankfurter Rundschau*, 15 Jan. 1992.

—— 'Die blockierte Erinnerung', *Kommune*, 6 (1992), 37–9.

—— 'Teile zu keinem Bild, oder: Das Puzzle von der geheimen Macht', in Schädlich (ed.), *Aktenkundig*, 62–91.

—— 'Ein Faltblatt mit Auszügen aus den Original-Stasi-Akten, kommentiert von Anton Gerhard Leitner', *Das Gedicht*, 1 (Oct. 1993), suppl.

—— and HAUSWALD, HARALD, *Berlin-Ost: Die andere Seite einer Stadt* (Berlin: BasisDruck, 1990).

ROSENTHAL, RÜGIGER, 'Hintergrund und Widerstand: die Parallelkultur in Berlin-Ost', in Kroh (ed.), *'Freiheit ist immer Freiheit ...'*, 141–54.

SCHEDLINSKI, RAINER, 'Zwischen Nostalgie und Utopie. Ein Postskriptum', in Michael Naumann (ed.), *"Die Geschichte ist offen": DDR 1990: Hoffnung auf eine neue Republik. Schriftsteller aus der DDR über die Zukunftschancen ihres Landes* (Reinbek bei Hamburg: Rowohlt, 1990) 183–6.

—— 'an das literaturinstitut der akademie der wissenschaften', *ariadnefabrik*, 5 (1988), repr. in *abriss der ariadnefabrik*, 203–4.

—— ' "Diese verdammten Erdbeeren im Winter!": Gespräch mit Elke Erb und Rainer Schedlinski', *Wochen-Zeitung*, 4 May 1990.

—— ' "Es gibt nichts Schlimmeres, als recht zu haben": Gespräch mit den DDR-SchriftstellerInnen Elke Erb und Rainer Schedlinski', *Volkszeitung*, 18 May 1990.

—— *die arroganz der ohnmacht: aufsätze und zeitungsbeiträge 1989 und 1990* (Berlin and Weimar: Aufbau, 1991).

—— ' "Was ein IM ist, weiss ich erst heute": Gesprach mit Rainer Schedlinski', *Neue Zürcher Zeitung*, 14 Jan. 1992.

—— ' "Nach vier Wochen hatten sie mich klein." Ein Gespräch mit dem Berliner Autor Rainer Schedlinski', *Berliner Zeitung*, 18/19 Jan. 1992.

—— 'Dem Druck, immer mehr sagen zu sollen, hielt ich nicht stand', *FAZ* 14 Jan. 1992.

—— ' "Wolltest Du nie bei der Stasi aussteigen?": Die Schriftsteller Rainer Schedlinski und Detlef Opitz im Gespräch', *Süddeutscher Zeitung* MAGAZIN, 16 Apr. 1992.

—— 'Die Unzuständigkeit der Macht', *NdL* 6 (1992), 75–105.

SCHMIDT, KATHRIN, ' "Es liegt an uns, Überkommenes aufzubrechen": *Temperamente* im Gespräch mit Kathrin Schmidt', *Temperamente*, 3 (1982), 39–44.

—— 'zwischen friß und stirb', *NdL* 12 (1990), 108–112.

Sprache & Antwort [see under Hesse above].

STÖTZER-KACHOLD, GABRIELE, ' "Denn wir haben uns nur bekämpft und verletzt": Gespräch mit Gabriele Stötzer-Kachold', *Freitag*, 3 Jan. 1992.

—— ' "Eine glaubhafte weibliche Ich-Figur kommt von einer glaubhaften weiblichen Identität": Birgit Dahlke, Gespräch mit Gabriele Stötzer-Kachold, *DB* 4 (1993), 243–58.

TÖRNE, DOROTHEA VON (ed.), *Vogelbühne: Gedichte im Dialog* (Berlin: Verlag der Nation, 1983).

—— (ed.), *Komm lies geh sprich: gedichte im dialog* (Berlin: Union Verlag, 1989).

vogel oder käfig sein [see under Michael and Wohlfahrt above].

Vogelbühne: Gedichte im Dialog [see under Törne above].

WENZEL, HANS-ECKARDT [see also under Mensching], 'Von meiner Hoffnung laß ich nicht. Vorrat Erich Mühsam', *Temperamente*, 4 (1979), 89–91.

—— 'Vier Fragen an Hans-Eckardt Wenzel', *NdL* 5 (1984), 71–5.

—— 'Traumhafter Ausflug des Dichters Steffen M. mit Rosa L.: Steffen Menschings "Traumhafter Ausflug mit Rosa L." ', in Hähnel (ed.), *Lyriker im Zwiegespräch*, 345–67.

—— 'Arbeit mit Geschichte', *NdL* 1 (1981), 108–111.

—— 'Bekenntnis', *Temperamente*, 4 (1984), 50–1.

—— 'Verlangen nach einem großen Platz', *NdL* 5 (1984), 63–71.

—— 'Allgemein wiederholte Auslassungen zu einem hinlänglich bekannten

Thema/Diskussionsschrift', in Eberhard Günther and Hinnerk Einhorn (eds.), *Positionen 2: Wortmeldungen zur DDR-Literatur* (Halle–Leipzig: Mitteldeutscher Verlag, 1986), 86–106.

—— *Stirb mit mir ein Stück*, Amiga VEB Schallplatten (1987).

—— 'Zeitfragen—Streitfragen', broadcast 25 Dec. 1987 by NDR.

—— 'Noch mal Gemeinsinn! Oder: Wem gehört die Wirklichkeit?', in Eberhard Günther und Hinnerk Einhorn (eds.), *Positionen 4: Wortmeldungen zur DDR-Literatur* (Halle–Leipzig: Mitteldeutscher Verlag, 1988), 46–52.

—— *Reisebilder*, Amiga VEB Schallplatten (1988).

—— *Reise-Bilder: Satiren, Berichte, Essays* (Halle–Leipzig: Mitteldeutscher Verlag, 1989).

—— 'Hans-Eckardt Wenzel: Den Begriff der Vernunft ausweiten', *Börsenblatt für den deutschen Buchhandel*, 1 (1990), 8–10.

—— *Malinche: Legenden von Liebe und Verrat* (Leipzig, Mitteldeutscher Verlag, 1991).

—— 'Rhythmische Veränderung einer Losung oder: Die Entstehung des Marsches aus dem Geiste des Tanzes', *Sondeur*, 2 (1990), 61–3.

—— 'Die herrenlosen Hunde des Mittags', *NdL* 2 (1991), 41–7.

—— 'Halteverbot in der Dunkelheit: Variationen zum Begriff der Geschichte', *NdL* 8 (1991), 53–65.

WESULS, ELISABETH, 'Sich einlassen auf das Langwierige', *NdL* 1 (1981), 75–8.

—— 'Die Erinnerungen der Nachgeborenen', *NdL* 4 (1983), 90–105.

WÜSTEFELD, MICHAEL, 'Jetzt drängt sie mit Macht ins Gedicht', *NdL* 2 (1994), 134–6.

Zellinnendruck [see under Hesse and Tannert above].

3. Round-Table Discussions

' "Vorbild—Leitbild". Joachim Nowotny im Gespräch mit den Studenten des Instituts für Literatur "Johannes R. Becher", Wolfgang Berger, Stephan Ernst, Ingrid Hildebrandt, Rainer Hohberg, Annerose Kirchner, Chistine Lindner, Thomas Rosenlöcher', *WB* 7 (1979), 11–22.

' "Zwischen Text und Szene". Peter Reichel im Gespräch mit Jürgen Groß, Günter Preuß, Uwe Saeger, Frieder Venus, Albert Wendt', *WB* 7 (1979), 23–40.

' "Ohne den Leser geht es nicht": Ursula Heukenkamp im Gespräch mit Gerd Adloff, Gabriekle Eckart, Uwe Kolbe, Bernd Wagner', WB 7 (1979), 41–52.

' "Eine eigene Sprache finden": Walfried and Christel Hartinger sowie Peter Geist im Gespräch mit den Lyrikern Thomas Böhme, Kurt Drawert, Kerstin Hensel, Dieter Kerschek, Bert Papenfuß-Gorek und Kathrin Schmidt', *WB* 4 (1990), 580–616.

II. OTHER PRIMARY AND SECONDARY SOURCES

For reasons of space, this list is confined to those secondary works which deal directly with the young writers and a select number of those other primary and secondary sources which I have found particularly useful.

Anon., 'Pegasus an der Stasi-Leine', *Der Spiegel*, 18 Nov. 1991, 276–80.

ANON., 'Der Verräter seiner Freunde', *Der Spiegel*, 9 Dec. 1991, 22–4.

ANON., 'Kein Verbrechen ohne Schuld', *Der Spiegel*, 23 Dec. 1991, 30–8.

ANON., 'Maßnahme Totenhaus', *Der Spiegel*, 23 Dec. 1991, 28–9.

ADORNO, T. W., *Gesammelte Schriften*, ed. Ralf Tiedemann (Frankfurt/ M.: Suhrkamp, 1974).

ALBRECHT, DAGNY, 'Leipziger Kolloquium "DDR Lyrik der siebziger/ achtziger Jahre" ', *WB* 7 (1991), 1089–94.

ANZ, THOMAS (ed.), *'Es geht nicht um Christa Wolf': Der Literaturstreit im vereinten Deutschland* (Munich: edition spangenberg, 1991).

ARENDT, ERICH, *entgrenzen* (Leipzig: Insel Verlag, 1891).

ARNOLD, HEINZ LUDWIG (ed.), *Bestandsaufnahme Gegenwartsliteratur: Bundesrepublik Deutschland, Deutsche Demokratische Republik, Österreich, Schweiz* (Munich: edition text + kritik, 1988).

—— (ed.), *Vom gegenwärtigen Zustand der deutschen Literatur, Text + Kritik*, 113 (Munich: text + kritik, 1992).

—— and MEYER-GOSAU, FRAUKE, (eds.), *Literatur in der DDR: Rückblicke Sonderband Text + Kritik* (Munich: edition text + kritik, 1991).

ASSHEUER, THOMAS, 'Den Versen den Verrat verraten', *Frankfurter Rundschau*, 23 Jan. 1992.

—— 'Jean meets Sascha', *Frankfurter Rundschau*, 5 Nov. 1991.

BACHMANN, INGEBORG, *Werke*, ed. Christine Koschel, Inge von Weidenbaum, and Clemens Münster (Munich: Piper, 1978, 3rd edn., 1984).

BALLUSEK, LOTHAR VON (ed.), *Dichter im Dienst: Der sozialistische Realismus in der deutschen Literatur* (Wiesbaden, Limes Verlag, 1956).

BARCK, KARLHEINZ, SCHLENSTEDT, DIETER, AND THIERSE, WOLFGANG (eds.), *Künstlerische Avantgarde: Annäherungen an ein unabgeschlossenes Kapitel* (Berlin: Akademie-Verlag, 1979).

BARON, ULRICH, 'Und die Moral von der Geschicht? Dichter, Denunzianten und die Wahrhaftigkeit der Literatur', *Rheinischer Merkur*, 28 Feb. 1992.

BATHRICK, DAVID, 'Kultur und Öffentlichkeit in der DDR', in Peter Uwe Hohendahl and Patricia Herminghouse (eds.), *Literatur der DDR in den siebziger Jahren* (Frankfurt/M.: Suhrkamp, 1983), 53–81.

BAUMGART, REINHARD, 'Ein Falschspiel nur', *Die Zeit*, 31 Jan. 1992.

—— 'Der neudeutsche Literaturstreit: Anlaß—Verlauf—Vorgeschichte—Folgen', in Arnold (ed.), *Vom gegenwärten Zustand der deutschen Literatur*, 72–85.

BECHER, JOHANNES R., *Über Literatur und Kunst* (Berlin, Aufbau, 1962).

—— *Gedichte 1936–1941* (Berlin and Weimar: Aufbau, 1966).

BENDER, HANS, *Was sing das dür Zeiten: Deutschsprachige Gedichte der achziger Jähre* (Munich: Hanser, 1988).

BENJAMIN, WALTER, *Gesammelte Schriften*, ed. Roy Tiedemann and Hermann Schweppenhäuser (Frankfurt/M.: Suhrkamp, 1974).

BERENDSE, GERRIT-JAN, *Die 'Sächsische Dichterschule'. Lyrik in der DDR der sechziger und siebziger Jahre*, Bochumer Schriften zur deutschen Literatur, 14 (Frankfurt/M.: Peter Lang, 1990).

—— 'Outcast in Berlin: Opposition durch Entziehung bei der jüngeren Generation', *ZfG*, 1 (1991), 21–7.

—— 'Zu neuen Ufern: Lyrik der "Sächsischen Dichterschule" im Spiegel der Elbe', in Margy Gerber *et al.* (eds.), *Studies in GDR Culture and Society 10* (Lanham, MD: University Press of America, 1991), 197–212.

—— 'Mit der Lücke leben', *SuF* 6 (1992), 1055–61.

—— ' "Ändern sich die Umstände, zeigen sich die Konstanten!". Deutsche Lyrik in der "Wende" zum Regionalen', *Germanic Review*, Theme Issue: 'The End of GDR Literature (Conclusion)', 4 (Fall 1992), 146–51.

BERNHARDT, RÜDIGER, ' " Vertrauliche Mitteilung" über Geschichte', *Wort Wechsel: Studien zur DDR-Literatur*, Wissenschaftliche Zeitschrift der Friedrich Schiller Universität Jena, 3 (1990), 151–5.

BERTAUX, PIERRE, 'Hölderlin und die Französische Revolution', in *Hölderlin-Jahrbuch*, 15 (1967–8), 1–27.

BIERMANN, WOLF, *Die Drahtharfe: Balladen Gedichte Lieder* (Berlin/W.: Klaus Wagenbuch, 1965, repr. 1981).

—— *Für meine Genossen: Hetzlieder, Balladen, Gedichte* (Berlin, Verlag Klaus Wagenbach, 1972).

—— *Verdrehte Welt—das seh' ich gerne: Gedichte* (Munich: dtv, 1985).

—— *Affenfels und Barrikade* (Cologne: Kiepenheuer & Witsch, 1986).

—— *Klartexte im Getümmel: 13 Jahre im Westen: Von der Ausbürgerung bis zur November Revolution*, ed. Hannes Stein, KiWi 217 (Cologne: Kiepenheuer & Witsch, 1990).

—— 'Auch ich war bei der Stasi', *Die Zeit*, 11 May 1990.

—— 'Nur wer sich ändert bleibt sich treu: Der Streit um Christa Wolf, das Ende der DDR, das Elend der Intellektuellen: Das alles ist auch komisch', *Die Zeit*, 24 Aug. 1990.

—— ' "Laß, o Welt, o laß mich sein": Rede zum Eduard-Mörike-Preis', *Die Zeit*, 15 Nov. 1991.

—— 'Stasi Akten explodieren. Eine kleine Ansprache' (Laudatio auf Utz Rachowski in Fellbach), *FAZ* 14 Nov. 1991.

—— 'Der Lichtblick im gräßlichen Fatalismus der Geschichte', *Die Zeit*, 25 Oct. 1991.

—— 'Ein öffentliches Geschwür: Offener Brief an Lew Kopelew', *Der Spiegel*, 13 Jan. 1992, 158–67.

—— 'Das Kaninchen frißt die Schlange: Die Stasi-Debatte und das Drehbuch meiner Ausbügerung', *Der Spiegel*, 2 Mar. 1992, 40–51.

—— 'Tiefer als unter die Haut: Über Schweinehunde, halbe Helden, Intimitäten und andere Funde aus meinen Stasi-Akten', *Der Spiegel*, 27 Jan. 1992, 180–5.

—— *Der Sturz des Dädalus, oder Eizes für die Eingeborenen der Fidschi-Inseln über den IM Judas Ischariot und den Kuddelmuddel in Deutschland seit dem Golfkrieg*, KiWi 294 (Cologne: Kiepenheuer & Witsch, 1992).

BISKUPEK, MATTHIAS, 'Wilde Künstlerbücher, Milde Kunstkäufer, Wüste Stasidichter, Deutsche Verschriftungen', *NdL* 7 (1992), 141–8.

BLÖDORN, URSULA, 'Revolution und Geschichte in der neuesten DDR-Lyrik. Zu einigen Aspekten im Schaffen Hans-Eckardt Wenzels', in Peter Richter (ed.), *Utopie und Realität im Funktionsverständnis von Literatur*, Greifswalder Germanistische Forschungen, 10 (Greifswald: [n.publ.], 1989), 74–81.

BLOOM, HAROLD, *The Anxiety of Influence* (Oxford: OUP, 1973).

BOBROWSKI, JOHANNES, *Gesammelte Werke in 6 Bänden* (Berlin: Union Verlag, 1897).

BÖCK, DOROTHEA, 'Fixierte Realität: Gabriele Kachold, "zügel los" ', *NdL* 11 (1990), 154–6.

BODEN, PETRA, 'Strukturen der Lenkung von Literatur. Das Gesetz zum Schutz der Berufsbezeichnung Schriftsteller', in Böthig and Michael (eds.), *MachtSpiele*, 217–27.

BÖHNKI, DETLEF, *DADA-Rezeption in der DDR-Literatur*, Kunstwissenschaften in der Blauen Eule, 4 (Essen: Verlag Die Blaue Eule, 1989).

BOHRER, KARL HEINZ, 'Kulturschutzgebiet DDR?', *Merkur*, 10/11 (Oct./Nov. 1990), 1015–18.

—— 'Die Ästhetik am Ausgang ihrer Unmündigkeit', *Merkur*, 10/11 (Oct./Nov. 1990), 851–65.

—— 'Provinzialismus', *Merkur*, 12 (1990), 1096–1102.

BORMANN, ALEXANDER VON, 'Wege aus der Ordnung', in Muschter and Thomas (eds.), *Jenseits der Staatkultur*, 83–107.

—— 'Rede-Wendungen: Zur Rhetorik des gegenwärtigen Gedichts in der DDR', in Cosentino, Ertl, and Labroisse (eds.), *DDR-Lyrik im Kontext*, 89–143.

—— 'Begrenzte Andersheit: Zur DDR-Lyrik der achtziger Jahre', *Der Deutschunterricht*, 4 (1990), 77–99.

BÖTHIG, PETER, 'die verlassenen worte—eine skizze (literatur in den 80ern)', *SitZ*, 112 (Dec. 1989), 262–5.

—— 'fertonung des orts & der zeit: Zu Bert Papenfuß-Gorek, "dreihzehntanz" ', *Temperamente*, 3 (1989), 146–50.

—— 'Möglichkeitsräume: Selbstverlegte Originalgrafisch-Literarische Zeitschriften in der DDR', in Henkel and Russ (eds.), *D1980D1989R Künstlerbücher und Originalgrafische Zeitschriften*, 95–100.

—— 'Wie man mit Wahrheit lügt. Eine Entgegnung auf Rainer Schedlinski, "Die Unzuständigkeit der Macht" ', *NdL* 10 (1992), 157–63.

—— 'Gedächtnisprotokoll mit Herrn K.', in Böthig and Michael (eds.), *MachtSpiele*, 288–95.

—— 'Spiele der Revolte', in Böthig and Michael (eds.), *MachtSpiele* 59–64.

—— 'Differenz und Revolte: Literatur aus der DDR in den 80er Jahren. Untersuchungen an der Rändern eines Diskurses' (unpublished dissertation, Humboldt-Universität, Berlin, 1993).

—— and MICHAEL, KLAUS (eds.), *MachtSpiele: Literatur und Staatssicherheit im Fokus Prenzlauer Berg*, Reclam-Bibliothek, 1460 (Leipzig: Reclam, 1993).

BRADY, PHILIP, ' "Wir hausen in Prenzlauer Berg": On the Very Last Generation of GDR Poets', in Pape (ed.), *1870/71—1989/90 German Unifications and the Change of Literary Discourse*, 278–301.

BRAUN, MICHAEL, 'Suchbewegungen im Sprachzerfall: Einige Bermerkungen zur Poetik der jüngsten Lyriker-Generation', *SitZ*, 111 (1989), 210–16.

—— 'Was alles hat Platz in einem Gedicht?: Sprachspieler, Sprachsaboteur, Sprachverrückte: ein Streifzug durch die bundesdeutsche und DDR-Lyrik der achtziger Jahre', *Badische Zeitung*, 12 June 1989.

—— 'Neufang oder Restauration?', *Universitas*, 7 (1989), 675–83.

—— 'Entfesselungsversuche: *zügel los*: Das Prosadebüt von Gabi Kachold aus der Ex-DDR', *Basler Zeitung*, 2 Nov. 1990.

—— 'Poesie in Bewegung: Kleine Abschweifung über Sprachbesessenheit in der jüngsten Lyriker-Generation', *Manuskripte*, 108 (1990), 69–72.

—— 'Traumstücke & Textmaschinen. Zu Gedichten von Dieter M. Graf und Jayne-Ann Igel (Bernd Igel)', *SitZ*, 122 (June 1992), 132–6.

—— 'Ende eines Mythos?', *Freitag*, 22 Nov. 1991.

—— 'Nerven aus Draht', *Freitag*, 31 Jan. 1992.

—— 'Kann Spitzel-Literatur gut sein? Michael Braun—Hajo Steinert: Ein Briefwechsel', *Basler Zeitung*, 1 Feb. 1992.

—— and THILL, HANS (eds.), *Punktzeit: Deutschsprachige Lyrik der achtziger Jahre* (Heidelberg: Verlag Das Wunderhorn, 1987).

BRAUN, VOLKER, *Provokation für mich* (Halle/S.: Mitteldeutscher Verlag, 1965).

—— *Vorläufiges* (Frankfurt/M.: Suhrkamp, 1966).

—— *Gegen die symmetrische Welt* (Halle: Mitteldeutscher Verlag, 1974).

—— *Es genügt nicht die einfache Wahrheit* (Leipzig: Philipp Reclam jun., 1975).

—— *Unvollendete Geschichte* (Frankfurt/M.: Suhrkamp, 1977).

—— *Training des aufrechten Gangs* (Halle–Leipzig: Mitteldeutscher Verlag, 1979).

—— 'Rimbaud. Ein Psalm der Aktualität', *SuF* 5 (1985), 978–8.

—— *Langsamer knirschender Morgen* (Frankfurt/M.: Suhrkamp, 1987).

—— 'Das Unersetzliche wird unser Thema bleiben', *NdL* 6 (1990), 6–9.

—— 'Monströse Banalität', *Die Zeit*, 22 Nov. 1991.

—— *Die Zickzackbrücke: Ein Abrißkalender* (Halle: Mitteldeutscher Verlag, 1992).

BRECHT, BERTOLT, *Gesammelte Werke in 20 Bänden*, ed. Suhrkamp Verlag in association with Elisabeth Hauptmann (Frankfurt/M.: Suhrkamp, 1967).

BRETTSCHNEIDER, WERNER, *Zwischen literarischer Autonomie und Staatsdienst: Die Literatur in der DDR* (Berlin/W.: Erich Schmidt Verlag, 1972; 2nd edn. 1974).

BREŽAN, JURIJ, 'Über Widerspiegel, das kleine und das große Erleiden und die Würde des Schriftstellers', *NdL* 4 (1982), 5–15.

BRINKMANN, RALF DIETER, *Westwärts 1 & 2 Gedichte* (Reinbeck bei Hamburg: Rowohlt, 1975).

BROCKMANN, STEPHAN, 'The Politics of German Literature', *Monatshefte*, 1 (spring, 1992), 46–58.

BULLIVANT, KEITH, 'The Divided City: Berlin in Post-War German Literature', in Glass, Rösler, and White (eds.), *Berlin: Literary Images of a City*, 162–77.

—— *The Future of German Literature* (Oxford, Berg, 1994).

BÜRGER, PETER, *Theorie der Avantgarde*, es 727 (Frankfurt/M.: Suhrkamp, 1974).

CHIARLONI, ANNA, ' "Entgrenzen"—The "Breaking of Bounds", in Recent GDR Literature', in Margy Gerber *et al.* (eds.), *Studies in GDR Culture and Society 5* (Lanham, MD: University Press of America, 1985), 125–40.

—— and PANKOKE, HELGA   (eds.), *Grenzfallgedichte. Eine deutsche Anthologie* (Berlin and Weimar: Aufbau, 1991).

—— SARTORI, GEMMA and CAMBI, FABRIZIO (eds.), *Die Literatur der DDR 1976–1986. Akten der Internationalen Konferenz in Pisa, Mai 1987* (Pisa: Giardini Edizione e Stampatori, 1988).

CLAUER, MARKUS, ' "Das endet dann in Mord und Totschlag": Der neudeutsche Literaturstreit zwischen Wolf Biermann und Sascha Anderson—Ein altes Trauma', *Die Rheinpfalz*, 15 Nov. 1992.

COHEN-PFISTER, LAUREL, 'Defining the End of GDR Literature: Making the Case for Young Literature', *Germanic Review*, Theme Issue: 'The End of GDR Literature (Conclusion)', 4 (Fall 1992), 151–8.

CORINO, KARL, 'Vor und nach der Wende: Die Rezeption der DDR Literatur in der Bundesrepublik und das Problem einer einheitlichen deutschen Literatur', *NdL* 8 (1991), 146–64.

—— 'Zerstörte Legende: Über den Fall Sascha Anderson', *Stuttgarter Zeitung*, 30 Nov. 1991.

—— 'Vom Leichengift der Stasi: Die DDR-Literatur hat an Glaubwürdigkeit verloren. Eine Entgegnung', *Süddeutsche Zeitung*, 6 Dec. 1991.

—— 'Absolution vor der Beichte?', *Die Welt*, 2 Jan. 1992.

—— ' "Anderson ist reif für die Therapie": Gespräch mit Karl Corino', *Hamburger Morgenpost*, 16 Jan. 1992.

COSENTINO, CHRISTINE, 'Gedanken zur jüngsten DDR-Lyrik: Uwe Kolbe, Sascha Anderson, Lutz Rathenow', *Germanic Review*, 3 (1985), 82–90.

—— 'Lutz Rathenows Lyrikband "Zangengeburt": Eine Stimme vom Prenzlauer Berg', in Margy Gerber *et al.* (eds.), *Studies in GDR Culture and Society* 5 (Lanham, MD: University Press of America, 1985), 141–151.

—— ' "ich bin kein artist": Volker Braun und Sascha Anderson zur Position des Dichters in der DDR', *Germanic Notes*, 1 (1986), 2–4.

—— ' "ich habe ausser meiner sprache keine | mittel meine sprache zu verlassen": Überlegungen zur Lyrik Sascha Andersons', in Cosentino, Ertl, and Labroisse (eds.), *DDR-Lyrik im Kontext*, 195–221.

—— ' "Aber die Sprache. | Warum spreche ich?": Zur "Metasprache" und Sprachhinterfragung in der Lyrik Uwe Kolbes', *GDR Monitor*, 18 (1987/8), 71–85.

—— 'Noch einmal Sascha Anderson', in Elrud Ibsch and Ferdinand van Ingen (eds.), *Literatur und Politische Aktualität*, ABznG 36 (Amsterdam: Rodopi, 1993), 3–20.

—— ERTL, WOLFGANG and LABROISSE, GERD (eds.), *DDR Lyrik im Kontext*, ABznG 26 (Amsterdam: Rodopi, 1988).

CZECHOWSKI, HEINZ, 'Es geht um die Realität des Gedichts', *SuF* 4 (1972), 897–902.

—— *Was mich betrifft: Gedichte* (Leipzig: Mitteldeutscher Verlag, 1981).

—— *Ich beispielsweise* (Leipzig: Philipp Reclam jun., 1982).

—— *Kein näheres Zeichen* (Halle–Leipzig: Mitteldeutscher Verlag, 1987).

—— *Nachtspur: Gedichte und Prosa 1987–1992* (Zurich: Ammann Verlag, 1993).

DAHLKE, BIRGIT, ' "Die Chancen haben sich verschanzt": Die inoffizielle Literatur-Szene der DDR', in Rainer Bohn, Knut Hickethier, Eggo Müller (eds.), *Mauer Show: das Ende der DDR, die deutsche Einheit und die Medien*, sigma medienwissenschaft, 11, (Berlin: edition sigma Rainer Bohn Verlag, 1992), 227–42.

—— ' "ein stück leibverantwortung": Gabriele Stötzer-Kachold: "grenzen los fremd gehen" ', *NdL* 6 (1993), 148–50.

—— ' "Im Brunnen vor dem Tore": Autorinnen in inoffiziellen Zeitschriften der DDR 1979–90', in Delabar, Jung, and Pergande (eds.), *Neue Generation—Neues Erzählen*, 177–94.

—— ' "Die romantischen Bilder blättern ab". Produktionsbedingungen, Schreibweisen und Traditionen von Autorinnen in inoffiziell publizierten Zeitschriften der DDR 1979–90' (unpublished dissertation, Freie Universität, Berlin, 1994).

DAHN, DANIELA, *Prenzlauer-Berg-Tour* (Halle–Leipzig: Mitteldeutscher Verlag, 1987; also published as *Kunst und Kohle: die 'Szene' am Prenzlauer Berg*, SL 785 (Frankfurt/M.: Luchterhand, 1987).

DAU, MATHILDE, 'Mit meinen Augen: Junge Lyrik beim Entdecken neuer Wirklichkeit', *Temperamente*, 3 (1979), 90–106.

—— 'Steffen Mensching: "Erinnerung an eine Milchglasscheibe" ', *WB* 7 (1985), 1193–6.

—— 'Vivisektion mit stumpfem Skalpell', *SuF* 2 (1986), 442–7.

—— 'Mythos und Geschichte in unserem Alltag: Zu Willhelm Bartsch, "Übungen im Joch" ', *Temperamente*, 3 (1987), 150–4.

—— ' "Meine utopische Taschenuhr": Zu Steffen Menschings Lyrikband "Tuchfühlung" ', in Siegfried Rönisch (ed.), *DDR-Literatur '86 im Gespräch* (Berlin and Weimar: Aufbau, 1987), 288–96.

—— 'Selbstporträt einer Generation. Zu: "Stilleben mit Zukunft" von Kerstin Hensel', *Temperamente*, 3 (1988), 145–8.

DAU, MATHILDE and RUDOLF, 'Noch einmal: Junge Lyrik am Ende der siebziger Jahre', *WB* 3 (1982), 152–6.

—— 'Steffen Mensching: "Traumhafter Ausflug mit Rosa L." ', in Horst Hartmann *et al.* (eds.), *Werkinterpretationen zur deutschen Literatur* (Berlin: Verlag Volk und Wissen, 1986), 257–63.

DAU, RUDOLF, 'Zum Sonettenkranz "Märchenland" ', *Temperamente*, 2 (1984), 31.

DAUTEL, KLAUS, 'Subjektivität und Unmittelbarkeit. Zur Entwicklung der DDR-Lyrik in den 70er Jahren', *Text & Kontext*, 1 (1979), 32–66.

DEICKE, GÜNTHER, 'Wiederbegegnung mit Hölderlin', *NdL* 5 (1970), 107–16.

—— 'Tübingen, Oktober', *NdL* 5 (1970), 116–18.

—— 'Auftritt einer neuen Generation', in Annie Voigtländer (ed.), *Liebes- und andere Erklärungen: Schriftsteller über Schriftsteller* (Berlin and Weimar: Aufbau, 1972), 36–7.

DEIRITZ, KARL, ' "Ich halt's halt mit der Kunst": Ein Gespräch mit Gerhard Wolf', in Deiritz and Krauss (eds.), *Verrat an der Kunst?*, 255–72.

—— 'Zur Klärung eines Sachverhalts—Literatur und Staatssicherheit', in Deiritz and Krauss (eds.), *Verrat an der Kunst?*, 11–17.

—— and KRAUSS, HANNES (eds.), *Der deutsch–deutsche Literaturstreit oder 'Freunde es spricht sich schlecht mit gebundener Zunge': Analysen und Materialien*, SL 1002 (Hamburg: Luchterhand, 1991).

—— —— *Verrat an der Kunst? Rückblicke auf die DDR-Literatur*, AtV 8005 (Berlin: Aufbau Taschenbuch Verlag, 1993).

DELABAR, WALTER, JUNG, WERNER, and PERGANDE, INGRID (eds.), *Neue Generation—Neues Erzählen: Deutsche Prosa-Literatur der 80er Jahre* (Opladen: Westdeutscher Verlag, 1993).

DEMANDT, ALEXANDER, *Metaphern für Geschichte: Sprachbilder und Gleichnisse im historisch-politischen Denken* (Munich: Beck, 1979).

DOMDEY, HORST, 'Die DDR-Literatur als Literatur der Epochenillusion. Zur Literaturgeschichtsschreibung der DDR-Literatur', in Ilse Spittmann and Gisela Hellwig (eds.), *Die DDR im vierzigsten Jahr. Geschichte, Situation, Perspektiven*, xxii. Tagung zum Stand der DDR-Forschung in der BRD 16–19 Mai 1989 (Cologne: Edition Deutschland Archiv, 1989), 141–9.

—— 'Duftmarken: Eine Anthologie über Kunst und Literatur aus unabhängigen Zeitschriften in der DDR 1979–1989', *Freitag*, 8 May 1992.

EGGERT, STEFAN, 'Der schwankende Mythos vom tapferen Partisanen: Das Druckhaus "Galrev" und die Affäre Sascha Anderson', *Frankfurter Rundschau*, 18 Nov. 1991.

EHLERT, MATTHIAS, 'Niemand hat uns was zu sagen', *Junge Welt*, 20 Dec. 1991, 13.

—— 'harri weiß bescheid', *Junge Welt*, 21 Dec. 1991, 14.

—— 'Zerfallen die Dichter', *Junge Welt*, 23 Dec. 1991, 13.

—— 'Unkraut als Züchtigungsobjekt im Gewächshaus? Wie die Stasi im Prenzlauer Berg literarische Opposition simulierte', *Berliner Zeitung*, 9 Jan. 1992.

EICH GÜNTER, *Gesammelte Werke*, ed. Suhrkamp Verlag in collaboration with Ilse Aichinger *et al.* (Fankfurt/M.: Suhrkamp, 1973).

ELIOT, T. S., *Selected Essays* (London: Fraber, 1957).

—— *The Waste Land: A Fascimile Transcript*, ed. Valerie Eliot (London: Faber, 1971).

EMMERICH, WOLFGANG, *Kleine Literaturgeschichte der DDR*, SL 801, extended and rev. edn. (Frankfurt/M.: Luchterhand, 1989). Quotations are taken from this edn. unless otherwise stated.

—— 'Status melancholicus: Zur Transformation der Utopie in der DDR', in Arnold and Meyer-Gosau (eds.), *Literatur in der DDR: Rückblicke*, 232–245.

—— 'Gleichzeitigkeit. Vormoderne, Moderne und Postmoderne in der Literatur der DDR', in Arnold (ed.), *Bestandsaufnahme Gegenwartsliteratur*, 193–211.

—— 'Für eine andere Wahrnehmung der DDR-Literatur: Neue Kontexte, neue Paradigmen, ein neuer Kanon', in Goodbody and Tate (eds.), *Geist und Macht*, 7–22.

—— 'Im Zeichen der Wiedervereinigung: die zweite Spaltung der deutschen Literatur', in Sekretariat für kulturelle Zusammenarbeit nichttheatertragender Städte und Gemeinden in Nordrhein-Westfalen, Gütersloh (ed.), *Kultur und Macht: Deutsche Literatur 1949–1989* (Bielefeld: Aisthesis, 1992), 26–40.

ENDLER, ADOLF, 'Czechowski und andere', *NdL* 11 (1963), 137–45.

—— 'DDR Lyrik Mitte der Siebziger. Fragment einer Rezension', *ABznG* 7 (1978), 67–95.

—— *Den Tiger reiten: Aufsätze, Polemiken und Notizen zur Lyrik der DDR*, ed. Manfred Behn, SL 898 (Frankfurt/M.: Luchterhand, 1990).

—— *Tarzan am Prenzlauer Berg: Sudelblätter 1981–1983* (Leipzig: Reclam, 1994).

ENGLER, JÜRGEN, 'Form und Haltung: Steffen Menschings "Erinnerung an eine Milchglasscheibe" ', *NdL* 11 (1985), 142–6.

—— 'Hans-Eckardt Wenzel: "Lied vom Wilden Mohn" ', *WB* 8 (1985), 1360–7.

—— 'Gedrängte Kränze? Bemerkungen zum Sonett in der jüngsten Lyrik', in Eberhard Günther and Hinnerk Einhorn (eds.), *Positionen 4: Wortmeldungen zur DDR-Literatur* (Halle–Leipzig: Mitteldeutscher Verlag, 1988), 149–68.

—— 'Das Spiel ist die Regel: Gerhard Wolfs "Janus press": Bücher von Róža Domašcyna, Jan Faktor, Bert Papenfuß-Gorek, Flanzendörfer und Franz Mon', *Freitag*, 8 May 1992.

ENZENSBERGER, HANS MAGNUS, *Museum der modernen Poesie* (Frankfurt/M.: Suhrkamp, 1960; here Munich: dtv, 1964).

—— *Einzelheiten.* (Frankfurt/M.: Suhrkamp, 1962).

—— 'Meldungen vom lyrischen Betrieb', *FAZ* 14 Mar. 1989.

ERB ELKE, *Der Faden der Geduld* (Berlin and Weimar: Aufbau, 1978).

—— 'Gib zu was wir wissen!', *CONstruktiv*, 12 Dec. 1991, 13.

ERB, ROLAND, *Die Stille des Taifuns* (Berlin and Weimar: Aufbau, 1981).

ERBE, GÜNTER, 'Zum Selbstverständnis junger Lyriker in der DDR: Kolbe, Anderson, Eckart', in Margy Gerber *et al.* (eds.), *Studies in GDR Culture and Society 4* (Lanham, MD: University Press of America, 1984), 171–85.

—— 'Schriftsteller in der DDR: Eine soziologische Untersuchung der Herkunft, der Karrierewege und der Selbsteinschätzung der literarischen Intelligenz im Generationsvergleich', *Deutschland Archiv*, 11 (1987), 1162–79.

—— 'Moderne, Avantgarde und Postmoderne: Zur neueren Rezeption in der Literaturwissenschaft der DDR', Margy Gerber *et al.* (eds.), *Studies in GDR Culture and Society 6* (Lanham, MD: University Press of America, 1986), 156–72.

—— 'Writers' Careers in the GDR: A Generational Comparison', in Margy Gerber *et al.* (eds.), *Studies in GDR Culture and Society 7* (Lanham, MD: University Press of America, 1987), 155–172.

—— *Die verfemte Moderne: Die Auseinandersetzung mit dem 'Modernismus' in Kulturpolitik, Literaturwissenschaft und Literatur der DDR* (Opladen: Westdeutscher Verlag, 1993).

FEHERVARY, HELEN, *Hölderlin and the Left: The Search for a Dialectic of Art and Life* (Heidelberg: Carl Winter Universitätsverlag, 1977).

FEIST, GÜNTER (ed.), in collaboration with GILLEN, ECKHART and Museumspädagogischen Dienst, Berlin *Kunstkombinat DDR: Daten und Zitate zur Kunst und Kunstpolitik der DDR 1945–1990* (Berlin: Verlag Dirk Nishen, 1990).

FLIEGER, JAN, and TILLER, PETER, Floßfahrt (Halle/S.: Mitteldeutscher Verlag, 1977).

FLORES, JOHN, *Poetry in East Germany: Adjustments, Visions, and Provocations, 1945–1970* (New Haven: Yale University Press, 1971).

FOX, THOMAS C., 'Oobliadooh or EIKENNGETTNOSETTISFEKSCHIN: Music, Language, and Opposition in GDR Literature', *Germanic Review*, 3 (summer 1986), 109–16.

FRANKE, KONRAD, *Die Literatur der Deutschen Demokratischen Republik* (Munich: Kindler Verlag, 1971).

—— 'Glauben ersetz' ich nicht durch weiteren Glauben. Neue Literatur aus der DDR in vier Anthologien', *Süddeutsche Zeitung*, 25/26/27 May 1985.

—— 'Fuchteln gilt nicht, Anmerkung zur absurden These, die DDR-Literaturgeschichte müsse umgeschrieben werden', *Süddeutsche Zeitung*, 2 Dec. 1991.

FRANZ, MICHAEL, ' "Offene Fenster"—Schülergedichte zwischen 1967–1977', *WB* 7 (1979), 149–3.

—— 'Steffen Mensching: "Erinnerung an eine Milchglasscheibe" ', *WB* 7 (1985), 1196–200.

FUCHS, JÜRGEN, *Gedächtnisprotokolle: mit Liedern von Gerulf Pannach und einem Vorwort von Wolf Biermann* (Reinbek bei Hamburg: Rowohlt 1977).

—— 'Landschaften der Lüge: Schriftsteller im Stasi Netz (I): Der "Operative Vorgang" Fuchs', *Der Spiegel*, 18 Nov. 1991, 280–91.

—— 'Landschaften der Lüge: Schriftsteller im Stasi Netz (II) Pegasus, Spinne, Qualle, Apostel', *Der Spiegel*, 25 Nov. 1991, 72–92.

—— 'Landschaften der Lüge: Schriftsteller im Stasi Netz (III)', *Der Spiegel* 2 Dec. 1991, 94–108.

—— 'Landschaften der Lüge (IV): "Aktion Gegenschlag" im Namen Fuchs', *Der Spiegel*, 9 Dec. 1991, 103–21.

—— 'Landschaften der Luge (V): Gegen die "Konterrevolution" in Polen', *Der Spiegel*, 16 Dec. 1991, 118–30.

GASKILL, HOWARD, McPHERSON, KARIN and BARKER, ANDREW (eds.), *Neue Ansichten: The Reception of Romanticism in the Literature of the GDR*, GDR Monitor Special Series, 6 (Amsterdam: Rodopi, 1990).

GAUCK, JOACHIM, *Die Stasi-Akten: Das unheimliche Erbe der DDR*, ed. Margarethe Steinhausen und Hubertus Knabe, rororo Aktuell, 13016 (Reinbek bei Hamburg: Rowohlt, 1991).

GEISEL, SIEGLINDE, ' "Der Müll zwischen Buna und Bitterfeld": Durs Grünbeins Gedichtband Schädelbasislektion', *Die Wochenzeitung*, 16 Apr. 1992.

—— ' "In die Gegenwart verwunschen": Gedichte von Barbara Köhler', *Neue Zürcher Zeitung*, 26 July 1991.

—— 'Walkman der Poesie': Sascha Andersons "Jewish Jetset" ', *Freitag*, 15 Nov. 1991.

—— 'Die Moral des Grenzhundes: Müssen Dichter gute Menschen sein?', *Freitag*, 14 Feb. 1992.

—— ' "Die alles umfassende Dechiffriermaschine": Rainer Schedlinski und andere Autoren vom Prenzlauer Berg sprechen in der Literaturwerkstatt', *Der Tagesspiegel*, 15 Feb. 1992.

GEIßLER, CORNELIA, 'Gerüchte, Mutmaßungen, Verdächtigungen. . . Der "Fall" Sascha Anderson: Mit der Frage seiner Stasi-Mitarbeit wird eine ganze literarische Generation in Mißkredit gebracht', *Badische Zeitung*, 30 Oct. 1991.

GEIST, PETER, 'Die Gefühle und die Dinge: Sonja Schüler, "Schimmel werden schwarz geboren" ', *NdL* 4 (1983), 153–6.

—— 'Gedicht-Schreiben in der DDR zwischen Mitte der siebziger und Anfang der achtziger Jahre: Positionen—Probleme—Tendenzen' (unpublished dissertation, Karl-Marx-Universität, Leipzig, 1987).

—— 'Zu Steffen Mensching: "Erinnerung an eine Milchglasscheibe" ', in Walfried Hartinger and Klaus Schumann (eds.), *Im Blick: Junge Autoren. Lesarten zu neuen Büchern* (Halle–Leipzig: Mitteldeutscher Verlag, 1987), 67–73.

—— 'Die Metapher in der poetologischen Reflexion und Dichtungspraxis von DDR-Lyrikern in den siebziger und achtziger Jahren—Eine Problemskizze', Cosentino, Ertl, and Labroisse (eds.), *DDR-Lyrik im Kontext*, 61–87.

—— 'Gruß, Gerade, Grat—Anmerkungen zur Mickel-Rezeption bei jüngeren Lyrikern aus der DDR', *Diskussion Deutsch*, 12 (1991), 619–37.

—— 'Lyrik aus der Lychener Straße, Karl-Chemnitz-Stadt und Niemands-Land. Weniger ein Rückblick', in Deiritz and Krauss (eds.), *Verrat an der Kunst?*, 233–54.

—— ' "Mit würde holzkekse kauen"—neue Lyrik der jüngeren Generation nebst Seiten- und Rückblicken', *NdL* 2 (1993), 131–53.

—— 'Die Schatten werfen ihre Eignisse voraus: Nachsichtendes zur Lyrik aus der DDR', in Reid (ed.), *Re-assessing the GDR*, 129–52.

—— HARTINGER, CHRISTEL and WALFRIED, and WERNER, KLAUS 'Unerhörte Nachrichten: Wilhelm Bartsch, "Übungen im Joch", Uwe

Kolbe, "Bornholm II", Volker Braun, "Langsamer knirschender Morgen" ', in Siegfried Rönisch (ed.), *DDR-Literatur '87 im Gespräch* (Berlin and Weimar: Aufbau, 1988), 128–57.

GELBRICH, DOROTHEA, 'Steffen Mensching: "Erinnerung an eine Milchglasscheibe", *WB* 7 (1985), 1200–4.

—— 'Meine epikureische Traurigkeit': Hans-Eckardt Wenzels "Antrag auf Verlängerung des Monats August" ', *NdL* 11 (1987), 161–5.

GIRSHAUSEN, THEO (ed.), *Die Hamletmaschine: Heiner Müllers Endspiel* (Cologne: Prometh Verlag, 1978).

GLASS, DEREK, RÖSLER, DIETMAR and WHITE, JOHN J. (eds.), *Berlin: Literary Images of a City. Eine Großstadt im Spiegel der Literatur*, Publications of the Institute of Germanic Studies, 42 (Berlin: Erich Schmidt Verlag, 1989).

GNÜG, HILTRUD, *Entstehung und Krise lyrischer Subjektivität: Vom klassischen lyrischen Ich zur modernen Erfahrungswirklichkeit*, Germanistische Abhandlungen, 54 (Stuttgart: Metzler, 1983).

GOHLIS, TOBIAS, 'Wo das Unverbrauchte ist: Ein Besuch bei der Dichterin Gabriele Kachold', *Stuttgarter Zeitung*, 30 Jan. 1991.

GOODBODY, AXEL, and TATE, DENNIS (eds.), *Geist und Macht: Writers and the State in the GDR*, German Monitor, 29 (Amsterdam: Rodopi, 1992).

GOYKE, FRANK, 'Zweiter Ausflug in "Böhmische Wälder", weniger tief: Zu Thomas Böhme, "Die Schamlose Vergeudung des Dunkels" ', *Temperamente*, 3 (1986) 146–9.

GRÄF, DIETER M., 'Der Dichter als aus Sprache erzeugtes Gesamtkunstwerk: Avantgardist und Mystiker zwischen Mauer und Mantra: Der Belfast "Unpop"-Dichter Bert Papenfuß-Gorek und seine neuen Gedichtzyklen "Soja" ', *Basler Zeitung*, 1 Feb. 1991.

GRANT, COLIN B., 'The Departure from Dialogue in GDR Reader–Writer Relations in the 1970s and 1980s', *GDR Monitor*, 22 (summer 1990), 69–82.

GRASS, GÜNTER, *Ein Schnäppchen namens DDR: Letzte Reden vorm Glockengeläut* SL 963 (Frankfurt/M.: Luchterhand, 1990).

GRATZ, MICHAEL, 'Drei programmatische Gedichte von Dreißigjährigen', *WB* 9 (1987), 1444–8.

—— 'Leben ohne die Notdurft zum Gleichnis: Uwe Kolbe, "Bornholm II" ', *NdL* 12 (1987), 130–5.

—— 'Reden gegen die Wand im Aufwind: Michael Wüstefeld: "Heimsuchung" ', *NdL* 1 (1989) 155–7.

—— 'Weiter im Text . . . oder raus ausm Text?: Zu Hans Brinkmann: "Federn oder Federn lassen" ', *Temperamente*, 4 (1989), 145–7.

—— 'Umbau der Bühne bei Laufende Probe: Gedanken zu Gedanken von Wenzel und Schedlinski', *WB* 6 (1989), 1052–4.

—— 'Schreiben gegen Verfestigungen: Zu Bert Papenfuß-Gorek,

"dreizehntanz", Rainer Schedlinski, "die rationen des ja und des nein" ', *NdL* 11 (1989), 163–8.

—— 'Sprachspiel gegen Bewußtseinsbesetzung. Eine andere politische Dichtung aus der DDR', *Diskussion Deutsch*, 12 (1991), 606–18.

—— 'Was sollte sich daran ändern? Anmerkung zur Debatte um DDR-Literatur und "Unterground-Kultur" ', *NdL* 4 (1992), 159–63.

GREINER, BERNHARD, 'Zersprungene Identität: Bildnisse des Schriftstellers in zeitgenössischen Dichtungen über Hölderlin', in Karl Lamers (ed.), *Die deutsche Teilung im Spiegel der Literatur: Beiträge zur Literatur und Germanistik der DDR* (Bonn: Verlag Bonn Aktuell; 2nd edn. 1978), 85–120.

—— *Literatur der DDR in neuer Sicht: Studien und Interpretationen*, Literarhistorische Untersuchungen, 5 (Frankfurt/M. Peter Lang, 1986).

GREINER, ULRICH, 'Das Phantom der Nation: Warum wir keine Nation sind und warum wir keine werden müssen—ein vergeblicher Zwischenruf im Intellektuellenstreit um die deutsche Einheit', *Die Zeit*, 16 Mar. 1990.

—— 'Mangel an Feingefühl', *Die Zeit*, 1 June 1990.

—— 'Was bleibt? Bleibt was?', *Die Zeit*, 1 June 1990.

—— 'Keiner ist frei von Schuld. Deutscher Literaturstreit: Der Fall Christa Wolf und die Intellektuellen', *Die Zeit*, 25 July 1990.

—— 'Die deutsche Gesinnungsästhetik. Noch einmal: Christa Wolf und der deutsche Literaturstreit', *Die Zeit*, 2 Nov. 1990.

—— 'Der Ursprung der Lüge: Die Auseinandersetzung über die Stasi-Vergangenheit läuft falsch', *Die Zeit*, 3 Jan. 1992.

—— 'Die Falle des Entweder-Oder', *Die Zeit*, 24 Jan. 1992.

—— 'Plädoyer für den Schluß der Stasi-Debatte', *Die Zeit*, 5 Feb. 1993.

GRIMM, ERIK, 'Der Tod der Ostmoderne oder Die BRDigung des DDR-Untergrunds: Zur Lyrik Bert Papenfuß-Goreks', *ZfG*, 1 (1991), 9–20.

GROSZ, CHRISTIANE, *Blatt vor dem Mund* (Berlin and Weimar: Aufbau, 1983).

GRUNENBERG, ANTONIA, *Aufbruch der inneren Mauer: Politik und Kultur in der DDR 1971–1990* (Bremen: Edition Temmen, 1990).

—— ' "Ich finde mich überhaupt nicht mehr zurecht . . ." Drei Thesen zur Krise in der Geschichte der DDR', in Ilse Spittmann and Gisela Hellwig (eds.), *Die DDR auf dem Wege zur deutschen Einheit. Probleme. Perspektiven. Offene Fragen*, xxiii. Tagung zum Stand der DDR-Forschung in der Bundesrepublik Deutschland (Cologne: Edition Deutschland Archiv, 1990), 47–58.

GÜNTHER, THOMAS, 'Die subkulturellen Zeitschriften in der DDR und ihre kulturgeschichtliche Bedeutung', in 'Aus Politik und Zeitgeschichte', *Das Parlament*, 8 May 1992, 27–36.

HAASE, HORST, 'Steffen Mensching: "Erinnerung an eine Milchglasscheibe" ', *WB* 7 (1985), 1204–6.

—— *et al.* (eds.), *Geschichte der deutschen Literatur von den Anfängen bis zur Gegenwart*, xi. *Literatur der DDR* (Berlin: Verlag Volk und Wissen, 1976).

HAASE, NORBERT, REESE, LOTHAR, and WENSIERSKI, PETER (eds.), *VEB Nachwuchs: Jugend in der DDR* (Reinbek bei Hamburg: Rowohlt, 1983).

HAFNER, KATIE, 'A Nation of Readers Dumps its Writers', *New York Times*, 10 Jan. 1993, 23–6 and 45–8.

HAGE, VOLKER, 'Kunstvolle Prosa', *Die Zeit*, 1 June 1990.

—— ' "Wir müssen uns dem Schicksal stellen": Über den Fall von Christa Wolf', *Der Spiegel*, 8 Feb. 1993, 197–9.

HAGEMANN, KATRIN, 'Die Analyse der Wertvorstellungen und Lebensorientierungen in der jungen Lyrik der DDR' (unpublished dissertation, Akademie für Gesellschaftswissen beim ZK der SED. Institut für marxistisch-leninistische Kultur und Kunstwissenschaften, Berlin, 1985).

HÄHNEL, INGRID (ed.), *Lyriker im Zwiegespräch. Traditionsbeziehungen im Gedicht* (Berlin and Weimar: Aufbau, 1981).

—— 'Steffen Mensching: "Erinnerung an eine Milchglasscheibe" ', *WB* 7 (1985), 1207–10.

—— and HÄHNEL, KLAUS-DIETER, 'Junge Lyrik am Ende der siebziger Jahre', *WB* 9 (1981), 127–53.

HAMM, PETER, ' "Glück ist schwer in diesem Land": Zur Situation der jüngsten DDR-Lyrik' in *Merkur*, 19 (1965), 365–99.

HARTINGER, CHRISTEL and WALFRIED, 'Unterwegs in der Erfahrung. Zeitgenossenschaft und lyrische Subjektivität', in Walter *et al.* (eds.), *Ansichten*, 340–469.

—— 'Zeitgenossenschaft und Lyrische Subjektivität (Lyrikdiskussion in Leipzig)', *WB* 10 (1977), 80–104.

—— 'Von Horizonten und Grenzen: Zum Charakter zeitgenössischer lyrischer Subjektivität', in Siegfried Rönisch (ed.), *DDR-Literatur '83 im Gespräch* (Berlin and Weimar: Aufbau, 1984, 268–94.

—— 'Zu Hans-Eckardt Wenzel: "Lied vom wilden Mohn" ', in Walfried Hartinger and Klaus Schuhmann (eds.), *Im Blick: Junge Autoren. Lesarten zu neuen Büchern* (Halle–Leipzig; Mitteldeutscher Verlag, 1987).

—— and WERNER, KLAUS, 'DDR Lyrik der siebziger und achtziger Jahre: Thesen', *WB* 12 (1990), 1986–92.

HARTINGER, WALFRIED, ' "Vom Machen einleuchtender Bilder": Versuche zur geschichtlichen Positionsbestimmung in der Lyrik in der DDR'. in Nalewski and Schuhmann (eds.), *Selbsterfahrung als Welterfahrung*, 5–20.

—— 'DDR-Debüts in der Reihe "Poesiealbum" ', *Temperamente*, 3 (1980), 148–53.

—— 'Gedichte im Gespräch: Zur Produktion, Vermittlung und Rezeption der DDR-Lyrik', in John L. Flood (ed.), *Ein Moment des erfahrenen Lebens: Zur Lyrik der DDR* (GDR Monitor Special Series, 5 (Amsterdam: Rodopi, 1987), 6–21.

HARTLEY, GEORGE, *Textual Politics and the Language Poets* (Bloomington and Indianapolis: Indiana University Press, 1989).

HARTMANN, ANNELI, *Lyrik-Anthologien als Indikatoren des literarischen und gestellschaftlichen Prozesses in der DDR (1949–1971)*, Deutsche Sprache und Literatur, 643 (Frankfurt/M.: Peter Lang, 1983).

—— 'Neue Tendenzen in der DDR-Lyrik', *Deutsche Studien*, 85 (1984), 5–29.

—— 'Der Generationswechsel—ein ästhetischer Wechsel? Schreibweisen und Traditionsbezüge in der jüngsten DDR-Lyrik', in Paul Gerhard Klussmann and Heinrich Mohr (eds.), *Jahrbuch zur Literatur in der DDR 4* (Bonn: Bouvier, 1985), 109–34.

—— 'Schreiben in der Tradition der Avantgarde. Neue Lyrik in der DDR', in Cosentino, Ertl, and Labroisse (eds.), *DDR-Lyrik im Kontext*, 1–37.

—— 'Berührung ist nur eine Randerscheinung', *Colloquia Germanica*, 21 (1988), 94–5.

HARTUNG, HARALD, 'Die ästhetische und soziale Kritik der Lyrik', in Hans-Jürgen Schmitt (ed.), *Die Literatur der DDR*, Hansers Sozialgeschichte der deutschen Literatur, xi. (Munich: Hanser, 1983).

—— *Deutsche Lyrik seit 1965. Tendenzen Beispiele, Porträts*, SP447 (Munich: Piper, 1985).

—— 'Tagträume in der Grauzone: Gedichte von Durs Grünbein', *FAZ* 24 Oct. 1988.

—— 'Placebos, Kwerdeutsch, Vaterlandkanal: Anmerkungen zur jungen Lyrik', *Merkur*, 12 (Dec. 1991), 1145–52.

—— 'Die Eltern sind viel zu nett. Lyrik auf dem Weg von Prenzlauer Berg in die Bundesrepublik', *FAZ* 8 Aug. 1991.

—— *Luftfracht: Internationale Poesie 1940–1990* (Frankfurt/M.: Eichborn, 1991).

—— ' "Klappe zu, Aleph tot": Bert Papenfuß-Gorek versucht sich als Anarchist', *FAZ* 14 Dec. 1992.

HARVEY, DAVID, *The Condition of Postmodernity: An Enquiry into the Origins of Cultural Change* (Oxford: Blackwell, 1990).

HASENFELDER, ULF CHRISTIAN, 'Die Generation, die nicht zu sich kommen durfte: Junge Avantgarde der ehemaligen DDR', *Der Literat*, 4 Apr. 1991, 18–20.

—— 'Die Generation, die nicht zu sich kommen durfte' (Fortsetzung), *Der Literat*, 5 May 1991, 16–19.

—— 'Kwerdeutsch. Die dritte Literatur in der DDR', *NdL* 1 (1991), 82–94.

HAVEL, VÁCLAV, *Václav Havel or Living in Truth*, ed. Jan Vladislav (London: Faber, 1986).

HEINRITZ, REINHARD, ' "Prenzlauer Berg": Über experimentelle Literatur und Politik', *Literatur für Leser*, 3 (1992), 181–93.

HENKEL, JENS, and RUSS, SABINE (eds.), *D1980D1989R: Künstlerbücher und Originalgrafische Zeitschriften im Eigenverlag: Eine Bibliographie* (Gifkendorf: Merlin, 1991).

HESSE, EGMONT, 'sprachabbruch und umbruch des sprechens', in *Zellinnendruck*, 16–20.

HEUKENKAMP, MARIANNE and URSULA, 'Fragen zwischen den Generationen: Kerstin Hensel: "Stilleben mit Zukunft" ', *NdL* 6 (1989), 132–6.

HEUKENKAMP, URSULA, 'Poesie und Poetik. Unmittelbarkeit in der Gegenwartslyrik', *WB* 10 (1977), 113–38.

—— 'Gedanken zur jungen Lyrik', *NdL* 2 (1978), 110–18.

—— 'Wandel einer Mitteilung', *SuF* 5 (1978), 1079–91.

—— 'Das Ungenügen an der Idylle', *SuF* 5 (1981), 1120–30.

—— 'Kunstbewußtsein und geistige Strenge. Zur Entwicklung der Lyrik in der DDR der siebziger Jahre', in P. U. Hohendahl and P. Herminghouse (eds.), *Literatur der DDR in den siebziger Jahren*, 82–113.

—— 'Dichterporträts', in Ingrid Hähnel (ed.), *Lyrik im Zwiegespräch*, 217–64.

—— 'Funktion und Ausdruck: Gedanken zu einer Anthologie neuer Lyrik', in Siegfried Rönisch (ed.), *DDR-Literatur '83 im Gespräch* (Berlin and Weimar: Aufbau, 1984), 295–302.

—— 'Metapher der Befreiung: Volker Braun, "Das innerste Afrika" ', in Siegfried Rönisch (ed.), *DDR-Literatur '87 im Gespräch* (Berlin and Weimar: Aufbau, 1988), 184–96.

—— KAHLAU, HEINZ, and KIRSTEN, WULF (eds.), *Die eigene Stimme: Lyrik der DDR* (Berlin and Weimar: Aufbau, 1988).

HEYM, STEFAN, *Auf Sand gebaut: Sieben Geschichten aus der unmittelbaren Vergangenheit* (Munich: Wilhelm Goldmann Verlag, 1990).

—— 'Aschermittwoch in der DDR', in Michael Naumann (ed.), *"Die Geschichte ist offen": DDR 1990: Hoffnung auf eine neue Republik. Schriftsteller aus der DDR über die Zukunftschancen ihres Landes*, rororo aktuell, 12814 (Reinbek bei Hamburg: Rowohlt, 1990), 71–8.

—— and HEIDUCZEK, WERNER, in collaboration with CZECHOWSKI, INGRID, *Die sanfte Revolution*, (Leipzig und Weimar: Gustav Kiepenheuer Verlag, 1990).

HILBIG, WOLFGANG, die versprengung: gedichte (Frankfurt/M.: Fischer, 1986).

—— 'Über Jayne-Ann Igel', *SuF* 2 (1991), 295–9.

—— *"Ich": Roman* (Frankfurt/M.: Fischer, 1993).

HÖBEL, WOLFGANG, ' "Auch ich habe Verhörprotokolle unterschrieben": Ein Porträt des Berliner Autors und Denunziationsopfers Rainer Schedlinski', *Süddeutsche Zeitung*, 28 Oct. 1991.

—— 'Gewitterwolken über die Oase. Die Vorwürfe gegen Sascha Anderson: Zerfällt der Mythos vom Prenzluaer Berg?', *Süddeutsche Zeitung*, 2 Dec. 1991.

HOHENDAHL, PETER UWE, and HERMINGHOUSE, PATRICIA (eds.), *Literatur und Literaturtheorie in der DDR*, es 779 (Frankfurt/M.: Suhrkamp, 1976).

—— *Literatur der DDR in den siebziger Jahren*, es 1174 (Frankfurt/M.: Suhrkamp, 1983).

HÖLDERLIN, FRIEDRICH, *Sämtliche Werke*, Große Stuttgarter Ausgabe, ed. Friedrich Beißner and Adolf Beck (8 vols.; Stuttgart: W. Kohlhammer Verlag, 1943–85).

HÖRNIGK, FRANK, 'Die künstlerische Intelligenz und der Umbruch in der DDR', in Ilse Spittmann and Gisela Hellwig (eds.), *Die DDR auf dem Wege zur deutschen Einheit. Probleme. Perspektiven. Offene Fragen*, xxiii. Tagung zum Stand der DDR-Forschung in der Bundesrepublik Deutschland (Cologne: Edition Deutschland Archiv, 1990), 137–45.

—— 'Die Literatur bleibt zuständig: Ein Versuch über das Verhältnis von Literatur, Utopie und Politik in der DDR—am Ende der DDR', *Germanic Review*, Theme Issue: 'The End of GDR Literature', 3 (summer 1992), 99–105.

HUTCHEON, LINDA, *The Politics of Postmodernism* (London: Routledge, 1989).

HUYSSEN, ANDREAS, 'After the Wall: The Failure of German Intellectuals', *New German Critique*, Special Issue on German Unification, 52 (winter 1991), 109–13.

—— and SCHERPE, KLAUS R. (eds.), *Postmoderne: Zeichen eines kulturellen Wandels* (Reinbek bei Hamburg: Rowohlt, 1986).

JÄGER, ANDREA, 'Schriftsteller-Identität und Zensur: Über die Bedingungen des Schreibens im "realen Sozialismus" ', in Arnold (ed.), *Literatur in der DDR. Rückblicke*, 137–48.

JÄGER, MANFRED, 'Subjektivität als politische Kategorie. Zur Emanzipationsgeschichte der Lyrik in der DDR', in Jordan, Marquardt and Woesler (eds.), *Lyrik von allen Seiten*, 304–16.

—— ' "Wem schriebe ich": Adressen und Botschaften in Gedichten jüngerer Autoren aus der DDR seit dem Beginn der achziger Jahre', in *Die andere Sprache*, 61–71.

JAMESON, FREDRIC, 'The Politics of Theory: Ideological Positions in the Postmodern Debate', *New German Critique*, 33 (Fall 1984), 53–65.

JANETZKI, ULRICH, and RATH, WOLFGANG (eds.), *Tendenz Freisprache: Texte zu einer Poetik der achtziger Jahre*, es 1675 (Frankfurt/M.: Suhrkamp, 1992).

JANKA, WALTER, *Schwierigkeiten mit der Wahrheit*, rororo aktuell, 12731 (Reinbek bei Hamburg: Rowohlt, 1989).

JARMATZ, KLAUS, 'Erkundungen, Erfahrungen, Erwartungen (I)', *NdL* 3 (1983), 124–35.

—— 'Erkundungen, Erfahrungen, Erwartungen (II)', *NdL* 4 (1983), 127–38.

—— 'Laß uns laufen lernen: Steffen Mensching: "Erinnerung an eine Milchglasscheibe" ', *Kritik 85: Rezensionen zur DDR-Literatur* (Halle–Leipzig: Mitteldeutscher Verlag, 1986), 145–8.

—— ' "Was bleibt, stiften die Dichter": Nachdenkliches zu einer Diskussion um die DDR-Literatur', *tacheles*, 10 (1990), 34–7.

JENNY-EBELING, CHARITAS, ' "mit doppeltem boden": Zum Beispiel: Rainer Schedlinski', *Neue Zürcher Zeitung*, 24 Mar. 1992.

—— ' "Jeder Text ist ein Wortbruch": Leonce-und-Lena-Preis an Kathrin Schmidt', *Neue Zürcher Zeitung*, 30 Mar. 1993.

JENS, WALTER, 'Plädoyer gegen die Preisgabe der DDR-Kultur: Fünf Forderungen an die Intellektuellen im geeinten Deutschland', *Süddeutsche Zeitung*, 16/17 June 1990.

JORDAN, LOTHAR, MARQUARDT, AXEL, and WOESLER, WINFRIED (eds.), *Lyrik von allen Seiten. Gedichte und Aufsätze des ersten Lyrikertreffens in Münster*, Collection S. Fischer, 2320 (Frankfurt/M.: Fischer, 1981).

—— *Lyrik—Blick über die Grenzen. Gedichte und Aufsätze des 2. Lyrikertreffens in Münster*, Collection S. Fischer, 2336 (Frankfurt/M.: Fischer, 1984).

—— *Lyrik—Erlebnis und Kritik: Gedichte und Aufsätze des 3. und 4. Lyrikertreffens in Münster*, Collection S. Fischer, 2359 (Frankfurt/M.: Fischer, 1988).

KANE, MARTIN, 'From Oobliadooh to Prenzlauer Berg: Literature, Alternative Lifestyle and Identity in the GDR', in Goodbody and Tate (eds.), *Geist und Macht*, 90–103.

—— (ed.), *Socialism and the Literary Imagination: Essays on East German Writers* (Oxford: Berg, 1991).

KARASEK, HELLMUTH, 'Selbstgemachte Konfitüre: Über die Diskussion um Christa Wolfs Erzählung "Was bleibt" ', *Der Spiegel*, 25 June 1990, 162–8.

KAUFMANN, HANS, 'Veränderte Literaturlandschaft', *WB* 1 (1981), 27–53.

—— and KAUFMANN, EVA (eds.), *Erwartung und Angebot. Studien zum gegenwärtigen Verhältnis von Literatur und Gesellschaft in der DDR* (Berlin: Akademie Verlag, 1976).

—— *et al.* (eds.), *Tendenzen und Beispiele. Zur DDR Literatur in den siebziger Jahren* (Leipzig: Verlag Philipp Reclam jun., 1981).

KEITH-SMITH, BRIAN, ' "Little Magazines from the Former German Democratic Republic—A Survey', *German Monitor*, 26 (1992), 64–93.

KIRSCH, RAINER, 'Meinen Freunden, den alten Genossen', *NdL* 11 (1963), 99.

KLEINSCHMIDT, CLAUDIA, 'Spannungszustände: Porträt Gabriele Kachold', *Sonntag*, 14 Jan. 1990.

KLUGE, GERHARD, 'Die Rehabilitierung des Ich: Einige Bermerkungen zu Themen und Tendenzen in der Lyrik der DDR', in Wolfgang Kuttenkeuler (ed.), *Poesie und Politik: Zur Situation der Literatur in Deutschland* (Stuttgart: W. Kohlhammer, 1973), 206–35.

KNABE, HUBERTUS (ed.), *Aufbruch in eine andere DDR: Reformer und Oppositionelle zur Zukunft ihres Landes* (Reinbek bei Hamburg: Rowohlt, 1989).

KOPELEW, LEW, 'Für Christa Wolf', *die tageszeitung*, 14 June 1990.

KORN, BENJAMIN, 'Bald Schwein, bald Schmetterling, oder: Die Moral der Kunst ist die Moral', *Die Zeit*, 20 Dec. 1991.

KORTE, HERMANN, *Geschichte der deutschen Lyrik seit 1945*, SM 250 (Stuttgart: Metzler, 1989).

KRAMER, JANE, 'Letter from Europe', *New Yorker*, 25 May 1992, 40–64.

KREUZER, HELMUT (ed.), *Pluralismus und Postmodernismus: Zur Literatur- und Kulturgeschichte der achtziger Jahre*, Forschungen zur Literatur- und Kulturgeschichte, 25, 2nd edn., rev. and expanded (Frankfurt/M.: Peter Lang, 1991).

KRIEGER, HANS, 'Die neue Unfähigkeit zu trauern. Nachbemerkung zu Wolf Biermann und seinen "lieben Ossis" ', *NdL* 1 (1992), 165–8.

KRIPPENDORF, KLAUS, 'Unruhestiftender Lärm oder Weltentwurf? Die Anfänge zweier Lyrikergenerationen', in Richter (ed.), *Generationen, Temperamente, Schreibweisen: DDR Literatur in neuer Sicht*, 242–71.

KROH, FERDINAND (ed.), *'Freiheit ist immer Freiheit . . .': Die Andersdenkenden in der DDR*, Ullstein Buch, 34489 (Berlin: Ullstein, 1989).

KRUSE, WERNER, CHRIST, RICHARD, and DEICKE, GÜNTHER (eds.), *Himmel meiner Stadt. Aus der Werkstatt der Gruppe 'alex 64'* (Berlin: Verlag der Nation, 1966).

KUHLBRODT, DETLEF, 'Café Kiryl am Prenzelberg: Jagdszenen und Alltagsnotizen aus Ost-Berlin', *Frankfurter Rundschau*, 22 Feb. 1992.

KUHN, ANNA K., 'Rewriting GDR history: The Christa Wolf Controversy', *GDR Bulletin*, 1 (1991), 7–11.

—— ' "Eine Königin Köpfen ist effektiver als einen König köpfen": The Gender Politics of the Christa Wolf Controversy', in Elizabeth Boa and Janet Wharton (eds.), *Women and the Wende: Social Effects and Cultural Reflections of the German Unification Process*, German Monitor, 31 (Amsterdam: Rodopi, 1994), 200–15.

KUNERT, GÜNTER, *Verkündigung des Wetters: Gedichte* (Munich: Hanser, 1966).

—— *Stilleben* (Munich: Hanser, 1983).

—— *Vor der Sintflut: Das Gedicht als Arche Noah* (Munich: Hanser, 1985).

—— *Berlin beizeiten* (Munich: Hanser, 1987).

—— (ed.), *Aus fremder Heimat. Zur Exilsituation heutiger Literatur* (Munich: Hanser, 1988).

—— 'Zur Staatssicherheit: Poesie und Verbrechen', *FAZ* 6 Nov. 1991.

—— *Der Sturz vom Sockel: Feststellungen und Widersprüche* (Munich: Hanser, 1992).

—— 'Fortgesetzt was geht', *NdL* 6 (1993), 5–11.

KUNZE, REINER, *Deckname 'Lyrik'*, Fischer Taschenbuch, 10854 (Frankfurt/M.: Fischer, 1990).

LAATZ, HORST, 'Keine Gerechtigkeit für IM "Hölderlin"?', *Das Parlament*, 29 Jan. 1993, 13.

LABROISSE, GERD, 'Neue Positionen in der DDR-Lyrik der 8oer Jahre?', in Ian Wallace (ed.), *The GDR in the 1980s*, GDR Monitor Special Series, 4 (Dundee: [n.pub.], 1984), 101–19.

—— 'Lyrische Frauenliteratur der DDR', in Chiarloni, Sartori, and Cambi (eds.), *Die Literatur der DDR 1976–1986*, 287–303.

—— 'Frauenliteratur-Lyrik in der DDR', in Cosentino, Ertl, and Labroisse (eds.), *DDR-Lyrik im Kontext*, 145–194.

—— 'The Literatur of the GDR and the Revoltion of 1989/90', *German Monitor*, 26 (1992), 37–49.

—— 'Das Erfahren von Geschichte in der DDR-Lyrik der 8oer Jahre', in Labroisse and Visser (eds.), *Im Blick behalten*, 135–52.

—— and VISSER, ANTHONYA (eds.), *Im Blick behalten: Lyrik der DDR*, Neue Beiträge des Forschungsprojekts DDR-Literatur an der Vrije Universiteit Amsterdam, German Monitor, 32 (Amsterdam: Rodopi, 1994).

—— and WALLACE, IAN (eds.), *DDR-Schriftsteller sprechen in der Zeit: Eine Dokumentation*, German Monitor, 27 (Amsterdam: Rodopi, 1991).

LASCHEN, GREGOR, *Lyrik in der DDR. Literatur und Reflexion* (Frankfurt/M.: Athenäum 1971).

LEEDER, KAREN, 'Towards a profane Holderlin: Representations and Revisions of Hölderlin in some GDR poetry', in Gaskill, McPherson, and Barker (eds.), *Neue Ansichten: The Reception of Romanticism in the Literature of the GDR*, 212–31.

—— ' "Poesie ist eine Gegensprache": Young GDR Poets in Search of a Political Identity', in Arthur Williams, Stuart Parkes, and Roland Smith (eds.), *German Literature at a Time of Change 1989–1990: German Unity and German Identity in Literary Perspective*, (Frankfurt/M.: Peter Lang, 1991), 413–28.

—— ' "eine abstellhalle des authentischen": Postmodernism and Poetry in the New Germany', in Arthur Williams and Stuart Parkes (eds.), *The Individual, Identity and Innovation: Signals from Contemporary Literature and the New Germany* (Frankfurt/M.: Peter Lang, 1994), 201–20.

LEISTNER, BERND, *Unruhe um einen Klassiker. Zum Goethe-Bezug in der neueren DDR-Literatur* (Halle–Leipzig: Mitteldeutscher Verlag, 1978).

—— ' "... Dich zu treiben bis aufs Blut": Steffen Mensching, "Erinnerung an eine Milchglasscheibe", Hans-Eckardt Wenzel, "Lied vom wilden Mohn" ', *SuF* 5 (1985), 1094–1102.

—— 'Einkehr in eine deutsche Tradition? Thomas Böhme: "Stoff der Piloten" ', *NdL* 1 (1989), 149–52.

LEISTENSCHNEIDER, PETER, 'Spiegelfrau und Rapunzel: Gedichte von Kerstin Hensel und von Barbara Köhler', *Freitag*, 13 Sept. 1991.

LEPENIES, WOLF, *Aufstieg und Fall der Intellektuellen in Europa* (Frankfurt/M.: Suhrkamp, 1992).

—— 'Das Ende der Utopie und die Rückkehr der Melancholie: Blick auf die Intellektuellen eines alten Kontinents', in Meyer (ed.), *Intellektuellendämmerung? Beiträge zur neuesten Zeit des Geistes*, 15–26.

LERMEN, BIRGIT, ' "Über die ganze Szene fliegt Ikarus": Das Ikarus-Motiv in ausgewählten Gedichten von Autoren aus der DDR', in Dieter Breuer (ed.), *Deutsche Lyrik nach 1945* (Frankfurt/M.: Suhrkamp, 1988), 284–305.

LETHEN, HELMUT, and BERENDSE, GERRIT-JAN, 'Im Zeichen der Kentauren: Überlegungen zu dem Gedicht "Die Elbe" von Karl Mickel (1973)', in Paul Gerhard Klussmann and Heinrich Mohr (eds.), *Jahrbuch zur Literatur in der DDR 6* (Bonn: Bouvier, 1987), 119–42.

LOEST, ERICH, *Der Stasi war mein Eckermann, oder, mein Leben mit der Wanze* (Göttingen: Steidl, 1992).

LORENC, KITO, *Wortland: Gedichte* (Leipzig: Verlag Philipp Reclam jun., 1984).

LYOTARD, JEAN-FRANÇOIS, *The Postmodern Condition: A Report on Knowledge*, tr. Geoff Bennington and Brian Massumi, Theory and History of Literature, 10 (Manchester: Manchester University Press, 1984; 5th edn. 1991).

MCCAFFERY, STEVE, 'The Death of the Subject: The Implications of Counter-Communication in Recent Language-Centred Writing', *L=A=N=G=U=A=G=E*, 1 (1980).

MCELVOY, ANNE, 'Staying on for Better or Worse', *The Times*, 15 Sept. 1989.

MADEA, ANDREJ, 'Das ES gegen das ICH: Neue Texte von Kerstin Hensel und Gabriele Kachold', *Freitag*, 21 Dec. 1990.

MADEI, PETER, 'Zu viel Sand in der Sanduhr? Zu Thomas Böhme, "Mit der Sanduhr am Gürtel" ', *Temperamente*, 3 (1984), 149–51.

MANGEL, RÜDIGER, SCHNABEL, STEFAN, STAATSMANN, PETER (eds.), DEUTSCH *in einem anderen* LAND: *Die DDR (1949–1990) in Gedichten* (Berlin: Edition Hentrich, 1990).

MARX, KARL, 'Der achtzehnte Brumaire des Louis Bonaparte', in *Karl*

Marx, Friedrich Engels, Sudienausgabe in 4 Bänden, ed. Iring Fetscher (Frankfurt/M.: Fischer, 1966; 9th edn. 1980) iv. 34–121.

MATT, BEATRICE VON, 'Generationswechel in der Literatur der DDR', *Neue Zürcher Zeitung*, 18 Apr. 1986.

MATTENKLOTT, GERT, 'Botschaften aus Retrograd: Aspekte der intellektuellen Situation', in Meyer (ed.), *Intellektuellendämmerung? Beiträge zur neuesten Zeit des Geistes*, 96–109.

MAYER, HANS, *Außenseiter*, st 736 (Frankfurt/M.: Suhrkamp, 1981).

—— *Der Turm von Babel: Erinnerung an eine Deutsche Demokratische Republik*, st 2174 (Frankfurt/M.: Suhrkamp, 1991, 2nd edn. 1993).

MEINHARD, PERSICKE, 'Tendenzen der Lyrik von Jugendlichen der 70er Jahre in der DDR 1973–1980' (unpublished dissertation, Pädigogische Hochschule, Dresden, 1984).

MEINICKE, MICHAEL, *Junge Autoren in der DDR 1975–1980*, (Düsseldorf: drei-ECK Verlag, [n.d.]).

MEYER, MARTIN (ed.), *Intellektuellendämmerung? Beiträge zur neuesten Zeit des Geistes* (Munich: Hanser, 1992).

MICHAEL, KLAUS, 'Die Dinge beginnen zu sprechen: Zu Rainer Schedlinski, "die rationen des ja und des nein"', *Temperamente*, 4 (1989), 147–50.

—— 'Papierboote', in Muschter and Thomas (eds.), *Jenseits der Staatskultur*, 62–82.

—— 'Einige junge Lyriker dezentralisieren: Sascha Anderson: Machtspiele und Freundesverrat in der Ostberliner Literatenszene', *Focus*, 4 (1993), 80.

—— 'In den Stasi-Akten findet sich der zweite Text der DDR. Pläydoyer für eine Weiterführung der Debatte über das Erbe des untergangenen Staates', *Berliner Zeitung*, 6/7 Mar. 1993.

MICKEL, KARL, 'Lesarten: Das Einfache das selten gelingt', *NdL* 8 (1980), 67–71.

—— 'Aussagen über Papenfuss', *SuF* 6 (1986), 1230–31.

MIKA, BASCHA, and SCHEUB, UTE, 'Untergrundhelden und Stasi-Spitzel am Prenzelberg', *die tageszeitung*, 11 Jan. 1992.

MIŁOSZ, CZESLAW, *The Captive Mind*, tr. Jane Zielonko (London: Penguin, 1981; repr. 1985).

MISCHKE, ROLAND, ' "Diese tierische Menschheit". Eine Anthologie mit "Neuer Literatur aus der DDR" ', *FAZ* 24 Sept. 1985.

MITSCHERLICH, ALEXANDER and MARGARETE, *Die Unfähigkeit zu trauern: Grundlagen kollektiven Verhaltens*, SP 168 (Munich: Piper, 1967; 21st edn. 1990).

MOHR, REINHARD, *Zaungäste: Die Generation, die nach der Revolte kam* (Frankfurt/M.: Fischer, 1992).

MÜHSAM, ERICH, *Gedichte Prosa Stücke* (Berlin: Verlag Volk und Welt, 1978).

Müller, Heiner, *Traktor*, in *Geschichten aus der Produktion 2* (Berlin/ W.: Rotbuch, 1974, repr. 1991), 9–24.

—— 'Wie es bleibt, is es nicht. Zu Thomas Braschs "Kargo" ', *Der Spiegel*, 12 Sept. 1977, repr. in Müller, *Rotwelsch*, 150–5.

—— 'Fatzer ± Keuner', in *Rotwelsch*, 140–9.

—— *Die Hamletmaschine*, repr. in *Mauser* (Berlin/W.:Rotbuch, 1980).

—— *Rotwelsch* (Berlin/W.: Merve Verlag, 1982).

—— *Verkommenes Ufer Medeamaterial Landschaft mit Argonauten*, in *Herzstück* (Berlin: Rotbuch, 1983), 91–101.

—— ' "Ohne Hoffnung, ohne Verzweiflung": Spiegel-Interview mit dem DDR-Dramatiker Heiner Müller in Ost Berlin', *Der Spiegel*, 4 Dec. 1989, 264–5.

—— '*Jenseits der Nation*', (Berlin: Rotbuch, 1991).

—— *Krieg ohne Schlacht: Leben in zwei Diktaturen* (Cologne: Kiepenheuer & Witsch, 1992).

—— *Gedichte* (Berlin: Alexander Verlag, 1992).

—— ' "Es gibt ein Menschenrecht auf Feigheit": Ein Gespräch mit dem Dramatiker Heiner Müller über seine Kontakte mit der Staatssicherheit', *Frankfurter Rundschau*, 22 May 1993.

—— ' "Stalingrad war eigentlich das Ende der DDR". Gespräch mit Heiner Müller über den 17. Juni und den Untergang des Realsozialismus', *Freitag*, 18 June 1993.

Müller, Veit-Ulrich, 'Stillhalteliteratur in Ost und West', *FAZ* 13 Oct. 1990.

Müller, Wolfgang, 'Recent Lyric Poetry in the GDR', *Germanic Notes*, 3 (1986), 37–40.

—— 'Personal Experience and Recent GDR Literature', *Monatshefte*, 1 (spring, 1989), 90–103.

—— 'Die Kunst der (simulierten?) Rebellion: Zur Lyrik aus Prenzlauer Berg', *GDR Bulletin*, 2 (Fall 1992), 21–6.

Muschter, Gabriele, and Thomas, Rüdiger (eds.), *Jenseits der Staatskultur: Traditionen autonomer Kunst in der DDR* (Munich: Hanser, 1992).

Nádas, Péter, 'Armer Sascha Anderson', tr. from the Hungarian Zsuzsanna Gahse, in *Kursbuch*, 108 (July 1992), 163–88.

Nagel, Ivan, 'Die Volksfeinde: Literaturstreit und Intellektuellenjagd', *Süddeutsche Zeitung*, 22/3 Dec. 1990.

Nalewski, Horst, and Schuhmann, Klaus, (eds.), *Selbsterfahrung als Welterfahrung: DDR Literatur in den siebziger Jahren* (Berlin and Weimar: Aufbau, 1981).

Naumann, Michael (ed.), '*Die Geschichte ist offen': DDR 1990: Hoffnung auf eine neue Republik. Schriftsteller aus der DDR über die Zukunftschancen ihres Landes*, rororo aktuell, 12814 (Reinbek bei Hamburg: Rowohlt, 1990).

NEUMANN, GERD, *Die Schuld der Worte* (Rostock: Hinstorff Verlag, 1979).

—— 'Geheimsprache "Klandestinität" ', in *Sprache & Antwort*, 129–44.

—— 'Die Wörter des reinen Denkens', in *abriss der ariadnefabrik*, 249–54.

New German Critique, Modernity and Postmodernity, 33 (Fall 1984).

New German Critique, Special Issue on German Unification, 52 (winter 1991).

NORRIS, CHRISTOPHER, *What's Wrong with Postmodernism: Critical Theory and the Ends of Philosophy* (New York, London: Harvester Wheatsheaf, 1990).

NOVAK, HELGA M., 'Offener Brief an Wolf Biermann, Sarah Kirsch und Jürgen Fuchs', *Der Spiegel*, 28 Oct. 1991, 329.

Oktober 1989: Wider den Schlaf der Vernunft [no editor] (Berlin/W.: Elefanten Press; Berlin: Verlag Neues Leben/Temperamente, 1989).

ORTHEIL, HANNS-JOSEF, *Schauprozesse: Beiträge zur Kultur der 80er Jahre*, SP 1180 (Munich: Piper, 1990).

PACKALÉN, STURE, *Zum Hölderlinbild in der Bundesrepublik und der DDR. Anhand ausgewählter Beispiele der produktiven Hölderlin-rezeption*, Studia Germanistica Upsalensia, 28 (Stockholm: Almquist and Wiksell, 1986).

PANNEN, STEFAN, *Wir Mauerkinder* (Weinhein: Quadriga, 1994).

PAPE, WALTER (ed.), *1870/71–1989/90 German Unifications and the Change of Literary Discourse*, European Cultures, 1 (Berlin, New York: de Gruyter, 1993).

PARROTTA, ASTRID, 'Große Lähmung. Ost-Autoren im westlichen Medienzirkus: ratlos', *Frankfurter Rundschau*, 21 Feb. 1990.

PERGANDE, INGRID [see also Ingrid Hähnel], ' "Volker Braun?—Da kann ich nur sagen, der Junge quält sich . . .": New Voices in the GDR Lyric of the 1980s', in Kane (ed.), *Socialism and the Literary Imagination*, 229–245.

PERLOFF, MARJORIE, *The Poetics of Indeterminacy: Rimbaud to Cage* (Princeton: Princeton University Press, 1984).

PETERS, PETER, 'Der Satellit—ein inoffizieller Mitarbeiter?', *NdL* 2 (1992), 163–9.

PEUKERT, TOM, 'Metaphern für eine neue Wildnis: Im Dickicht des Nicht-Ich: Die Gedichte von Durs Grünbein', *Der Tagesspiegel*, 17 May 1992.

PIETRASS, RICHARD, 'Raum des Lebbaren: Interview mit Christian Löser', *NdL* 9 (1976), 119–21.

—— *Notausgang* (Berlin and Weimar: Aufbau, 1980, 2nd ed. 1988).

PLAVIUS, HEINZ, 'Positionsbestimmung', *WB* 6 (1980), 136–47.

RADDATZ, FRITZ J., *Marxismus und Literatur: Eine Dokumentation in drei Bänden* (Reinbek bei Hamburg: Rowohlt, 1969).

—— *Traditionen und Tendenzen: Materialien zur Literatur der DDR* (Frankfurt/M.: Suhrkamp, 1972).

—— ' "bebe go ehed". Lyrik von Flanzendörfer, Jan Faktor, Bert Papenfuß-Gorek und anderen: Rückblick auf die alternative Literatur der DDR', *Die Zeit*, 8 May 1992.

—— 'Von der Beschädigung der Literatur durch ihre Urheber': Bemerkungen zu Heiner Müller und Christa Wolf', *Die Zeit*, 29 Jan. 1993.

RADISCH, IRIS, 'Warten auf Montag. Anderson, Biermann und die Stasi: Zwischenrufe in einer endlosen Affäre', *Die Zeit*, 22 Nov. 1991.

—— 'Die Krankheit Lüge: Die Stasi als sicherer Ort: Sascha Anderson und die Staatssicherheit', *Die Zeit*, 24 Jan. 1992.

RADLACH, SIEGFRIED (ed.), *Aufbruch. Ankunft. Ausbruch: 30 Jahre DDR–Kunst und Literatur*, Schriftenreihe DDR-Kultur, 1 (Berlin/W.: Paul-Löbe-Institut, 1981).

RAMM, KLAUS J., 'Revolte gegen eine erdrosselte Sprache: Gabriele Kacholds Prosatexte "Zügel los" ', *Der Tagesspiegel*, 2 Oct. 1990.

REID, J. H. (ed.), *Re-assessing the GDR*, German Monitor, 33 (Amsterdam: Rodopi, 1994).

RESCHKE, RENATE, 'Fortgesetzte Faszination: Literarische Annäherungen an Hölderlin', *WB* 1 (1990), 74–99.

RICHTER, HANS, (ed.), *Schriftsteller und literarisches Erbe. Zum Traditionsverhältnis sozialistischer Autoren* (Berlin and Weimar: Aufbau, 1976).

—— *Generationen, Temperamente, Schreibweisen: DDR-Literatur in neuer Sicht* (Halle–Leipzig: Mitteldeutscher Verlag, 1986).

—— 'Zum Thema Generation(en): Thesen und Gedanken, vorgetragen in der Werkstatt Junge Kunst II der Akademie der Künste der DDR, 20 März 1988', *Temperamente*, 1 (1989), 66–73.

—— 'Dialoge mit Kathrin Schmidts Gedichten', *WB* 6 (1989), 990–5.

RIETZSCHEL, THOMAS, 'Kalauer und geliehene Fragmente: Gedichte der DDR verlieren ihren Reiz', *FAZ* 12 Feb. 1990.

—— (ed.), *Über Deutschland: Schriftsteller geben Auskunft* (Leipzig: Reclam, 1993).

RIMBAUD, ARTHUR, *Œuvres complètes. Correspondance*, ed. Louis Forestier (Paris: Laffont, 1992).

RÖNISCH, SIEGFRIED, 'Notizen über eine neue Autorengeneration', *WB* 7 (1979) 5–10.

ROSENLÖCHER, THOMAS, 'Die unentwegte Suche nach dem Verbindungsstück: Zu einem Gedicht von Hans-Eckardt Wenzel', in Eberhard Günther and Hinnerk Einhorn (eds.), *Positionen 3: Wortmeldungen zur DDR-Literatur*, (Halle–Leipzig: Mitteldeutscher Verlag, 1987), 115–121.

ROSELLINI, JAY, 'Subjektivität contra Politik? Anmerkungen zur Lyrik der

DDR', in Manfred Durzak (eds.), *Deutsche Gegenwartsliteratur: Ausgangspositionen und aktuelle Entwicklungen*, (Stuttgart: Philipp Reclam jun., 1981), 517–51.

ROSINSKI, STEFAN, 'Der Fall Schedlinski oder Konjekturen des Unglücks', in Böthig and Michael (eds.), *MachtSpiele*, 64–73.

ROTHBAUER, GERHARD, 'Viermal junge lyrik—Bilanz: offen', *Temperamente*, 2 (1984), 145–51.

RUMP, BERND, *Poesiealbum*, 141 (Berlin: Verlag Neues Leben, 1979).

—— 'Diskussion', *NdL* 9 (1983), 161–2.

—— *Sing-Gedichte* (Leipzig: Philipp Reclam jun., 1983).

RÜTHER, GÜNTHER, '*Greif zur Feder Kumpel': Schriftsteller, Literatur und Politik in der DDR 1949–1990* (Düsseldorf: Droste Verlag, 1991).

SACHSE, CORNELIA, 'Vage Zagenvragen', in *vogel oder käfig sein*, 401–2 (see under Anthologies above).

—— 'Die Orange Leben: ein abwesender Essay über die Abwesenheit der abwesenden Autorinnen', in *vogel oder käfig sein*, 402–4 (see under Anthologies above).

SCHÄDLICH, HANS JOACHIM (ed.), *Aktenkundig* (Berlin: Rowohlt, 1992).

SCHEER, REGINA, and WIEKE, THOMAS, 'Senden auf verschiedenen Frequenzen: Notiert zu Kerstin Hensel und Ralph Grüneberger', *Temperamente*, 2 (1987), 149–53.

SCHIRRMACHER, FRANK, ' "Dem Druck des härteren strengeren Lebens standhalten": Auch eine Studie über den autoritären Charakter: Christa Wolfs Aufsätze, Reden und ihre jüngste Erzählung "Was bleibt" ', *FAZ* 2 June 1990.

—— 'Abschied von der Literatur der Bundesrepublik. Neue Pässe, neue Identitäten, neue Lebensläufe: über die Kündigung einiger Mythen des westdeutschen Bewußtseins', *FAZ* 2 Oct. 1990.

—— 'Ein grausames Spiel: Der Fall Sascha Anderson und die Stasi-Akten' *FAZ* 25 Oct. 1991.

—— 'Verdacht und Verrat: Die Stasi-Vergangenheit verändert die literarische Szene', *FAZ* 5 Nov. 1991.

—— 'Der große Verdacht: Am Beispiel der Akten. Literatur und Stasi', *FAZ* 23 Nov. 1991.

—— 'Aufgeklärt. Der Fall Anderson', *FAZ* 8 Jan. 1992.

—— 'War da irgendein Mythos?: Porträt des Künstlers als junger Grenzhund', *FAZ* 28 Mar. 1992.

SCHLENSTEDT, DIETER, 'Lyrik als Empfindungskorrelat der Welt: Gespräch mit Georg Maurer', in Anneliese Löffler (ed.), *Auskünfte: Werkstattgespräche mit DDR-Autoren*, (Berlin and Weimar: Aufbau, 1974), 15–40.

—— (ed.), *Wirkungsästhetische Analysen: Poetologie und Prosa in der neueren DDR Literatur* (Berlin: Akademie Verlag, 1979).

—— 'Eine kleine Geste. Zu einem Gedicht von Steffen Mensching', in

Siegfried Rönisch (ed.), *DDR-Literatur '83 im Gespräch* (Berlin and Weimar: Aufbau, 1984), 320–5.

—— 'Entwicklungslinien der neueren Literatur in der DDR', in Chiarloni, Sartori, and Cambi (eds.), *Die Literatur der DDR 1976–1986*, 29–54.

—— 'Laudatio: Heinrich Heine Preis für Steffen Mensching und Hans-Eckardt Wenzel', *NdL* 4 (1990), 164–75.

SCHLENSTEDT, SILVIA, ' "Nur ich allein bin mir zu wenig": Hans-Eckardt Wenzel, "Lied von wilden Mohn" ', *Kritik '85: Rezensionen zur DDR-Literatur* (Halle–Leipzig: Mitteldeutscher Verlag, 1986), 228–32.

—— 'Das Individuum in der Geschichte: Erkundungen in der Lyrik der DDR', in Eberhard Günther and Hinnerk Einhorn (eds.), *Positionen 3: Wortmeldungen zur DDR-Literatur* (Halle–Leipzig: Mitteldeutscher Verlag, 1987), 81–109.

—— 'Umgang mit einer mythischen Figur: Das Ikarus-Motiv in der neueren DDR-Lyrik', *NdL* 8 (1987), 94–109.

—— 'Fragen der Nachgeborenen. Aspekte gegenwärtiger Lyrik in der DDR', in Margy Gerber *et al.* (eds.), *Studies in GDR Culture and Society 9*, (Lanham, MD: University Press of America, 1989), 85–99.

SCHMID, THOMAS, 'Ikarus bei Meißen: Sascha Anderson und Ralf Kerbach, "Totenreklame. Eine Reise" ', *Lesezeichen* (spring 1983), 27.

SCHMIDT, KARL-WILHELM, 'Grenzüberschreitungen: Über Leben und Literatur ehemaliger DDR-Autoren in der Bundesrepublik. Eine Bestandsaufnahme kulturpolitischer Folgen der Biermann-Ausbürgerung', in Kreuzer (ed.), *Pluralismus und Postmodernismus*, 149–89.

SCHMIDT, KATRIN, 'Ebenfalls zu Kathrin Schmidts Gedichten', *WB* 6 (1989), 995–9.

SCHMIDT, RICARDA, 'Im Schatten der Titanin: Minor GDR Women Writers—Justly Neglected, Unrecognized or Repressed?', in Goodbody and Tate (eds.), *Geist und Macht*, 151–62.

SCHMIDT, ULRICH, 'Engagierter Ästhetizismus. Über neudeutsche Literaturkritik', in Arnold (ed.), *Zum gegenwärten Zustand der deutschen Literatur*, 86–96.

SCHNEIDER, ROLF, *Volk ohne Trauer: Notizen nach dem Untergang der DDR* (Göttingen: Steidl, 1992).

SCHRÖTER, ULRICH, 'Wie wurde man ein IM?: Viele Gesprächspartner der Stasi waren Spitzel—aber nicht alle', *Die Zeit*, 6 Mar. 1993.

SCHÜTTE, WOLFRAM, 'Auf dem Schrotthaufen der Geschichte. Zu einer denkwürdig-voreiligen Verabschiedung der "bundesdeutschen Literatur" ', *Frankfurter Rundschau*, 20 Oct. 1990.

—— 'Doppelzüngler. Jagdszenen um Christa Wolf', *Frankfurter Rundschau*, 22 Jan. 1993.

SERKE, JÜRGEN, 'Was bleibt, das ist die Scham', *Die Welt*, 23 June 1990.

—— 'Lawinen mit Lügen bekämpft. Stasi und kein Ende: Das (viel zu späte) Geständnis Rainer Schedlinskis', *Die Welt*, 15 Jan. 1992.

SINGLDINGER, JOSEF, 'Sich einlassen auf ein Stück möglicher Selbsterkenntnis: Anmerkungen zum Umgang der Medien mit der Staatssicherheit der DDR', *Publizistik & Kunst. Zeitschrift der IG Medien*, 3 (1992), 10–14.

—— 'Literatur, Politik, die Dichter und ein Verlag. Der Prenzlauer Berg und seine mehrdimensionalen Geschichten', *Publizistik & Kunst. Zeitschrift der IG Medien*, 5 (1992), 27–9.

SOMMERHAGE, CLAUS, 'Einsätze: Barbara Köhlers Gedichte', *SuF* 4 (1992), 668–78.

STEINERT, HAJO, 'Lyrik mit Nadelstreifen: Entgrenzungen der Literatur im Kölner Filmhaus', *FAZ* 26 May 1988.

—— 'Die neuen Nix-Künstler: Die DDR-Literatur ist tot, es lebe die DDR-Literatur!', *Die Zeit*, 7 Dec. 1990.

—— 'Die Szene und die Stasi: Muß man die literarischen Texte der Dichter vom Prenzlauer Berg jetzt anders lesen?', *Die Zeit*, 29 Nov. 1991.

STEPHAN, ALEXANDER, 'Ein deutscher Forschungsbericht 1990/91: Zur Debatte um das Ende der DDR-Literatur und den Anfang einer gesamtdeutschen Kultur', *Germanic Review*, Theme Issue: 'The End of GDR Literature', 3 (summer 1992), 126–34.

STREISAND, JOACHIM, *Deutsche Geschichte von den Anfängen bis zur Gegenwart. Eine marxistische Einführung* (Cologne: Pahl-Rugenstein, 1976).

STRUZYK, BRIGITTE, *Leben auf der Kippe: Gedichte* (Berlin and Weimar: Aufbau, 1984).

—— *Der wild gewordene Tag: Gedichte* (Berlin and Weimar: Aufbau, 1989).

SUBIOTTO, ARRIGO, 'Volker Braun, Rimbaud und die DDR', in Chiarloni, Sartori, and Cambi (eds.), *Die Literatur der DDR 1976–1986*, 241–51.

TANNERT, CHRISTOPH, 'Rock aus dem Unterholz', in Muschter and Thomas (eds.), *Jenseits der Staatskultur*, 155–78.

TATE, DENNIS, 'The Socialist Metropolis? Images of East Berlin in the Literature of the GDR', in Glass, Rösler, and White (eds.), *Berlin: Literary Images of a City*, 146–61.

THEOBALDY, JÜRGEN (eds.), *Und ich bewege mich doch . . . : Gedichte vor und nach 1869* (Munich: Beck, 1977).

THOMAS, RÜDIGER, 'Selbstbehauptung', in Muschter and Thomas (eds.), *Jenseits der Staatskultur*, 11–42.

THULIN, MICHAEL [i.e. Klaus Michael], 'die metaphorik des todes: die texte sascha andersons', *ariadnefabrik*, 1 (1988), 6–11.

—— 'Die verschwundenen Gegenstände: Sprache und Sprachkritik am Ende der achtziger Jahre', *SitZ* 111 (Sept. 1989), 222–33.

—— 'Sprache und Sprachkritik: Die Literatur des Prenzlauer Bergs in Berlin/DDR', in Arnold and Wolf (eds.), *Die andere Sprache*, 234–42.

—— 'Das Subjekt und sein Spiegel: das dezentrierte subjekt in den texten Rainer Schedlinskis', in Arnold and Wolf (eds.), *Die andere Sprache* 158–61.

—— 'Die Imagination der poetischen Sprache. dichtung und arkdichtung von Bert Papenfuß-Gorek', in Arnold and Wolf (eds.), *Die andere Sprache*, 114–19.

—— 'Das Unikat Syndrom', *vogel oder käfig sein*, 295–8 (see under Anthologies above).

TIMMS, EDWARD, and KELLY, DAVID, (eds.), *Unreal City: Urban Experience in Modern European Literature and Art* (Manchester: Manchester University Press, 1985).

TÖRNE, DOROTHEA VON, Jeder Killer hat seinen Killersatelliten: Der Fall Sascha Anderson oder Wie Gespaltenheit zur Überlebensstrategie wird', *Neue Zeit*, 4 Jan. 1992.

TREBEß, ACHIM, ' "wir würschten" in den Kämpfen unserer Zeit: Porträtgedichte junger Autoren', in Ingrid Hähnel (ed.), *Lyriker im Zwiegespräch*, 312–31.

—— ' "im rechten augenblick das linke tun": Spracherneuerung in Texten von Bert Papenfuß-Gorek', *WB* 4 (1990), 617–36.

TREICHEL, HANS-ULRICH, 'Ein Grabstein für die Zukunft', *Die Welt*, 8 Oct. 1991.

'Umfrage zur Situation der Literatur-, Kunst- und Kulturwissenschaften', in *WB* 1 (1991), 9–54, and 'Fortsetzung', *WB* 2 (1991), 234–84.

VINKE, HERMANN (ed.), *Akteneinsicht Christa Wolf: Zerrspiegel und Dialog: Eine Dokumentation* (Hamburg: Luchterhand, 1993).

VISSER, ANTHONYA, 'Überlegungen zur Lyrik Uwe Kolbes', in Cosentino, Ertl, and Labroisse (eds.), *DDR-Lyrik im Kontext*, 297–334.

—— *'Blumen im Eis': Lyrische und literaturkritische Innovationen in der DDR. Zum kommunikativen Spannungsfeld ab Mitte der 60er Jahre*, Amsterdamer Publikationen zur Sprache und Literatur, 107 (Amsterdam: Rodopi, 1994).

VORNBÄUMEN, AXEL, 'Mit Phänomenen wie Chaos und Liebe kam die Stasi nicht klar', *Frankfurter Rundschau*, 9 Jan. 1992.

WAGNER, BERND, *Zweite Erkenntnis* (Berlin and Weimar: Aufbau, 1978).

—— *Der Griff ins Leere: 11 Versuche* (Berlin: TRANSIT, 1988).

WALLACE, IAN, ' "Das Dennoch und der Triumph der Selbstbehauptung": Indentitässuche und Zivilisationskrise bei Volker Braun', in Klussmann and Mohr (eds.), *Jahrbuch zur Literatur deer DDR 3*, (Bonn: Bouvier, 1983), 185–208.

—— (ed.), *The GDR in the 1980s*, GDR Monitor Special Series, 4 (Dundee: [n.pub.], 1984).

—— (ed.), *The Writer and Society in the GDR* (Tayport: Hutton Press, 1984).

—— 'The Failure of GDR Cultural Policy under Honecker', in Gert-Joachim Glaeßner and Ian Wallace (eds.), *The German Revolution of 1989: Causes and Consequences* (Oxford: Berg, 1992), 100–23.

—— 'The Politics of Confrontation: The Biermann Affair and its Consequences', in Goodbody and Tate (eds.), *Geist und Macht*, 68–77.

—— 'Writers and the *Stasi*', in Reid (ed.), *Re-assessing the GDR*, 115–28.

WALTER, JOACHIM *et al.*, *Protokoll eines Tribunals: Die Ausschlüsse aus dem DDR-Schriftstellerverband 1979* (Reinbek bei Hamburg: Rowohlt, 1991).

WALTER, KLAUS *et al.* (eds.), *Ansichten: Aufsätze zur Literatur der DDR*, (Halle/S.: Mitteldeutscher Verlag, 1976).

WANGENHEIM, INGE VON, 'Genosse Jemand und die Klassik', *NdL* 3 (1981), 99–119.

WEBER, RITA, 'Der Eintritt einer neuen Generation in die Literatur-Schaffensfragen junger Lyriker, die bereits mit der sozialistischen Gesellschaft heranwuchsen' (unpublished dissertation, Institut für Gesellschaftswissenschaften beim ZK der SED. Lehrstuhl für marxistisch-leninistische Kultur und Kunstwissenschaften, Berlin, 1973).

WEERDENBURG, OSCAR VAN, 'Hölderlin am Prenzlauer Berg. Zur Hölderlin Rezeption Hans-Eckardt Wenzels', in Gerd Labroisse and Gerhard P. Knapp (eds.), *Literarische Tradition Heute: Deutschsprachige Gegenwartsliteratur in ihrem Verhältnis zur Tradition*, ABznG 24 (Amsterdam: Rodopi, 1988), 61–77.

WEIMANN, ROBERT, 'Realität und Realismus. Über Kunst und Theorie in dieser Zeit', *SuF* 5 (1984), 924–51.

WELSCH, WOLFGANG (ed.), *Wege aus der Moderne. Schlüsseltexte der Postmoderne-Diskussion* (Weinheim: VCH Verlagsgesellschaft, 1988).

WICHNER, ERNEST, 'Halb Zombie, halb enfant perdu: "Schädelbasis-lektion", der zweite Gedichtband von Durs Grünbein', *Süddeutsche Zeitung*, 9/10 Nov. 1991.

—— and WIESNER, HERBERT (eds.), *Zensur in der DDR. Geschichte, Praxis und 'Ästhetik' einer Behinderung der Literatur* (Berlin: Literaturhaus Berlin, 1991).

WIEKE, THOMAS, ' "ich sitz im Gold, daß ich zu Stroh verspinn . . .": Anmerkungen zu Kerstin Hensels Gedichten', *Temperamente*, 3 (1986) 149–51.

—— 'Lieber Hans-Eckardt Wenzel', *Temperamente*, 4 (1987), 154–8.

WITTSTOCK, UWE, 'Aus der Hauptstadt verbannt. Vom Schicksal eines kaum bekannten Schriftstellers drüben', *FAZ* 1 Apr. 1985.

—— 'Ohne Mauer im Kopf: Der DDR-Schriftsteller Sascha Anderson', *FAZ* 23 June 1983; repr. in a slightly different form in Wittstock, *Von der Stalinallee zum Prenzlauer Berg*, 258–64.

—— 'Literatur als Zuflucht in der Haft': "brunnen randvoll"—Prosa und Lyrik von Sascha Anderson', *FAZ* 9 July 1988.

—— ' "Ich bin bereit zur Herrschaft über mich selbst": Uwe Kolbe—Porträt eines Lyrikers als junger Mann', *Neue Rundschau*, 2 (1988), 88–100.

—— *Von der Stalinallee zum Prenzlauer Berg: Wege der DDR-Literatur 1949–1989*, SP1136 (Munich: Piper, 1989).

—— 'Die Dichter und ihre Richter: Literaturstreit im Namen der Moral: Warum die Schriftsteller aus der DDR als Sündenböcke herhalten müssen', *Süddeutsche Zeitung*, 13/14 Oct. 1990.

—— 'Wieviel Literatur im Leben, wieviel Politik in der Poesie?: Eine Umfrage unter deutschen Schriftstellern der Jahrgänge 1950–1966', *Neue Rundschau*, 2 (1992), 95–130.

—— 'Generationswechsel? Ja. Aber wie? Was tut sich bei dieser Umfrage unterm Strich? Nachbemerkung ohne Gewähr', *Neue Rundschau*, 2 (1992), 131–3.

WOLF, CHRISTA, *Der geteilte Himmel* (1963; and Munich: dtv, 1973).

—— *Die Dimension des Autors: Essays and Ausätze, Reden und Gespräche 1959–1985*, ed. Angela Drescher (Berlin and Weimar: Aufbau, 1986).

—— *Im Dialog. Aktuelle Texte* (Frankfurt/M.: Luchterhand, 1990).

—— *Was bleibt: Erzählung* (Frankfurt/M.: Luchterhand, 1990).

—— and WOLF, GERHARD, *Ins Ungebundene gehet eine Sehnsucht: Gesprächsraum Romantik: Prosa und Essays* (Berlin and Weimar: Aufbau, 1985).

WOLF, GERHARD, *Im deutschen Dichtergarten. Lyrik zwischen Mutter Natur und Vater Staat: Ansichten und Porträts*, SL 626 (Darmstadt and Neuwied: Luchterhand, 1985).

—— *Wortlaut—Wortbruch—Wortlust. Dialog mit Dichtung: Aufsätze und Vorträge* (Leipzig: Philipp Reclam jun., 1988).

—— 'Befindlichkeit der Sprache: Befindlichkeit des Sprechenden. Zu einem Aspekt junger Lyrik in der DDR', *bateria: Zeitschrift für künstlerischer Ausdruck*, 7/8 (1988), 4–13.

—— *Sprachblätter Wortwechsel: Im Dialog mit Dichtern* (Leipzig: Reclam, 1992).

WOLFF, LUTZ-W. (ed.) *Fahrt mit der S-Bahn: Erzähler der DDR* (Munich: dtv, 1971).

WÜLLENWEBER, WALTER, *Wir Fernsehkinder: Eine Generation ohne Programm* (Reinbek bei Hamburg: Rowholt, 1994).

WÜST, KARL HEINZ, *Sklavensprache: Subversive Schreibweisen in der Lyrik der DDR 1961–1976*, Europäische Hochschulschriften Reihe 1, Deutsche Sprache und Literatur, 1129, (Frankfurt/M.: Peter Lang, 1989).

ZEKERT, RAINER, ' "Von mir aus"—Inventur und Programm: Steffen Mensching, "Tuchfühlung" ', *NdL* 5 (1988), 145–148.
—— 'Das Wagnis Metapher. Kathrin Schmidt: "Ein Engel fliegt durch die Tapetenfabrik" ', *NdL* 6 (1989), 157–61.

ZIMMERMANN, MONIKA, 'Teuflische Provokateure oder Die Unschuldslämmer von Prenzlauer Berg', *Neue Zeit*, 2 Nov. 1991.

INDEX

Notes: 1. Page references for **quoted texts** are in **bold** figures. 2. Lengthy titles are shortened and omissions shown by dots, e.g. *Jeder Satellit. . . .* 3. Items are only included from Notes where discussed in detail.